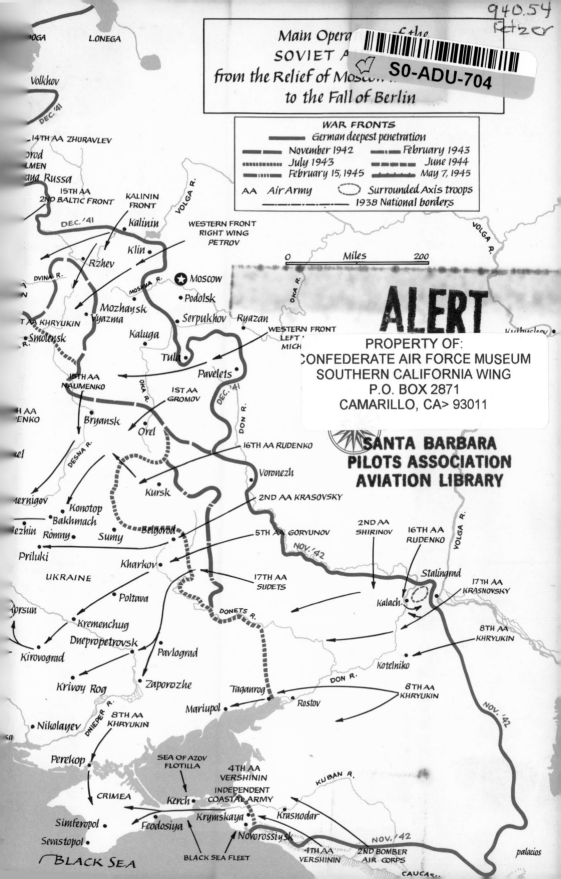

THE SOVIET AIR FORCE IN WORLD WAR II

THE SOVIET AIR FORCE IN WORLD WAR II

THE OFFICIAL HISTORY, ORIGINALLY PUBLISHED BY THE MINISTRY OF DEFENSE OF THE USSR

Translated by Leland Fetzer
Edited by Ray Wagner

Doubleday & Company, Inc., Garden City, New York
1973

ISBN: 0-385-04768-1

Library of Congress Catalog Card Number 72–76158

Copyright © 1973 by Doubleday & Company, Inc.

FOREWORD BY THE AMERICAN EDITOR

The role of the Soviet Air Force in World War II is of great importance to Americans interested in military aviation. The Soviet Air Force is the strongest air force, outside the United States, in the world. Knowledge of its experience, methods, organization, and traditions is essential to understanding today's strategic balance.

For those interested in World War II fighting, this Soviet history offers the first balance to the postwar Eastern Front books by Germans, whose natural bias makes an objective account difficult. In the Soviet history, one reads the other side of the war's most costly, hard-fought theater. All the major air campaigns are described, as well as uniquely Soviet aspects of air war, such as mid-air ramming and women combat pilots.

The original Russian text, as published in the Soviet Union, has been translated and edited by an American team. No factual content has been omitted from the translation, and the Russian text has been rendered into English as closely as possible. All names of commanding officers and leading pilots have been retained, but lists of subordinates have been omitted. German terms are given in the style used in wartime German documents.

Background material on the war, the aircraft, and the German forces, as well as all the subheads, have been added by the editor to make the book more useful to the American reader, but no attempt has been made to change or evaluate the content of the Russian text.

Readers will make their own judgments of the factual content, aware that wartime claims of enemy losses were frequently in excess of the facts; for example, the RAF's estimate of enemy losses in the Battle of Britain were double those of actual losses. The Russian text is usually reticent about their own losses, but their statement of a loss for each 32 sorties in 1941, applied to the first

250,000 sorties, indicates that more than 7800 aircraft were lost in the war's first three and one-half months—surely the highest aircraft loss of any such period in history. This book indicates some of the reasons for such losses, including the lack of radar and the almost complete lack of radio on the fighter planes.

Although this book is published with Soviet permission, Americans are entirely responsible for the translation and the editorial additions. They do not endorse the political views of the history, which are those usual to official history, and American readers will make their own evaluation of the content.

It will also be noticed that this history's scope is quite parochial; it confines itself to major Soviet air campaigns only, and does not go into aspects of the war in which their air force was not the largest participant. Therefore there is no mention of the Soviet Navy ships, or of the defense of Sevastopol in 1942, or of associated Allied actions such as the convoys to Murmansk, or the USAF "shuttle" raids to Poltava in June 1944.

Illustrations were added to the American edition by courtesy of Sovfoto, except for German aircraft photos contributed by H. J. Nowarra, James V. Crow, and the Bundesarchev.

R. W., *October 1972*

CONTENTS

ADVANCES / PERSONNEL / INFLUENCE OF THE WAR
ON TODAY'S AIR FORCE.

LIST OF ILLUSTRATIONS

The TB-3, world's first four-engined bomber to reach mass production, still served as a transport into 1942.

Modernized TB-3s flew to the North Pole in May 1937.

A TB-3 shown in 1938 in China; this model was used as a night bomber in 1941.

An I-15 fighter in Spain, 1936.

The I-152, or I-15bis, in China, 1938, and still used in 1941.

The I-153, last of the biplane fighters, is shown here in 1941 with pilots and a starter truck.

The I-16 was still the most widely used fighter when the war began.

The SB-2 bomber.

This damaged SB-2 fell into enemy hands when its air base was overrun in the war's first days.

An SB-2bis, with M-103 engines, of a night-bombing unit.

The DB-3 long-range bomber built before the war.

INTRODUCTION

The Great Patriotic War* between the Soviet Union and Fascist Germany was, especially in its early period, a severe test for all the Soviet people and their armed forces. Before beginning their attack, the German fascist command concentrated 190 well-equipped and well-trained divisions with 3500 tanks and more than 50,000 guns and mortars on our borders. The Luftwaffe and its allied air forces had almost 5000 war planes. The enemy had a four- or fivefold advantage in men and materials in those areas where he struck.

At dawn on June 22, 1941, the German fascist armies without a declaration of war attacked us with powerful blows from their air forces, artillery and tanks. This sudden and treacherous attack put our ground forces, fleet, and air forces in a difficult position. The mass attacks by the Luftwaffe on our airfields, barracks, railroad lines, and population centers in the very first hours of the war led to significant losses in men, supplies, and military equipment, including aircraft. Control and communication between the border garrisons, troops in the field, and aircraft were lost. The German fascist air forces seized the initiative in the air, and thereby created optimum conditions for tank and motorized units to pierce the border and to drive deep into Soviet territory.

The enemy fell on our country just when the air forces in the Western border military districts were in the process of reorganizing and receiving new equipment, and when extensive construction and remodeling was under way on our airfields. Our air units still had a large number of antiquated aircraft.

* World War Two is described by two separate terms in the USSR. The term *Great Patriotic War* is used for the fighting between the Soviet Union and Germany and her allies, while *World War II* covers the entire 1939–45 period. This distinction is maintained in the English text, except for the book title itself, where it was feared the original *Patriotic War* term would not be recognized by many American readers. ED.

Under such difficult and complex conditions, the Soviet Air Force had to begin its military operations. It had to simultaneously fulfill several assignments: carry on intense battles with enemy aircraft, strike against his tank and motorized columns, operate against industrial targets and the administrative centers of Fascist Germany, and conduct aerial reconnaissance.

The air force personnel, educated by the Communist party, morally stalwart and boundlessly dedicated to their socialist Motherland, and possessing excellent aerial skills, displayed high courage in their bitter struggle with a powerful and experienced foe. During the defensive operations carried out by the ground forces and their necessary retreat toward Leningrad, Moscow, and Kiev, our air power during the summer and fall of 1941 attacked and wore down the advancing enemy armies and his air forces.

For the first time in World War II, the Red Army with the help of air power decisively defeated German troops and then threw them back 350 kilometers (217 miles) in the winter of 1941–42. The plan of Hitler's command for a blitzkrieg was decisively disrupted, and the legend of the invincibility of the German fascist Army and its Luftwaffe was dispelled. In this historic battle for Moscow our air power provided major support for the ground forces, acquired control of the air, and in cooperation with the men of Air Defense won security for the capital city. The defeat of the German fascist Army near Moscow was the beginning of the great reversal in the course of the war.

The subsequent military operations of our air forces in the summer and fall of 1942 also occurred under unfavorable conditions. The armed forces of the United States and England were not carrying on active military operations against Germany. Taking advantage of this situation, the German fascist troops made a massive attack on the southern front. However, in spite of great enemy superiority in both men and material, our ground forces with the help of our air forces were able to stop his troops in intense and extended battles on the shores of the Volga and in the northern Caucasus, and to win the time necessary to train the Red Army for the transition to offensive operations.

Thanks to the exemplary efforts of the workers at the rear, production of the new types of aircraft increased 3.3 times from December 1941 to December 1942 and aircraft engines increased 5.4 times. This made it possible, in addition to replacing losses, to increase the size, improve the qualitative level of the air forces in the front, and in May 1942 to begin a fundamental reorganization— to create air armies on the fronts, and uniform air divisions, and to form reserve air corps for the Supreme Command. In March 1942 the Long-range Air Force was reorganized into an independent Air Force for Long-range Operations.† A system established at the beginning of the war and then revised, for the formation and outfitting of air units and the training and retraining of flying and ground crews made it possible to successfully comply with Supreme Command measures to further strengthen the air force.

With the massive introduction and assimilation of new air technology, the command, staffs, and the flight and ground crews of the air force acquired experience in the organization and conduct of military operations; the aircraft at the front became more active and increased their strikes against enemy troops and airfields, and navy aircraft were active at sea. The AFLRO struck at targets deep in the rear and on the battlefield. By November 1942 the conditions had been created for a basic reversal in the war's course in favor of the Soviet Union.

In the second period of the war (November 19, 1942, to December 1943) our troops aided by air power surrounded and destroyed 300,000 German fascist troops at Stalingrad, caused serious losses to German troops near Kursk, and then liberated the left bank of the Dnieper. The Red Army victory at Kursk was one of the decisive events that gave a successful course to the war and led to the resolution of World War II.

The Soviet Air Force caused great losses to German fascist aircraft in the counterattack at Stalingrad, and then at Kursk it firmly seized and held control of the sky along the entire Soviet-German front until the end of the war. This domination of the air made it possible for the ground forces to conduct offensive operations simultaneously in several sectors.

The self-sacrificing labor of the Soviet people in the rear contributed significantly to Soviet Army successes at the front. In 1943 our industry produced 34,000 aircraft, and 40,000 in 1944. This greatly increased the aircraft reserves at the front. Both a quantitative and a qualitative superiority over the enemy was achieved in aircraft technology.

† The new force included both bombers and transport aircraft. ED.

The war's second period was marked by a new, higher development in the tactics of different kinds of aircraft, and was a period of acquiring and perfecting battle experience by the flying, ground crew, and command personnel. This made it possible to successfully utilize air power with ground operations, to perfect coordination with the ground forces, to guarantee flexible control over air units, and more effectively to conduct combat with enemy aircraft.

In the third period of the war, embracing the Red Army operations in 1944–45, the Soviet Air Force consistently ruled the air and rendered general support to ground forces and the fleet so that they might achieve decisive victories over the enemy. This period saw the use of great numbers of aircraft in offensive operations.

In the last years of the war the Soviet Air Force advanced along a difficult, but glorious, road. Its personnel successfully completed their assignments, were tempered in severe battles, and acquired rich experience in the organization, conduct, and maintenance of military operations by various types of aircraft under difficult conditions.

The Communist party, the Soviet government, and the Supreme Command appreciated the military services of the air force. Supreme Commander of the Soviet Armed Forces J. V. Stalin, in his order of August 19, 1945, noted: "In the Great Patriotic War, our air forces with honor fulfilled their debt to the Motherland. The glorious falcons of our Fatherland in arduous aerial battles smashed the much-praised German air forces, thereby guaranteeing freedom of action for the Red Army and freeing the population of our country from enemy air attack. Together with the whole Red Army, it made crushing attacks against the enemy, destroying his men and equipment. The skilled actions of our illustrious air forces constantly contributed to the success of our ground forces and helped to achieve a final victory over the enemy."

The present work is a brief military history dedicated to air force operations in the major battles of the Great Patriotic War. The issuing of this work will contribute toward the improved training and education of Soviet airmen and the younger generation in the spirit of a boundless dedication to the Communist party and the socialist Motherland, toward a more profound study and utilization of the past war's experience, and toward an increased understanding of the air force traditions.

Part One

THE AIR FORCE IN THE PERIOD OF
REPELLING FASCIST GERMANY'S
TREACHEROUS ATTACK
(June 22, 1941, to November 18, 1942)

I

THE SOVIET AND GERMAN AIR FORCES
AT THE WAR'S BEGINNING

The Communist party and the Soviet government, relying on V. I. Lenin's instructions to guard "the military preparedness of our country and our Red Army, like the apple of our eye," constantly displayed concern for raising the defensive power of the socialist state and strengthening its armed forces.

Aircraft Development before the War. The air force received great attention. Its constantly increasing role in military action was correctly evaluated, and consideration was given to the primitive state of the industrial base which we inherited from old Russia. Acting on this premise, the party and the government in the prewar years took broad measures to create and develop a powerful aircraft industry, to train flight and ground personnel, to develop scientific and experimental work, and to organize design facilities.

Even when the First Five-Year Plan began in 1928, most of the aircraft in the Red Army Air Force were of Soviet construction. During the years of the First Five-Year Plan, production of numerous types of aircraft was begun. Our aircraft industry, among other new aircraft, produced a considerable number of TB-1s and TB-3s (heavy bombers*), making it possible for us to create the best heavy

---

* The twin-engined TB-1's all-metal, low-wing monoplane structure was far more advanced than the fabric-covered biplane bombers then common. Designed by Andrei N. Tupolev, the prototype (ANT-4) appeared in November 1925, and 216 were produced up to 1932. After retirement from the bomber units they were designated G-1 for cargo use.

Tupolev's larger TB-3 was the first four-engined monoplane bomber in mass

bomber force in the world at that time, which significantly increased the striking power of our air force.

Significant successes were also achieved in aircraft construction in the Second Five-Year Plan (1933–37). The air force accepted these new types of aircraft: the DB-3 long-range bomber, the SB fast bomber, and the I-15 and I-16 fighters. The speed and altitude capabilities of these planes were 1.5 or 2 times the capabilities of the older types of aircraft. The range and bomb-carrying capacity of these bombers was 3 times greater.†

---

production anywhere, and so is a forerunner to bombers like the famous Boeing B-17. Its prototype, ANT-6, was first flown on December 22, 1930, by Mikhail Gromov, and mass-produced TB-3s went into service in 1932. Early models had open cockpits, dual landing wheels, and M-17 engines, but modernized versions had enclosed nose, amidships, and tail turrets, M-34 engines, and more streamlined airframes by 1936. Some 818 were built, and many remained in service in 1941 as night bombers or in transport configuration as the G-2.[1] ED.

† Both the I-15 and I-16 fighters designed by Nikolai Polikarpov were compact, short-nosed single-seaters powered by M-25 radials (the Soviet-built Wright Cyclone). While the I-15 was a biplane with the upper wings gulled into the fuselage, the I-16 became the world's first low-wing monoplane fighter with retractable landing gear to go into mass production.

First flown in October 1933 and reaching service the following year, the I-15 became world-famous after it entered combat near Madrid on November 4, 1936. It was flown by Russian, Spanish, and also by American volunteers fighting for the republic in the Civil War.[2]

Some 674 I-15s had been built when production shifted in 1937 to the I-15bis, or I-152, an improved version with a straight upper wing and a deep cowl over the 750 hp. engine. Like its predecessor, it was armed with four 7.62 mm. guns and racks for four small bombs, and had 9 mm. pilot armor. This type first appeared with the Soviet volunteer pilots in China in November 1937. Of 2408 built, some still remained in service in 1941, probably with ground-attack units.

The remarkable I-16 monoplane was first flown on December 31, 1933, by Valeri Chkalov. When it went into service in 1935 with a 715 hp. M-25 engine and two 7.62 ShKAS wing guns, it was the world's fastest (454 kilometers per hour or 282 miles per hour) fighter in squadron service, and remained so when it reached Spain in October 1936. After 2200 were built, models appeared in 1937 with 750 hp. and four guns, and this type was used in both Spain and China in 1938.

In contrast to his bulky TB designs, Tupolev had produced a smaller, streamlined bomber in his SB, or ANT-40, series. The first prototype (SB-1) was flown on October 7, 1934, with two M-25 radial engines, but the

The aircraft industry increased the production of aircraft, engines, and other military equipment during the Second Five-Year Plan by 5.5 times.[3] As a result, the total number of military aircraft in the air force regiments more than doubled.[4]

The rapid development of Soviet aviation technology made it possible to carry out during the 1930's a series of long-range flights, including several intercontinental flights. The entire world knows of the intercontinental flights of V. P. Chkalov, G. F. Baldukov, and A. V. Belyakov; M. M. Gromov, A. B. Yumashev, and S. A. Danilin; V. K. Kokkinaki and A. M. Bryandinsky. These were triumphs of our own national air technology and indicated great flying skills.‡

The Soviet Air Force's high capabilities were demonstrated at the annual Red Army parades in Moscow. From 400 to 600 aircraft flew over Red Square at one time according to precise schedules. More than 100 aircraft took off from some airfields. The foreign press reported on the precision and tight control of the aircraft at these parades.

However, under the conditions of very rapid change in aviation technology, the aircraft in the field quickly became outmoded. When World War II began in 1939 the question had to be faced of improving the quality of our aircraft reserves. At this time there were outmoded aircraft in some air forces units.

---

second, flown on December 30, had two M-100 in-line engines behind frontal radiators. This model went into mass production as the SB-2 and entered service early in 1936. A three-seat, midwing monoplane carrying four guns and a 1320 lb. bomb load, it was then faster than any other bomber, or most fighters, but its range was short. Some were used in the Spanish Civil War and the Sino-Japanese conflict.

For long-range bombing, the design bureau headed by Sergei Ilyushin had produced the prototype for the DB-3 in 1936. Powered by two M-86 radial engines, it could carry up to 5500 lb. of bombs 800 miles or 1100 lb. up to 2485 miles. The DB-3, of which 1528 were built, entered service in 1937, and was still active in 1941. ED.

‡ Chkalov and his crewmen made the first nonstop flight from Moscow to the U.S. in June 1937, by flying an ANT-25 over the North Pole and landing in Vancouver, Washington. Less than a month later, Gromov's crew flew a similar aircraft over that route and reached San Diego, turning back to land at San Jacinto, setting a 6262-mile world's nonstop distance record. Vladimir Kokkinaki became known in America with his flight from Moscow in April 1939 in the DB-3 prototype, which he had to land in Canada instead of New York. ED.

Among these antiquated aircraft were the I-16 and I-153 fighters.* Although they had been modernized, at the war's beginning they nonetheless were inferior to German fighters in a number of tactical and technical aspects, particularly in speed and rate of climb.

The I-16 fighter was widely used during the entire first period of the war. Skillfully employing its superiority to the Bf-109 in maneuverability, as well as its great firepower and rocket armament, Soviet fliers caused serious losses to the enemy both in the air and on the ground. The I-153 was employed mostly for ground attack during the first part of the war.

The basic bomber used at the front was the SB, accepted for service in 1934–35, which was inferior to the German Ju 88 and He 111 in speed by 50 kilometers per hour (31 miles per hour) and with only half the bomb capacity and range. (Production of the SB series had continued until 1940, with 6656 built, later models using M-103 engines. About 200 were finished as dive bombers with M-105 engines, wing brakes, and the designation SB-RK, or Ar-2. ED.)

The aviation industry began mass production of the latest aircraft types† in the second half of 1940, but naturally was not able to produce the required number of fighters, bombers, and ground-attack planes before the war began.

Combat Aircraft Types in 1941. The Soviet Air Force began the war with the following new types of aircraft:

* Production of the I-16 had continued to 1940, with a total of 6555 built. Later models used the M-62 engine, and 737 had two 20 mm. guns fitted in the wings as well as racks for two 100 kg. (220 lb.) bombs or two 100 liter fuel tanks. Underwing rails could be added for six RS-82 rockets, an innovation first used in combat on August 20, 1939.[5]

That summer, provocations near Khalkhin-Gol, on the Mongolian-Manchurian border, caused fighting between Japanese and Soviet armies from May 11 to August 31. During this incident the I-153 fighter entered combat in July. Developed from the I-15, this gull-wing biplane had retractable wheels, an M-62 engine, four 7.62 mm. guns, and racks for bombs or rockets; 3437 were produced in the 1939–40 period. ED.

† Designations also changed for newer Soviet aircraft. Instead of nomenclature such as I for fighter and DB for long-range bombers, aircraft were named for their designers, and given odd numbers for fighters and even numbers for other types: for example, the Yak-1 fighter and the Pe-2 bomber. ED.

Fighters. The MiG-3, designed by A. I. Mikoyan and M. I. Gure-vich; the Yak-1, designed by A. S. Yakovlev; and the LaGG-3, designed by S. A. Lavochkin, V. P. Gorbunov, and M. I. Gudkov.

The MiG-3 was planned as a high-speed interceptor for Air Defense, but in fact became the basic fighter at the front. Thus, of the 980 newer fighter planes in the Western Frontier military districts, 886 were MiG-3s. This plane could fly both higher and faster than all other Soviet fighters. Fliers in MiG-3s successfully carried on air battles with the numerically superior enemy.

The Yak-1 and LaGG-3 were adequate for their time in design and engine power. In order to improve the Yak-1, at the beginning of 1942 the M-105 engine was replaced by the M-105P engine, which was significantly more powerful at low altitudes. As the result of the engine change and other aerodynamic improvements the aircraft designed by A. S. Yakovlev were successful in fighting with German Messerschmitts.

In the first part of 1942, the LaGG-3 was removed from production and then modified by the designer Lavochkin by replacing the in-line M-105 engine with the ASh-82 radial, which gave better flight characteristics to the later series of La-5 and La-7. Thus, the fighters of Yadovlev and Lavochkin, which were sent to the Red Army Air Force before the war, were constantly being improved during the war.

All the new fighters were made of wood with the exception of the fuselage structure of the Yak-1 (which was made from tempered tubing), the metal-covered forward fuselage, and the control surfaces. In later modifications, the percentage of metallic components was increased.‡

‡ The first of these new fighters to go into service, the Yak-1, was also the most successful. A low-wing monoplane with an in-line engine, like its two contemporaries, it was armed with one 20 mm. and two 7.62 mm. guns in the nose and six RS-82 rockets, and had the 9 mm. pilot back armor usual to the Soviet fighter. First flown as the I-26 prototype January 1, 1940, it went to special test squadrons in 1940, but less than 100 were in the Western border districts before the war.

The weaknesses of the faster MiG-3 were its armament, one 12.7 mm. and two 7.62 mm. guns, and insufficient maneuverability. Production had been ordered even before the prototype's (I-200) first flight on April 5, 1940, and MiGs were the majority of fighters delivered in early 1941. When battle experience exposed its weaknesses, its AM-35 engine was discontinued to

Ground-Attack Aircraft. The one-place armored ground-attack bomber Il-2, designed by S. V. Ilyushin, was first supplied to air units on the eve of the war. Experience in the war's first days immediately showed that it was an irreplaceable means of supporting ground troops in all kinds of operations. The effectiveness of this aircraft was assured by the excellent armor around the engine and the pilot's cockpit, its large machine gun, cannon, and bomb capacity, its successful integration of the armor with the fuselage structure, and the powerful 1600 hp. AM-38 engine. These features gave it liveliness, maneuverability, and great firepower for use against ground targets, all essential for ground-attack operations. *

---

expedite AM-38s for the Stormovik, and MiG-3 production ended in favor of more Yaks.

The LaGG-3 was first flown on March 30, 1940, as a prototype (I-22), and entered service in 1941 armed with one 20 mm. and one 12.7 mm. gun. Its successor the La-5 reintroduced the air-cooled radial engine and was armed with two 20 mm. guns; production deliveries began in July 1942.

Fighter production in 1940 was still mostly I-153 and I-16 types, with only 64 Yak-1 and 20 MiG-3s.[6] In the first half of 1941, 1946 of the newer types were produced, including 335 Yak-1s, 322 LaGG-3s, and the rest MiG-3s; but in the second half of 1941, 1019 Yak-1s and 2141 LaGG-3s were delivered.[7] MiG-3 production stopped in November 1941 with a total of 3322, while Yak-1s continued with 8721 aircraft, and 6528 LaGG-1s were made before factories shifted late in 1942 to newer models.

The Yak-7 first appeared in 1942 as a two-place fighter-trainer, but was modified into the Yak-7B single-seat fighter and joined at the end of 1942 by the Yak-9. The lighter Yak-3 did not reach quantity production until 1944, when it was produced parallel with improved Yak-9 models until 1945. Production totaled 6399 Yak-7s of all models, 4848 Yak-3s, and 16,769 Yak-9s.

Over 10,000 La-5s were built by 1944, and followed by 5753 La-7s. While the latter Yaks usually had one 20 mm. and two 12.7 mm. guns, all three of the La-7's guns were 20 mm. caliber. ED.

* While 249 Il-2s were delivered by the end of June 1941, 1293 more were produced by year's end. The first armored prototype appeared with an AM-35 engine as the BSh-2, or TsKB-55, flown by Kokkinaki in 1939. A stronger AM-38 was specified for the production Il-2, whose prototype, TsKB-57, flew on October 12, 1940. The 1941 "Stormoviks" were single-seaters armed with two 20 mm. and two 7.62 mm. guns in the wings, and fittings underneath for eight RS-82 or RS-132 rockets, or 880 to 1320 lb. bomb load. More power, 23 mm. wing guns, and a rear gunner with a 12.7 flexible gun were seen on the Il-2M3 appearing at the front on October 30, 1942. Ilyushin also built the superior Il-10 used at the front in 1945.[8] Total production, beginning in March 1941, was 36,163 Il-2s and 4966 Il-10s. ED.

Bombers. The Pe-2 dive bomber, designed by V. M. Petlyakov in 1939–40 and used in day operations and in dive-bombing, was only slightly slower than German fighters and exceeded in speed the German He 111 by more than 100 kilometers per hour (62 miles per hour) and the Ju 88 by 75 kilometers per hour (46 miles per hour). Its speed made it possible to use it in day operations during the entire war. However, at the beginning of the war there were few Pe-2s assigned to bomber units at the front.

Another attack bomber was built by the design team of A. N. Tupolev—the 103—but its tests had not been completed by the war's start. The mass production of this aircraft with two Ash-82 engines was begun in 1942, and in this form it bore the name Tu-2. Its flight characteristics made the Tu-2 the best attack bomber of World War II.

The Il-4 medium bomber was a modification of the DB-3 Ilyushin developed in 1935. It met the demands of its time for night operations and was the basic aircraft for long-range operations. In addition to the Il-4, other aircraft were built by the designers N. N. Polikarpov, V. M. Myasishchev, and V. G. Yermolayev. The long-range heavy bomber, the Pe-8 designed by V. M. Petlyakov, was used against targets deep in the rear. The Li-2 was used to transport troops, to maintain liaison with partisans, and in part for night bombing.†

† The twin-engined, three-place Pe-2 had been first flown as the PB-100 prototype on December 22, 1939. One or two production Pe-2s were ready in 1940; 458 were built in the first half, and 1405 in the second half, of 1941. Wartime production finally totaled 11,426, including the improved version introduced in 1943. Armament usually comprised up to 2200 lb. of bombs, and two fixed and two flexible guns.[9]

At the same time, 5256 four-place Il-4s were built for the long-range units. The type had been tested in 1939 as the DB-3F, and reached production in 1940 with two 950 hp. M-87A radials. In 1942, because of a scarcity of metal, wooden components were utilized, and the M-88B engine standardized. Armament included three flexible guns, 1100 to 5500 lb. of bombs, or a torpedo on those used by naval units.

The largest Soviet bomber was the Pe-8, developed from the TB-7 of 1937, and delivered in 1941 with four AM-35 engines. But when this powerplant was discontinued, M-82 radials were utilized in 1942. Armament included a 20 mm. gun in the tail and in the dorsal turret, twin 7.62 mm. guns in the nose turret, a 12.7 mm. gun behind each inner engine nacelle, and up to 11,600 lb. of bombs.

Since the air force wanted to use its resources on smaller aircraft for ground attack, only 79 Pe-8s were built, and the Il-4 was dropped from production in 1943.

On the other hand, the small two-place light bombers in production at the war's beginning did not last long. The Su-2 had a single radial engine, four 7.62 guns in the wing, and another in a rotating turret for the second crewman, and could carry a 880 lb. bomb load, or 10 rockets. First flown in August 1937 as the ANT-51 prototype, it went into production as the BB-1, and was redesignated Su-2 in 1941. While the 1941 model had a 950 hp. M-88B, the 1000 hp. M-82 was used later.

Two in-line M-103 engines were used on the twin-tailed BB-22 light bomber which went into production in 1940, but was redesignated Yak-2. This model was quickly superseded by the Yak-4, which had M-105 engines, and dive brakes. Armament included a 7.62 fixed gun, another for rear defense, and a 880 to 1320 lb. bomb load.

As the Yak-4 was found less useful at the front than the Il-2 or Pe-2 types, production ceased before the end of 1941, and the remainder served as reconnaissance types. The Su-2 was also withdrawn, for the same reason, in 1942.

The only new bomber type introduced at the front during the war was the twin-engined, four-place Tu-2. First flown as the ANT-58 prototype with in-line M-37 engines on January 29, 1941, it had a long development delayed by the necessity of shifting to the M-82 radial. The standard Tu-2 did not arrive at the front in large numbers until 1944, with 1111 delivered before Germany surrendered, and production of 2527 continuing until 1947. Armament comprised two 20 mm. fixed guns, three 12.7 mm. flexible guns, and up to 6600 lb. of bombs.[10]

The other aircraft mentioned in the preceding section, the Li-2, is very familiar to Americans as the DC-3 transport. A license to manufacture this type had been procured from Douglas in 1937, the Soviet version being similar in appearance to the U.S. C-47, except that a gunner's position was sometimes added to the roof top.

Reconnaissance types had been declining in importance before the war. In 1929, 82 percent of the air force consisted of recon types: slow, two-seat biplanes. In 1934, only 26 percent, and in 1938, only 9.5 percent, were recon types, while fighters increased from 25 percent to 38.6 percent.[11]

In 1929, the principal recon type was still the R-1, based on a World War I de Havilland design with numerous struts and a Soviet-built M-5 (Liberty) engine. From 1930 to 1937, the principal recon type was the R-5 biplane two-seater designed by Polikarpov. Over 7000 were built, most with M-17 (BMW), in-line engines, and R-34 engines on the later R-Z model.

Although a monoplane two-seater, the R-10, powered by an M-25V, entered production in 1937, it was soon displaced by the trend toward using fast bomber types for recon work. Yet the R-5 biplane soldiered on into the war years, operating on liaison and utility tasks.

The most unlikely looking warplane of the 1941–45 period was the U-2 light two-seater, the biplane in which most Soviet aviators of the time had learned to fly. Designed in 1927 by Polikarpov as an inexpensive, easily produced and operated primary trainer, the U-2 had been built by the

The proportional share of the different aircraft types at the war's start was as follows: In the air forces of the Western border military districts, 59 percent of the planes were fighters, 31 percent bombers, 4.5 percent ground-attack bombers, and more than 5 percent reconnaissance planes.

In addition to the creation of new types of aircraft and engines, much attention was devoted to developing new types of armament and special equipment. Pneumatic and electric gun turrets, automatic temperature regulators in engine systems, new types of ammunition, and 20 mm., 23 mm., and 37 mm. cannons were designed, and air-launched rockets were developed. Rockets were used on fighters as early as at the battles at Khalkhin-Gol.

In March 1941 the government took measures to establish navigational equipment both in aircraft and on the ground for flying in bad weather.

Air Force Organization. The air forces (VVS) were divided into the:

1. Long-range Air Force of the High Command, which had five corps and two separate divisions. (Of bombers and transports. ED.)

2. Air force of each front, or military district, consisting of fighter divisions and short-range bomber divisions. Each regiment had 60–64 aircraft. (Usually three regiments per division. ED.)

3. Air force component of each land army. These had only begun to be formed, and consisted of composite divisions. (A composite, or mixed, division combined fighter, bomber, and ground-attack regiments. ED.) At the war's beginning, only a few armies had such divisions, so most air divisions were those which made up the district air force (above), and were under the commander of that district's troops.

4. Military service air force, made up of individual communication (liaison) squadrons subordinate to infantry and mechanized corps commanders.

---

thousands before the war. Production had continued throughout the war as a liaison type serving the army, and with racks fitted for small bombs, it was issued to night bombing regiments formed to harass the Nazis after dark. The U-2 was renamed Po-2, in July 1944, after the designer's death. ED.

5. Naval Air Service. (Divided among the four fleets; Baltic, Black Sea, Northern, and Pacific. There were over 2500 Navy aircraft, including 763 fighters. ED.)

Based on a decision of the Communist party's Central Committee, and the USSR Council of People's Commissars, support elements of the air force were reorganized to insure high flexibility among the units during military operations. Regions for air support were set up on the eve of the war in the Western border districts, which included air bases each having four or five service battalions intended to give material and technological support for combat units. This reorganization was supposed to have been completed by fall 1941.

The increase in air force size‡ and the supply of new aircraft types meant more intensive training for both flight and ground crews. Therefore the number of aviation schools was significantly increased. This made it possible to train and send to their units about 10,000 specially trained men in 1940.

Manpower. The training of personnel became especially crucial beginning in fall 1939 as World War II began. In order to guarantee enough men for the air force the principle was established in December 1940 of taking men from the regular Red Army draft calls to support the growing need for men in the air force.*

Another important order of the party and government issued four months before the beginning of the Great Patriotic War established a new system for training men in both wartime and peacetime for the air force. Airmen were to be trained in three types of schools: primary military air schools with a training period of four months in peacetime, and three in wartime; in military schools for pilots where the training period was to be nine months in peacetime and six months in wartime; and in aviation institutes with a training period of two years in peacetime and one year in wartime. Navigators were trained in aviation schools for machine-gunner bombardiers, and in aviation institutes. In addition, a series of

‡ Between 1939's beginning and the spring of 1941, the total number of aircraft in the air force doubled; most, however, were the older models, except for the DB-3Fs (Il-4s).[12] ED.

* The air force had 414,370 of the 4,200,000 men in the Red Army on January 1, 1941. By June, the Red Army had increased to nearly 5,000,000 men, but Germany on May 31, 1941, had 7,200,000 men in her armed forces.[13] ED.

educational institutions was established for improving the training of flight crews, which consisted of courses for squadron commanders, and higher schools for air navigators.

Measures were also taken to improve the training of command personnel with advanced military backgrounds. For many years this had been carried out only at the Zhukovsky Air Force Academy and in the M. V. Frunze Military Academy's Air Department. In March 1941, the Air Force Academy for Command and Navigator Personnel was created from the Command and Navigational Departments of the Zhukovsky Air Force Academy (now the Red Banner Air Force Academy). The Air Force Engineering Academy was opened in spring 1941 in Leningrad. (Later this academy was given the name of A. F. Mozhaysky.) At the same time, courses to improve the training of engineering personnel were set up in Leningrad and also advanced tactical courses for training staff officers. Thus, by the war's beginning, personnel with advanced and technical skills were being trained at three air force academies and one general army academy, with political officers trained at the V. I. Lenin Military-Political Academy.

A significant contribution toward the formation and strengthening of Soviet Air Force power was made by the Volunteer Defense Society, which conducted propaganda activities promoting aviation affairs among the broad masses of the workers and actively contributed to the training of aviation personnel.

These activities were carried on in close cooperation with the Comsomols (Young Communists. ED.). The call of the IX Comsomol Congress—"Comsomol—to your plane!"—brought a large flow of young people to aviation clubs and discussion groups. With their own hands the Comsomols and other young people built many club buildings and sport airfields in their spare time, including the Chkalov Central Aviation Club of the USSR.

Groups of public-minded amateurs built new airplanes, gliders, and parachutes, and carried out scientific and technical experiments with rockets. Many well-known designers began their work in the Volunteer Defense Society, such as A. K. Antonov, S. V. Ilyushin, A. S. Yakovlev, and the scientists V. S. Pyshnov and F. A. Tsander.

In 1940 the Volunteer Defense Society had 182 airfields, 4 aviation schools for training instructors, 36 glider clubs, and 12 air mechanics' clubs. Besides these, there was also a broad network of aviation circles in factories, collective farms, and educational institutions. In the years before the war the Volunteer Defense Society trained tens of thousands of fliers, glider pilots, parachutists, and aviation technicians in sport-training organizations. Many fliers who became famous in Great Patriotic War battles received their first training in these circles and clubs, such as three-time Heroes of the Soviet Union A. Pokryshkin and I. Kozhedub, and two-time Heroes of the Soviet Union A. Molodchy, and N. Skomorokhov, A. Borovykh, G. Rechkalov, M. Odintsov, and G. Parshin.

The problem of training personnel for the air force was also being solved. Most air regiments were supplied with well-qualified flying and command personnel before 1939–40. Some crews from flights, squadrons, regiments, and divisions had battle experience which they had acquired in Spain, China, at Khalkhin-Gol River, and in the Soviet-Finnish War. Flying crews had practical experience with bombing over bombing ranges, aerial gunnery, high-altitude and long-distance flying, night operations, and flying during difficult weather conditions.

The military training level among the air units was equal to the demands of the time. Most bomber crews at the fronts were trained to fly by the compass or by ground landmarks, and to drop bombs in level flight by daylight under favorable weather conditions. Some Long-range Air Force crews were prepared to fly and drop bombs at night or under difficult weather conditions. A special air regiment staffed with crews who had mastered blind flying and dive-bombing operated effectively in the war with Finland in 1939–40. This regiment carried out operations for 63 days out of 70 both by day and night, while other units could operate only 6 to 8 days during the same period because of the weather conditions. On the basis of the experiences of this regiment, systems were worked out both for ground and flight equipment, a program was initiated to train flight crews for activities in bad weather conditions, and a new manual for navigation (NShS-40) was prepared.

Because of the increasing threat of an attack on the USSR, the plan for developing the air force during the Third Five-Year Plan (1938–42. ED.) was re-examined with the intent of hastening its completion. It was intended to increase the number of military aircraft, and more than 100 new air regiments were to be formed in 1941. These measures were to be carried out at the end of 1941 and the beginning of 1942.

At the beginning of 1941, formation was begun of many new air units in accordance with this plan, to which were contributed experienced flying and command cadres from old, well-trained, and well-organized air regiments. One should note that not all newly formed air units were completely equipped with aircraft or flight and technical crews. The young flight crews sent to these units were not adequately trained because, beginning at the end of 1940 and the first part of 1941, flight schools began to train crews according to an abbreviated program and they had only a small amount of flying time.

The engineering and technical crews of the air force had some experience with aircraft under battle conditions. A new manual for technical service in the air force of the Red Army had been worked out (NETS-40), which was introduced in October 1940. In it were described all the problems solved by the engineering and technical staffs when preparing and maintaining equipment under varying conditions.

Training of the engineering and technical staff was conducted at the aircraft plants, in the Zhukovsky Academy, and at military-technology schools. A considerable proportion of the technicians or young specialists got their training in the air units themselves.

Measures were also taken to expand the airfields system in order to insure aircraft dispersion, particularly in the Western military districts. In the spring of 1941 work was expanded on the construction, enlarging, and redesign of runways on more than 200 airfields located in the new border zone resulting from the reuniting of the western regions of White Russia and the Ukraine, and the entry of Latvia, Lithuania, and Estonia into the USSR. Here the airfield system was weak, and normal conditions for basing our air forces were not present. Because there were not enough airfields some air units were concentrated densely on their bases.

By a decision based on the experience of the Soviet-Finnish War, all military aircraft in the winter of 1940–41 were to be flown henceforth during the entire year equipped with landing gear with wheels. (This was instead of the temporary skis that reduced performance. ED.) This meant that measures had to be taken to insure flights during the winter weather.

Air Strategy. Soviet military strategy in the period before the war gave great importance to air power in any future war. These ideas on the use of air power were based on assumptions of achieving victory in battle, campaigns, and war by the combined efforts of all types of armed force.

Offensive operations made by ground forces must have decisive goals for destroying the enemy's defense concentrations and must be carried out deep into the rear.

The Red Army field order issued in June 1941 foresaw the assignment of air units to coordinated efforts with the ground forces and fleet, and to carry out independent operations for the High Command. Air power was considered to be a powerful means for striking at the enemy, destroying his air forces and annihilating important targets.

During general offensive operations made by the ground forces the air force was to carry out the following tasks: seizure of control of the air; cooperation with the ground forces to break through the enemy's tactical defense zone and to expand the operation in his immediate rear; protecting men and targets in our rear; striking against the enemy's reserves; protecting landings and supporting airborne troops; and carrying out aerial reconnaissance.

Much concern was given to the use of paratroops during a general offensive, the use of which was possible thanks to the heavy bombers, and later the long-range bomber forces, which were also employed for dropping troops and equipment. However, there were no aircraft in the air force designed for transport alone.

Basic assignments were also given to bomber and fighter units in instructions issued before the war (1940), as well as combat plans, battle formations, and communication plans for all types of aircraft. Great attention was given to aerial reconnaissance. Thus in a field order of 1941 we find the following: "Air power is one of the basic methods for reconnaissance, surveillance of the field of battle, and communications."

Simultaneously, fundamental principles were worked out for organizing and conducting independent operations by the air force. Provisional instructions for independent Red Army Air Force operations were issued in 1936. Here it was pointed out that "military aviation, thanks to the power of its armament, its speed, and operational range can have a great effect in all periods of a war." In accordance with these instructions, the air force, in the initial period of a war and later, was to carry out aerial operations to annihilate enemy aircraft, to destroy military-industrial and administrative targets, and to disrupt rail, maritime, and road transportation. Air operations were to be carried out by heavy bombers of the air armies belonging to the High Command reserves, and after these had been reorganized, it was assumed that long-range bomber corps and the air forces of the fronts would be utilized for this purpose.

There were also a number of other works published separately and in the periodical press, which, based on actual conditions and the possibilities of air power, explored the contents and sequence for fulfilling the assignments of aircraft in battle, in support, and as a whole. Much attention was given to the problem of working out the possibilities in a struggle for control of the air. A notable contribution to this problem was made by the work of Brigadier Commissar A. N. Lapchinsky, who made bold and accurate predictions about air force military operations in the initial period of a war, and in particular, about the question of control of the air in his book *The Air Army*. In his book he said, "Air power participated as a major factor in offensive operations, expanding the front both to the rear and laterally, but it did not replace the ground forces."[14]

A number of articles about new forms and procedures for gaining control of the air were published in the years 1937–41 as monographs, in the journal *The Air Force Herald,* and in the newspaper *Red Star*. Basic principles were developed in them concerning the necessity for carrying out air operations according to a unified plan over a large area and with the combined forces from several fronts, the decisive significance of the first strike against the basic air units of the enemy, and other questions involving the application of air power. The military academies' teaching staffs and the military leaders F. K. Arzhenukhin, P. P. Ionov, S. A. Mezheninov, B. L. Teplinsky, and V. V. Khripin, among others, made significant contributions in questions in the theory of the art of air operations and tactics for different types of aircraft.

These questions were discussed by the Supreme Military Council of the Red Army to work out a unified approach to the character and manner of air operations under combat conditions. Thus, General P. V. Rychagov, head of the Air Force Supreme Command, made a report in which he pointed out that during offensive operations the struggle with enemy air power is of extreme importance and would have great significance both for military operations and units in the rear. Simultaneously, he noted that mastery over the air could be achieved by destroying enemy aircraft at their bases by coordinated attacks against his fields at the front, repair facilities, fuel and materiel dumps, and by destroying enemy aircraft in the air. Co-ordinated mass attacks on the central airfields of the enemy was considered to be the best method for destroying his aircraft.

The operational and tactical training of command personnel in the air force in the years 1936–40 was carried out in accordance with the basic principles of regulations, manuals, and instructions concerning the role of air power and its tasks during the course of a major offensive.

Problems concerning the use of aircraft for paratroop operations were worked out during exercises and maneuvers in the prewar period. Large paratroop operations were deployed during exercises and maneuvers in the Kiev, White Russia, and Moscow military districts in 1935 and 1936.

It was noted in the report of the People's Commissar for Defense for the year 1936 that "the fundamental and most difficult step in paratroop operations—mastering of the jump technique by large numbers of men—may be considered to have been made." Thus, these first paratroop exercises made it apparent that a new kind of military unit—paratroops—and a new application for air power had appeared—the supplying of men and materiel from the air.

Political Indoctrination. The Bolshevik party Central Committee and the Soviet government never ceased to devote attention to the ideological and political indoctrination of personnel and to the strengthening of party-political work in air force units. In 1938 the Supreme Military Council, including air force representatives, was formed under the People's Commissar for Defense of the USSR. At the end of 1939, about 100 political workers were sent into the air force units from among the fliers who completed study at the Lenin Military-Political Academy or specially organized courses. During the war years many of them were designated as commanders of regiments or divisions and demonstrated their abilities as mature and independent leaders. Various political organizations and party organizations were set up. They increased their influence on all aspects of both the military and political life of the air units, especially after the Eighteenth Congress of the Bolshevik party. Party organizations became stronger and more robust. At the beginning of 1940, 41 percent of the original party organizations had fifty or more party members. About 60 percent of the air force personnel were either party members or members of the Comsomols.[15]

In 1940 the number of party organizations in the air force increased by 17 percent and the Comsomol organizations by 38 percent.
Seventy-eight percent of the air force officers were party members.
Communists and members of the Comsomol played the role of the
advance guard in the military and political training of air force
personnel.

In the prewar years much attention was devoted to training of
our troops for military actions against a powerful and well-armed
foe. Profiting from the experience of our army in military operations
at Lake Khasan,† on the Khalkhin-Gol River, against the White-
Finns, and the first battles of World War II, the Bolshevik party
plenum in March 1940 came to the conclusion that it was necessary
to improve the military and political training of our ground and air
force. In August, Supreme Command for Political Propaganda issued the directive "The Re-structuring of Political and Party Work,"
in which commanders, political workers, and party organizations were
told that all party-political work among the troops was to have a
militant aggressive character, so that it might eradicate all vulgar-
ization and conventionality in the training of our fighters, improve
discipline and organization, and increase the authority of the com-
mander-leaders.

The Political Propaganda Command, with the help of the commanders and political workers in the air force, profited from the
experience in party-political work among the troops and the air
force during the military operations on the Khalkhin-Gol River and
in the Soviet-Finnish War.

Military leaflets were systematically distributed among air units,
both at bases and during flights, that stressed the advance-guard role
of the Communists and the Comsomols. Socialist competition was
widely developed, which improved the quality of training among air
units.

In April 1940 there was a conference in the air force on the
question of training and safety. Participating at this conference were
command personnel from air force units.

The political organizations, the party, and Comsomol organizations
directed all their work to aid the commands to improve the military
training, lift the fliers' moral-political level, strengthen military dis-

† On the Soviet-Manchurian border near the Pacific, where a battle with
Japanese troops was fought from July 21 to August 11, 1938. ED.

cipline, improve safety conditions, master new aircraft and promote patriotic feelings and dedication to the socialist Motherland.

In the prewar years many measures were taken to increase the size and all-around strength of the air force. These measures played an important role in improving the battle proficiency of the air force. Soviet fliers distinguished themselves by their high moral-political and military characteristics. This was brilliantly demonstrated by the famous flights across the Arctic to America made by the crews of V. P. Chkalov and M. M. Gromov, by the exploits of our fliers during the Civil War in Spain and the battles on the Khalkhin-Gol River, and by the successes in mastering new aviation technology.

At the beginning of the war, the German fascist air force had both a qualitative and quantitative superiority over our air forces in the border military districts. For example, in the area of the Western special military district, the enemy had a 50 percent superiority in military aircraft. In the areas where the major attacks were made this superiority was even greater. The air regiments in the border military districts lived the routine life of peacetime drills; there were training flights and new airplanes were being introduced. Part of the fliers were in training centers being retrained for equipment. Thus, our air force began repelling the aggressor's sudden attack under the most unfavorable conditions—in a state of reorganization, rearming, and retraining the flight personnel for the new types of aircraft.

The Luftwaffe. The over-all planning of Fascist Germany's air forces (Luftwaffe) and the basic principles of their application in battle were based on the high-risk blitzkrieg theory. It was officially admitted that a powerful air force was one of the basic requirements for successfully conducting a blitzkrieg. Therefore the German military leaders gave high priority to aviation development.

Much work was done in the creation of military aircraft. In the years 1935–36 reliable aircraft appeared which developed into the basic air weapons of Fascist Germany during the early years of World War II.

Fighters. The fundamental fighter of the Luftwaffe, the Me 109,‡ made its appearance as early as 1935. It was used in the Spanish

---

‡ The official German designation was Bf 109, but many foreign publications used *Me* for the designer Willy Messerschmitt. ED.

Civil War and subsequently in the campaigns of World War II. With various modifications, it was used until 1945. In addition to the Me 109, the two-motored Me 110 was also used on the Soviet-German front. But this aircraft was employed most frequently against ground targets.

Another fighter type was the Fw 190, which became one of the basic German fighters; it appeared in 1943 (on the Eastern Front; it was used in France in 1941. ED.). Aircraft armament consisted of two 20 mm. cannons mounted on the wings, and two 7.9 mm. machine guns synchronized to fire through the propeller. Later a 20 mm. or even 30 mm. cannon was mounted to fire through the engine as well as heavy 13 mm. machine guns. (This version was the Ta 152. ED.)

Ground-Attack and Light Bombers. The Hs 129, an armored aircraft, the Me 110 fighter, and later the fighter-bomber version of the Fw 190 were used as ground-attack aircraft.

The Ju 88 and He 111 were the basic light bombers and reconnaissance aircraft during the entire course of the war. The Dornier Do 215 was used for the most part for reconnaissance and night operations.

Heavy bombers were employed in Germany only for special tasks and their numbers remained small. Transport aircraft and gliders were used in some operations.

Germany devoted much attention to development of high-altitude reconnaissance aircraft. They were constructed as modifications of standard reconnaissance aircraft with the installation of turbo-superchargers, which significantly increased the engines' altitude capabilities by utilizing exhaust gas energy. There were also increases made in the wing surfaces. By these methods altitudes of 12–13 kilometers, (7 to 8 miles) were attained.

At the beginning of 1941 Germany had 135 aircraft construction plants and 35 aircraft engine factories. Her aircraft industry was undergoing rapid growth. In 1933, 20 aircraft were being produced each month; in 1939 production had reached 8295 aircraft; and in 1940, over 10,000.[16] In addition to this, after 1940 there were 57 aircraft plants and 17 aircraft engine plants in occupied countries that were producing aircraft for Germany. Thus, when the USSR was attacked Germany had a powerful aircraft industry that was turning out over 1000 aircraft every month, and there were 20,700 aircraft in her air force, of which 10,980 were ready for battle and located in military units.[17]

Most of the German aircraft in service were bombers (57.8 percent). Fighters and reconnaissance aircraft amounted to 31.2 percent and 11 percent of the total, respectively. These proportions were in accordance with the enemy's intent of striking our ground and air forces with heavy attacks from tanks in coordination with bomber attacks.

It was also not without importance that the German Air Force had had much valuable experience in warfare against Poland, Norway, France, and England in 1939–40 before the attack on the Soviet Union.

German Plans and Deployment. In Directive 21, dated December 18, 1940 ("Barbarossa"), it was stated that the task of the Luftwaffe would be to paralyze and liquidate so far as it was possible the Russian Air Force, and also to support the German armies in decisive areas. In order to concentrate all possible battle forces against the enemy air force and to give direct support to the army, it was deemed not necessary to attack industrial targets during major offensives.[18]

In further extension of the "Barbarossa" plan the directive dated January 31, 1941, stated that "highest priority must be given to concentrating all air power in the struggle against the enemy Air Force and to the direct support of the ground forces. Attack against industrial centers must not be made until the ground troops have achieved their operational goals."

The military-political situation at the beginning of the Great Patriotic War favored Germany. Imperialist circles of the United States and England favored the aggressive plans of Hitler's followers. The advantageous strategic situation and the absence of active military operations in Western Europe made it possible for the German command along with its allies to concentrate nearly 5000 aircraft, including about 1000 Finnish and Rumanian planes, on the western frontier of the USSR. These aircraft were divided into four large groups, corresponding to the strike groups of the German forces. Nine hundred aircraft were held in readiness on Finnish soil, 400 aircraft of the Fifth Air Fleet and 500 aircraft of the Finnish Air Force. In East Prussia there were 1070 aircraft of the First Fleet. In the border region near Minsk were 1680 aircraft of the Second Air Fleet, and opposite Kiev were concentrated 1300 aircraft, about 800 planes of the German Fourth Air Fleet and about 500 Rumanian aircraft.*

Hitler's government considered an official declaration of war to be an antiquated international tradition. War was to begin suddenly with a powerful air strike.

In accordance with the high-risk blitzkrieg theory, air power together with armor was given a decisive role in attaining victory. Prime importance was given to aerial reconnaissance, so that even before the war began, reliable data was obtained concerning all the targets of the initial strike. German reconnaissance planes systematically intruded into the airspace of our country. In the period from January 1 to June 21, 1941, they crossed the national boundaries of the USSR 152 times,[20] surveying airfields and their locations in the border regions, counting aircraft, and drawing conclusions about the grouping of Soviet aircraft in the areas to be attacked. To a significant degree this contributed to the success of the sudden air attack against Soviet air forces on the war's first day.†

* How many German aircraft were used against the USSR in 1941? There is a great discrepancy between the 3950 cited above and the 2000 given by certain postwar German writers.

German writers reach their estimates by omitting transport, liaison, and all reconnaissance aircraft attached to the army, and assume only ten aircraft per squadron and thirty per group at the opening of the war. Other evidence, however (see p. 42), indicates that fighter and dive-bomber groups were at full strength before the invasion began.

Soviet estimates include all types of aircraft, and assume most units began the war at full strength; twelve per squadron, forty per group.

The deployment of the Luftwaffe in summer 1941 is given, as far as is known, at the end of this chapter, on pp. 29–30, to indicate the actual situation. Unfortunately, the actual June 22 strengths of most units are not available.[19]

† *German Estimate of Soviet Air Strength.* The photos taken by the high-altitude reconnaissance planes, as well as information gathered by listening to Soviet Air Force radio traffic, enabled the Germans to form an estimate of Soviet strength in Europe as it stood before the invasion.[21]

In the German estimate, there were about 50 Soviet air divisions with 162 air regiments; 3 regiments in each bomber or fighter division, and 3 or 4 in the composite, or mixed, divisions directly attached to the ground armies. Each regiment was assumed to have 4 squadrons, with 48 aircraft in the single-seat fighter or ground-attack regiments, or 36 in the bomber or recon

Summary. During the prewar years the Communist party and Soviet government gave serious attention to air force development. New units and combinations were formed, and the Soviet aircraft industry began production of new types of aircraft. Great numbers of aircraft were competently employed in exercises and maneuvers. But it was not possible to carry out completely measures under way to strengthen the air force before the war.

The theoretical principles for the use of air power in war were at the level required at that time.

---

regiments, although 60 aircraft was the authorized strength, including reserves.[22]

Deployment of these aircraft throughout the Soviet military districts in Europe was considered to be[23]:

	Bombers & Recon	Fighters	Total
Leningrad Military District			
HQ Leningrad	570	585	1,155
Baltic Military District			
HQ Riga	315	315	630
Western Military District			
HQ Minsk	660	770	1,430
Kiev Military District			
HQ Kiev	460	625	1,085
Other European Districts			
Odessa, Kharkov, and Caucasian	395	445	840
Moscow and Orel	320	240	560
	2,720	2,980	5,700

To these 5700 aircraft, the Germans added an estimated 1800 noncombat transport and liaison aircraft, and supposed there were some 3000 more Soviet aircraft in Asia. The latter would probably have to remain in position against a possible attack from Japan, and only a third were of modern types, in any case.

Afterwards, the Germans realized that their estimates had been too low, not taking into account the aircraft in reserve parks. These, of course, were of the outmoded types, there being less than 3000 of the new generation of combat types delivered before the war. Little was known in Germany of these newer models. The MiGs seen, for example, were incorrectly named I-18.

Serviceability of Soviet aircraft was guessed to be only 50 percent of aircraft available, compared to about two-thirds expected of German groups. Above all, German confidence was inflated by their two years of successful combat from 1939 to 1941. ED.

On the whole the Soviet Air Force, in spite of its inadequacies, had at its disposal great resources for the support of ground forces to defeat the enemy and to carry out its own tasks.

One may characterize the Luftwaffe at the eve of the Fascist German attack on the Soviet Union as possessing entirely modern aircraft, a large aircraft industry for producing these planes, and fliers who, for the most part, had battle experience.

The German suppositions on the role, character, and application of air power in warfare were totally connected with the high-risk theory of the blitzkrieg. This led to an overestimate by the Fascist command of the role of their own air force in the war and to an underestimate of the power and possibilities of Soviet air power.

The Luftwaffe in 1941. For the American reader, a description of German Air Force organization is added here. The tactical unit was the *Staffel* (squadron), which was usually assigned twelve aircraft. If a reconnaissance unit, it operated from a single airfield, and had only nominal relationships with the next level, the *Gruppe*.

Fighter aircraft, however, usually operated from a single air base as a *Gruppe* (group) of three squadrons, plus a three-plane staff flight, totaling 39 aircraft. Above them was the *Geschwader* (no exact English term), which usually comprised three groups plus a staff flight, or 120 aircraft. There were ten single-engined fighter *Geschwader* in the Luftwaffe in 1941, along with 15 bomber *Geschwader* of similar organization, although several groups had only nominal attachments to *Geschwader*.

These units, along with specialized dive-bomber and twin-engined fighters, were distributed among the five large *Luftflotten* (air fleets) according to wartime needs. Intermediate commands, either geographical, or as *Fliegerkorps* (flying corps), were set up when needed.

The exact number of aircraft available in each unit at any time varied with production deliveries, repair status, and operating losses, but had increased in the months preceding June 1941. Of some 100 combat groups, 67 were used against the Soviet Union in summer 1941, along with at least 72 of the 87 long-range, close, and sea recon squadrons.

Air Fleet 1 was assigned to help Army Group North destroy Soviet forces in the Baltic republics and advance to capture Leningrad. It comprised nine groups of Ju 88A bombers, and JG 54 with the new Bf 109F model fighter. Its twenty reconnaissance squadrons included two attached to the Air Fleet Command, four long-range and 11 short-range squadrons attached directly to the ground troops, and a seaplane group to work over the Baltic. For support, a Ju 52 transport group and five Fi 156 liaison squadrons were attached.

Air Fleet 2 was the largest German air force, and was to support Army Group Center in its effort to encircle and destroy the Soviet armies in the west, and advance to Moscow. This air fleet concentrated seven Stuka groups with 282 Ju 87 dive bombers, later joined by Hs 123 biplanes of the special ground-attack group. The twin-engined Bf 110 fighters were also concentrated there, including those of the SKG bomber-fighter unit. The fighters included the strongest *Geschwader*, JG 51, the only one with four groups, and led by their foremost ace, Moelders. The bombers were joined in July by the special KGr. 100 pathfinder group, while 18 recon squadrons and the usual support units were attached.

Air Fleet 4 supported Army Group South when it overran the Ukraine, and had 21 groups and 22 squadrons, along with the 504 first-line planes of the Rumanian Air Force. After Hungary declared war on June 27, its 368 aircraft were added to the enemy.

In the north, German plans involved collaboration with Finland, who began secretly mobilizing on June 17. Field Marshal Mannerheim was to attack toward Leningrad, and into Karelia, supported by the Finnish Air Force of 550 aircraft.[24] In the Arctic, a German force from Norway had entered Finland, and was to attack toward Murmansk, supported by elements of Air Fleet 5. Luftwaffe participation was limited by the bases available, but by June 21, the 42 dive bombers of the Stuka group were at Kirkenes, along with a fighter and a long-range recon squadron. The close recon squadron was forward in Finland, while a new bomber base at Banak received its first squadron of Ju 88s from KG 30 in June. The bomber and fighter elements were enlarged to group size in July.

The remainder of the Luftwaffe forces left facing Britain were Air Fleet 3, will 11 groups ranged from Holland to France, X Flying Corps in the Mediterranean with eight groups, and home defense forces with seven fighter groups.

The following table gives the deployment of the Luftwaffe in summer 1941. Official German abbreviations for the units are used; prefixes with Arabic numbers denote squadrons, Roman numbers, groups; capital letters, the primary organization:

(F)	Long-range recon squadrons
(H)	Close recon squadrons
JG	Fighter, single-seat, *Geschwader*
K.Fl.Gr.	Coastal Group
KG	Bomber *Geschwader*
KGr.	Bomber Group
LG	"Instructor" *Geschwader*
NJG	Night-fighter *Geschwader*
Ob.d.L.	High Command recon squadron
SAG	Seaplane Recon Group
SKG	Fast Bomber-fighter *Geschwader*
St.G	Dive-bomber *Geschwader*
ZG	Twin-engined *Geschwader*

Air Fleet 1

IN EAST PRUSSIA WITH ARMY GROUP NORTH
HQ INSTERBURG, COLONEL-GENERAL ALFRED KELLER
INCLUDES I AIR CORPS AND AIR COMMAND BALTIC

Bombers	*9 groups*	
	II, III/KG 1 "Hindenburg"	Ju 88A
	KG 76	Ju 88A
	KG 77	Ju 88A
	K.Fl.Gr. 806	Ju 88A
Fighters	*3⅔ groups*	
	JG 54 "Green Heart"	Bf 109F
Recon	*20 squadrons*	
Long-range	2(F) Ob.d.L.	Do 215B
	5(F) 122	Ju 88D
	4 squadrons with army	
Close	11 squadrons with army	Hs 126
Sea	SAGr 125	Ar 95, Ar 196, He 114
Support	*8 squadrons*	
	1 transport group	Ju 52
	5 liaison squadrons	Fi 156

Air Fleet 2

IN POLAND, WITH ARMY GROUP CENTER
HQ WARSAW, FIELD-MARSHAL ALFRED KESSELRING
INCLUDES II AND VIII AIR CORPS

Bombers	*11 groups*	
	I, II/KG 2 "Wooden Hammer"	Do 17Z
	I, II/KG 3 "Lightning"	Ju 88A
	III/KG 3 "Lightning"	Do 17Z
	KG 53 "Condor Legion"	He 111
	I, II/KG 4* "General Wever"	He 111
	KGr. 100*	He 111
Dive bombers	*8⅓ groups*	
	II, III/St.G 1	Ju 87
	I, III/St.G 2 "Immelmann"	Ju 87
	St.G 77	Ju 87
	II(S)LG 2*	Bf 109E, Hs 123

Fighters	*9 groups*	
	II, III/JG 27	Bf 109E
	JG 51 "Moelders"	Bf 109F
	JG 53 "Ace of Spades"	Bf 109F
Fighters (2 engines)	*4 groups*	
	I, II/ZG 26 "Horst Wessel"	Bf 110
	I, II/SKG 210	Bf 110
Recon	*18 squadrons*	
Long-range	1, 5(F) 122	Ju 88D
	2(F) 17	Do 17P
	+4 sq. with army	Do 17, Ju 88
Close	11 sq. with army	Hs 126
Support	*9 squadrons*	
	1 transport group	Ju 52
	6 liaison squadrons	Fi 156

* Exact June 22 location uncertain, but unit in Russia later that summer.

Air Fleet 4

IN POLAND AND RUMANIA WITH ARMY GROUP SOUTH HQ RZESZÓW, COLONEL-GENERAL ALEXANDER LOEHR INCLUDES II AIR CORPS IN RUMANIA, AND V AIR CORPS

Bombers	*12 groups*	
	KG 51 "Eidelweiss"	Ju 88
	I, II/KG 54 "Death's-Head"	Ju 88
	KG 27 "Boelcke"	He 111
	KG 55 "Griffon"	He 111
	III/KG 4* "General Wever"	He 111
Fighters	*9 groups*	
	JG 3 "Udet"	Bf 109F
	I, II/JG 52	Bf 109F
	(III/JG 52 near Bucharest)	
	II, III/JG 77	Bf 109E
	I(J)LG 2	Bf 109E
Recon	*22 squadrons*	
Long-range	3, 4(F) 121	Ju 88D
	4(F) 122	Ju 88D
	+5 sq. with army	Ju 88
Close	14 sq. with army	Hs 126
Support	*14 squadrons*	
	2 transport groups	Ju 52
	8 liaison squadrons	Fi 156

* Exact June 22 location uncertain, but in Russia later that summer.

Air Fleet 5

IN NORWAY
HQ OSLO, COLONEL-GENERAL HANS STUMPF
INCLUDES AIR COMMANDER KIRKENES

Bombers	*4 groups*	
	*KG 30 "Eagle"	Ju 88A
	I/KG 26 "Lion"	He 111H
Dive bombers	*1 group*	
	*IV(St.)LG 1 (Later I/St.G 5)	Ju 87R
Fighters	*2⅓ groups*	
	I/JG 77	Bf 109T
	*13/JG 77	Bf 109E
	III/JG 1	Bf 109
Recon	*9 squadrons*	
Long-range	*1(F) 120	Ju 88D
	1(F) 124	Ju 88D
Close	*1(H) 32	Hs 126
Sea	*1, 3/K.Fl.Gr. 406	He 115, Do 18G
	2, 3/K.Fl.Gr. 506	He 115, BV 138B
	I/K.Fl.Gr. 706	He 115, Ar 196
	3/K.Fl.Gr. 906	Do 18G
Support	*4 squadrons*	
	Transport group	Ju 52
	1 liaison squadron	Fi 156

* Operated against USSR in summer 1941.

Air Fleet 3

IN FRANCE AND NETHERLANDS
HQ PARIS, FIELD-MARSHAL HUGO SPERRLE
INCLUDING IX AIR CORPS AND AIR COMMANDER ATLANTIC

Bombers	*5 groups*	
	I/KG 40	Fw 200
	II/KG 40	Do 217
	III/KG 40	He 111
	II/KG II	Do 217
	KGr. 606	Ju 88
Fighters	*6 groups*	
	JG 2 "Richthofen"	Bf 109F
	JG 26 "Schlageter"	Bf 109F

Fighter (2 engines)	*1 group*	
	I/ZG 76	Bf 110
Recon	*8 squadrons*	
Long-range	1, 3(F) 33	Ju 88
	1, 2(F) 123	Ju 88
Sea	1, 3/K.Fl.Gr. 106	He 115
	5/K.Fl.Gr. 196	Ar 196
	1/K.Fl.Gr. 906	He 115

X Air Corps

IN MEDITERRANEAN
HQ TAORMINA, SICILY, GENERAL HANS GEISLER

Bombers	*5 groups*	
	LG 1	Ju 88
	II & III/KG 26	He 111
Dive bomber	*3 groups*	
	I/St.G 1	Ju 87
	II/St.G 2	Ju 87
	I/St.G 3	Ju 87
Fighter	*2 groups*	
1 engine	I/JG 27	Bf 109E
2 engine	III/ZG 1	Bf 110D
Recon	*5 squadrons*	
Long-range	1(F)121	Ju 88
	102(F)122	Ju 88
	2(F)123	Ju 88
Close	4(H)12	Hs 126

IN GERMANY
INCLUDING DEFENSE AND MARINE FORCE

Fighter	*7 groups*	
Day	I, II/JG 1	Bf 109
Night	NJG 1	Bf 110
	I/NJG 2	Ju 88C
	I/NJG 3	Bf 110
Recon	*5 squadrons*	
Sea	2.K.Fl.Gr. 106	Do 18G
	1/K.Fl.Gr. 196*	Ar 196
	2/K.Fl.Gr. 406	BV 138
	1/K.Fl.Gr. 506	BV 138
	2/K.Fl.Gr. 906	BV 138

* Operated in the Baltic against the USSR in summer of 1941. ED.

II

AIR POWER IN THE 1941 SUMMER CAMPAIGN

Fight on the Frontiers, June 22–July 10. At dawn on June 22, 1941, the fascist German army treacherously attacked the Soviet Union with millions of men. A blow of immense force suddenly crashed against our ground forces, airfields, railroad systems, army bases, and cities located in the border zone. After massive preliminary artillery and air attacks, German troops invaded the territory of the USSR. Over a huge expanse from the Baltic to the Black Sea unfolded bloody and ferocious battles on a scale hitherto unknown.

In order to seize control in the air, Hitler's command assigned more than 50 percent of its air power to this area. On June 22, more than 1000 German bombers attacked more than 66 of our airfields, often several times, on which were based the core of the air forces of the Western border districts. The first to be attacked were those airfields at which were based regiments equipped with the latest-type aircraft. At the same time, German fighter planes fought our planes in the air and also attacked antiaircraft units at the airfields.

As the result of these sudden mass strikes at our airfields and intense aerial battles, the air forces of the Western districts in the first day of the war lost around 1200 airplanes, including 800 that were destroyed on airfields.*

However, the attempts of the enemy to completely destroy the Soviet Air Force and to crush the will of our fliers to fight was not

---

* German claims for the whole front were 322 in the air and 1489 on the ground. Part of the discrepancy in the ground totals may be aircraft thought repairable at the time, but many of these were lost when their airfields were overrun; the Germans claimed 242 aircraft captured by July 8 by their Army Group Center.

Wartime claims of enemy losses were usually excessive, as in the Battle of Britain, where claims were double actual German losses. The Germans admitted the loss of only 35 aircraft on June 22.[25] ED.

crowned with success. The experience in aerial warfare which the German fliers had obtained in campaigns in Poland, France, Belgium, and in the air battles over England did not support the hopes of Hitler's High Command. In spite of the difficulties and the complexities of the situation, Soviet fliers manfully entered into battle with the fascist Luftwaffe. On the first day of the war, our air force made 6000 sorties and destroyed in aerial combat more than 200 enemy planes. "In spite of the suddenness of the German attack," admit the fascist officers and generals, "the Russians were able to find the time and the forces to render firm resistance."

Five Fronts.   The general military assignments of the air force along the front were outlined in the order of the People's Commissar for Defense (Marshal S. K. Timoshenko until July 19, when J. V. Stalin assumed the post, and Timoshenko took command of the Western Front. ED.) that went out to the air force at 7:15 A.M. on June 22. (In the first days of the war the Leningrad, Baltic, Western, Kiev, and Odessa military districts were reorganized respectively into the Northern, Northwestern, West, Southwestern, and Southern Fronts.) The major task of our air force was battle with the Luftwaffe. However, the rapid and extensive advance of the German armies within the boundaries of our territory required the Soviet command to revise this original decision and to direct both the forces at the front and the long-range bombers to destroy the tank and motorized columns of the enemy and to support our defensive units. In addition, our long-range bombers began to strike at railroad lines and at military-industrial targets behind the front.

The military operations of our air force (Commanding General P. F. Zhigarev) began almost simultaneously along the whole Soviet-German front, but differed according to circumstances.

Northwestern Front.†   Units of the Northwestern Front Air Force (Commanding General L. P. Ionov) on the night of June 21 were carrying out training flights. In the morning when the flights had been completed and the support team was engaged in inspection and

---

† Hitler's Army Group North, according to the Nazi plan, advanced through Lithuania and Latvia, where they were to reach Riga in a week. Then, as its left wing moved into Estonia, the Panzer group would enter Russia itself at Pskov, to open the way to Leningrad. Success would depend on crushing the Northwestern Front armies and air force. ED.

servicing their equipment, German bombers appeared in the sky. In spite of the suddenness of the attack, the enemy did not succeed in causing real losses either at the airfields or in the air.

The air force initiated military operations at ten or eleven o'clock. Bombers and ground-attack bombers in groups of from 10 to 18 planes began to strike at enemy tank columns near Tilsit, Taurage and Palukne, and at crossings on the Niemen River. Fighters began battle with fascist bombers. During the war's first day, the air force on this front flew more than 2000 sorties. In air battles Soviet fliers destroyed more than 20 enemy planes.

Despite the stubborn and heroic resistance of the Soviet armies and air forces, the enemy's tank and motorized divisions on the war's first day succeeded in penetrating 20 to 50 kilometers (12½ to 31 miles) into Soviet territory. Many airfields were in danger of capture. Our air forces found it necessary to shift to the east, to the Mitavia and Dvinsk regions in Latvia.

Struggling to restrain the enemy's advance, troops on the Northwestern Front, in accordance with a directive from the General Headquarters of the High Command (hereafter *Stavka* ED.), on June 23–25 made a counterattack toward Sauliai and Tilsit. Almost all the aircraft of the Front and the 1st Long-range Bomber Corps were engaged in the support of this counterattack. The battle raged for three days in this area on the ground and in the air.

Soviet fliers destroyed German tanks and troops in the battle area, flew cover for the 8th and 11th Armies and also for units of the 12th and 3rd Mechanized Corps, and bombed railroad lines, stations, and reserves moving toward the front. Our fliers flew more than 2100 sorties in filling these assignments. But the efforts of the Soviet Air Force in this period were scattered over a wide front, not concentrated in specific directions, and the air force did not have firm communications with the ground forces. This resulted in an unsatisfactory operational effectiveness. In addition, our fighters did not succeed in providing constant and reliable protection for our strike forces on the ground, who suffered serious losses from enemy bomber attacks.

After stubborn and bloody battles with the superior forces of the enemy, the troops on the front were forced to retreat to the northeast. Having seized the initiative, the enemy by July 10 had advanced toward Leningrad and Pskov as much as 500 kilometers (310 miles).

In the first 18 days of the war, the air force on the Northwestern

Front flew more than 8000 sorties, causing significant losses in men and equipment. But our air force also took serious losses in violent battles.

Western Front. Yet more serious was the situation in the air over the Western Front. In this strategically most important quarter, German bombers made intensive attacks on 26 airfields, at which were based our best-trained and most effective fighter regiments, which had been equipped with new types of fighters (MiG-3 and Yak-1). Certain airfields (Tarnovo and Dolubovo) located directly on the border were even shelled by the enemy's long-range artillery.‡

In spite of this difficult situation, the Front Air Force heroically fought with the enemy and on June 22 carried out 1900 sorties. Bomber groups attacked the enemy at Sokolov, Dedlets, Lukow, and Biala Podlaska airfields, and also tank concentrations in enemy columns in the regions of Tsekhanovets, Konstantinov, Avgustov, and Suvalki. Front fighter planes repelled numerous enemy bomber attacks and destroyed in the course of the day more than 100 German planes.

Resisting the sudden fascist attack, Soviet fliers carried out their military operations at a high level, displaying heroism and daring. A squadron commander of the 127th Fighter Regiment, I. I. Drozdov, on the first day of the war flew five sorties and shot down two German planes in aerial combat, and Senior Political Instructor A. A. Artemyev made nine sorties and shot down three planes. Many Soviet fliers, when all their ammunition had been expended, courageously and with determination rammed enemy planes to prevent the enemy from attacking equipment and ground forces. On June 22 on the Western Front ramming attacks were made by Deputy Squadron Commander of the 123rd Fighter Regiment, Lt. P. S. Ryabtsev; Deputy Squadron Commander for Political Affairs, Senior Political Officer A. S. Danilov; and Second Lt. D. V. Kokorev.

In subsequent battles along the border, the major efforts of the

‡ Soviet losses were concentrated in this district, which lost 528 aircraft on the ground and 210 in the air, of the 1200 lost altogether on the war's first day.[26] Many more with repairable damage had to be abandoned in the hasty withdrawal. Loss of most of the district's aircraft placed this front at a great disadvantage. The Germans advanced with two Panzer armies, acting as jaws of a movement which encircled Red Army troops between Bialystok and Minsk, when the two tank forces met near Minsk on June 27. ED.

Front Air Force were directed at the destruction of the great tank concentrations in the Suvalki salient.

Individual strikes by our bombers against enemy troops along roads and in areas of troop concentrations were very successful. Thus, on June 24, 13th Bomber Division crews commanded by General F. P. Polynin successfully attacked a column of German tanks in the regions of Grudopole, Pilovidy, and Ivantsevichi. The strike was made sequentially by three flights of nine planes just at the time when the tank units were concentrated at the crossing on the Shara River. The enemy, not expecting attacks from the air, lost many tanks and soldiers.

On June 25, during the counterattack by units of our 11th and 6th Mechanized Corps near Grodno, air regiments of the 12th and 13th Bomber Divisions, the 43rd Fighter Air Division, and the 3rd Long-range Bomber Corps carried out 780 sorties and destroyed about 30 tanks, 16 guns, and 60 armored vehicles together with their crews.

The struggle against the Luftwaffe in this period was marked by constant and intense aerial warfare. German bombers continued to attack the fields where our aircraft were stationed. However, as the result of the increasing resistance of our fighters, dispersal of units, and camouflage of aircraft, losses on the airfields were significantly lowered.

In spite of a difficult situation, the Air Force of the Western Front during the first eighteen days of the war flew around 7000 sorties, inflicted significant losses on the enemy, and also acquired battle experience which made it possible to increase resistance to the enemy both on the land and in the air.*

Southwestern Front.† On the Southwestern Front (commanded by Air Force General E. S. Ptukhin, and from July 1941, General

---

* By July 1, no more than 120 aircraft remained of the Western Front's air strength, front air Commander I. I. Kopets was a suicide, and front Commander D. G. Pavlov was removed. Command of the front was given to the People's Commissar for Defense, Marshal Timoshenko, and his deputy, Yeremenko, and on July 1 the first reinforcement of 30 fighters arrived. ED.

† The German's Army Group South aimed its main blow toward Kiev, and after bitter tank battles, captured Lvov on June 30, and reached Zhitomir on July 9. Its right wing, in Rumania, facing the Soviet Southern Front, had orders to remain in place, at the Prut River, except for winning a bridgehead and containing Soviet forces there. ED.

F. A. Astakhov) the appearance of enemy aircraft was met by fighter units which took off at the sound of warning sirens. In the very first air battles, our fliers knocked down several planes and scattered the formations of German bombers. However, it was not possible to curtail their operations completely. Striking at 23 airfields of the air force on this front, the enemy took out of action around 200 of our aircraft.

Air force units received their military assignment at 10:00 A.M. and began operations in the afternoon on June 22. The bombers of the front made several strikes at the tank columns of the enemy near Grubeshov and Ustilug, making 240 flights in regimental groups. Fliers of the fighter units fought intense battles from the moment of the enemy attack. At 4:25, First Lt. I. I. Ivanov, a flight commander of the 46th Fighter Regiment, having exhausted his ammunition, resorted to ramming and knocked down an enemy bomber. This feat was performed in the Zholkva region, not far from the place where the famous Russian flier P. N. Nesterov, in August 1914, for the first time in history, rammed an enemy plane in aerial warfare.‡ On August 2, 1941, Lt. I. I. Ivanov was awarded the title of Hero of the Soviet Union. On the same day, fighter pilot Second Lt. L. G. Butelin on the Southwestern Front rammed another fascist aircraft.

In all during the war's first eighteen days the Air Force of the Southwestern Front flew approximately 10,000 sorties, aiding the ground forces in destroying the enemy and restraining his advance.

Southern Front. The Air Force of the Southern Front began its military operations under less difficult conditions (under Commander of the Air Force, General F. G. Michugin). In the several days before the war began, the Odessa military district command was in the process of verifying the operational preparedness of its troops and aircraft. In this connection, aviation units were dispersed onto field air bases where their aircraft were scattered and camouflaged, and flight equipment was in a state of heightened military preparedness. In the fighter regiments, flights were organized and measures were taken to alert flight personnel. The military district's air force

‡ Nesterov rammed Austria's Baron von Rosenthal on August 26, 1914. Both pilots were killed. ED.

staff was moved from Odessa to Tiraspol, from where it had time to organize communications with subordinate units.

Thanks to these measures the fighter pilots met the attack of the German Air Force opportunely and without confusion, resisting it stubbornly and causing serious enemy losses. The attacks of the German bombers on the airfields of the air force on this front were not effective. The enemy attacked six airfields, for the most part empty or mock fields, and put out of commission six of our planes, but lost thirty bombers.

But there was also a temporary loss of communications and control by the air force staff over the units on the Southern Front. However, the air regiments' commanders, not waiting for orders for military action from above, independently made decisions for repelling the flights of the enemy. Such a decision was made, for example, by the commander of the 67th Fighter Regiment, Major B. A. Rudakov. Under his command, pilots on the first day of the war made 117 combat flights and successfully repelled four attacks from enemy bombers. In aerial combat they destroyed thirteen planes, while they themselves lost two fighters. In these battles First Lt. A. I. Moklyak, a flight commander, especially distinguished himself, shooting down with machine-gun fire two German planes, and rammed a third.

Lieutenant Colonel V. P. Ivanov, 55th Fighter Regiment commander, also displayed intelligent initiative and courageous action. When he received the alarm that enemy planes had violated the border and that twenty bombers and eighteen fighters were approaching the Beltsy airfield, he immediately sent the squadron on duty into the air with eight MiG-3s. Attacking the enemy directly, the fliers scattered the German bombers and forced them to jettison their bombs in disorder without reaching their targets. Hearing the alarm, the rest of the regiment's fliers bravely went into battle and drove the enemy into flight. Only individual bombers were able to break through to damage insignificantly three of our planes and to ignite a gasoline storage area.

The Southern Front command concentrated its efforts in attacking the troops of the enemy who had invaded our territory. The first dive-bomber attacks were made on the Prut River crossings and against the enemy troop columns. The effective actions of our air force caused significant losses to the enemy both in men and materiel. "Both the command and the men," it was stated in the telegram of the

9th Army Council of War, "give comradely thanks to the fliers of the 21st Composite Air Division (Commander Col. D. P. Galonov) and the Night Bomber Regiment commanded by Lt. Col. F. P. Kotlyar, for their active help in the destruction of the enemy. Thanks to the outstanding activities of the air force, the enemy, who had crossed the borders of our land, was so demoralized that he had to quickly retreat, mercilessly attacked by the accurate fire of the airmen."

Altogether, during the first eighteen days of the war the Air Force of the Southern Front flew more than 5000 sorties and destroyed 238 enemy aircraft in aerial combat or on airfields. During this period the total number of aircraft belonging to the front decreased insignificantly; taking into account replacements; this amounted to 734 planes.

*Northern Front.** The enemy armies on the northern wing of the Soviet-German front began their attack on the seventh day of the war, June 29. However, our air force began its military operations in this area on the third day of the war.

On June 25 according to a *Stavka* directive, the Northern Front Air Force (commanded by General A. A. Novikov), together with the Air Force of the Red Banner Baltic Fleet (Commanding General V. V. Yermachenkov) and the Air Force of the Northern Fleet (Commanding General A. A. Kuznetsov), made a massive attack on 19 airfields in Finland and northern Norway where were stationed German 5th Air Fleet units and the Finnish Air Force. The attack purpose was to weaken the enemy's northern air forces and to prevent attacks on Leningrad.

This bombing attack made by our air force was preceded by detailed aerial reconnaissance that analyzed the types of aircraft on the air bases and the location of the aircraft on the ground. Early in the morning, 236 bombers and 224 fighters appeared precisely over the assigned targets. The enemy, caught in confusion, did not have time to offer organized resistance. Our fliers, without hindrance, dropped their bombs on planes on the ground, fuel supplies, and military supplies. As a result of this first attack 41 enemy planes were destroyed or damaged. Our planes suffered no losses.

---

* While Finland had secretly mobilized its forces by June 17, it was not intended to begin the northern offensive until a week after the invasion had begun on the main front. Then the Finns were to attack toward Leningrad, and the German corps in the north toward Murmansk. ED.

During the next six days several effective raids were made against these same airfields. According to data taken from aerial photographs, our fliers put out of action more than 130 planes.

Bombers of the 2nd, 41st, 55th, and 5th Composite Air Divisions vigorously bombed troops on the battlefield, as well as those coming up from the reserves. With the intent of disrupting the transportation and mobility of the enemy forces, the air force on this front from July 1 to July 5 bombed the Finnish ports on the Gulf of Bothnia and the most important bridges, dams, power plants, and sections of railroad. Successful attacks on these targets disrupted rail movements and therefore retarded the grouping of enemy troops preparing to advance.

At the beginning of July, two regiments of the 2nd Composite Air Division were transferred from the airfield at Staraya Russa for action on the Northwestern Front, where a very difficult situation had developed. Carrying out their assignments under difficult weather conditions and without fighter cover, the bombers of these regiments in four days completed more than 530 sorties, dropping 250 tons of bombs and inflicting serious losses on enemy forces. Somewhat later, two more air divisions (the 41st Composite and the 39th Fighter Divisions) of the Northern Front were transferred to the section of the front held by troops defending the border at the Velikaya River.

Simultaneously, in the Leningrad area our fighters were actively engaged in destroying enemy aircraft in the air. The first meeting with fascist aircraft took place in this area on June 23. That day Second Lt. A. V. Chirkov detected and shot down an enemy reconnaissance plane and the next day First Lt. P. S. Pokryshev destroyed a plane. Soon pilots over Leningrad were to become famous, such as First Lt. S. I. Zdorovtsev and First Lt. P. T. Khariton, who rammed German bombers, and Second Lt. M. P. Zhukov, who shot down several enemy planes. On July 8, 1941, M. P. Zhukov, S. I. Zdorovtsev, and P. T. Khariton became the first men in World War II to receive the high honor of Hero of the Soviet Union.

Altogether in the first eighteen days of the war, the Air Force of the Northern Front carried out approximately 10,000 sorties. By July 10, there were 837 aircraft in the units of this front.

Long-range Bombers of the High Command. Together with the air forces of the Fronts, the Long-range Air Force (ADD) was also active in destroying the enemy forces. In the first three days of the war, the long-range bombers attacked industrial and military targets in the cities of Koenigsberg, Danzig, Bucharest, Constanţa, and Ploeşti.

The attacks of these long-range aircraft caused much damage to the enemy. In addition, they forced Hitler's command to maintain large numbers of antiaircraft guns and fighter planes in the rear to protect targets. These flights had great moral and political significance because they revealed the falsity of Hitler's claims that the Soviet Air Force had been completely destroyed.

Later, in connection with the swift movement of enemy troops deep into our country, the Long-range Air Force operated largely against the motorized equipment and the tank columns of the enemy and against battlefield troops, causing great losses to the enemy and therefore slowing the rate of his advance. To complete this assignment, during the first eighteen days of the war the ADD units completed 2112 sorties (this was 95 percent of all their sorties).

The crew of a long-range bomber flown by squadron commander Captain N. F. Gastello provided a brilliant example of fearlessness and devoted service to the Motherland. When attacking a German motorized column on the Molodechno-Rodoshkevichi road on June 26, 1941, his Il-4 was hit by antiaircraft fire. There was no opportunity to save the aircraft, but to abandon it and to take to parachutes meant to fall into the hands of an enraged enemy. The plane, wrapped in flame, was flown into a troop concentration and equipment center. For this exemplary and heroic feat, Captain N. F. Gastello was posthumously awarded the title of Hero of the Soviet Union, and his name was entered into the rolls of the 207th Long-range Air Division. His navigator Second Lt. Skorobogaty, and aerial gunner-radioman Second Lt. A. A. Burdenyuk, and the aerial gunner Tech. Sgt. A. A. Kalinin, were posthumously granted medals of the USSR.

The Fleet Air Force, from the first day of the war, was also involved in the battle against the advancing enemy in the coastal regions.

The Frontier Air Battles Summarized. Thus, during the first eighteen days of the war the entire Soviet Air Force made more than 47,000 sorties to repel the foe and to support our troops.

The major effort of the air force—47 percent of all military flights —was made to support ground troops, which was appropriate to the situation in the field. Attack weapons included high-explosive and fragmentation bombs of both small and medium size, as well as machine-gun fire and rockets. The major targets of our aircraft were tanks, artillery, and mortars in firing position, tank and motorized columns, vehicle concentrations, river crossings, reserves, and troops on the battlefield.

Beginning in July, our air force began to attack enemy airfields more actively. At the beginning of that month, the air force commander ordered the commanders on the Northern, Northwestern, Western, and Southwestern Fronts together with the Long-range Bomber Corps to attack 31 enemy airfields. Only unfavorable weather conditions made it impossible to carry out this plan completely. Only a few airfields were attacked and this for the most part in the area of the Western Front.

Five days later attacks were made simultaneously against the enemy airfields along almost the whole Soviet-German front. On the eve of this attack it had been ascertained by all types of reconnaissance that on the morning of July 8 the German Air Force intended to attack all our airfields. In connection with this the *Stavka* demanded from all commanders on the fronts that a decisive strike be made against the German airfields. At dawn on July 8 the combined units of the Long-range Air Force and the air forces of the five fronts made bombing attacks on 40 airfields. The Air Force of the Western Front alone destroyed or damaged 54 German planes.

All in all, during the first eighteen days of the war the air forces of the fronts made more than 1000 sorties in strikes against enemy airfields, and put out of commission 348 enemy planes, and destroyed 752 aircraft in aerial battles.†

Reorganizing under Attack. Under the difficult conditions at the first period of the war, the party, the government, and the High Command took many measures to strengthen the air force. The Air Forces of the Fronts were organized on the foundation of the Air Forces of the Border Districts. With the intent of coordinating their efforts, on July 10 headquarters for air forces on the Northwestern, Western, and Southwestern Fronts were formed. By a *Stavka* order on June 29, the Chief of Operations of the Red Army Air Force was replaced

† During this period, the invaders had overrun most of the border area, and inflicted heavy losses on the Soviet Union. Aircraft losses in 1941 were to average 1 per 32 sorties, indicating that around 1500 Soviet planes were lost in the air, while over 1000 were lost in the airfields due to surprise attacks, or abandonment during the first two weeks' activities.[27] ED.

by the office of the Air Force Commander of the Red Army with the rights of a Deputy People's Commissar of Defense. To this office was named General P. F. Zhigarev, for whom was created a military council and a staff. After June 23, 1941, the Civil Air Fleet aircraft were assigned operationally to the People's Commissar for Defense. From the Civil Air Fleet were carved air units, subordinate units, and detachments which entered into the organization of the Fronts' air forces.

For training flight personnel in new technology and their general preparation for military action, reserve air regiments and brigades were created. Within the internal military districts, new air units were quickly formed and sent to the front.

Simultaneously, measures were taken to remove deficiencies in organization, operation, and supply in the air forces by the *Stavka*, the General Staff, and the Air Force Command of the Red Army.

In order to lower the losses in aircraft, beginning in the first part of July 1941, planes were used for the most part at high altitudes and at night. During day operations, long-range bombers were used at medium altitudes with secure protection from fighter planes and after antiaircraft fire had been dampened.

Trying to increase troop support and to raise the effectiveness of operations against the enemy, *Stavka* ordered the command of the air force "to destroy tanks, troops, fuel supplies, air bases and machine guns on those bases by incendiary bombs." In the directive instructions were given "to immediately organize an attack on the major and most dangerous enemy concentrations from the air by subordinate aircraft armed with granulated phosphorus, thermite, and also charges with inflammable mixtures. . . ."

Generalizing on the experiences of the war's first two weeks, the Red Army's Air Force commander on July 9 issued a directive in which he demanded that the command of the air force of the Fronts, "When basing aircraft on an airfield, have on each of these no more than nine to twelve aircraft. After the planes have landed, they are to be immediately dispersed into field locations, camouflaged and put under cover. Trenches are to be dug for the support crews. Camouflage must be rigorously maintained on the airfields, and there is to be no walking or riding of automobiles on the runways." In the same directive, measures are given to improve air watch and to raise the military effectiveness of antiaircraft units and fighter units to repel enemy air attacks. Meeting the demands of this directive gave positive results. The loss of our aircraft from enemy air strikes against airfields decreased.

During the very first days of the war the Communist party expanded its party-political and educational work within the Red Army. Many responsible and experienced party officials were sent to the air force.

The political organizations, together with the party and the Comsomol organizations in the air units, rendered daily service to commanders in the struggle against various elements of complacency and carelessness; they made it clear to all aviators that mortal danger loomed over our Motherland, and helped them to organize military operations. All this was favorably reflected in an improvement in the air force military preparedness. The morale and political outlook of our aviators was high. In these difficult conditions, in innumerable battles with the enemy, Soviet fliers daily carried out heroic feats. Our best warrior-fliers—pilots, navigators, machine gunners, engineers, technicians, and specialists in the rear—requested membership in Lenin's party, demonstrating a son's love for the Motherland. Thus, from June 22 to July 8, 1941, more than 70 men were taken into the party from the 18th Long-range Bomber Division, and 68 from the 55th Composite Air Division, and 98 men from the 5th Composite Air Division. The increase in the numbers of party organizations in the air force demonstrated the indissoluble tie between the Communist party and the masses of the country. Together with the Comsomols, membership in the party at that time was from 65 percent to 85 percent of the personnel of the aviation units.

The German Advance Continues, July 10–September 30, 1941.‡

Leningrad Is Surrounded. In the period from July 10 to September 30, our air forces protected and supported ground troops in all defense operations carried out by the Red Army with the purpose of

‡ By July 10, 1941, the invaders had reached a line running from Pskov in the north down to Vitebsk, Mogilev, and Zhitomir. The greatest danger came from Hitler's intention to "annihilate" the Soviet army with encirclement battles, using armored spearheads to prevent "withdrawal to the rear," in the words of the Barbarossa directive.

In the northwest, the Nazi plan to destroy Leningrad began with an advance to surround Leningrad with the help of a Finnish offensive from the north. By September 8, the enemy reached Petrokrepost on Lake Ladoga, cutting Leningrad off by land from the rest of Russia. ED.

stopping the offensive of the enemy, wearing down and exhausting his offensive forces, and disrupting his plan for a blitzkrieg.

In the northwest area the German troops of Army Group North, after passing the line of Pskov-Ostrov-Opochka-Idritsa, attempted to capture Leningrad with the aid of Finnish troops. The enemy had a fourfold superiority in guns and mortars, twofold in infantry, and one and a half fold in tanks and aircraft. He had 1900 aircraft* out of which 1200 operated directly over Leningrad. Our aircraft from the air forces of the Northern and Northwestern Fronts, the Baltic Fleet Air Force and the 7th Fighter Air Corps of Air Defense (ADF) had 1300 mainly outdated aircraft.

In order most effectively to employ our air power, *Stavka* subordinated the air forces of the Fronts, the navy, and also the 7th Fighter Air Corps (ADF) to the Northwestern Front commander, General A. A. Novikov, who coordinated the actions of the air units and directed their basic efforts toward completion of their major tasks.

The defensive efforts of our troops on the approaches to Leningrad began on July 11. The enemy's tanks and motorized divisions with the support of their aircraft went on the offensive simultaneously in the directions of Luga, Novgorod, Olonets, and Petrozavodsk. But the most dangerous of all were the enemy troops moving on Luga and Novgorod, who were attempting to break through on the shortest road to Leningrad. Therefore, around 70 percent of our air power was concentrated on the battle with the enemy in these areas.

Operating in squadrons and flights, bombers and fighters struck at the enemy columns on the roads, destroying the enemy crossings on the Luga River and tanks and troops on the battlefield. On July 11 and 12 alone, Soviet fliers put out of commission in the Luga area 15 tanks and 90 armored vehicles, and destroyed 2 bridges.

Our aircraft in the Novgorod area were not less successful. From July 14 to 18 they actively supported the 11th Army of the Northwestern Front, which was counterattacking in the area of Soltsy. To support the 11th Army, not only the Air Force of the Northwestern Front, but also the 1st Corps of the Long-range Bombers and the 2nd Composite Air Division of the Northern Front Air Force were involved—in all around 235 planes. By day and night, the enemy troops were subjected to attacks from Soviet aircraft which during the five days of battle made 1500 sorties over targets in the area of

---

* Combined strength of 1st and 5th Air Fleets, plus Finns, ED.

Soltsy. In close cooperation with the air force, our troops caused many losses to the 8th Panzer Division of the enemy, throwing it back 40 kilometers (25 miles). The threat of a German breakthrough to Novgorod was averted for the time being.

The former chief of the German Army General Staff, General Hadler, wrote in his diary during this period: "The enemy's aircraft are very active . . . they are making strikes on the combined Rhineguard Corps and our infantry divisions, which are advancing along the eastern bank of Lake Chudskoye. . . . One is aware in general that in the enemy air force there is firm and effective command."

In these intense battles the strong and weak aspects of the enemy aircraft became apparent, while there also appeared inadequacies in the operations of our fliers, and energetic measures were taken to eliminate them. Thus, the experience of the first days of the war showed that the German fighters attempted to break up the large flights of the Soviet aircraft and attack them in small units. Therefore, our bombers began to carry out operations in close order, organizing a shield against enemy fighters. When protecting ground troops and important targets, Soviet fighter planes maintained formations consisting of attack and cover groups. The attack group struck at enemy bombers and the second group protected the attack group. When this was done, the characteristics of the new planes, the MiG-3 and Yak-1, and the older I-16 and I-153, were taken into account.

By the end of July, the enemy offensive on Leningrad had been stopped. In the twenty-two days of battle on the distant approaches to the city, our air force flew 16,567 sorties and caused the enemy not inconsiderable losses.

Once they had regrouped their troops and drawn up their reserves, the German armies with the support of 1500 aircraft undertook a new drive on Leningrad. This time they struck from the west, the southwest, and the northwest, attempting to surround and destroy the Soviet armies near Leningrad and to capture the city.

On July 31, seven Finnish divisions with aircraft support took the offensive on the Karelian Isthmus. Having a great superiority in forces, they advanced to the old frontier. But their attempts to break through the Karelian defense region were not successful.

Fliers of the 5th Composite Air Division and the 41st Bomber Air Division, which during a sixteen-day period flew approximately 1100 sorties, aided the troops of the 23rd Army which defended this region. In this battle the fliers of the ground-attack squadron under the command of First Lt. N. I. Svitenko were especially successful. During a seven-day period they destroyed 30 enemy vehicles with infantry and shot down 7 aircraft in air battles. In one of these flights the airplane of First Lt. Svitenko was hit by antiaircraft fire. The flier landed on territory occupied by the enemy. His death seemed inevitable. But the flier and Comsomolets A. M. Slonov came to the rescue of his commander; Slonov landed near the damaged aircraft in full sight of the enemy, picked up his commander, and returned to his unit.

In support of our troops in the war against enemy tanks advancing from the south toward Leningrad, the Soviet Command drew on the basic forces of the Air Force of the Northern Front (350 aircraft), part of the aircraft of the Baltic Fleet, and the 7th Fighter Air Corps, ADF.

The bloody battle continued for thirty days and nights. The attacks of the enemy tanks and infantry followed one after another. German bombers in groups of 30 and 40 planes attacked the defensive positions of our troops, trying to clear a path to Leningrad for their Panzer divisions.

In order to reduce the intensity of the attacks from enemy aircraft, our fighters began to protect our troops during the daylight hours with constant patrols. Intense air battles resulted, which at various points on the front became wholesale battles with each side participating with 100 to 150 aircraft. The 39th Fighter Air Division under the command of Colonel Ye. Ya. Kholzakov displayed a high level of skill and great daring in these battles. In August alone they destroyed around 100 German aircraft; of these Second Lt. A. V. Chirkov shot down 7; First Lt. A. N. Storozhakov, 8, and First Lt. P. A. Podryshev, 4.

Our bombers also attacked 10 enemy airfields on August 25 and 28 on which our aerial reconnaissance had discovered large concentrations of aircraft. The attacks on the airfields were carefully prepared. In each squadron certain crews were assigned to destroy enemy antiaircraft. The moment of the attack was skillfully chosen—dawn —when aircraft were located on the airfields. All of this guaranteed high results for our aircraft, which flew more than 250 flights and destroyed more than 40 aircraft. Losses to German aircraft in the month of August amounted to 213 planes in this segment of the front. The level of enemy bomber flights noticeably declined.

In this period the fliers of the 2nd Bomber, 41st Fighter Air Divisions, and the 7th Fighter Air Corps (ADF) constantly supported the defensive armies in the field, making four or five sorties each per day, putting many tanks out of commission, setting fire to as many as 200 armored vehicles, and killing many enemy soldiers and officers.

On August 22, thanks to the combined efforts of the ground troops and the air forces, the offensive of the Germans on the southern approaches to Leningrad was stopped. The front was to be stabilized at the line from Gatchina to Oranienbaum until the middle of September.

The enemy went on the offensive on August 10 in the area of Novgorod and Lake Chudskoye. Attempting to smash the offensive units of the 39th German Mechanized Corps, the combined forces of the 11th and the 34th Armies of the Northwestern Front counterattacked near Staraya Russa. In support of these troops the fliers of the front and long-range bombers flew 460 sorties. They operated against troops in the field and reserves moving toward the front, flew patrols over ground troops, and attacked railroad targets and rolling stock in the yards at Gulbene, Valka, and Pskov.

Fliers of the 288th Ground-Attack Air Regiment, commanded by Major I. V. Delnov, were especially successful in these attacks. These fliers daily had to participate in military operations under difficult air and ground conditions and they invariably displayed high skill, persistence, and daring.

On August 14, aerial reconnaissance discovered an enemy column consisting of as many as 150 vehicles along with infantry advancing toward Soltsy. The 288th Ground-Attack Air Regiment was ordered to attack this column. First they attacked the troop carriers, which stopped the column, and then they sprayed the troop concentration with machine-gun fire from very low altitudes. As a result of the attack more than 50 vehicles were destroyed or damaged and the advance of the column was delayed for three hours.

The counterattack, with the help of aviation, destroyed several German divisions and the survivors were pushed back as far as 60 kilometers (37 miles). Hitler's command was forced to throw into the region of Staraya Russa additional forces drawn from other segments of the front including the Smolensk region.

At the same time, *Stavka* strengthened the Russian forces and air units near Leningrad. During the first half of August, 4 air regiments arrived as reinforcements, and in September, 9 more. In order to improve the command over military activities of both ground and air forces, on August 23 the Northern Front was split in two: the Leningrad and Karelian Fronts. Correspondingly, the Air Force of the Leningrad Front (Commanding General A. A. Novikov) and the Air Force of the Karelian Front (Commanding General T. T. Khryukin) were organized.

After regrouping their troops Hitler's armies renewed their attacks. The most difficult period in the struggle for Leningrad began.

More than 600 aircraft of the Leningrad Front and 200 aircraft of the Baltic Fleet Air Force were involved in the support of our troops. In addition to these, the fliers of the 7th Fighter Air Corps (ADF) successfully operated in the air over the battlefield. During September, in support of the ground forces, our aircraft flew more than 17,000 sorties. The Air Force of the Leningrad Front alone destroyed or damaged scores of enemy tanks as well as many guns and vehicles. With the help of the air forces and the ships of the Baltic Fleet, our ground forces broke the next attempt of Hitler's men to seize Leningrad. At the end of September the enemy, having suffered great losses without accomplishing their goals, ceased their offensive operations.

During the period of defense operations on the distant and near approaches to Leningrad our aircraft, in addition to attacking the armies of the enemy, also carried out operations against his air forces. More than 15,000 sorties were flown to further this aim. Attacks on the enemy airfields were carried out according to a plan worked out by the air force staff of the Leningrad Front. Altogether, in the period from July 22 to September 22, Northwestern Front aircraft made 1760 sorties against enemy airfields, destroying and damaging as many as 500 German aircraft.

Air warfare was also conducted according to a unified plan. Aircraft from units of the 7th Fighter Air Corps (ADF), the Air Force of the Front and the Baltic Fleet Air Force defended the city against attacks from enemy aircraft. The fighter divisions were strengthened for fighting the enemy aircraft in the air. For defense against mass flights of enemy bombers over Leningrad, the general command for all aircraft was assumed by the commander of the 7th Fighter Air Corps of the ADF, Col. S. P. Danilov. For controlling fighters in the air, control points were organized, from which fighter planes were directed against enemy aircraft with the help of radio. Groups of fighter planes patrolled constantly over Leningrad, Kronstadt, and other important targets.

From July to September 1941, 4306 German aircraft took part in attacks against Leningrad. But thanks to the active resistance of all resources of the Air Defense, especially the fighter planes, only 508 bombers broke through to the city during that period. In aerial combat 333 enemy aircraft were destroyed.

The engineers, technical personnel, and drivers, under the command of Brigade Engineer A. V. Ageyev, labored manfully and unselfishly. Specialists in the rear worked well preparing an airfield system and guaranteeing the all-around battle efficiency of the air units. The aircraft, which were almost constantly in action, often returned to the airfields with numerous bullet holes and other serious damage, but within a few hours the competent hands of the technical crews, working without sleep or rest, made them ready for action.

Personnel worked under artillery fire and bomb attacks. Take-offs were made directly out from under cover, regardless of wind direction. Upon landing, the aircraft taxied into cover at high speeds. At the signal of a bell, the technical crews ran out of their trenches, secured the aircraft, and once more took cover.

Altogether during the period of summer warfare near Leningrad (until September 30, 1941) our aircraft made about 60,000 sorties. The average performance was three or four flights per day for fighter planes and two or three for bombers.

After Leningrad had been cut off by land (September 8. ED.), the efforts of our aircraft were directed to the defense of the besieged city. Soviet fliers along with ground forces protected the road across Lake Ladoga and delivered military supplies, arms, and food to the city, and evacuated the wounded and ill soldiers and city residents.

Loss of the Smolensk Region. The situation along the Western Frontier was still more tense. After the enemy had crossed a line from the Western Dvina to the Dnieper, he attacked toward Yelnya, Roslavl, and Velikie Luki, pursuing his goal of smashing the troops of the Western Front in a short time and capturing Smolensk, and then turning his 3rd Tank Group to the north for joint action with Army Group North to seize Leningrad. Furthermore, Hitler's Command planned to use the Smolensk region as a starting point for the offensive on Moscow.

Army Group Center, advancing in this direction, had a huge advantage in men and materials over the Soviet forces. In the air, the

German troops were supported by the 2nd Air Fleet, which had a thousand aircraft. At this period, the Air Force of the Western Front had in all around 370 aircraft. In addition to this, as reinforcements for the Air Force of the Western Front, there were 120 bombers of the Long-range Force's 3rd Corps and 150 aircraft from the Air Force of the Reserve Front. (Commanding the Air Force was General B. A. Pogrebov. Note: After August 1, the commanding general was Ye. M. Nikolayenko.) Colonel N. F. Naumenko of the Western Front Air Force was in charge of the entire coordination of air power in any given area.

The first five days of the Smolensk defense operation were characterized by stubborn battles to hold the line of the Dvina-Dnieper. All possible aircraft were recruited to support and cover the troops defending the Dnieper and the Western Dvina. Soviet fliers attacked river crossings, tank columns, troops in battle, and enemy aircraft on the ground. Bridges were attacked by small groups of bombers and ground-attack bombers. Demolition and antipersonnel bombs, and incendiary mixtures, which were especially effective in wooded areas, were employed. Motor columns were attacked for the most part on roads in wooded areas or on roads that cut through swampy areas.

The command of the Western Front, in its communications with *Stavka,* paid tribute to the military operations of our aircraft: "The Air Force, beginning on July 13, made intensive attacks against the enemy in the region of Vitebsk and is continuing systematic action against the columns of the enemy in this region. Simultaneously the enemy's bridge near Shklov was destroyed by an aerial attack and his columns have been subjected to constant attacks in the region of Gorki. On July 14, many enemy troops were killed by air attacks."

In spite of the Soviet troops' stubborn resistance and active support of the air forces, the enemy, at the cost of many losses, succeeded in forcing the Western Dvina and the Dnieper and overwhelming the defenses of our troops near Vitebsk, Orsha, and Shklov. From this base the Germans began their attack in the general area of Smolensk, attempting to surround and destroy our troops that were defending the Vitebsk-Shklov line.†

---

† Smolensk fell on July 19, and a second battle of encirclement went on in the area. Throughout this struggle, vigorous counteractions were launched by the Red Army in its efforts to aid the escape of its troops from the Smolensk pocket. ED.

With the aim of disrupting the plan of the enemy, the armies of the Western Front, from July 23 to 25, made counterattacks near Roslavl, Beloye, and Yartsevo. Almost all the air units and combined units of the Western and Reserve Fronts and the 3rd Corps of the Long-range Air Force were involved in the support of the ground forces. In order to insure close cooperation between the air units and the ground forces, the Western Front Air Force Staff sent its representatives to the headquarters of the counterattacking group, who by radio informed the aviation commanders of the ground and air conditions, transmitted reports from the ground forces on the attacks from the air, and worked out a system of mutually understood signals for the selection of targets. Before the beginning of the counterattack the 47th Composite and the 43rd Fighter Air Divisions were shifted close to the area of military activity. The regiments of these divisions were divided into elements consisting of 1 or 2 squadrons which were stationed on temporary fields from 11 to 20 kilometers (7 to 12½ miles) from the front lines. This made it possible to increase the number of flights and to intercept advantageously enemy planes in the air.

Constant battles occurred both on the ground and in the air for three days. Before the counterattack, the Soviet air forces attacked the reserves that were moving up, airfields (Ulla, Beshenkovichi, Krupka, Pukhovichi, Vilnius, Osipovichi, and others), and the rail centers of Orsha and Vitebsk, where aerial reconnaissance had discovered enemy troop trains. On the morning of July 23, when our infantry divisions supported by tanks, began their attack, ground-attack and heavy bombers in small groups began to wipe out enemy tanks and guns directly in front of the attacking armies.

As the result of the counterattack, the troops of the Western Front caused serious losses to the enemy and pinned down large forces near Yartsevo, Beloye, and Roslavl. This also improved the situations of the 20th and 16th Armies, which were fighting in the Smolensk region.

At the same time the troops on the left wing of the Western Front, with the help of three air divisions, in bitter fighting, stopped the advance of the enemy 2nd Army and the 2nd Panzer Group. On July 26, 1941, the Central Front was formed in this area from units of the Western Front, including the 12th and 21st Armies. The Air Force of the Western Front was also organized (Commanding

General G. A. Vorozheykin), including the 11th and 28th Composite and the 13th Bomber Air Divisions.

By the end of July the enemy advance had been halted. During the period from July 10 to July 31, the Soviet air forces flew about 5200 sorties to support and protect the troops in the area of Smolensk and Soviet fliers shot down 200 fascist aircraft. Substantial aid was provided for the ground forces.

On August 8, Hitler's command sent a part of the troops of the Army Group Center (the 2nd Army and the 2nd Panzer Group) toward the south with the aim of smashing the troops of the Central Front and developing an offensive against Konotop and Chernigov, with an extension toward the rear of the Southwestern Front.

The troops of the Central Front, inferior both in forces and equipment, could not withstand the enemy offensive and began to retreat. In order to protect the sector around Bryansk, the Bryansk Front was created on August 16, together with its air force (Commanding General F. P. Polynin). The troops of this front had the tasks of making two counterattacks—one against the flank of the 2nd Panzer Group near Starodub and the second in cooperation with the Reserve Front near Roslavl—and stopping the enemy. (The Bryansk Front had 159 aircraft at its formation, consisting of the 11th Composite Air Division. ED.)

At the same time the *Stavka* ordered the Red Army Air Force to carry out an aerial operation on August 29–31, 1941, in order to disrupt the advance of the 2nd Panzer Group. For this purpose, 450 aircraft were drawn from the air force of the fronts of the Western region and the Long-range Bomber Force. The Air Force Staff of the Red Army worked out a plan for aerial operations, which was approved by the Supreme Commander.‡

Aerial operations lasted for six days. Bombers and ground-attack planes began constant strikes on August 29 against enemy tank columns near Unecha, Starodub, Trubchevsk, and Novgorod Seversk. Deficiencies in the aircraft that were apparent during combat were compensated for by great efforts of the crews. Thus, on August 30 and 31, fliers in the TB-3 heavy four-motor bombers made two flights per night; in the SB, Pe-2, and Il-2 bombers, three or four flights; and in fighter planes, six or seven flights per day. All in all, during the operation more than 4000 sorties were flown.

‡ J. V. Stalin became Supreme Commander on August 7, 1941. ED.

The commander of the Bryansk Front, General A. I. Yeremenko, recalling the activities of the air forces, wrote in his memoirs: "The Air Force of the Front, utilizing every flying day, caused great losses to the enemy. On August 30 and 31 alone, around 1500 sorties were flown, 4500 bombs were dropped, more than 100 tanks and 20 armored vehicles were destroyed, a fuel dump was blown up, and 55 aircraft were destroyed. The air attacks were closely coordinated with operations on the ground west of Trubchevsk."[28]

The fliers also received high praise from the Supreme Commander, who in a telegram to the commander of the troops on the front wrote, "The air forces are operating well, but they would do better if reconnaissance planes would summon the bombers quickly and over radios, and not after they had returned to their landing places. . . . I wish you success. Greetings to all fliers."

During the operation our air force made effective attacks also against the airfields of the enemy. On August 30, Soviet fliers attacked eight German airfields, on which 57 aircraft were destroyed, and on September 1 and 2, nine more airfields. The decisive actions of our aircraft had their influence on the situation both in the air and on the ground.

As the result of the strong counterattack made by our troops and the strong actions of our air force the strike group of the enemy suffered serious losses. Hitler's command was required to turn part of the divisions assigned to attack toward the south against the troops of the Bryansk Front, which retarded the movement of the 2nd Panzer Group toward Konotop.

Not less severe was the battle at the same time to the east of Smolensk where the troops of the Western and the Reserve Fronts with air support continued to wear down the main force of the enemy. During the course of the counterattacks near Dukhovshchina and Yelnya the enemy took serious losses. In the region of Yelnya alone, around 50,000 German soldiers and officers were wounded or killed. Yelnya was liberated and the enemy thrown back 25–30 kilometers (15–19 miles).

The successful actions of our aircraft were several times noted by the commander of the troops on the front. In his report, the Western Front Commander, Marshal S. K. Timoshenko, pointed out that "on the 21st and 22nd of August, the enemy tried to stop the movement of our troops, introducing great concentrations of tanks and motorized troops, and with great assurance attacked

our units. But the days of easy victories for the enemy have passed.
. . . the glorious 64th and 50th Infantry Divisions and the illustrious 47th Air Division (the 61st and 215th Ground-Attack and
the 129th Fighter Air Regiments) smashed the fascist tanks and
forced Hitler's men to retreat in disorder. The enemy lost as many
as 130 tanks, more than 100 vehicles, many guns, supplies, and
1000 men killed and wounded."

Striving to weaken the effect of the German air power on our
troops, the Western Front Air Force and the fliers of the Long-range
Bomber Forces from July 10 to July 14 attacked 33 enemy airfields, damaging and destroying as many as 100 aircraft. But
the fascist aircraft also increased their flights against our airfields.
However, they were not as effective as they had been during the first
days of the war, because our aircraft were well camouflaged and
dispersed, and the watchfulness and military preparedness of the
Air Defense forces had improved. Simultaneously, the activities of
our fighter pilots increased and they made it their first order to destroy
enemy bombers.

Aircraft of the 401st Fighter Air Regiment equipped with MiG-3s
commanded by the Hero of the Soviet Union and famous test pilot
Lt. Col. S. P. Suprun, had great success in their battles with the
enemy. Under his command the fliers made five or six flights per
day. On July 4, S. P. Suprun died gallantly in an air battle with
overwhelmingly superior enemy forces. On July 22, 1941, he was
posthumously awarded a second "Gold Star." He was the first two-
time Hero of the Soviet Union in World War II.*

Moscow Is Attacked. As the enemy troops advanced deep into
our country, the Luftwaffe made bombing attacks on Vyazma,
Bryansk, Moscow, Leningrad, and other Soviet cities. As is widely
known, on July 8 Hitler issued an order to the German Air Force
to destroy Moscow by mass bombardment. The first attack on the
capital was made on the night of July 22, 1941. In this attack
250 bombers participated.† To repel this attack 170 aircraft were

---

* When the war began, U.S.-born Stepan Suprun was testing the first Yak-1M.
He organized fellow test pilots into the special 401st Regiment, which arrived
at the front near Mogilev July 1. ED.

† German sources say 127 bombers (Ju 88 and He 111) were used on
the first Moscow raid, but this number rapidly declined for the remaining
75 German raids made in 1941.[29] ED.

collected, which, together with antiaircraft artillery, destroyed 22 fascist aircraft. Only isolated bombers broke through to Moscow. By the order of the People's Commissar for Defense dated July 23, 1941, the fliers of the 6th Fighter Air Corps of the ADF (commanded by Colonel I. D. Klimov) were given thanks for their successful participation in repelling the attack on Moscow.

During the period from July 22 to August 15, 1941, there were 18 night attacks on Moscow. In 8 of these, there were 120 bombers participating; and in the remainder, from 50 to 80 aircraft. The fighter pilots and the antiaircraft artillery of Air Defense successfully met their assignment to drive off the German air attacks. The great mass of bombers could not break through to the city. Of the 1700 aircraft that participated in the attacks, only around 70 reached the city.

In the air battles to repel the enemy flights, deputy squadron commander of the 177th Fighter Air Regiment, Second Lt. V. V. Talalikhin fought heroically. On the night of August 7, he engaged a bomber in battle on the approaches to Moscow. Exhausting all his ammunition, the daring flier rammed and destroyed the enemy plane. This was one of the first aerial rammings that took place at night. By order of the Supreme Soviet Presidium of the USSR, he was granted the title of Hero of the Soviet Union. In later battles Talalikhin destroyed four more planes. On October 27, he was killed in an air battle. By order of the Minister of Defense, V. V. Talalikhin was eternally entered into the rolls of the 177th Fighter Air Regiment.

A significant role in the defense of the capital from air attacks was played by units of the Western Front Air Force and the Long-range Bomber Forces. In the period of the most frequent attacks on Moscow (July 22 to August 15, 1941) they struck at 118 enemy airfields, as the result of which the Luftwaffe activities noticeably decreased. During the second half of August and in September, the flights of the fascist bombers consisted of only small groups of planes or single planes and on the whole had only a diversionary character.

During July the Western Front Air Force was very active, receiving as reinforcements more than 900 aircraft. But as the result of losses and transfer of units to other fronts, the total number of planes in comparison with the number for July 10 was cut in half. At the beginning of August it had only 180 aircraft. But the number of German aircraft in this sector was reduced to almost one-fourth of its previous figure. Luftflotte 2 had 250 aircraft. All of this led to a reduction in air force activity on both sides. Nonetheless, air warfare did not cease. During August, the Air Force of the Western Front made 188 strikes against airfields and put about 70 German aircraft out of commission. Our losses on airfields during that period amounted to only 1 aircraft.

Defense operations near Smolensk played an important role in destroying Hitler's plan for a blitzkrieg. By the admission of the German command, their motorized and tank divisions lost half of their equipment and their losses amounted to as many as 450,000 men. Our air force carried out around 22,000 sorties and rendered significant help to the ground forces in the fulfillment of their tasks.

The Ukraine Is Overrun.   In the Southwestern Sector, Hitler's command gave to Army Group South the task of capturing Kiev and surrounding and destroying the Soviet troops on the right bank of the Dnieper. On the side of the enemy was a double superiority in tanks, guns, and infantry. His air strength (the German 4th Air Fleet and the Rumanian Air Force) was 1150 planes. Our air force had almost the same number of aircraft, but 75 percent of them were older types. The coordination of the activities of the Southern Front Air Force (Commanding General P. S. Shelukhin; after September 24, 1941, Col. K. A. Vershinin) and the Southwestern Front Air Force (Commanding General F. A. Astakhov) was carried out by the air force commander of the Southwestern Front, General F. Ya. Fala-leyev.

On July 10, fourteen German divisions, with the support of their air forces, went on the offensive. Breaking through our defense, they rushed toward Kiev. It appeared possible that the enemy would seize the Ukrainian capital. Intending to disrupt the enemy's plans, Soviet troops with the support of aviation made a counterattack against the flank of the enemy toward Novgorod Volynski and Chervonoarmeysk. Heavy fighting raged for about a month in the area of Kiev. Having lost his best troops, the enemy ceased his offensive.

Our air power played not a small role in thwarting the enemy offensive by employing mass flights effectively in the decisive sectors of the front. To support the 5th Army, which was carrying out the counterattack, six air divisions from the Front and two corps of long-range bombers were employed. Our fliers carried out their operations at a high level, making four or five flights every day. They attacked tank and motorized columns on the road between Zhitomir and Kiev, destroying troops in the field and aircraft on airfields, and protected Kiev from the air, as well as crossings and bridges over the Dnieper, and the railroad centers in Nezhin and Chernigov. Nearly 5000 sorties were flown to carry out these objectives.

In the battles near Kiev, the 62nd Bomber Division fliers commanded by Hero of the Soviet Union Col. V. V. Smirnov, and the 36th Fighter Division, under the command of Hero of the Soviet Union Col. V. V. Zelentsov, were especially successful. For their active support of the ground troops in repelling the enemy's attack, the fliers of these divisions received praise from the Military Council of the Southwestern Front.

On the extreme southern wing of the Soviet-German front, our troops were supported by four air divisions of the Southern Front and the Air Force of the Black Sea Fleet, which in a forty-five-day period flew more than 10,000 sorties.

In these battles, the 210th Bomber Air Regiment displayed high skill, daring, and heroism. On July 31, near Golovanevsk, enemy tanks and infantry attacked units of the 17th Infantry Corps. The German artillery was also very active. To aid the Soviet troops, the bomber regiment units were brought into action, and they suppressed enemy artillery fire, blew up a storage area, and destroyed several enemy tanks. Thanks to these efforts our troops escaped from the advance of the overwhelming forces of the enemy. The Military Council of the 18th Army commended the personnel of the 210th Bomber Air Regiment. From August 14 to 16, in the Bashtanka and Barmashev regions, and near Yavkino station, bombers of the 210th Regiment destroyed up to eight tanks and 30 armored vehicles, which aided the 18th Army units in their escape from enemy entrapment. For these actions the fliers were praised a second time by the command. Later on, when carrying out operations near Dnepropetrovsk, the 210th Bomber Regiment crews, on only the two days of August 25–26, put out of action several tanks and eighteen vehicles with infantry, and destroyed a crossing over the Dnieper. Thirteen fliers were granted medals for their great services to the Fatherland.

The 5th Bomber Air Regiment crews were not less successful.

On July 15 near Leovo they helped elements of the 2nd Infantry Corps to repel an attack made by enemy tanks. On July 21, the fliers of this regiment, together with fighter planes of the 67th Fighter Air Regiment, caused great losses to an enemy division, and on July 23 destroyed two river crossings near Yampol and Soroki. The 131st Fighter Air Regiment's fighters also fought well. In a four-month period during the war, they flew 1500 sorties in ground-attacks against troops in the field alone. Although this regiment had older types of planes, the fliers fought many aerial duels, destroying 63 fascist aircraft and losing 38 of their own.

First Lt. A. I. Pokryshkin, now General-Colonel of Aviation and three times Hero of the Soviet Union, received his baptism of fire in battles in this area as commander of a flight in the 55th Fighter Air Regiment. On July 20, he flew on a reconnaissance flight to the region of Beltsy. While he was carrying out this mission his MiG was hit by antiaircraft fire. It was impossible to continue his flight. Landing on territory occupied by the enemy, Pokryshkin destroyed his plane. He was then able to make his way through the front lines and returned to his unit three days later. A few days later he began once more to carry out his military assignments. In one of his flights First Lt. Pokryshkin set fire to railway equipment and silenced artillery fire from a German battery near Akimovka. The precise and decisive attacks of his fliers helped our troops to drive the Fascists out of a populated area.

Having regrouped their troops and strengthened their southern strike group with two armies brought from the region of Smolensk, the German command renewed the offensive. The balance of forces in this area was sharply altered to the advantage of the enemy. The troops of the Southwestern and Southern Fronts were in a difficult position. They were supported from the air by a combination of aviation from the fronts and two divisions of long-range bomber aircraft. In addition, the 4th and 5th Reserve Air groups were sent to this area, which included four fighter, three ground-attack, and two bomber air regiments.

During September Soviet aircraft flew about 10,000 sorties in this area. About 80 percent of the planes were engaged in battle with the German 1st and 2nd Panzer Groups and in destroying their crossings over the Desna and Dnieper rivers. However, the superiority of the enemy was overwhelming and these tasks could not be completed. Continuing to press their advance, Fascist troops on September 9 surrounded part of the troops of the Southwestern Front in the Kiev, Priluki, and Piryatin region.‡

The command and staff of the Front's Air Force and also the personnel of several air divisions found themselves surrounded. The deputy to the commander of the 62nd Bomber Division, General G. I. Tkhor, trapped near the city of Piryatin, headed a group of officers and sergeants from the command organization of the air force who began to fight their way free. In an unequal battle with superior enemy forces he was seriously wounded and while unconscious was captured by the enemy.

In the Gestapo prison in Berlin, Hitler's men tried in many ways to force Tkhor to betray his Motherland. But the patriot remained true to her and accomplished much among prisoners of war. In the camp at Hammelburg, General Tkhor headed an underground organization of Soviet officers and generals. Under his direction an underground committee under the harshest conditions of Fascist terror organized a celebration of the twenty-fifth anniversary of the Great October socialist Revolution and trained prisoners for a mass escape.

According to documents from the German archives, General Tkhor in December 1942 was transferred in irons to the Nuremberg prison where he underwent inhuman torture, and then was transferred to the concentration camp at Flossenburg, which was under direct Gestapo control. The Fascists were not able to break the will of the Soviet warrior-Communist by any tortures or trials. In January 1943 General Tkhor was shot. His boundless dedication to the Motherland and his faithfulness to his military oath may serve as a brilliant example even in our time for all fighters in the Soviet armed forces. By order of the Ministry of Defense General G. I. Tkhor was eternally entered in the rolls of the first squadron of the bomber regiment in which he served.

Battles on the Black Sea Coast. Military operations on the approaches to Odessa began on August 10. The Soviet air forces in this

‡ The largest of 1941's encirclement battles ended in near catastrophe. The front commander at Kiev requested permission to withdraw from the city on September 11, but Stalin refused. On September 14, Romny, 200 kilometers (124 miles) to the east, was lost, the two German tank groups closed the last gap on September 16, and Kiev itself given up on September 19. The encircled Soviet forces were then defeated by the enemy by September 26.[30] ED.

area were small in number, amounting to only one-fourth or one-fifth of the enemy's.* The Independent Maritime Army had only one air regiment, the 69th, with thirty aircraft. The Air Force of the Black Sea Fleet and a unit of the Civil Air Fleet had only a small number of aircraft.

In the battles above Odessa the 69th Fighter Regiment Commander L. L. Shestakov, and the regiment's commissar, Battalion Commissar N. A. Verkhovets, especially distinguished themselves. They personally carried out four or five flights a day and with their courageous actions inspired other fliers to heroic deeds. On August 9 a group of fighters headed by Major Shestakov, after ground attacks against troops in the Katarzhino region, joined battle against twelve Bf 109s and shot down nine of them without any Soviet losses.

Major L. L. Shestakov, who was at the front from the first days of the war, bravely and decisively destroyed the enemy both on the land and in the air. Under his command, the fliers successfully completed their military assignments, aiding the troops in the defense of the city, for which the regiment was reorganized into a guard regiment and granted the Order of the Red Banner. Twelve fliers of the regiment received the titles of Hero of the Soviet Union. Shestakov during the two and a half years of the war made more than 200 flights. He made more than 65 attacks on ground targets and engaged in 32 air battles, in which he personally shot down 15 planes, including 11 in one formation. On March 13, 1944, he died the death of the brave in an air battle near Proskurov. For his outstanding services in commanding military units, for his selfless bravery and daring, the Hero of the Soviet Union, Col. L. L. Shestakov was eternally enrolled in the rolls of the fighter regiment in which he served.

On September 22, after reinforcements had arrived, our troops made a coordinated counterattack against the enemy from both the front and the rear. The night before a regiment was landed near Grigorevka. Three minutes before the landing, Black Sea Fleet aircraft dropped troops behind the lines who disrupted communications and caused panic among the enemy ranks. Air support for the landing was provided by the Black Sea Fleet Air Force, the 69th Fighter Regiment, and a Civil Air Fleet unit. On September 22 our air forces made several strikes against airfields, putting as

---

* The Rumanian Air Force had 500 first-line aircraft. ED.

many as 20 enemy aircraft out of action and restraining enemy troops on the battlefield as well as reserves coming up to the front. The units which had landed and the Odessa garrison soldiers, with the help of aircraft, attacked and smashed two enemy divisions, throwing the survivors back 5 to 8 kilometers (3 to 5 miles). The enemy lost as many as 2000 troops killed or captured. The fascists were prevented from shelling the port with their artillery. The position of the Odessa garrison was somewhat improved. During the three-day period our air forces flew more than 1500 sorties and destroyed twelve enemy aircraft in air battles.

But at the same time, after the enemy broke through the defensive positions at Perekop, the situation in the Crimea became much worse. It appeared that Sevastopol might be lost, disrupting the sea communication lines with Odessa by which reserves and supplies were brought to support ground forces and warships of the fleet. Therefore the staff of the Supreme Command ordered that troops be brought from Odessa to strengthen the defense of the Crimea.

During the evacuation of Odessa (October 1–16, 1941) Soviet fighter planes flew constant day patrols, protecting ships at sea and the troop movements; they attacked enemy troops on the battlefield and aircraft on airfields.

Our aircraft flew more than 8000 sorties during the defense of Odessa and gave great support to ground troops and to the fleet. Squadron Commander Major A. P. Tsurtsumiya was posthumously granted the title of Hero of the Soviet Union; Capt. A. A. Gnedoy, Major P. N. Akkuratov, Captain A. M. Bondarenko, and many others distinguished themselves. The defense of Odessa has gone down in history as a model of persistence and heroism displayed by Soviet fighters, competent utilization of forces and men, and close cooperation between ground forces, the fleet, and aircraft in a struggle with superior enemy forces.

Thus, our air forces took a very active role in all defense operations in the southwestern sector. From July 11 to September 30, 1941, they flew more than 59,000 sorties, of which the Air Force of the Southwestern Front made 21,000; the Air Force of the Southern Front, about 19,000; the Air Force of the Black Sea Fleet, more than 17,000; and the Long-range Bomber Air Force, 2300 flights.

The basic efforts of air power were dedicated to the destruction of enemy equipment, battlefield troops, and reserves in the rear. Only 245 sorties were made against airfields during the first three months of the war, but their effectiveness was high. Thus, from July 1 to August 10, 1941, the Air Force of the Southwestern Front destroyed 72 aircraft on the ground, while the losses to our forces on the ground in that period amounted to 44 aircraft. Soviet fliers conducted themselves more effectively than in the first days of the war. The major effort was expended on the destruction of bombers. The air force command of the Southwestern Front competently managed its forces and increased its numerical superiority in the most important segments of the front, which made it possible in the most important periods to maintain the initiative in the air.

Long-range Raids. The military operations of the Long-range Bomber Forces during the summer were carried out in conjunction with the ground forces and with the front air forces. Most of its flights were made to destroy enemy troops. Of the total 11,186 sorties, 70 percent were made in the day and 30 percent at night. Nine percent of the flights were directed against airfields. Most of the strikes were made against distant airfields, from which enemy bombers made attacks on Moscow, Leningrad, and other cities. During the war's first three months, the crews of the long-range bombers damaged or destroyed 414 enemy aircraft on the ground.

The long-range bombers, together with the Air Force of the Black Sea and Baltic Fleets, at times struck against military-industrial targets deep in the rear of the enemy from the very first days of the war. From July 10 to 30, the 4th Air Corps of long-range bombers made eight attacks on targets deep in the rear of the enemy.

In August 1941, because of the systematic flights of German aircraft against Moscow and Leningrad, the Supreme Command directed corresponding attacks against the capital of Fascist Germany, Berlin. A group of the 1st Bomber Regiment of the Red Banner Baltic Fleet Air Force, thirteen Il-4s (the regiment commander was Col. Ye. N. Preobrazhensky), was given this assignment. On the night of August 8 this group made the first attack on Berlin. During the course of one month, 72 sorties were flown against targets in Berlin.

Besides the Baltic Fleet Air Force, the 81st Air Division of long-range bombers also made flights against Berlin. (The commander was Col. N. I. Novodranov.) During August and September the division made a series of successful flights against military targets in Berlin and other cities in Germany. For these successful operations against targets in Berlin many fliers were given medals, and the most outstanding, including Captain V. G. Tikhohov and Lt. V. I. Lakhonin, were granted the title of Hero of the Soviet Union.

Summary of Summer 1941 Operations. The military operations of the Soviet air forces in the summer of 1941 were carried on simultaneously along a front stretching for 3000 kilometers (1864 miles) from the Barents to the Black Sea. The fighting was fierce and demanded the greatest physical and moral efforts from the airmen and was marked by the stubborn resistance of the Soviet fliers. As the result of the sudden attack by a strong and experienced enemy, the air forces of our border districts suffered extensive losses. However, in spite of the extremely difficult conditions, the Soviet air forces rendered great aid and support to the ground forces to disrupt the plan for a blitzkrieg.

The fundamental efforts of the Soviet air forces were directed against the tank and motorized troops of the enemy. The air forces also destroyed enemy aircraft in the air and on the ground, attacked railway complexes and river crossings, and carried out aerial reconnaissance. During the first three and a half months of the war, our fliers flew 250,000 sorties to carry out these assignments. Soviet ground-attack planes and heavy bombers caused the enemy serious losses, lowered the attack capabilities of the German Army, and retarded its advance deep into our country. The Luftwaffe was weakened significantly. During the first three months of the war the air forces of the fronts in air combats and on airfields destroyed as many as 3500 fascist aircraft. The Soviet Air Force played a very important role in repelling the flights of enemy bombers over Moscow, Leningrad, and other cities.

Together with these actions in support of the ground forces, the long-range bombers and the aircraft of the fleets attacked military-industrial centers and ports of the enemy, including Berlin. These attacks above all had great political and moral significance for the Soviet people and the fighters of the Red Army.

During the course of the 1941 summer operations, the organization and conduct of military operations by the air force under difficult ground and aerial conditions was constantly improved. By the end of the summer campaign, air power was used more effectively. Its efforts were concentrated, as a rule, to smash the main concentrations of the enemy. Communications were improved and the cooperation of the air force with the ground forces was made more efficient.

The directing and mobilizing role of the Communist party was particularly apparent in strengthening the Soviet Air Force in the very difficult conditions during 1941. The party-political work within the air force directed by the Central Committee of the party aided the successful completion of military assignments, the maintenance of high morale, and the inculcation of courage, daring, and an unshakable faith in victory over the hated foe.

Simultaneously, imperative measures were taken to train air crews and new air units and to develop the production of aircraft equipment in the eastern areas of the country.†

III

THE BATTLE OF MOSCOW

Enemy Goals and Soviet Forces.   At the beginning of October 1941 the situation on the Soviet-German front remained tense. The enemy had a superiority in men and matériel and was attempting to expand his successful offensive. On the Northwestern Front, the Germans were preparing to attack Tikhvin with the goal of a total blockade of Leningrad. On the southern front they intended to complete the seizure of the Kharkov industrial region, the Don basin, and the Crimea.

The main enemy attack was on the Western Front with the goal of capturing Moscow. With this in mind a huge offensive operation was prepared by Army Group Center with support from the Luftwaffe's Second Air Fleet, which had around 1000 aircraft. The

† "The aircraft industry was endangered in the fall of 1941 by the enemy advance. Many factories, with their machinery and workers, had to be moved to safety in Asia. During the move, plane output dropped in November to about 30 percent of September's output: there was no means of replacing the heavy losses suffered by our air force. . . ."[31] These losses amounted to 1 for each 32 sorties in 1941. Workers in the relocated plants made strenuous efforts, resumed, and even increased production past previous levels within three months. ED.

scheme involved powerful strikes with the goal of destroying the major Soviet forces and surrounding Moscow from the north and south. Beginning in the second half of September, the fascist air force doubled its activities. These attacks were against railroad targets, troops, and airfields. Many reconnaissance flights were made. Eleven flights were made over Moscow. As the result of the strong opposition from our aircraft and antiaircraft artillery, only about 51 enemy bombers broke through to the city.

On the Moscow front the defensive positions were occupied by troops of the Western, Reserve, and Bryansk Fronts, who were supported by 364 front aircraft, more than 50 percent of which were older models. In addition to these, nearly five divisions of long-range bombers operating against the enemy's rear were brought in as reinforcements for the Front air forces and the 6th Fighter Air Corps (ADF) protecting Moscow.

The training of Soviet ground and air forces for defensive operations began in the second half of September. The over-all command of air forces was held by *Stavka* through General P. F. Zhigarev, commander of the Red Army Air Force, and Corps Commissar P. S. Stepanov, member of the Military Council, both of whom were based in Moscow with their operational groups.

Air operations were organized in agreement with the orders of the commanders of the front's troops and the commander of the Red Army Air Force. The Western Front Air Force (Commanding General F. G. Michugin, and after December 25, 1941, General N. F. Naumenko) concentrated its basic forces on the front's left wing. The Air Force of the Reserve Front (Commanding General Ye. M. Nikolayenko) was engaged in the support of the 24th and 43rd Armies, which defended the areas where it was assumed the enemy would attack. The Bryansk Front Air Force (commanded by General F. P. Polynin) was assigned to the support of the left wing of the front.

The Bryansk/Vyazma Battles. Battle began when the enemy's southern attack group on the distant approaches to Moscow went on the offensive on September 30. With the help of air power they broke through the tactical defense zone on the left wing of the Bryansk Front and then, two days later, on the right wing also. By October 6, the Soviet troops of this front were split into three parts. All attempts to counterattack were unsuccessful. The enemy seized Bryansk, Orel, and continued to advance toward Tula.

The Supreme Command took a number of measures to stop the enemy troops. All possible means of transportation, including aircraft, were employed to bring up reserve units to the region of Mtsensk, from which were formed the First Guards Infantry Corps. The Moscow Aviation Group of the Civil Air Fleet and units of the Long-range Bomber Force successfully completed their assignment to bring arms and men from the regions of Teykovo and Yaroslavl, in the course of three days transporting nearly 5500 men and officers and about thirteen tons of military supplies.

Five air regiments, from which was formed the Sixth Reserve Air Group (Commanding General A. A. Demidov), were shifted to airfields near Mtsensk. The air regiments of this group carried out incessant operations to destroy enemy troops on the approaches to Mtsensk, to protect our own troops, and to carry out aerial reconnaissance. In these days many fliers displayed daring, courage, and mutual assistance. On October 5, Second Lt. V. Ya. Ryaboshapko, when flying a ground-attack plane in strikes against a tank column, saw that flight commander Second Lt. A. V. Yakushev had been forced to make an emergency landing of his damaged aircraft, landed his own plane, picked up the other flier, and returned to his base. Sergeant P. V. Dubina did the same thing, rescuing his comrade M. P. Vovkogon. Second Lt. G. M. Moshinets, flight commander in the 74th Ground-Attack Air Regiment, gave a brilliant example of flying skill. Three Il-2s under his command, when making a low-level attack, suddenly surprised and bombed a motorized column on the road from Orel to Mtsensk, destroying fifteen armored cars and three gasoline trucks.

For several days the military operations of the Bryansk Front Air Force had to be conducted under poor weather conditions, which seriously limited the number of sorties. In addition, the rapid retreat of our troops forced the air units to shift their bases several times, which also had a negative effect on air operations. Because of the dangerous position of the Bryansk Front troops and the limitations on its air power, the *Stavka* ordered into this area six divisions of long-range aircraft, which day and night struck effectively against enemy rail lines to destroy enemy troops, especially on the Sevsk-Kromy-Orel line.

In support of the Bryansk Front troops, our planes flew 1700 sorties in an eleven-day period in spite of the small number of operational aircraft; 65 percent of the attacks were made against the enemy's 2nd Tank Army. These systematic attacks hampered the advance of the enemy toward Tula and helped several of our infantry divisions to escape encirclement.

The enemy began his Western Front offensive on October 2, 1941, with a heavy artillery barrage and air attacks. With overwhelming forces he made his major attack at the juncture of the 30th and 19th Armies and a second attack toward the town of Bely, broke through our lines, and with active air support began to expand his attack in the rear. Our troops had no success with their counterattack and our air power was limited by losses, technical problems, and the shift of aircraft to field air bases, in part not suitable for operations in the autumn. As a result, our planes made only 100–200 sorties per day against the enemy.

To support the Front's troops, the 6th Fighter Air Corps (ADF), the Air Force of the Moscow Military District, several divisions of the Long-range Bomber Force, and two divisions of the Air Force of the Northwestern Front were shifted to this area. For several days they attacked enemy concentrations near Vyazma. The coordination of all the air units' operations was carried out by the *Stavka* representative, Military Council member of the Red Army, Air Force Corps Commissar P. S. Stepanov, who was located at the Western Front Air Force command post along with his operational group.

As the result of these reinforcements, the activities of our aircraft on the Western Front noticeably increased. During the course of nine days they made about 2850 sorties in support of the Front's troops, causing serious losses to the enemy. But nonetheless, the enemy, although he had sustained losses, was not stopped. His aircraft were very active, flying in this period as many as 4000 sorties in the area of the front. Nevertheless, Soviet fliers were very active in resisting the fascist aircraft. On October 5, Pe-2s of the 39th Bomber Air Regiment, commanded by Air Squadron Commissar First Lt. B. K. Gorelikhin, while returning from a mission were attacked by ten Me-109 fighters. In this unequal battle, three enemy fighters were shot down.

In the area of the Reserve Front, the enemy's offensive also began on October 2. Having broken through the line of defense, he expanded his offensive in the rear. The few aircraft of this front had to carry out operations under the difficult conditions of the retreat of our troops and with frequent loss of communications with them and between air units. Carrying out at first as many as 100 sorties per day, our aircraft flew against motorized columns around Yukhnov. Three days later parts of the Moscow Military District Air Force, the 6th Fighter Air Corps (ADF), and the Long-range Bomber Force were assigned to this region. As a result, in a nine-day period Soviet aircraft in support of the troops of the front made 1340 sorties. On October 10 the Reserve Front force was dissolved and its troops and aircraft transferred to the Western Front.

The Mozhaisk Front. After eleven days of heavy defensive operations (September 30 to October 10, 1941), the troops of the Western, Reserve, and Bryansk Fronts retreated to the Mozhaisk defense line, having significantly retarded the advance of the enemy's strike group. A not unimportant role in these operations was played by Soviet aircraft, which flew 8500 sorties in defense of Moscow, 68 percent in support of troops and 32 percent over Moscow.

After October 10 fierce fighting developed along the Mozhaisk defense line in the Kalinin and Tula areas.*

Stavka took a number of measures to concentrate reserves in support of the defense troops, especially in the near approaches to Moscow. The 5th Army and its aircraft, more than eighty planes, were concentrated in the Mozhaisk region. Two long-range bomber divisions were brought from the Transcaucasian Front. Besides these, two newly formed air units were brought up from the rear.

Attacking on October 14, the enemy seized Kalinin and tried to advance toward Torzhok, but was stopped by the counterattack of our troops with the active support of aircraft from the Western and Northwestern Fronts, and long-range bombers, which flew 1500 sorties. Our planes in constant attacks caused great losses to the enemy troops, especially on the roads south of Kalinin,† and our fighter planes, attacking the enemy airfield in the Kalinin region, destroyed or damaged more than forty enemy aircraft. As the result

---

* At this point, Moscow's situation became so precarious that part of the government was moved to Kuibyshev.[32] Kaluga was taken by enemy forces on October 12, Kalinin on the fourteenth; the aircraft designers, including Ilyushin and Yakolev, were ordered to leave Moscow[33]; and a state of siege was declared in Moscow on October 19. ED.

† The Kalinin Front was formed on October 17 together with its air force of five air regiments commanded by Air Force General N. K. Trifonov. ED.

of the stubborn defense of our troops with effective air support, the enemy's further advance in this quarter was stopped by the end of October.

During the battles on the Mozhaisk defense line our command became aware, on the basis of all kinds of intelligence, that the enemy was preparing for a mass air attack against the defenses and targets in the rear of the Moscow region on October 12 and 13. Three hundred sorties were flown as a strike against twenty enemy airfields. As the result of the blow against enemy aircraft both on the ground and in the air, the effectiveness of enemy air power in the zone of the Western Front was reduced by three-fourths.

There was diversity in the intensity of the battles along the Mozhaisk line in different sectors, depending on the enemy's advance. To repel these discontinuous attacks in the Borovsk area, support was rendered by the Moscow Military District Air Force (Commanding General N. A. Sbytov) and the 81st Long-range Division (commanded by Colonel A. E. Golovanov), which struck against troops on roads there and also in the Yukhnov region, and the stations of Ugryumovo, Medyn, Borovsk, Maloyaroslavets, and Myatlevo; they destroyed the crossing of the Ugra River in the Yukhnov and Kaluga sectors and destroyed a fuel center. They destroyed or damaged forty enemy aircraft on the ground.

The enemy offensive was halted at the end of October on the Nara River when the 33rd Army's divisions were brought into the battle, and several air regiments of the Western Front Air Force, long-range bombers, and the 6th Fighter Air Corps (ADF) were brought up. Soviet aircraft made more than 2300 sorties in this area from October 11 to 31, giving substantial support to the front's troops.

At the same time there were bitter battles under way in the Kaluga area, where enemy troops had broken through toward Tarusa and Aleksin. The greater part of our aircraft was concentrated in operations against enemy troops in these regions. On October 23, the enemy was stopped west of Serpukhov, thanks to the joint efforts of ground and air forces. That day fliers of the 120th Fighter Air Regiment especially distinguished themselves. Five times they flew in groups of six to seventeen aircraft in ground attacks on the battlefield. Soviet aircraft flew 1800 sorties in a twenty-day period in the Kaluga area supporting the 49th Army troops.

Defensive battles in the Mozhaisk region began on October 14.

The 5th Army, with support from the air, stopped the enemy to the west of Kubinka by the end of October. In a twenty-day period, Soviet aircraft flew more than 3100 sorties as air support, more than 40 percent of which were intended to destroy enemy troops in the regions of Gzhatsk, Mikhaylovskoye, and Vereya. Ground-attack aircraft were especially effective against enemy troops. On October 20, five ground-attack planes, Il-2s, of the 47th Composite Air Division accompanied by six fighters under the command of Captain Romanov attacked a column of troops west of Mozhaisk. Seventeen vehicles and several tanks were damaged or destroyed as a result. The success of our ground forces and airplanes made it possible for the fighters of the 6th Fighter Air Corps (ADF) to go over to flying systematic air cover for the troops of the front, which lowered the level of activity of enemy aircraft.

In the Volokolamsk area the enemy offensive began on October 17, but it was stopped nine days later. The increasing activity of our air force played a significant role in this process, smashing enemy troops in the Volokolamsk, Shakhovskaya, and Ostashevo regions. The enemy bore heavy losses. Groups of ground-attack bombers, under the command of V. M. Romanov and others, on October 29 destroyed or damaged fifteen tanks and sixty other vehicles.

By the end of October the enemy attack groups had been stopped in the zone of the Western Front. In twenty days our air force flew 10,200 sorties in support of our troops. This increase in activity was furthered by the regrouping of our aircraft onto the airfields of the Moscow Military District with good technical services and the cover provided by the system of Air Defense. The enemy suffered serious losses in aircraft and his air activities became less intense. The situation in the air began to shift to the advantage of our air force.

The troops of the Bryansk Front, restraining the enemy advance in the area of Mtsensk on October 10–24, retreated to new lines. By the end of October the Bryansk Front troops, under pressure from overwhelming enemy forces, withdrew to the line of Tula-Yefremov-Livny-Tim. In this area Soviet aircraft in a twenty-day period flew 3750 sorties, of which more than 50 percent were to support the troops of the front.

During the course of these defense operations from September 30 to October 31, 1941, our aircraft flew more than 26,000 sorties, 80 percent of which were to support or protect ground troops. According to the data collected by the staff of the Western Front Air

Force alone, the enemy lost 228 aircraft, of which 120 were destroyed in aerial battles; many tanks were destroyed, also 2500 vehicles with loads and crews, 130 guns, and a significant amount of equipment. The total losses of the Luftwaffe in the Moscow area from September 30 to October 14 amounted to 1020 planes, 54 percent of which were destroyed on the ground and 30 percent in aerial battle, and 16 percent shot down by antiaircraft artillery.

Fighting with enemy aircraft, our fliers displayed daring and bravery, struggling with all possible means to destroy the enemy. On October 29, Second Lt. B. I. Kovzan, of the 184th Fighter Air Regiment, returning from his mission, attacked an enemy aircraft; having exhausted his ammunition, he rammed the enemy plane near Zaraysk. The Motherland valued highly the glorious exploits of her son, granting to Second Lt. B. I. Kovzan the high honor of Hero of the Soviet Union.

In addition to supporting the men on the front, Soviet aircraft took an active part in driving off enemy raids from Moscow and other targets in the rear. In October 1941, 31 enemy raids were made on Moscow with from 10 to more than 50 planes in each raid, but in all only 72 aircraft broke through to the city.[34] Fliers of the 6th Fighter Air Corps and the Western Front Air Force in close cooperation with antiaircraft artillery conducted operations day and night at a high level, displaying high skill and courage.

Failure of the Nazi Offensive. Not having attained their goal in October, Hitler's command concentrated the major forces of Army Group Center in the middle of November for a new offensive, whose purpose was to deal encircling blows on Moscow by means of tanks from the north and the south with the support of 950 planes from the 2nd Air Fleet.

The defense positions before Moscow were occupied by troops of the Kalinin, Western, and the right wing of the Southwestern Front (on November 1941 the Bryansk Front was dissolved and its men transferred to the Southwestern Front), who were somewhat reinforced in the middle of November. However, the enemy still had the advantage in men and materiel.

Our air force was becoming stronger. Its bases were protected by the Air Defense of the Moscow zone, and its numerical strength was sufficient for considerable latitude of action. The presence in the Moscow region of aviation factories, repair shops, supplies, good roads, and wire communications created favorable conditions for carrying out military operations. The support crews took the necessary measures to insure the success of aircraft under winter conditions.

On the whole, the situation of the ground troops and air forces in the Moscow region in the middle of November 1941 was somewhat better than it was at the beginning of October, but there was still the very real danger of a new enemy attack. With this in mind the *Stavka* concentrated large strategic reserves directly before and also north and south of the capital.

The basis for the organization of the Western Front troops before Moscow was the possibility that the enemy might attack at several points. As part of this defense plan, the air force was to participate actively in the counterattacks made by the 16th and 49th Armies with a preliminary attack on enemy aircraft on the ground. Therefore the Front Air Force staff worked out an operational defense plan involving different types of aircraft. The plan included various options on the basis of the possible enemy attack areas.

The Kalinin Front Air Force was to destroy enemy troops in that region, and to protect the communication lines running up to the front. The air force of the former Bryansk Front, concentrated on the right wing of the Southwestern Front, was to be involved in destroying enemy troops as they came up to the front and also to protect our troops.

Preparations for battle in November were better organized and more efficacious than they had been in October. They coincided with the twenty-fourth anniversary celebration of the Great October Revolution. The appeals of the party's Central Committee became a battle plan for the universal mobilization of the Soviet people and its armed forces to smash the enemy, and had a great influence on the moral-political uplift of the troops and was fundamental in the party-political work in air force units.

At the same time that our air force was preparing to repel a new enemy offensive, it remained constantly active; from November 1 to 14, the air force flew 9400 sorties against enemy troops in the Kalinin region, at Volokolamsk, Mozhaisk, Tula, and Yefremov, and to protect our troops.

On November 15 the enemy began a new offensive against the Kalinin Front troops, and the next day also against the Western Front's right wing. In a ten-day period under bad flying conditions more than 1300 sorties were flown to support the troops on the

Western Front's right wing. Dozens of tanks were destroyed or damaged as well as hundreds of other vehicles and many soldiers and officers killed, retarding the German advance.

However, the enemy, utilizing a considerable gap between the 30th and 16th Armies, on November 28 broke through to the Moscow-Volga Canal and crossed it near Yakhromy. But as the result of a counterattack made by the 1st Shock Army with the help of air power, the German troops were thrown back into the west bank of the canal. Three air divisions formed into one group (commanded by the deputy to the Red Army Air Force commander, General I. F. Petrov) supported the troops of the 1st Shock Army. Daily they flew 150–180 sorties to destroy troops near Yakhromy, Klin, and Solnechnogorsk. As the result of the actions of our ground and air forces the enemy was compelled to cease his offensive against the 30th Army.

At the end of November and the beginning of December our troops with the active support of our air power made a series of counterattacks causing serious losses among German troops. The 6th Air Corps fighters added their efforts to those of bombers and ground-attack aircraft. On December 2, the 65th Ground-Attack Air Regiment destroyed a column of up to 100 vehicles near Solnechnogorsk. The enemy air force was also suffering serious losses. The night of December 2, bombers of the Moscow Military District Air Force destroyed nearly twenty enemy aircraft on an airfield near Klin. As the result of the combined efforts of our ground and air forces, which flew 5660 sorties over a ten-day period, the enemy suffered perceptible losses and by December 5 was forced into defensive operations to the north of Moscow.

On the left wing of the Western Front, the enemy broke the defensive lines southeast of Tula and seven days later came up to Venev and Kashira. To support the 50th Army in the Tula region, an air group was formed commanded by Colonel Shcherbakov. For operations against the enemy advancing on Mikhailov and Pavelets, another air group was formed in the Ryazhsk regions, commanded by General G. P. Kravchenko, two times Hero of the Soviet Union.

As the result of these measures, our air force in this area doubled its level of operations. On November 27, the reinforced 1st Guards Cavalry Corps, supported by tanks and part of the front's air force, the 6th Fighter Air Corps, and one division of long-range bombers, counterattacked against the enemy 17th Tank Division which had broken through at Kashira, and forced it to retreat. At the same time the 10th Army, with the support of the 28th Composite Air Division (commanded by Colonel S. Ya. Mozgovoy) moved toward Mikhailov from the Ryazan region. Our aircraft were effective against enemy trooops east of Tula.

As the result of the operations of our ground and air forces the enemy also ceased his offensive toward Ryazan by the end of November. His attempt to seize Tula from the north was a failure. The result of the bitter defensive struggle on the left wing of the Western Front was that the enemy was decisively halted.

Troops of the Western Front in conjunction with our air power had disrupted enemy attempts to surround Moscow from the north and south and caused him great losses.

Our troops were involved in a stubborn defense operation on the right wing of the Southwestern Front in the grip of overwhelming enemy forces. The air power of the front, two divisions and several regiments of long-range bombers, every day completed 100 sorties in support of ground trooops, striking against the advancing enemy on the approaches to the city of Yefremov and the Pavelets area. This made it possible for the men of the 3rd Army to take strong positions on the line Shakhovskaya-Lyubimovka, east of Yefremov.

Beginning on November 27 the enemy began an offensive near Yelets in the defense zone of the 13th Army, which was compelled to retreat. The low level of enemy efforts in the air made it possible to use fighter planes for ground attack; these fliers effectively struck at the enemy, displaying heroism and daring. On November 29, three 165th Fighter Regiment planes attacked a large column of vehicles northwest of the settlement of Ptan. The plane of the flight commander, Second Lt. Yevstafiyev, was damaged by antiaircraft fire and he was forced to make a landing on territory occupied by the enemy. The rest of the fliers of the group dispersed the column, destroying about twenty vehicles. Later, Second Lt. N. I. Musatov, with cover provided by Second Lt. Kalinin, landed near the damaged aircraft, picked up Yevstafiyev, and returned to his base.

Thanks to the stubborn and energetic defense made by Soviet troops and the intense efforts of our aircraft the enemy offensive was finally stopped. During a twenty-day period, Soviet aircraft flew more than 15,840 sorties in support of ground forces, giving substantial aid to the troops, while the German aircraft made only

3500 sorties. In November the enemy made 41 raids over Moscow, but only 28 aircraft broke through to the city, which was only 40 percent of the total in October.

The intense two-month battle on Moscow's approaches was the most important event of the entire 1941 summer-autumn campaign. The German military strategy here suffered its first major failure. The chief concentration of German troops and air power, whose task was the capture of the Soviet capital, was drained of its strength and went over to defense operations, and Hitler's command lost the strategic momentum which it had obtained with its sudden attack.

The enemy offensive was decisively halted on the approaches to Moscow by the heroic efforts of our ground and air forces. During the defense of Moscow our air force flew 51,300 sorties, of which 86 percent were ground support and 14 percent were in defense of Moscow. The enemy lost about 1400 planes in the Moscow sector, 85 percent of them the result of the operations of our air force, which made it possible for our air force to claim control of the sky and to disrupt the enemy advance on Moscow.

The Soviet government recognized the exemplary fashion in which the fliers had fulfilled their military assignments, displaying courage and heroism. By the order of the People's Commissar dated December 6, 1941, the 29th and 129th Fighter Regiments and the 215th Ground-Attack Regiment (commanded respectively by Majors Yudakov and Yu. M. Berkal and Lt. Col. L. D. Reyno) were designated as Guards Regiments and the 61st Ground-Attack Air Regiment was awarded the Order of the Red Banner. These were the first units honored as Air Guards Regiments.

For military exploits 1254 fliers received medals. In the first period of defensive operations, dozens of daring fliers were given the high title of Hero of the Soviet Union.

It was during the defense operations near Moscow that for the first time, front aircraft, long-range bombers, and fighters from Air Defense were united under the command of the commander of the Red Army Air Force. Military operations showed that in great defensive operations the most effective use of air power was possible with centralized control, which guaranteed operational cooperation and tactical joint efforts with the ground forces.

During the defense operations, it was confirmed that what was important were attacks on enemy communications, general attacks on his aircraft on the ground and troop concentrations preparing for attack, and also the carrying out of constant aerial reconnaissance.

The Soviet Counteroffensive.   By the beginning of December 1941, the situation on the Soviet-German front had changed sharply. The enemy was worn down and exhausted by the Red Army defense operations, which made it possible to shift to a counterattack in the Moscow area. The most immediate task of the coming offensive was to smash the enemy shock troops and to liquidate the direct threat to Moscow. The plan for the counterattack was for two major blows to be made by the forces of the Western Front to destroy the enemy shock troops northwest of Moscow and in the Tula region with the help of troops from the Kalinin Front and the right wing of the Southwestern Front.

The preparations for the counterattack were made during bitter defense operations and in a very short time, which did not make it possible to concentrate adequate men and materials. The troops of the three fronts were inferior to the enemy in artillery, mortars, and tanks in the following proportions respectively: 1.1, 1.8, and 1.4 times. We had an advantage only in air power, because reserves had been drawn into the fronts' air forces from the 6th Fighter Air Corps (ADF) and units from the *Stavka*'s long-range bombers.

At the time the counterattack began we had about 1200 aircraft and the enemy had about 700.[35] When one takes into account the fact that about 35 percent of our aircraft were irreparably damaged then our superiority over the fascist Air Force was not large. In addition, one must remember that older types of aircraft still predominated in the Soviet Air Force.

The moral and political spirit of our fliers was high, they had become more experienced in tactics, and air commanders and staffs at all levels had acquired considerable experience in the control and direction of air operations, which even the German command noted. "At this stage of the war," wrote Hitler's generals, "both the command and the flying crews had become far more experienced. One was struck by the efforts of the Russians to concentrate their forces and also their more effective tactical utilization." The increasing resistance and increase in the activities of our aircraft shook the faith of the German fliers in a quick and easy victory.

As the result of our air force's increased strikes on enemy airfields, the enemy pulled back his aircraft to the rear and dispersed them, which further lowered his activity level. The air forces of the fronts had the task of supporting and protecting the ground forces. The Moscow Military District Air Force, the air group of General I. F. Petrov, and part of the 6th Fighter Air Corps were brought into action in the area of offensive operations of the Western Front. Long-range aircraft were to destroy enemy rail communications.

As a rule, air operations in the counterattack were planned on a twenty-four-hour basis. Control over the air complexes and units was maintained from the command posts of the commanders of the air forces of the fronts. Coordination between air forces and ground forces was organized by the commanders and staffs of the air forces of the fronts and the air forces of the armies. Air representatives for working out and coordinating operations and signals for combined operations, and also for sharing information about land and air conditions, were sent to the command posts of the commanders of ground armies.

Great attention was devoted to operations in the rear of the air force to guarantee the effectiveness of aviation during offensive operations. On the basis of special orders from *Stavka,* the command of the Red Army Air Force worked out measures to prepare the rear for serving the aircraft of the fronts.

Before the counterattack was begun, air bases were built from 15 to 30 kilometers (9½ to 19 miles) from the front where interceptors could wait in ambush and ground-attack bombers be sent quickly into the air. The air force units that carried out military operations from these bases were supported by teams sent from the air-base service battalions and supplies were maintained for two or three sorties by an air regiment. Supplies for the air force of a front were located 250–400 kilometers (155 to 250 miles) from the front lines and were sufficient for fifteen to twenty days of military operations. Such careful and all-encompassing planning guaranteed successful and continuous operations for aircraft in the counterattack near Moscow.

Party-political work was closely connected with the assignments of the air force. Party and Comsomol meetings were held in the air regiments, in which questions of increasing the responsibility of the soldiers for the fate of their Motherland, the teaching of self-confidence in one's ability, and the possibilities of defeating the enemy were discussed.

In spite of the complexity of the situation under conditions of constant military operations, the command and the staffs were able to carry out reassignments and concentration of air forces, and to prepare them for the coming battles.

The air force began its operations in the counterattack on December 5 by providing support for the 31st Army of the Kalinin Front. The basic efforts of our air force were concentrated on bombing the enemy's troops and artillery positions. Expanding the offensive, our troops on December 16 liberated Kalinin and advanced 15–30 kilometers (9½ to 19 miles) on the left wing of the front. The air force of the front flew 560 sorties under unfavorable weather conditions. After our troops had broken through the tactical defense zone of the enemy, the air force went over to attacks against his retreating troops on roads, protecting our troops and our crossings over the Volga and carrying out aerial reconnaissance.

The offensive on the right wing of the Western Front began on December 6. The attack was preceded by an aerial attack on the previous night, consisting of 150 sorties. For the most part enemy staff headquarters, communication lines, and reserve concentrations in the areas were subjected to major attacks. Simultaneously a strike was made against enemy airdromes near Klin and Vatulino.

The efforts of General Petrov's air group were devoted to supporting the 1st and 30th Shock Armies, and the air force of the front and other units supported the 16th Army and particularly the 20th Army. Aircraft attacked enemy troops near Dmitrov, Klin, Solnechnogorsk, Kryukovo, and Krasnaya Polyana. Stretching the limits of their capabilities, they flew 800 sorties in three days of the offensive. Enemy aircraft in small groups tried to bomb our advancing troops, but meeting stiff resistance from our fighter planes they could not really hamper the advance of our troops.

With the active support of air power, our troops broke through the enemy's tactical defense zone and sought to surround his troops at Klin. On December 9, aerial reconnaissance established the beginnings of a mass enemy retreat, especially along the road from Klin to Teryayeva Sloboda. The basic efforts of the air force were directed to the destruction of the retreating enemy. In order to cut the fascist escape route on the night of December 15, 415 parachute troops were dropped to the west of Teryayeva Sloboda. They completed their assignment and at the end of December rejoined the 30th Army.

Abandoning their equipment, artillery, and vehicles, the enemy retreated rapidly, suffering heavy losses from the blows of our ground and air forces. The roads between Klin and Teryayeva Sloboda were covered with corpses and burned and damaged vehicles and tanks. On December 16, the troops of the right wing of the Western Front in pursuit of the enemy emerged onto the line of Dorino–Vysokovsk–Novo Petrovskoye. Our aircraft flew more than 3600 sorties in a ten-day period to support our forces. These strikes were very effective. On December 13, five of our fighters attacked an airfield in the Vatulino region where they destroyed or damaged seven planes. On December 15, five fighters of the 43rd Composite Air Division under the command of T. K. Romanenko entered into an unequal battle with forty enemy bombers and fifteen fighters, trying to break through to Moscow. During the battle they destroyed three enemy aircraft and without any losses returned to their base.

On the left wing of the Western Front, the 10th Army with air support went on the offensive near Mikhailov. Simultaneously the 50th Army and the 1st Guard Cavalry Corps, expanding their counterattack, continued to follow the enemy east of Tula. Because of bad weather conditions, our aircraft flew only 90–100 sorties every day, attacking enemy troops on the battlefield and on roads. The enemy, deprived of air support and tied down by battles north of Moscow, was compelled to retreat rapidly. Soviet troops with the help of air power did not allow him to regroup at intermediate points and by December 16 the demoralized units of his 2nd Tank Army had retreated 130 kilometers (80 miles). Our aircraft with their attacks disrupted the organized retreat of the enemy and caused him great losses.

As the result of the counterattacks of the first ten days, the enemy troops of both shock groups lost many men, and favorable conditions were created for our troops to pursue and annihilate the enemy.

Our air forces gave great aid to the ground troops, making 5400 sorties in bad weather. In German documents seized by our troops, it was noted that there were great losses to tanks, trucks, and other vehicles, as the result of Soviet air attacks.

In order to support the offensive on the left wing of the Western Front, on December 6 and 13 the 3rd Army of the Southwestern Front struck against the enemy concentration at Yelets, forcing him to retreat. Aircraft supporting the offensive flew sixty sorties a day, attacking enemy troops for the most part on the battlefield. Fliers of the Long-range Bomber Force rendered great aid day and night, striking against enemy troops on the battlefield and vigorously attacking his train movements on the lines Novgorod-Pskov and Sumy-Kiev.

At the end of the ten-day counterattack Soviet troops had broken through the enemy's tactical defense zone and begun to pursue his retreating troops. Our aircraft, supporting the troops of three fronts and protecting Moscow, flew about 6950 sorties.

Hitler's command sought to halt the offensive by means of stubborn resistance and a firm defense, deploying their Luftwaffe in the support of their troops. Taking advantage of the favorably developing situation, *Stavka* decided to continue the counterattack, hoping to be able to surround and destroy the entire enemy troop concentration. To carry out this plan, the Kalinin Front was given the task of destroying the enemy concentration near Kalinin. The Western Front, continuing the pursuit of the enemy north and south of Moscow by going on the offensive in the central sector, was to split the major forces of the enemy in order to surround and destroy them. In order to support the counterattack of the Western Front from the south, on December 18 the Bryansk Front was revived with its air force consisting of three air divisions (commanded by General F. P. Polynin). The 4th Reserve Air Group, commanded by Colonel Yu. A. Nemtsevich, was sent to strengthen the Bryansk Front Air Force.

The Kalinin Front commander decided to crush the enemy troops by means of a strike from the north (the 22nd, 39th, and 29th Armies), and from the east (the 30th and 31st Armies) in the general area of Staritsa, concentrating the major air strikes in the support of the 30th and 31st Armies, which were most deeply involved. During the offensive, which began on December 17, aircraft struck against the retreating enemy on the roads. Air power was especially effective in the region of Staritsa where on December 24, sixty vehicles were destroyed or damaged.

The decision of the Western Front commander was to continue the pursuit and destruction of the retreating enemy. On December 18, the 33rd and 43rd Armies went on the offensive, each one having for support a composite air division. The troops of the front's right wing, with the help of air power, during their pursuit of the enemy, liberated Volokolamsk and a number of other populated points, and on December 21 reached the line of the Lama and Ruza rivers, where they met an organized enemy defense. To support the ground forces, an air group of two air divisions commanded by General Ye. M. Nikolayenko was created, which with the Air Defense fighters, and the Moscow Military District Air Force, attacked the enemy on the Klin–Teryayeva Sloboda road and west of Volokolamsk under difficult weather conditions.

On the Western Front's left wing, the enemy continued to retreat to Kaluga and Belev under attack from our troops. In support of these troops on the Western Front's left wing, the air force in bad weather in an eight-day period flew 380 sorties. The 28th Composite Air Division devoted itself to supporting the offensive of the 1st Guards Cavalry Corps.

Our aircraft made 2360 sorties in support of the Western Front from December 17 to 24. The enemy was thrown back to the line of the Lama and Ruza rivers, and the towns of Naro-Fominsk, Kaluga, and Belev.

The Bryansk Front had the task of exploiting its advance toward Orel. The major assignment was given to the 61st Army and the operational group under General Kh. U. Kostenko, to whom was given most of the air power of the front. On December 18–25 the troops of the front with air support crushed an enemy concentration and came to the Orlovka-Lipitsy-Verkhovye line.

The long-range bombers continued to attack enemy rail communications in the general area from Pskov to Kiev. As the result of these strikes, about fifty trains were blown up and the lines cut in many sectors and at some stations.

As the result of these offensive operations, our troops, with the help of aviation, threw the enemy back 20–60 kilometers (12–37 miles) to the west in the period of December 17–24. In this period the Luftwaffe in the area of the three fronts flew only about 300 sorties. Our aircraft, with superiority in the air, made 3200 sorties, the Western Front Air Force alone destroying or damaging 30 tanks, 1200 other vehicles, 340 carts, 36 guns, and 50 railroad trains.

The troops of the Kalinin Front, in coordination with the Western Front, had the task of surrounding and destroying the retreating enemy in the areas of Staritsa and Rzhev, and on December 26, after a softening up from the air, they attacked anew near Rzhev. Our fliers damaged or destroyed 40 vehicles and 30 wagons, and on December 29 near Rzhev, 190 vehicles, 130 wagons, and 15 self-propelled guns. The concentration of the basic efforts of our air power in support of the 39th Army helped it to advance as much as 80 kilometers (50 miles), reach the Volga, overwhelm the German defense, and surround the enemy's Rzhev troop concentration from the west.

In the central sector of the Western Front, the 33rd and 43rd Armies with the addition of reserve units and air power (five air divisions) broke through the enemy defenses on December 24. The air force concentrated its efforts in strikes against enemy defensive lines, troops, and reserves. These efforts were made in a narrow part of the offensive.

Under pressure from the 33rd and 43rd Armies, the enemy continued to retreat to the west. The intensity of operations of our air force increased to 200 or more sorties per day. As a result, enemy losses increased and he was deprived of the opportunity of taking a stand along a defense line. Our troops, increasing their rate of advance, captured the enemy defense positions at Borovsk and Maloyaroslavets on January 4.

On the left wing of the Western Front, the 49th Army with air support liberated Kaluga and began the battle for Sukhinichi. After January 4, the efforts of the troops were directed toward surrounding and crushing the enemy's Medyn-Kondrovo troop concentration. For additional support to these troops, especially for the 1st Guard Cavalry Corps, the air group commanded by General Ye. M. Nikolayenko was shifted to the area of Serpukhov and Tula. The decision was made to drop 2000 parachute troops, intending to cut the enemy's escape route out of Medyn.

This attack was to be carried out by the front air force and the Civil Air Fleet. Reconnaissance was necessary for this operation and observation of the enemy airfields, and the decision was also made to deliver distracting strikes against enemy troops near Gzhatsk, Mozhaisk, and Yukhnov. On the night of January 4, 1942, air strikes were made against enemy airfields in the regions of Vyazma and Yukhnov. However, that same night only 416 men could be dropped in the Myatlovo region.

When the counterattack was completed, the Western Front troops with air support had thrown the enemy back 40–100 kilometers (25–62 miles), and the Bryansk Front troops on the right wing had advanced 20–70 kilometers (12–43 miles).

Our air force during a thirty-three-day period flew about 16,000 sorties, which was a great aid to the ground troops and partisans who were successfully completing the counterattack near Moscow.

The air force's central task was the destruction of enemy troops and materials, and about 50 percent of all its efforts were in this direction. Such successful military operations by the air force would have been impossible without the manifold support from the workers at the rear, the soldiers of the air engineering service, rear support, and the air force navigational and meteorological services.

January Offensive. Profiting from the success of the Soviet counterattack near Moscow, the *Stavka* in January 1942 organized an offensive on all strategic sectors. The major attack near Moscow was made by the Kalinin and Western Fronts, which were to surround and crush the major forces of the German Army Group Center in conjunction with the Northwestern and Bryansk Fronts. The balance of forces on the Western Front as far as infantry and artillery were concerned was equal, and we had an advantage in tanks of 1.3 times. As the troops moved to the west, the 6th Fighter Air Corps, remaining in the Moscow region, could no longer make a major contribution. Losses, dispersal of aircraft, and large numbers of crippled aircraft significantly lowered the effectiveness of our air power.

The further advance of the troops on the Kalinin and Western Fronts led to a difficult situation and to the absence of any superiority over the enemy. Although our troops could neither crush the enemy nor liberate Rzhev, Gzhatsk, or Vyazma, the enemy also found himself in a difficult situation. A considerable number of our troops and partisans were operated in his rear. Support and cover for troops for the most part was flown by the numerically weak aircraft of the Fronts. Besides flying against enemy troops, destroying railroad lines, struggling for control of the air, and conducting aerial reconnaissance, our aircraft also participated in parachute drops. From January 18 to 31 our aircraft dropped more than 3600 men into the enemy's rear, as well as a large quantity of supplies and armament. In February the 4th Parachute Corps, around 10,000 men, was dropped in the enemy's rear.

As the result of stubborn and bitter fighting on the Western Front our troops destroyed sixteen enemy divisions and one brigade, threw the enemy back 100–250 kilometers (62–155 miles), cut the main line from Vyazma to Bryansk, and threatened the basic forces of the enemy from the south, all of which had great military and political significance. During the offensive the Moscow, Tula, and parts of the Kalinin and Smolensk districts were liberated. Soviet aircraft rendered great aid to the ground forces in the solution of these problems. In spite of difficult weather conditions, they operated at a high level. More than 49,000 sorties were flown in January–March 1942, causing great losses to the German fascist troops and their aircraft in order to support and protect ground forces, drop parachute troops, and carry out aerial reconnaissance.

Results of the First Soviet Victory. The Red Army offensive at Moscow was the first great military and political event of the Great Patriotic War, the beginning of the fundamental reversal in the course of the war. For the first time in World War II, Hitler's forces suffered a great defeat. The legend of the invincibility of his army and Luftwaffe was dispelled. The Red Army went from a strategic defense to a decisive offense, seizing the initiative from the hands of the enemy. The immediate threat to Moscow was removed and the enemy plans for uniting the German and Finnish troops in the capture of Leningrad were disrupted.

Instead of a further advance to the east, the enemy was thrown back a considerable distance under the blows of our ground and air forces. The victory of the Soviet ground and air forces had great political significance. It convincingly showed the real possibility of defeating the German fascist troops and encouraged the freedom-loving peoples of Europe to believe that they might be liberated from fascist slavery.

Our air force made a major contribution to the Soviet offensive. The systematic support given to ground forces on the battlefield, attacks on enemy reserves, disruption of railroad lines, destruction of retreating troops, and the capturing of supremacy in the air, made it possible for our troops to attack under conditions of parity with the enemy. The former commander of the Western Front, G. K. Zhukov, in his recollections about air operations during the offensive, wrote: "The fliers operated competently and with self-sacrifice. Thanks to the combined efforts of the Front Air Force, Long-range Bomber Force, and the Air Defense Force, for the first time since the Great Patriotic War began, the initiative in the air was seized from the enemy. Our air power systematically supported our ground forces, struck at artillery positions, tank units, and command posts. When the German fascist armies began their retreat, our aircraft constantly made both ground attacks and high-altitude bombing raids against enemy columns. As the result, all the roads to the west were clogged with equipment and vehicles abandoned by Hitler's troops."

The victory at Moscow represented an important step in the development of the operational skills of the air force. Considerable experience was acquired in the transition in a brief period of time from defense operations to the support of troops engaged in a counterattack. During the course of the offensive, complete confirmation was found for a basic principle of Soviet military doctrine concerning the application of air power: concentrating basic efforts on the major area of attack, utilizing reserves, the air force of the neighboring fronts, Long-range Bomber Force, and the aircraft of the Air Defense. This was especially so during the first days of the counterattack, when up to 75 percent of all our air power on the Western Front was involved in the strike against the enemy's powerful troop concentration northwest of Moscow.

Experience was also acquired in the organization and operation of coordinated action with ground forces and among the air forces of several fronts, and also with the Long-range Bomber Force and the aircraft of the Air Defense of Moscow, which was to be utilized in succeeding operations of the Great Patriotic War and to be further refined.

The organizational structure of the air force was tested in the battle for Moscow. Experience showed that the existence of air forces in ground armies and composite air groupings much complicated the disposition and the massed utilization of air power in the most important sectors of the front. In order to concentrate air power in a few hands and to further enhance its application in battle, air armies were created from the air forces of the fronts according to the *Stavka* decision in May–November 1942. Such an organizational structure for air combinations gave positive results and existed for the rest of the Great Patriotic War. At the same time it was recognized that it was reasonable to separate units of long-range bombers and to create an air force for long-range operations, directly subordinate to *Stavka*.

In the battle for Moscow and in operations on other sectors of the Soviet-German front, units of the reserves were brought up to strengthen the air forces of the fronts. However, the small number of such units and their low complement could not guarantee superiority over the enemy's air forces and therefore to strengthen the air forces of the fronts it was necessary to involve units from other branches of the air force.

The experience of this operation showed that it was necessary to create powerful air reserves. In summer and fall of 1942 ten fighter, ground-attack, and bomber air corps of the reserves were created, which was one of the most important conditions for fulfilling the tasks assigned to the air force.

In the offensive near Moscow, all the positive aspects of the organizational measures for strengthening the structure of the air force units in the rear made in August 1941 became strikingly clear. The battalions for airfield service became mobile and as air-base administration became more experienced it improved its operations. The air force units in the rear within a short time became skilled at preparing new field bases and at advantageously creating on them the essential material and technological organization. The new structure made it possible to improve the control, planning, and organization for rear services for the air force in an operation carried out by several fronts. The engineering-air service acquired great experience in supporting military operations and in repairing damaged aircraft.

There was some development in the tactics for employing different kinds of aircraft.

Fighter aircraft acquired experience in protecting ground troops by patrolling and alerts at air bases. Patrolling by aircraft groups over their territory and take-offs for interceptions on the basis of information from the observation posts of Air Warning, given the absence of radio communications, was not sufficiently effective. Air units armed with new fighter types began to follow the procedure of meeting their assignments in pairs.

Ground-attack aircraft on the whole operated against enemy troops on the battlefield at ground level, but at the same time they began to make strikes from as high as 300 meters (985 feet) in a glide which increased their effectiveness.

The difficult situation when operations began, and the absence of adequate fighter cover, forced our bombers to fly alone or in flights. Later, as the situation in the air improved, they began to strike in groups of six to nine aircraft, which made them more effective. During the battle for Moscow, light bomber regiments were used, equipped with Po-2 and R-5 biplanes. They successfully operated at night as single bombers at an altitude of 400–1000 meters (1320–

3200 feet) over the battlefield and they were used widely for the rest of the war.

The unselfish support of the entire people multiplied the strength and contributed to the determination of the Soviet fighters in the battle for Moscow. About 300,000 German soldiers found a grave on the approaches to the capital and more than 1600 enemy aircraft were destroyed. For their active participation in the defense of the capital, more than 1,000,000 people, including thousands of airmen, received the medal "In the Defense of Moscow."

IV

DEFENSE OPERATIONS ALONG THE VOLGA

In spring 1942 the Red Army, consolidating the successes of its winter offensive, temporarily took a defensive position. The situation on all parts of the Soviet-German front was stabilized. Soviet troops, having undergone the failures and the joys of its first major victories, became more experienced, better organized, and stronger.

Thanks to the heroic efforts of the Soviet people, directed by the Communist party, by the middle of 1942 the restructuring of all branches of the economy to supply the needs of the front had been completed. The aviation industry not only had regained its lost capability, but had significantly exceeded it and produced 25,240 aircraft in 1942, 21,342 of them military aircraft. The modern aircraft Yak-1, Il-2, and Pe-2 had entered service. The production of the newest fighter, the La-5, had begun. Aid from our allies, England and the United States, lend-lease, was insignificant. On May 1, 1942, in our air force there were only 249 foreign aircraft of the older types: Hurricanes, Kittihawks, and Tomahawks.*

In addition to the production of piston-type aircraft, measures were taken to produce jet aircraft. On May 15, 1942, test pilot

* See appendix on lend-lease aid.

Captain G. Ya. Bakhchivandzhi tested the first rocket aircraft designed by V. F. Bolkhovitinov.†

There were also improvements in the air force organizational structure. In March 1942 the Air Force for Long-range Operations (AFLRO), Commanding General A. Ye. Golovanov, subordinate to the General Headquarters of the Supreme Command (*Stavka*), was formed from long-range aircraft units of the air force. In the beginning of May, formation began of front air armies with air divisions consisting of one type of aircraft, and at the end of the summer of 1942, Air Corps of the Supreme Command Reserve.‡ There was an intensive retraining of flight crews for new equipment. A regular system was worked out for training and retraining flight and maintenance crews, and the network of reserve air regiments and brigades was expanded and they were specialized by aircraft types and even by individual aircraft models. Within the air armies for the purpose of retraining flight crews, separate training air regiments were formed. Battle experience was analyzed and on this basis the operational skills of the air force and tactics for different aircraft types were perfected.

The volume of work for personnel of the engineering-air services during the first half of 1942 increased greatly, because the quality of the aircraft produced by the factories moved to the east was lower. This required a greater amount of maintenance work to keep aircraft in a battle-ready condition. Because the air force was not supplied with necessary materials and spare parts the repair of damaged aircraft was retarded. However, thanks to the labor heroism, creative initiative, and help from the experts of the air industry, crews were able to reduce the number of inoperable aircraft.

Hitler's command also took a number of important measures with the purpose of strengthening their ground and air forces on the Soviet-German front. By forming new divisions and utilizing units from among their allies they were able to maintain a superiority in men and materiel for the course of the entire war. Here were concentrated most German aircraft, although the quality of flying crews

---

† The BI-1 interceptor.[36]

‡ The only corps formed before the war were the five long-range bomber corps, and the two fighter air defense corps added on June 21, 1941. Ground-attack and two-seat light bombers operated as regiments within composite divisions in 1941, but in 1942 separate divisions of each type were included in the new air armies. ED.

declined. Having suffered great losses during the war's first year, the German command had to fill out their crews with the inadequately trained flyers from the class of 1942.

Hitler's Summer 1942 Offensive. By means of a decisive offensive, the Fascists calculated on seizing the strategic initiative, capturing the most important political and economic centers of the USSR and ending the war in the east. The great offensive operation at the begining of summer 1942 was planned on the southern wing of the front. Its basic goal was destruction of our troops west of the Don and capture of the Caucasus with its oil and agricultural resources.

The Soviet Supreme Command planned to initiate several offensive operations in summer 1942 on almost the entire front, but the major operation was planned for the Kharkov area. When this summer 1942 campaign was being planned, *Stavka* assumed that the offensive operations of the Red Army would be combined with powerful attacks from our allies, Anglo-American troops, against Germany from the west. But this did not happen.

In May the relative calm on the front was replaced by bitter fighting. The most difficult situation for the Soviet troops developed in the Crimea and in the region of Kharkov. The misfortunes of our troops near Kharkov compelled the Red Army to refrain from offensive plans and once more, just as in summer 1941, to resort to a strategic defense along the entire Soviet-German front. Again the initiative in the war's conduct passed to the enemy.

Possessing an advantage in men and materials, the enemy in June came up to Voronezh and the upper basin of the Don and captured the Don basin industrial area. The defense line of our troops between the Northern Donets and Don rivers, was pierced in an area of up to 170 kilometers (106 miles) in breadth. The German troops had the opportunity to expand the offensive, utilizing their major forces, into the Caucasus and to the Volga. In order to strengthen the defense forces the Stalingrad Front was created on July 12 (commanded by Marshal S. K. Timoshenko), consisting of the 63rd, 21st, 62nd, and 64th Armies and the 8th Air Army commanded by General T. T. Khryukin.

The German command concentrated about thirty divisions and 1200 aircraft in the Stalingrad region.[37] In the major areas of attack the enemy had twice the manpower and materials of the 62nd and 64th Armies. Among his air forces were crack units equipped with Bf 109s, Bf 110s, He 111s, Ju 87s, and Ju 88s. The 8th Air Army of the front had more than 300 aircraft on July 17. In addition to these, there were also 150–200 long-range bombers and 50–60 fighters from the 102nd Fighter Air Division of the ADF.

Because of the withdrawal of air units to the Stalingrad area, a difficult situation developed at the rear of the 8th Air Army (Deputy Commander for the Rear, General V. I. Ryabtsev). The air units of the army were based on airfields located on the right bank of the Don in immediate proximity to the enemy. On July 14 the order was given to relocate the bases in four regions, including thirty battalions of airfield service units, to the left bank of the Don.

The withdrawal of these rear units of the air army was fraught with great difficulties, because the enemy was systematically attacking the crossings on the Don, causing great losses to these units. During the retreat almost all tractors were lost, as well as a large quantity of special vehicles. Transport facilities deteriorated. Rubber was an especially difficult problem. Supplies from the airfields on the right bank of the Don were not completely evacuated and part of them were destroyed. Thus, difficult conditions existed for our aircraft at the beginning of the bitter fighting on the far approaches to Stalingrad.

Air operations on the distant approaches to the city began on July 17, 1942. For the first six days of battle the 8th Air Army was engaged in support of the advance units of the 62nd and 64th Armies fighting on the Chir and Tsimlya rivers. The basic efforts of our aircraft were directed against enemy shock troops. On the first day of battle, bombers and ground-attack planes made thirteen group attacks against tank columns and vehicles on the road from Nizhny Astakhov to Morozovsk, and the airfield and station at Morozovsk. Protection for our troops and the river crossings was provided by fighters in groups of four or six.

The AFLRO gave great support to the ground forces, operating against troop concentrations and enemy crossings over the Don and Chir rivers and his reserves in the regions of Ostrogozhsk, Rossosha, Boguchar, and Kantemirovka over a period of six nights.

Under overwhelming pressure from the enemy, the advance units of the 62nd and 64th Armies retreated to a firm defense line at Kletskaya, Kalmykov, and Suvorovsky. On July 23 two strong enemy groups struck at one area near Kalach, and having broken through our defense line, in two days reached the Don in the Kamensk region, surrounded part of the 62nd Army, and tried to break through to the Volga on the most direct route. At this period all the forces of the 8th Air Army were concentrated in the support of the 1st and 4th Tank Armies, which were counterattacking against the enemy troops that had broken through our lines. The enemy suffered significant losses and for the time being was halted, while the 62nd Army units slipped out of the trap.

As bitter fighting began the Supreme Command reinforced the ground and air forces. Units from the Supreme Command reserves were sent to the 8th Air Army, which made it possible to raise the level of operations. The enemy suffered great losses from these attacks. On July 28 alone, thirty tanks and thirty armored vehicles were destroyed or damaged, as well as two batteries of antiaircraft artillery and sixteen enemy aircraft.

During the battles for the river crossings near Kalach, an observation post was set up for directing fighter planes from which the following operations were carried out: surveillance of the situation in the air; guiding fighters to enemy planes from the ground by radio and directing them so long as they were in sight, and increasing our units in the air by calling up groups of fighters. The deputy to the 8th Air Army commander was located at this post. At times commanders of air fighter units were also there. This contributed to the improvement of operations and control over air units, increased pressure on the enemy, and led to the discovery and elimination of inadequacies in our air operations.

Simultaneously, the close proximity to the front of patrolling groups of fighters and their assignment to differing altitudes increased the effectiveness of air operations and decreased losses among our aircraft. Our fliers began to operate according to the principle: fly separately, but fight together. Such an arrangement in groups for protection made it possible to maneuver freely and to take offensive positions.

For the most part our bombers and ground-attack planes flew in groups of four to six with two to four fighter planes as escorts. Areas where there were concentrations of enemy men and materials sometimes were subjected to attacks by larger groups. For example, on July 31 four strikes were made against troops and river crossings near Kalach with more than 160 aircraft participating. As a result more than 30 tanks were destroyed or damaged, along with 150 other vehicles, 50 carts with military supplies, and 3 guns. Day attacks were supplemented by night raids made by the front air forces and long-range bombers. The enemy found himself under constant air attacks and his advance slowed.

As the intensity and effectiveness of our air power increased, the enemy made greater efforts to protect his ground forces and began to attack our airfields frequently. However, the enemy could not reduce the activity of Soviet aircraft. Fliers of the 434th Fighter Regiment, commanded by Major I. I. Kleshchev, were especially effective in this period. During the first eighteen days of battle they were involved in 144 air battles and shot down 36 enemy aircraft, showing themselves to be models of bravery and heroism. Second Lt. Kukushkin and Sergent Smirnov, when returning to their base after completing their mission, met nine German bombers escorted by twelve fighters. In spite of the enemy superiority in numbers and low fuel reserves, our fliers entered into an unequal battle, shot down five enemy aircraft, and disrupted their attack on our troops. The commander of the flight, Second Lt. Kukushkin, died a hero's death in this battle.

Major I. I. Kleshchev at this period was one of the innovators in the tactics of fighter aviation, every day perfecting his skill and studying enemy tactics. He always sought out the enemy and fought aggressively. This he taught to his subordinates. Their sudden attacks insured them of success. Major Kleshchev trained dozens of heroes.

Crews of the 150th Bomber Regiment, Regimental Commander Lt. Col. I. S. Polbin, who were flying Pe-2s, were especially active. They utilized dive-bombing, which was suited to the aircraft's capabilities, and caused serious enemy losses.

The attack of Polbin's fliers against the enemy fuel dump in the region of the Morozovsk farm was particularly interesting. This fuel dump had been carefully camouflaged by Hitler's forces. Moreover, it also contained a large amount of antiaircraft artillery and fighter planes. Nonetheless, two Soviet dive bombers broke through to it by daylight and on the second run ignited the fuel tanks. Because German tanks had inadequate fuel supplies, they could not enter into battle.

The enemy's advance toward the Caucasus and Stalingrad at the end of July aggravated the situation. Fighting bitterly and with heavy losses, Soviet troops retreated, abandoning rich industrial and agricultural regions to the enemy. Because of this, the People's

Commissar in his Order 227 dated July 28, appealed to the armed forces, describing the dangerous situation developing in the south, and in the name of the Motherland called on them to increase their resistance to the enemy and to halt his advance. The order appealed to officers and generals to increase the resistance of the ground and air forces, to reconstitute party-political work among the troops, and to mobilize all men and materials to withstand the enemy. Awareness of the mortal danger poised over the Motherland gave the soldiers new strength and stiffened their resistance.

Having failed in their attempt to break through to the Volga from the west, Hitler's command regrouped their men for an offensive from the southwest. They directed the 4th Tank Army from this quarter toward the Caucasus. On July 31, this army with air support went on the offensive and within two days it had reached the Kotelnikovo region. This was a threat to the flank and rear of the 62nd and 64th Armies. To combat the advancing enemy, an operational group of the front was formed, commanded by General V. I. Chuykov, supported by the 8th Air Army, which made as many as 600 daily sorties. There was a fierce air battle above the battlefield.

On the first of August air reconnaissance discovered near the railroad stations at Abganerovo and Plodovitoye a great enemy troop concentration, which went on the offensive on August 5 toward the Tinguta station. Most of our bombers and ground-attack planes were devoted, therefore, to the support of the 64th Army. In one day, our air forces flew 265 sorties in strikes against the enemy. The LaGG-3, a fighter plane equipped with 37 mm. cannons, was successfully employed in strikes against tanks. For example, eight fighters on August 5 destroyed four tanks, six armored vehicles, and a fuel dump.

More enemy aircraft were destroyed by effective strikes against airfields. On August 5, seven aircraft of the 268th Fighter Air Division attacked the airfield at Bolshaya Donshchina, where about eighty enemy aircraft were located. As the result of the battle, eight planes were put out of commission, and a few days later eight Il-2s of the 228th Ground-Attack Division made a strike against the airfield at Oblivskaya where ninety enemy aircraft were located. As the result of this strike about forty enemy aircraft were put out of commission.

In support of bombers and ground-attack planes, groups of fighters from time to time were sent into the strike areas to clear them of enemy planes. In spite of the fact that the enemy had control of the air, our fliers bravely entered into air battles and caused him losses. Fifty-four enemy aircraft were destroyed in 115 air battles and 28 on the ground in the first five days of August alone.

The great length of the Stalingrad Front (700 kilometers or 435 miles) complicated the problem of coordinating military activities. Therefore on August 5 it was divided into two fronts, the Stalingrad Front and the Southeast Front, and the 16th Air Army (commanded by General P. S. Stepanov; after September 28, 1942, by General S. I. Rudenko) was formed to support the Stalingrad Front.

The 4th German Tank Army renewed its offensive on August 6 and reached the station at Tinguta. Three days later our 64th Army, strengthened with reserve units and with the help of air power, made a counterattack against the advancing enemy units. As the result of this attack, three enemy infantry regiments were routed and dozens of tanks were destroyed or damaged. The enemy was pushed back and once more our troops occupied the external defense ring of the city. The 8th Air Army, which at that time had 250–300 functioning aircraft, operated at a high level, carrying out 400–600 sorties every day. On the basis of experience gained in the battle for Moscow and in order to increase the attacks against the enemy, the 102nd Fighter Air Division (ADF) assigned to Stalingrad's protection used its fighters as ground-attack planes.

Fighter pilots displayed great eagerness in the struggle for victory in those difficult days of constant battle. On August 6 a 183rd Fighter Air Regiment flight commander, First Lt. M. D. Baranov, who commanded a patrol of four Yak-1s over the crossings on the Don, entered into battle with 25 enemy fighters and on the very first attack shot down one enemy fighter, and then attacked approaching bombers, damaging one and forcing it to land behind our lines.

In the meantime the German fighters were attacking our ground-attack planes. Then Baranov came to their aid and shot down another Bf 109. When all his ammunition was exhausted, he rammed another plane, striking its tail with his wing, while he himself escaped by parachute. Thus, in the course of a few minutes the daring flier knocked down four enemy aircraft. During a brief period he destroyed 24 fascist aircraft, for which he was awarded the title of Hero of the Soviet Union. M. D. Baranov died the death of the brave in 1943.

Our troops with the help of our air power and by means of their strenuous efforts disrupted the enemy plan for reaching the Volga nonstop. In a thirty-day period, and at the price of great losses, the enemy advanced only 60–80 kilometers (37–50 miles). During that same period our planes flew about 15,500 sorties, destroying 567 enemy aircraft either in the air or on the ground.

Attack on Stalingrad. Military operations on the near approaches to Stalingrad began on August 17. After the failure of the plans for capturing the city from the west and south, the German command decided to make two drives with a single goal from the regions of Trekhostrovsky and Abganerovo. The German strike groups with the support of 1000 aircraft, concentrated in small sectors of the front, had a twofold or threefold superiority over our troops.

From August 17 to 23, the efforts of the 8th and 16th Air Armies were directed to the destruction of the river crossings near Vertyachy and Peskovatka. More than 1000 sorties were flown. At that time part of our air power was supporting troops of the 64th Army southwest of Stalingrad. But that effort was not sufficient and the enemy held control of the air.

Taking into consideration the difficulties of the situation, *Stavka* on August 20, 1942, ordered five divisions of AFLRO to be brought from the Moscow region closer to the area of operations, which made it possible to increase the strikes against the enemy.

The increase in the efforts of the air forces made it possible to strike more perceptible blows at the enemy. But the situation was still difficult.

On August 20, the 287th Fighter Air Division (commanded by Colonel S. P. Danilin), which had recently been retrained in the new La-5 fighters,* arrived as reinforcements for the 8th Air Army. On the very next day they began battle. In a twenty-seven-day period the fliers of this division successfully participated in 299 air battles and destroyed 97 enemy planes.

The Enemy Reaches the Volga. Utilizing his superiority in forces, the enemy broke through our defenses on August 23, reached the Volga in the Latoshinka and Rynok regions and split the troops of the Stalingrad Front into two parts separated by an 8-kilometer (5-

* The La-5 was the first new fighter to use a radial engine and was armed with two 20 mm. guns. ED.

mile) corridor, while paying a price in great losses. His aircraft, moved up to advanced fields, increased their activities and later that day made a mass raid against Stalingrad in which several hundred aircraft participated, making about 2000 sorties during the entire day. Fires broke out in the city. This was a barbaric destruction of a city with thousands of peaceful inhabitants. On this same day our fighters participated in 25 dogfights over the city and, together with antiaircraft artillery, they knocked down 90 fascist aircraft.

The crews of the rear units worked with self-sacrifice to create the essential conditions for supporting the military operations of the air regiments. Special attention was given to air-base construction, maintenance of vehicles, and organization of supplies. Fifty new airfields were completed on the far side of the river. For this purpose three engineering-airfield battalions and eight airfield service battalions were rushed to this region and 3500 local civilians were mobilized by the regional committee of the party and the regional executive committee. As the result of these measures the maintenance of aircraft became almost completely dependable.

From August 23 to September 2, the efforts of the air force were concentrated on the support of troops who were counterattacking against enemy troops who had broken through our lines. Soviet fliers both by day and night struck against the enemy north of the city. Together with the ground forces they did not allow the enemy to overrun Stalingrad. On September 7 all kinds of reconnaissance revealed that the enemy was concentrating great forces preparatory for an offensive in the region of Gumrak. The 272nd Night Bomber Air Division on the night of September 8 made a concentrated raid against the shock group and, as it later became clear, prevented it from attacking at the designated time.

At the suggestions of the 16th Air Army fliers, the engineering-technical crews of the air regiments installed cockpits for machine gunners on the Il-2 ground-attack aircraft. Machine gunners were not provided in personnel allotments for these aircraft, and at first mechanics, technicians, specialists in aircraft armaments, and equipment specialists flew in this capacity. Carrying out their regular duties as members of the technical crews, many of them flew in addition two or three sorties per day. Beginning early in November, the aviation industry began to send two-seater Il-2s to the front. Thus, air force circumstances and needs had a great influence on the improvement of aircraft capabilities. All of this contributed to the improved operation of the ground-attack aircraft and lowered their losses.

Hitler's soldiers called the Il-2s "Black Death." On September 7 the commander of a ground-attack air squadron, Captain P. S. Vinogradov, who was leading an attack of seven Il-2s on tanks and infantry on the battlefield, was attacked by four Bf 109s. Skillfully organizing a defense and maneuvers for the ground-attack planes, he himself entered into an unequal battle with the enemy fighters and shot down two of them. Wounded in battle, the daring commander, with cover from his subordinates, brought back his damaged aircraft to the airfield. By order of the People's Commissar for Defense, Captain P. S. Vinogradov was promoted to lieutenant colonel, assigned as commander of the 69th Ground-Attack Air Regiment, and awarded the Order of Lenin.

During the course of intense fighting, Soviet fliers often used fighting techniques that were avoided by German fliers: high-speed frontal attacks and ramming. Ramming was utilized in decisive moments of a battle, when there was no hope of knocking down an enemy plane by other means. The young flier B. M. Gomolko gave an exemplary exhibition of bravery at this time. On September 8, 1942, fighters from the 520th Fighter Regiment, when flying cover for our ground forces, met ten German bombers. Technical Sergeant Gomolko, making his first battle sortie, courageously sliced into the enemy's formation and shot down one bomber. In subsequent attacks, when he had exhausted all his ammunition and was wounded, he attempted ramming. He cut off the tail of one enemy bomber with his plane's propeller, and then abandoned his own plane. As his parachute was descending he saw other German fliers also landing by parachute. He shot one of them as he tried to run away, and he captured two others whom he delivered to the headquarters of his air regiment. Shortly afterwards, Technical Sergeant B. M. Gomolko was commissioned second lieutenant and granted the Order of Lenin.

It was in the Volga skies that V. D. Lavrinenkov began his great and glorious military career. In one dogfight he was seriously wounded, but was able to land his plane at his field. When he had recovered from his wound, the daring flier once more took his fighter into the air.

While patrolling over our river crossings, Master Sergeant Lavrinenkov noticed two groups of enemy bombers and decided to attack them. Before the attack he was joined by another flier from a a different air regiment, who, apparently, had become separated from his group.

"Let's get them!" Lavrinenkov cried over his radio.

A long round of cannon fire from the unknown flier missed an enemy plane, but Lavrinenkov with a short burst of machine-gun fire shot down the enemy lead plane. Two other fascist planes burst into flame. In a second attack Lavrinenkov set fire to a Ju 87. His companion, dipping his wings, began to drop to the side, but at that moment four enemy fighters appeared. Lavrinenkov and the other flier of the La-5, whom Vladimir did not know, immediately rushed into a frontal attack. The German fliers did not enter into battle, but turned back. Lavrinenkov, later twice Hero of the Soviet Union, destroyed sixteen German aircraft in one month over the Volga. In the same regiment with Lavrinenkov also bravely fought Hero of the Soviet Union A. V. Alelyukhin, who later won a second Gold Star.

Almost every day our fliers entered battle against large groups of enemy aircraft. This testified to the great daring and courage of Soviet fliers, who attacked the enemy regardless of his numerical superiority. In the very first day of the Stalingrad battle, eight fighters commanded by Major I. N. Stepanenko attacked eighteen bombers flying with an escort of eight fighters and shot down four aircraft, two shot down by the group commander. His aircraft was seriously damaged in this battle but Stepanenko did not abandon the field, but continued to direct his subordinates until the rest of the German aircraft fled.

On September 14 Major Stepanenko, leading six fighters flying cover over the 62nd Army fighting near the Stalingrad railroad station, attacked thirty enemy bombers accompanied by twelve fighters. During the battle he shot down three aircraft, and our fliers compelled the remaining bombers to drop their bombs in disorder outside the target area and turn back. Early in October, when carrying out aerial reconnaissance, Stepanenko's aircraft was attacked by four fighters. He shot down two of them and the rest of them disappeared into the clouds. For his outstanding successes in battle, Major I. N. Stepanenko later was twice awarded the title of Hero of the Soviet Union.

Together with success in battle, there were also inadequacies. Fighter planes did not always reliably escort bombers and ground-attack planes. Air regiments that had arrived as reinforcements were in brief time sent into battle. There were also deficiencies in staff control over fighter planes when they were in the air, but these deficiencies were quickly eliminated during offensive operations.

The commander of the Red Army Air Force ordered the organization of a radio network for target control within the 16th Air Army. General V. N. Zhdanov, deputy commander of the Leningrad Front's 13th Air Army, was summoned to organize it, although he had no experience controlling aircraft from ground radios. The target control network consisted of a central radio station, located near the 16th Air Army headquarters, radio stations in divisions and regiments located on airfields, and also stations for target control located along the line of the front, which had direct communications with fighter pilots in the air. Target control stations had the following tasks: informing fliers in the air concerning the situation in the air; warning about enemy aircraft that might appear; summoning fighter planes from airfields and reassigning them to new targets. Twenty-five commanders of air regiments from reserve air brigades were recruited as controllers with the intent of giving them battle experience. On the basis of this experiment the Red Army Air Force worked out and introduced in September 1942 the first manual for directing fighter planes by radio, which was an invaluable document and practical aid for air units.

Thus, the arrival of new types of aircraft, increase in the number of aircraft available, improvement in air tactics, and the acquisition of experience by both command and flight personnel contributed to the successful solution of military problems. During a twenty-seven-day period, our planes flew about 16,000 sorties on the near approaches to Stalingrad, destroying 655 enemy aircraft and causing great losses to enemy troops and equipment. During that period our aircraft doubled their night activities. Air power increased its total efforts.

The formation of Air Corps of the General Headquarters Reserve consisting of two to four divisions, began in the summer of 1942. Groups of "hunters," consisting of four to eight fliers, were established within fighter air divisions. The complement of fighter regiments was increased from 22 to 32 aircraft. Air regiments were filled out in the course of operations. This raised the battle capabilities of the regiment and increased the time it could carry out operations. The basic battle unit became the flight, consisting of two pairs of aircraft. Attacks against enemy aircraft were made for the most part from the rear and from above. Machine guns were fired in shorter bursts.

The Soviet government and commands took a number of measures to give firm resistance to German aircraft and thereby to improve the situation of our aircraft. A number of orders were issued by the People's Commissar for Defense and the air force with this in mind. In one of them the statement was made: "Only that flight of fighter planes in which contact is made with an air enemy and an air battle is conducted, is to be considered a combat sortie, and when flying protection for ground-attack planes or bombers, a flight is to be considered a combat sortie only when no ground-attack planes or bombers are lost to enemy interceptors." The strictness of this order raised the effectiveness of fighter operations.

Our command in every way encouraged decisive independent actions on the part of our fliers. It insisted that fighter planes must above all attack enemy bombers.

Lessons learned from battle operations were very important in developing aerial tactics, especially for interceptors, and were utilized in the *Guide for Interceptor Operations*, developed by the air force command and published in December 1942.

At the middle of September the situation in the Stalingrad region remained tense. Enemy troops reached the city's defense ring, broke through the line between the 62nd and 64th Armies, captured several elevations, and were only 3 or 4 kilometers (2 or 2½ miles) from the center of the city.

The Stalingrad Front troops had the task of holding the city, preventing the enemy from forcing the Volga and gaining its left bank, while the Don Front troops were to halt the enemy advance to the north of the city, to cause him heavy losses and to gain time to muster a counterattack.

The enemy, having seized advantageous locations and having drawn up his reserves, began the siege of the city. From September 13 to 27, there were intense battles in the southern and central parts of the city. Having paid a huge price in losses, Hitler's forces reached the Volga in a number of places. From the very first days of the battle for the city, units of the 8th Air Army and the AFLRO smashed the enemy as he advanced into the city and his reserves as they moved up to the front.

In order to halt the enemy advance and hinder the transfer of reserves to the north where the troops of the Stalingrad Front were to counterattack, troops of the 62nd Army, with support from the 16th Air Army, on September 19 counterattacked from the northern part of the city. At the same time the 8th Air Army and the AFLRO were attacking enemy reserves advancing out of the Gorodishche region. Six hundred sorties were flown in this region in only two nights. As the result of this coordinated action between ground and air forces, the enemy was not able to utilize his reserves.

Our bomber and ground-attack strikes were made alternately from one region of the city to another. On September 23, aircraft of the 8th and 16th Air Armies and the AFLRO hit the enemy in the central section of the city, and on September 24 they were active in the southern part of the city. The commanders of ground forces many times gave positive reports about the successful activities of our fliers. Night bombing raids were very important in this period.

During the battle for Stalingrad, our air forces gave ground forces support and also obtained much experience in operations against enemy troops in a large city. The most important targets were individual buildings occupied by the enemy, artillery, mortars, tanks, and troop and supply dumps.

Our air forces worked in close conjunction with the ground troops. Ground-attack planes and fighters operating with infantry and artillery attacked the enemy right on the front line, and aircraft of the front and long-range bombers struck against reserves, artillery and troops located 2 to 5 kilometers (1¼ to 3 miles) from the front line. Groups of ground-attack planes were directed to their target by artillery officers from command posts or observation posts belonging to the commanders of infantry regiments by means of rockets, smoke signals, or tracer bullets.

In addition to supporting ground forces, bombers of the front, ground-attack planes, and long-range bombers from time to time attacked enemy rail communications and aircraft on the ground. Fighter units, which had been strengthened, began to go over to the offensive more often. Losses of enemy aircraft increased. In September alone the fliers of the 16th Air Army destroyed 290 enemy aircraft in the air. The decrease in German air activity was noticeable in the curtailment of strikes against our airfields and targets in the rear and also a reduction in the flights made by German "hunters." This was testimony to the significant losses among the enemy's best flying personnel.

Changes in Tactics. The Red Army Air Force commander, General A. A. Novikov, who was in the battle region, took appropriate measures for more effective utilization of air power. He insisted that its efforts be concentrated on decisive areas, that there be strong centralization in the control of military operations, that part of the aircraft be held in reserve, and that aerial reconnaissance be carefully organized to increase the effectiveness of strikes against the enemy.†

The command of the Red Army Air Force made the following demands of air power: to strike systematically against enemy airfields, removing them from operations; to increase the efforts of "hunters"; to drive enemy air power out of its forward airfields, hampering its activities on the battlefield; to give fighter planes their choice to attack targets in whatever manner they wished; to assign a significant part of fighter strength beyond the front lines so that they might attack enemy aircraft as they approached our lines; to create conditions for increasing the victories of outstanding pilots, who were to be encouraged and given command posts, replacing incompetent commanders; to develop new tactics for fighter planes in order to attract the best commanders and fliers; to inculcate the best tactical procedures in all units; and not to send young fliers into battle until they had had basic testing and training.

In the period from September 27 to November 18, the battle shifted from the city's center to the workers' residential and factory districts. The troops of the front not only repelled numerous attacks from the enemy, but they themselves often counterattacked. There was bitter fighting for every street, every building. Day and night our aircraft carried out operations in support of the ground troops, striking against airfields, railroad targets, and enemy reserves.

Every day the resistance, courage, and heroism of the fighters increased. Communists and Comsomols displayed themselves as models of bravery. The 291st Fighter Air Regiment commissar, Battalion Commissar L. I. Binov, shot down one enemy aircraft, rammed a second with his wings, and then landed his aircraft. During the battles in the center of the city, Second Lt. A. A. Rogalsky

† Alexander A. Novikov was Northern Front Air Force Commander in 1941, and commanded the whole Red Army Air Force from April 1942 until the end of the war. His predecessor, P. F. Zhigaren, was given a Far Eastern air army command. ED.

The TB-3, world's first four-engined bomber to reach mass production, still served as a transport into 1942.

Modernized TB-3s flew to the North Pole in May 1937.

A TB-3 shown in 1938 in China; this model was used as a night bomber in 1941.

An I-15 fighter in Spain, 1936.

The I-152, or I-15bis, in China, 1938, and still used in 1941.

The I-153, last of the biplane fighters, is shown here in 1941 with pilots and a starter truck.

The I-16 was still the most widely used fighter when the war began.

The SB-2 bomber.

This damaged SB-2 fell into enemy hands when its air base was overrun in the war's first days.

An SB-2bis, with M-103 engines, of a night-bombing unit.

The DB-3 long-range bomber built before the war.

The Il-4 was the standard wartime long-range bomber.

The fastest Soviet fighter in 1941 was the MiG-3.

The LaGG-3 fighter of 1941–42.

The La-5s of the Czech regiment in 1944.

The most successful Soviet fighter available in 1941 was the Yak-1.

achieved immortal fame. During a ground attack against the enemy he repeated Gastello's exploit. His aircraft was set afire by enemy antiaircraft fire. Rogalsky guided his burning Il-2 into a concentration of German tanks and vehicles.

Second Lt. V. Ye. Pyatov twice rammed an enemy aircraft in one aerial battle, which crashed to the ground after the second blow. The hero-pilot, after displaying himself as a model of courage and high flying and battle skill, managed to land on his airfield. The number of examples of self-sacrifice and heroism increased with every day. Government organs and party and Comsomol organizations gave the widest publicity to the experiences of the hero-fliers in newspapers, battlefield bulletins, banners, posters, at party and Comsomol gatherings, and in discussions.

Battle amity and mutual cooperation developed among the fliers of the air units operating together. In a letter dated September 18, 1942, the fliers of the 783rd Ground-Attack Air Regiment expressed their warm comradely recognition to the 581st Fighter Air Regiment's fliers for their dependable support when accompanying them to their target and back. In the answering letter, the fighter pilots bound themselves to faithfully support the military operations of the ground-attack planes. The fliers of both regiments took an oath to defend the city.

The heroic resistance and courage of our troops and the active support of our air power both day and night caused great losses to the enemy ground and air forces. During the twelve days of battle from September 27 to October 8, the enemy was able to advance only several hundred meters (about 1300 feet).

After he had captured the Tractor Factory, the enemy concentrated his major forces on the complete destruction of the 62nd Army. But at that time fresh reserves came to the aid of the defenders of the city. In addition, on October 19 the troops of the Don Front counterattacked in the area north of the city. (On September 30, 1942, the former Stalingrad Front had been renamed the Don Front, and the Southeastern Front became the Stalingrad Front.)

The 272nd Night Bomber Air Division (commanded by Col. P. O. Kuznetsov) was very active, making 375 sorties. Every regiment was given specific targets on the property of the Tractor Factory, direction of approach to the target, and time of attack. The enemy was subjected to attacks every three to five minutes. To insure successful operations, experienced squadrons of "hunters" attacked the antiaircraft defenses in the target area. The bombing raids not only caused great losses to the enemy, but wore down his troops all night. They helped the 62nd Army to halt the further advance of the enemy. In October, Po-2 crews were very active, making seven to ten sorties per night and dropping from 180 to 350 kilograms (396 to 772 pounds) of bombs on the enemy from each plane.

Much attention was devoted to the question of perfecting night operations. The most-experienced and best-trained fliers began to carry out their assignments as "hunters" for attacks on railroad trains both under way and at stations. Attacks on such targets even when carried out by one aircraft gave very high results. For example, the 272nd Night Bomber Division in only two nights destroyed railroad lines at nine points, blew up two locomotives and eight cars, and ignited about fifteen fires at railroad stations. For eight to twelve hours, all rail traffic was immobilized.

Simultaneously with intensive military operations, fliers in Po-2s brought military supplies and food to the ground forces. During the period of September–December 1942, 1008 flights were made in support of the 62nd Army on the right wing of the front, delivering about 200 tons of cargo.

The 709th Air Regiment fliers (commanded by Major M. G. Khoroshikh) especially distinguished themselves. For their successes in battle with the enemy and in transporting cargoes to the ground forces this regiment was reorganized as a guards regiment by the order of the People's Commissar for Defense dated November 27, 1942, and then given the designation "the Moscow Regiment" by the order of the People's Commissar for Defense dated May 4, 1943. This name was given to the regiment because it was formed for the most part from a Moscow flying club of the October region in Moscow in December 1941.

The tactics were also improved for "hunter" interceptors, who more and more flew behind the lines seeking out and destroying single planes, moving railroad trains, staff automobiles, radio stations, artillery, etc.

A fighter air regiment, "Masters of Air Battle," was formed in the 8th Air Army from experienced fighters. They began to practice more extensively the procedure of ambushing enemy planes from concealed locations. Communications were improved. A control and communication center within the 287th Fighter Air Division was formed in October 1942 beyond the Volga in the settlement of Burkovsky.

Ground-attack techniques were also improved and these planes now attacked their targets in groups of six or nine planes. Great attention was given to the suddenness of the attack, and ground-attack planes were now utilized successfully for day operations and for attacking and destroying enemy bombers in the air.

The AFLRO was now much more active than it had been in 1941 and its planes flew only at night. Raids were flown against a small number of targets in one area. Flight over the target and the dropping of bombs was done by planes at two-minute or three-minute intervals. The approach to the target was carried out after calculation of the time available and the course, landmarks, and control lights on the ground. Troops marked their positions by lighting bonfires 1 or 1½ kilometers (.62 or .93 mile) from the front lines, and also with rockets, tracer rounds, and vehicle head-lights. The use of control lights and marking lights by our troops gave good results.

When our troops and air force were involved in bitter defensive fighting, they were also devising favorable conditions for the future counterattack. As the result of instructions from *Stavka* on October 27–29, in order to seize control of the air and to weaken the enemy's air power, the forces of the 8th Air Army and AFLRO raided thirteen airfields and made 502 sorties, destroying several dozen German aircraft and damaging the landing strips on a number of airfields, which curtailed German air activities and forced them to shift their forces toward the rear. There were more than 260 mass air battles in October near Stalingrad, in which about 200 German planes were shot down and more than 80 were destroyed on the ground.

Thus, the increased numbers of aircraft, improvement in their quality, use of radio communications, better support work done by the Engineering Air Service, and the elimination of inadequacies in tactics employed by differing types of aircraft all increased the role of air power in the support of ground forces in a period of intense fighting. During sixty-seven days of defense operations at the city our aircraft flew 45,325 sorties, dropped 15,440 tons of bombs, and fought more than 1000 air battles. Nine hundred and twenty-nine enemy aircraft were destroyed in air battles, on the ground, or by antiaircraft fire.[38]

Results of the Stalingrad Defensive Battle. As the result of the Stalingrad defensive operations carried out by Soviet troops, the plan of Hitler's command for the 1942 campaign was disrupted. Favorable conditions were created for the Red Army to initiate a decisive counterattack.

Our air power actively supported ground troops in holding defensive lines both on the near and distant approaches to the city and in battle in the city, helped our troops to hold defensive lines along rivers, supported counterattacks, attacked enemy reserves, and protected ground forces and important installations. In addition, air groups of the Civil Air Fleet and some AFLRO units transported military material, personnel, ammunition, and food to the ground troops, and evacuated the wounded to the rear.

Our air force rendered invaluable aid to the ground forces so that they could retain their bases at Stalingrad, wore down the enemy troops, and destroyed a significant part of the best German fliers.

During the whole defense operation the aircraft of the fronts, AFLRO, and the fighter aircraft of ADF made 77,000 sorties (the AFLRO made more than 11,000). Twenty-three thousand tons of bombs were dropped on enemy troops and other targets, and 38,000 rockets, 1,200,000 cannon shells, and about 4,000,000 bullets were fired. The enemy suffered great losses from our raids. More than 2100 of his planes were destroyed in the air and on the ground.

In comparison with the defense operations around Moscow, our air power in the operations between the Don and the Volga was employed in greater concentrations. This was accomplished for the most part by concentrating the efforts of the two air armies of the fronts, the air reserves of the *Stavka,* a significant part of the AFLRO, and the fighter air divisions of ADF. Centralized control, achieved when the air armies and groupings of one type of aircraft were created, facilitated the mass utilization of air power in important areas.

Coordination of the efforts of different types of aircraft, first carried out by representatives from the *Stavka,* justified itself. In the defense operation radio communication was now used for controlling the activities of fighters and ground-attack aircraft.

There was constant improvement in the organization of joint efforts with the ground troops. There were always air unit representatives on the army staffs who coordinated joint operations.

Compared with the operation of our troops in 1941 the proportion of night operations in the Battle of the Volga was significantly higher (about 47 percent of all sorties), so that air power was now involved with the enemy continuously, both by day and night.

At the time when the Luftwaffe was concentrating over the battle-field, most of our battles with their forces took place in the air, and it was here that 76 percent of their losses occurred.

Aerial reconnaissance was a great aid both to ground and air force commands. It aided in the advantageous discovery of enemy reserve concentrations, shock troops, and aircraft. In addition to special reconnaissance aircraft, other experienced flight crews, flights, and squadrons of all kinds of aircraft were utilized for aerial reconnaissance. Visual observation of enemy movements was supplemented by photographs, and radio reports concerning the enemy were transmitted by radio from the reconnaissance planes.

The experience gained in troop support during the long Stalingrad battle was to find broad application during the war in subsequent sieges of large cities.

A new development in ground-attack tactics was the wide use of these aircraft as short-range bombers in the daytime and, to a certain extent, at night. Thus, ground-attack aircraft began to operate not only at ground level, but also from intermediate and high altitudes. For longer operations against enemy troops and to increase their defensive capabilities, our aircraft in the target area began to use more widely the defensive "circle" formation.

For the most part, the usual procedure for our fighters when protecting ground troops and targets in the rear was systematic day patrols. The new fighter types, Yak-7B, and La-5, could climb and dive faster in dogfights. By the end of the defense operation flights of two pairs of aircraft became the basic tactical unit.

End of the Commissar System.   During the defense operation, party-political organs and party and Comsomol organizations were carrying out much ideological and educational work, whose major purpose was the strengthening of morale and the promotion of a spirit of boundless dedication to the Motherland and courage and decisiveness in battle.‡

‡ The system of military commissars used in the Red Army during the Civil War had been revived in July 1941. Every military unit was assigned a party official who shared command responsibility with the commanding officers. These commissars were responsible for the political reliability of the

Great attention was given to teaching affection and respect for one's commanding officer and the strengthening of one-man authority. When the Presidium of the Supreme Soviet of the USSR issued its directive "Concerning the Establishing of Complete One-man Authority and the Abolishing of the Institute for Military Commissars in the Red Army" there were party and Comsomol meetings, discussions, lectures, and reports, in the air force units, in which the significance of dedication and faith in one's commanding officer, especially at the time of fulfilling a battle assignment, was discussed. Unswerving and accurate compliance to a military order was the first law for the airman. This law was inviolable in all conditions, even the most difficult ones. The feeling of elevated responsibility, faith in one's abilities, and mutual comradely support helped fliers to emerge as victors, even in battle against a numerically superior foe. The will to victory and contempt for death were marked features of Soviet fliers.

It was explained to the air force personnel that the peoples of the entire Motherland were working for victory over the enemy: fighters in the army, air force, and navy at the front, and laborers in the rear lines. In the air units there were discussions of letters received from workers in Leningrad, Moscow, the cities of the Urals, Kazakhstan, Uzbekistan, and other republics. Exchanges of letters and delegations were arranged between workers at the aircraft factories and fliers. The custom developed for representatives from the workers to deliver airplanes with given names to outstanding fliers at ceremonies on airfields at the front, in reserve units, or at aircraft plants. Airmen-laborers at the rear took oaths to work better and fliers to fight courageously and stubbornly at the front until total victory was achieved over the enemy.

The exploits of flying and technical crews were given wide publicity. Meetings were held in the regiments when individual fliers were granted medals. Awards, as a rule, were granted at airfields with all personnel present.

Outstanding deeds of fliers were described in special military bulletins, "lightning-bulletins," and also in division, army, and front newspapers. Warm letters were sent to the families of hero-fliers and

---

commanders, as well as the political indoctrination of the men. On October 9, 1942, the government abolished the system, retaining the political officer only as a subordinate to the commander, and responsible primarily for political education. ED.

also to factories or kolkhozes where they worked before entering the air force. In the air regiments the practice was widespread of conducting meetings and discussions between young fliers and veteran airmen, Heroes of the Soviet Union, who shared their experiences.

The fliers' heroic exploits and great military acts were highly appreciated by the Communist party. In the period from July 17 to October 1, 1942, in the 8th Air Army alone, six daring fliers were given the title of Hero of the Soviet Union, and more than 1030 fliers were given orders or medals.

Multifaceted and constant party-political work supported high patriotic consciousness, battle training, courage in battle, and heroism among the personnel of the air units during the period of defensive operations, and prepared them morally for the coming counterattack.

SUMMARY AND CONCLUSIONS

Seventeen Months of Defensive Battle.   The first period of the Great Patriotic War, lasting almost seventeen months, was an extremely difficult and painful period for the Soviet armed forces. During this period of almost one and a half years the German Fascist armies twice conducted great offensive operations in their attempt to crush the Red Army. But these attempts did not reach their desired goal. Our ground forces, with active support from the air force, dealt the enemy a major defeat in the winter of 1941–42, and then a second one in the fall of 1942, thereby creating conditions for a fundamental reversal in the course of the war.

Events of the armed conflict during the first period of the war on the Soviet-German front made it clear that this was not only the major front of the war, but also that it was decisive in the course of World War II. Total losses among the German armies from June 22, 1941, to June 30, 1942, on our front amounted to nearly 2,000,000 men and officers. Our armed forces crushed Hitler's plan for a blitzkrieg. Germany was compelled to conduct a protracted war.

The Soviet Air Force took an active part in the struggle with the German Fascist aggressors. During this first period of the war the front aviation and AFLRO flew 858,000 sorties (footnote: of this number 57,000 were flown by the AFLRO), and 6,215,000 bombs with a total weight of 170,000 tons were dropped on enemy soldiers, equipment, and various targets in the rear (footnote: of these, 55,000 tons were dropped by the AFLRO). More than 15,700 enemy aircraft were destroyed in the air or on the ground by Soviet planes. Losses of German aircraft in the other theaters of the war in this period amounted to around 3400 aircraft.

Our aviation had as its major task the comprehensive support of the ground forces. Its major efforts were directed to the destruction of the enemy's tank and motorized columns. This made it possible to give significant aid to the troops of the fronts in the conduct of both defensive and offensive operations and to wear down the enemy. Simultaneously the air force carried out aerial reconnaissance, periodically struck at military-industrial and political targets deep in the rear, and supported partisans.

Our air force and Air Defense force prevented the destruction of the major administrative and industrial centers of the USSR, including Moscow, and protected the blockaded city of Leningrad and its one tie with the rear—the ice road across Lake Ladoga. Enemy bombers were not able to deal serious blows to the most important industrial centers: Baku, Gorki, Saratov, Kuibyshev, etc.

The Soviet government highly regarded the services of the airmen and their contribution to the attainment of victory over the enemy. During the years of 1941–42, 269 of our finest airmen were given the title of Hero of the Soviet Union and tens of thousands were granted medals. Three air regiments were given medals, while 38 front regiments and five regiments of the ADF were given guards status.

During the first period of the war when the strategic defense of our troops was under way and the enemy had control of the air and the situation on the ground was difficult, our planes had great successes in individual air battles with well-armed enemy aircraft which appeared without warning. They dealt the enemy serious losses in aircraft and experienced fliers. The Soviet aircraft industry was gradually achieving rear successes in the production of the most modern aircraft and armament. During 1941–42 it delivered 33,857 aircraft to the front, while the German aircraft industry and its allied states produced 20,857 aircraft. The successes at the front and in the rear guaranteed superiority both qualitatively and quantitatively over German aircraft and created the essential conditions for a final conquest of the air by Soviet aircraft in the second period of the war.

Much work was done in training flight and technical personnel: during the first eighteen months of the war, air force educational institutions trained about 90,000 men, including 41,224 flight personnel.

The system for training, recruiting, and forming air units and groupings, which was created at the beginning of the war, contributed to the strengthening and battle proficiency of the air force. During 1941–42, 570 air units were trained and sent to the front. In 1942 the average flier spent twice as much time in the air and the number of military sorties increased nearly 2.5 times when compared with 1941, which contributed much to the military capabilities of the flight personnel.

During the first part of the war much attention was given to creating an air reserve for the Supreme Command. Because so many planes had been lost and the situation in the air was so dangerous, reserve air combinations were formed within the air force beginning in July 1941, to strengthen the forces at the front in the most important areas.

At the beginning of the war, air groupings of the AFLRO of the Supreme Command, and also aircraft from the air forces of military districts at the rear were utilized as reserves. The first reserve, later strike air groups, were formed in August 1941, each of which consisted of four to six air regiments.

Completion of the aviation industry's evacuation to the east and adoption of aircraft mass production by summer 1942 created favorable conditions for the formation of stronger reserves for the air forces of the fronts and insured a greater increase in the number of aircraft at the disposal of the air armies. By the middle of November 1942, ten air corps of the Supreme Headquarters had been created, which amounted to more than 32 percent of the total number of aircraft of the fronts, making it possible to increase the flexibility of the air forces and to create large air concentrations in the most important sectors of the Soviet-German front.

From the beginning of the war, instructors and participants from air clubs were sent to air units and groups. Many regiments of night bombers were formed from the members of a number of air clubs. During the war, the organizations of the Volunteer Defense Society continued to train glider pilots, parachutists, parachute packers, and other specialists. Among the population, propaganda was disseminated popularizing the heroic exploits of airmen and the military operations of the air force. On the initiative of the organizations of the Volunteer Defense Society, collections of funds were made in both country and city for the construction of military equipment.

Concern for strengthening the power of the Red Army and Air Force and the united struggle of all the Soviet people to achieve victory over the Fascist invaders was expressed in the work of the Volunteer Defense Society. The patriotic activities of the Volunteer Defense Society were deeply appreciated. When noting its twentieth anniversary in 1947 the Presidium of the Supreme Soviet of the USSR granted the Volunteer Defense Society the Order of the Red Banner for its successful work in strengthening the defense of the country.

*Rebuilding the Air Force.** Successful completion of the aircraft industry evacuation to the east and the increased production of aircraft and other equipment improved the quality and quantity of the aircraft fleet and increased air force power. The proportion of bombers and ground-attack planes in the air force reached 66 percent of the total and the bomb-carrying capacity doubled. The ground forces received more substantial help from the air and as a result their resistance in defense and successes in offense were increased.

Operational mobility within the air force was one of the most important conditions necessary for successful operations. However, before summer 1942 it was impossible to concentrate efforts in the decisive sectors because aircraft were scattered among the armies of the fronts. The organization of air armies increased aircraft mobility in the first period of the war. The further increase in the number of air armies, and the formation of ten air corps for the Supreme Headquarters in fall 1942, contributed much flexibility in the use of air power in the war's second period.

The command of the Red Army Air Force organized coordinated operations between the air forces of the fronts, aircraft of the Air Defense Force, the reserves, and the strike air groups for joint efforts during the first war years. Members of the Red Army Air

---

* Increase of aircraft production from 15,735 in 1941 to 25,436 in 1942, was aided by reducing the number of types in production. The MiG-3, Pe-8, Yak-4, and Su-2 went out of production, allowing more concentration on the Il-2, Il-4, and Pe-2. The LaGG-3 and Yak-1 were replaced by the faster and more heavily armed La-5, Yak-7B, and, in December 1942, the Yak-9. ED.[39]

Force Military Council were sent into the operational areas for this purpose. Beginning in summer 1942, at the battle of Stalingrad, the commander of the Red Army Air Force as a representative of the *Stavka* coordinated joint efforts between the air forces of the front, the AFLRO, and ADF aircraft. The presence of a representative for aviation from the *Stavka* contributed to the successful operations of the air force.

After the air armies came into existence there was more effective coordination between the air and land forces. The staffs of the air units began to work out coordinated plans that indicated the assignments of both the ground and air forces, air bases, number of sorties to be flown, recognition signals to be exchanged, etc.

Coordination between the ground and air forces during offensive operations did not take final form in the first period of the war. Prior to an offensive, the air force attacked the enemy at his airfields, his rail lines, and approaching reserves. During a breakthrough into the enemy's defense zone, the efforts of the air force were directed to cooperation with the ground troops, the struggle for control of the air, interdiction of reserves, and reconnaissance. Subsequently, aircraft had a series of other assignments: support of ground troops to repel enemy counterattacks, to seize intermediate defense lines, and to pursue retreating enemy troops; parachute troops were also dropped and they were supported in the rear of the enemy.

Later on, the development of the theory of air force operations permitted the utilization of a more effective technique for employing air power during offensive operations, the air offensive. New concepts for artillery and air offensives were introduced into the *Infantry Military Manual* issued by the People's Commissar for Defense on November 9, 1942. Its basic purpose was to be a "constant support for the infantry in the form of massed effective fire from artillery, mortars, and the air during the entire course of the offensive." A more complete definition of an air offensive was given in the *Field Manual of the Red Army:* "An air offensive has two parts: preparation for the attack, and support for the attack and infantry and tank operations deep in the enemy's rear." An air offensive was seen as a concentration of air power in the major attack area of the troops of the front, and as strikes against the most important targets in the tactical and operational rear of the enemy.

In the operations in the first period of the war there was an increase in the continuity and effectiveness of the air strikes against the enemy. In the summer of 1941, the aircraft of the fronts carried out their assignments for the most part by daylight and in good weather, but by autumn they were operating in bad weather and at night. Night light bomber air regiments equipped with Po-2s and R-5s were formed for the purpose. Long-range bombers began to operate at night, complementing the strikes of the daytime bombers and ground-attack planes. As a result the proportion of night operations became noticeably larger. During the first six months of the war 6 per cent of all air force sorties were night bomber flights, but during the Battle of the Volga this increased to around 47 percent.

To promote the safety of night flights and flights under bad weather conditions, the navigational service of the Red Army Air Force in the autumn of 1941 organized a ground directional system, additional radio and light equipment were installed on aircraft, bombers were more often directed to their targets from the ground, and aerial photos were taken to assess the results of bomber raids. Thus, even under extremely difficult conditions the Soviet command, utilizing all possible resources, including antiquated aircraft, competently supported the continuity of air attacks against the enemy.

During the period of defensive operations the air force became experienced in supporting counterattacks, and during offensive operations, in dropping parachute troops and partisans and transporting men and material by air. The regiments of AFLRO and Civil Air Fleet units were widely used for this purpose. During the first year and a half of the war, 58,000 sorties were flown in support of partisans, including 4645 which involved landing behind enemy lines. In 1942 alone the units of the Civil Air Fleet and the AFLRO transported more than 38,000 men and 6400 tons of cargo.

In the first period of the war, much experience was gained in the struggle for control of the air. Out of a total of 803,000 sorties made by the aircraft of the fronts, our fighter planes made 184,686 to protect ground troops and important targets in the rear and 69,397 as cover for other types of aircraft. In attacks against enemy airfields 22,851 sorties were flown. More than one-third of the efforts of the aircraft of the fronts were expended in the struggle for the control of the air. The struggle to control the air was one of the most important tasks of our air force. In spite of the limited number of attacks against enemy airfields, 33 percent of all enemy planes destroyed were on airfields. During the war's first year, of 13,156 enemy planes destroyed on the Soviet-German front, 4316 were destroyed on airfields, 6891 were shot down in aerial battles, and 1949 were knocked down by antiaircraft artillery.

From data gathered by most of the air armies, it is known that about 70 percent of the enemy aircraft on field would be destroyed on a first strike, 19 percent on the second, and 10 percent on a third. Consequently, the destruction of enemy aircraft was most probable at a first strike.

In the war's first period, experience was gained in operations against the enemy's reserves, which in a number of cases involved enemy air operations. For example, the operation conducted by the Front and the AFLRO against the enemy's 2nd Tank Group in 1941 was of great aid to the ground forces by causing numerous enemy losses and retarding the enemy's tank offensive. However, the difficult situation in the air and the necessity of concentrating almost all our air power in the direct support of our ground troops on the battlefield limited the employment of air power against the enemy's operational reserves.

Improvements in Tactics. As our aircraft increased in numbers and improved in quality, battle skills were learned and assimilated, command personnel began to display creative initiative, and the air force perfected and developed tactics for different types of aircraft. The skilled, independent efforts of our personnel had a real influence on the successful completion of military assignments, a heightened effect on enemy troops, and the lowering of our losses. Bombers from the air forces of the fronts became the basic means for destroying the enemy's ground forces. Bomber techniques changed as more battle experience was acquired, new types of planes were acquired, and there was increased opposition from the enemy's air defenses. At the beginning of the war our bomber units operated in regiment-sized groups. After eight to ten days, because of losses, they operated in teams: at daytime in flights and squadrons, and at night as single planes. Beginning in summer 1942, when there were more planes and our crews were more experienced, our Front aircraft and AFLRO began to make concentrated strikes.

The day formation employed by our bombers, "the wedge," and "the line," a column of flights, squadrons, and air regiments, provided defense capability, flexibility, and precision in a strike against enemy targets. When a tight formation was maintained and when an organized pattern for machine-gun defense against enemy interceptors was organized, losses were lowered, and a more effective attack against the target could be made.

Bombs were dropped, as a rule, from horizontal flight. Because flight crews were not well trained, dive-bombing was not widely used, which limited the employment of the Pe-2 and hindered effective attacks against the enemy, especially against small targets.

The altitude from which bombs were dropped was determined for the most part by the size of the target, type of bomb, the effect of its explosion, and the extent of antiaircraft defenses. When the war began, bombers operated from an altitude of 2000–3000 meters (6560–9840 feet). But raids from this altitude did not insure the destruction of the target, especially if it was small. In order to increase the effectiveness of the raids, especially against tank or motorized columns, two weeks after the war began bombers started to operate at altitudes of 600–1000 meters (1968–3280 feet) and, when there was weak antiaircraft fire, from even lower altitudes.

At night, light bombers operated as solitary aircraft at intervals of five to fifteen minutes. If the target was important the strength of the blow was increased by utilizing more aircraft flying simultaneously at different altitudes. The approach to the target was made, as a rule, from one direction in a glide with the motors shut off, which increased the unexpectedness of the attack and reduced losses. The long-range bombers (Il-4, TB-3, Pe-8, Li-2) operated individually at night. During a short period of time 80–100 or more aircraft struck at targets from an altitude of not more than 2000 meters (6560 feet).

At the beginning of the war, ground-attack aircraft attacked tank and motorized columns and directly supported ground troops for the most part. Subsequently they began to attack railroad communications, reserves, and enemy aircraft on the ground. Assignments were carried out by ground-attack planes in small groups distributed in depth. When larger numbers of Il-2s were available, the ground-attack planes began to make concentrated attacks in groups of several squadrons. When the weather was bad, fliers employed the technique of flying as free "hunters."

As more experience was acquired, the tactics, formations, and organizational structure of ground-attack units were altered. In 1941, the three-plane flight met its assignments in a "wedge" (or V) formation; by 1942 the "line" was used; and by the fall of 1942, the fundamental unit was a pair of aircraft, and a flight consisted of four aircraft. The most maneuverable and most invulnerable unit consisted of a group of six or eight aircraft. The "line" became the formation employed by such a group. Bombs were dropped on the initiative of each flier or at a signal given by the leader of the group.

Attacks on the targets were usually carried out by individual ground-attack aircraft and flights at ground level, or from an altitude of 150–300 meters (492–984 feet) on one approach, and when there was no antiaircraft fire, several approaches would be made from different directions. Beginning in 1942 a number of ground-attack air regiments, in addition to ground-level attacks, began to attack at an angle of 20–35 degrees from an altitude of 800–1200 meters (2624–3936 feet), which made their attacks more accurate.

It was essential that ground-attack planes have fighter protection both to and from their targets. However, because we had so few fighter planes until fall 1942, ground-attack planes were not rarely compelled to operate without cover, which increased losses. When there was a larger pool of fighter planes then fighter cover became systematic. In summer 1942, the Il-2s were equipped with a second cockpit with a machine-gun mount in the Air Force of the Northwestern Front, then in the autumn the planes of the 16th Air Army, and then later in the planes of all the air armies. This made it possible for the ground-attack planes to successfully repel attacks from enemy interceptors. Larger gasoline tanks, better armor, and replacement of machine guns by 23 mm. cannons increased the effectiveness of ground-attack aircraft, particularly against enemy tanks, and reduced losses.

Fighter aircraft were involved most of all in the struggle for control of the air. They protected ground forces, important targets in our rear, the air bases of the Fronts, and from time to time flew escort for bombers and ground-attack aircraft. In addition, part of them were engaged in constant aerial reconnaissance and free "hunting," and periodically they were used as ground-attack aircraft against enemy troops and equipment on the battlefield.

In the daytime, cover for ground forces was provided by patrols and by groups of interceptors on alert on air bases and on temporary fields. When there were no radio-directional facilities, air patrols were the basic method of protecting our troops and targets in the rear. Interceptors at alert on the ground had positive results so long as enemy aircraft were numerous and constantly active. The considerable distance between the air bases and the front (80–100 kilometers, or 50–62 miles), the small number of aircraft available, and the poor utilization of radio communication for aircraft control over the battlefield before autumn 1942 had a negative effect on fighter operations.

During the battle for Moscow the first transition was made to a new battle formation consisting of pairs of interceptors. In September 1942, orders were issued to employ a four-aircraft flight. This transition to a new battle formation increased the effectiveness of fighter aircraft, contributed better cover for ground troops and escorting of other aircraft, and lowered losses.

In the battle for the Volga, experience was gained in protecting troops by assigning groups of fighters to different altitudes, dividing them into strike and cover groups, and shifting patrol zones across the front lines into territory occupied by the enemy.

By the end of the first period of the war, fighter planes had experience in making vertical attacks, which contributed to their effectiveness in covering troops, shifting to offensive operations, and increased their effectiveness in the struggle for the control of the air.

Development of interceptor tactics during the war's first period advanced along the line of increased flexibility of battle order, operations in pairs of aircraft, distribution of aircraft in depth, division of aircraft into groups for direct cover and a strike group, an improvement in the organized coordination between these groups and attack echelons, and the perfecting of the technique of vertical attack.

Organizational Development. Support of air force battle operations was one of the major obligations of the command personnel, political and party organizations, the personnel of engineering air service, the men at the rear, and other services.

Party-political work had the goal of supporting the air force in the fulfillment of its assignments and the strengthening of the political-moral resolve and military discipline of the airmen. The basic forms and methods of party-political work were as follows: regular visits for managerial workers from political organizations and military councils to the air regiments and squadrons; conferences; conventions; party and Comsomol gatherings; meetings; reports; lectures; discussions; daily news sheets; and readings from the most important information from the press. Individual and group discussions were the most effective forms of such work. They made it possible to communicate the needs of the Motherland opportunely and completely to the airmen, as well as orders from the command, to clarify the conditions of a situation as it was developing, and to publicize the advanced military experience and the exploits of our fliers.

Front, army, and divisional newspapers, wall newspapers, and bulletins which served as the basic medium for all education and political work in the air force, had great educational significance. On their pages was explained the policy of the Communist party and the goals and problems of the war; information was given concerning the workers behind the lines, the engineering and technical staffs, and air force units at the rear; and the outstanding experiences of our best fliers were given publicity.

The difficult situation at the beginning of the war caused great problems for commanding officers with authority over military operations. The creation of an institute for military commissars had great influence on the strengthening of the Red Army, including the air force. During this difficult period of the war the military commissars gave great help to command personnel in the raising of discipline and the improvement of the organizational structure and the effectiveness of the air force, in addition to broadening both the extent and content of party-political work.

The political workers popularized the experiences of the progressive commanding officers of regiments, squadrons, and flights, the heroic deeds of the engineering and technical staffs, and the air force fighters at the rear. Great help was given to the commands in publicizing progressive experiences by the timely publication of sketches, bulletins, memoirs, albums, and other materials. It was found worthwhile to honor fliers and crews that had successfully completed 25, 50, 100, 150, and 200 sorties. As a rule, on the same day that this was done, government awards, orders of gratitude, and commanders' letters to outstanding fliers were also handed out.

Under difficult conditions and in fierce battles, Communists and members of the Comsomol were found in the front ranks and with their personal example encouraged confidence in their own forces and weapons among the other men, arousing their military and moral enthusiasm, and teaching them love for the Motherland and burning hatred for the fascist invaders. Many political workers not only successfully organized party-political work, but they themselves personally took an active part in sorties. For example, squadron military commissars, senior political instructors A. S. Danilov, A. M. Sokolov, N. M. Dubinin, and Battalion Commissar A. P. Chulkov, and many others, were granted the title Hero of the Soviet Union because of their courage and exemplary conduct in innumerable battles, where they inspired their subordinates to heroic deeds and contributed to the military glory of Soviet aviation.

To give greater encouragement to fighters who successfully completed their military assignments, the Presidium of the Supreme Soviet of the USSR established the Orders of Suvorov, Kutuzov, Alexander Nevsky, and the Great Patriotic War, and medals for the defense of the hero-cities in 1942. Air units that especially distinguished themselves were designated as guards units. Commanders of air units were given the right to grant orders and medals to outstanding fliers. All of these measures contributed toward the strengthening of morale, lifting of battle capabilities, and the attainment of victory in bitter fighting.

Party Indoctrination of Airmen. The difficult experiences and the sacrifices connected with the conduct of the war did not weaken the ranks of the Communists and the party organizers of the air force. They became constantly stronger and grew in numbers by enrolling progressive fighters, especially after the decisions of the Central Committee of the party dated August 19 and December 9, 1941, which eased the conditions for entering the Communist party for outstanding fighters in the battle with the enemy. Therefore the party organizations of the air force, in spite of great losses, not only filled their ranks but also constantly increased them. The more difficult the situation became at the front, the more airmen joined the ranks of the party to replace those who had fallen in battle.

On January 1, 1941, there were 58,013 members of the party or candidates for membership in the air force. By January 1, 1942, party membership had grown by 16,193 members, i.e., by nearly 30 percent, and there were now 74,206 Communists in the ranks. In 1942 party ranks in the air force grew at yet a greater rate. During the first six months they increased more than in all of 1941. On July 1, 1942, there were 91,127 party members or candidates for membership in the air force, and at the end of 1942 this number was 123,102 (about 7 percent of all the Communists in the Red Army).

There was a constant increase in the percentage of Communists in the air force. On January 1, 1941, this was 14 percent, and on July 1, 1942, 22 percent. It was still higher among flying personnel, reaching 50 percent. The majority of the commanding officers of the air force were in the party, including 99 percent of all division and regimental commanders, 95 percent of all squadron commanders, and 70 percent of all flight leaders. As a rule, it was the brave, fearless fighters, heroes of numerous air battles or ground-attack and bombing raids which caused great losses to the enemy, who entered the party. With the example of their courage they taught hundreds, thousands of new courageous and brave fliers.

Reconnaissance. Aerial reconnaissance was extremely important. Because reconnaissance units had not been completely staffed at the beginning of the war, because there were no special reconnaissance aircraft, and because of losses in the very first days of the war, the commanders of the Front air forces had to employ considerable numbers of aircraft from regular units for aerial reconnaissance. The major task of aerial reconnaissance was daily observation of the enemy from the air. Its basic attention was turned to the discovery and observation of the enemy's major troop concentrations and airfields, and particularly his tank units and reserves. A number of measures were taken to support aerial reconnaissance operations: an institute for aerial reconnaissance fliers was created in April 1942 and in May, formation of reconnaissance air regiments in all armies was begun.

Aerial reconnaissance was carried out using two different techniques: visual observation and photography. In 1941, 2741 sorties were flown for aerial reconnaissance, and in 1942, 10,054. Aerial reconnaissance was flown at the following altitudes: in daylight, from ground level to 8000 meters (26,240 feet) and at night from 300 to 1500 meters (984–4920 feet). Concealment and surprise in aerial reconnaissance was attained by skilled utilization of weather conditions and ground relief.

Information concerning the enemy was reported by our reconnaissance planes after they had landed on their airfields. Radio communications for this purpose were first widely used in the summer of 1942. Only tactical reconnaissance was carried out for the most part in the first period of the war. Insufficient attention was devoted to the problems of operational and strategic reconnaissance.

Support Services. Navigational services were inadequate in a number of ways when the war began. There were more cases of lost aircraft than there had been before the war. There was not always precision in bombing raids made from altitudes of 2000–3000 meters (6560–9840 feet) and especially against small targets. A number of measures were taken to overcome these difficulties. The order of the commander of the Red Army Air Force dated September 10, 1941, forbade sorties without plotting, study, and calculation of the course. Senior navigators were subordinated to their commanders in squadrons, regiments, and divisions, who gave them assignments and verified their fulfillment. Beginning in August 1941, control-pass points were set up to insure that aircraft could return to their camouflaged airfields, and crews were trained for operations at night and under difficult weather conditions. Navigators from air regiments and squadrons were trained at advanced schools; navigational flights were introduced for all students at flight schools and fliers of reserve air regiments; a series of guides and manuals was developed on navigation; recording and analyses of causes of lost aircraft were set up; the formation of a unit for ground service for aircraft direction in the air forces of the fronts was accelerated; a number of training sessions concerning AFLRO radio navigation for navigational assistants within air regiments and divisions of AFLRO were set up; and the utilization of the powerful radio stations of the country for aircraft direction was begun. The introduction of these and other measures, in spite of bad weather conditions, cut in half the number of lost aircraft in November and December of 1941.

Great attention was given to increasing the effectiveness of air operations. The commander of the Red Army Air Force on March 19, 1942, demanded that the commands of the air forces of the fronts and armies provide concrete targets and demand specific results from the air regiments, and that the staffs of the air force support the air crews with reliable reconnaissance data concerning the targets of the raid, and with photographs, sketches, and large-scale maps of the operational area. Bomber units were forbidden to make strikes without using sights, and obligatory photo control of the results of raids was introduced. Special sniper bomber crews were designated for raids against small targets. New types of bombsights were ordered from industry to be used both by day and by night. All these measures insured a rise in the precision and effectiveness of bomber raids against the enemy.

The meteorological services also had great significance. At the beginning of the war, as part of support operations, weather stations were formed within the airfield service battalions, and weather bureaus were set up within the staffs of the air forces of the fronts and armies. In July 1941 the Hydro-meteorological Service of the USSR was combined with the military Meteorological Service. Supplying air units with meteorological data was the central task of the Air Force Meteorological Service. In many cases the success of an air operation depended on the degree of reliability and promptness of reports on weather conditions and predictions.

A number of measures were taken to improve the air force meteorological services: their structure and the utilization of specialists were improved, the collection of weather data from the weather stations of the air forces of the fronts and from ground troops was organized, the procedure was begun of regular broadcasts of weather information over the radio and their dissemination over wire communications was accelerated, and regular weather reconnaissance was begun over territory occupied by the enemy. In February 1942, a meteorological department was set up in the staff of the Red Army Air Force, weather bureaus were organized in the air divisions, and the AFLRO got its own meteorological service. All these measures contributed toward the improvement of the meteorological services in support of the air force.

Experience in the first period of the war showed that the organization of mobile radio-meteorological centers and weather bureaus in the air divisions, the wide utilization of information derived from aerial weather observation, the assignment (beginning in spring 1942) of meteorologists to division and regiment command posts, and the technique of systematic consultations between the Central Weather Institute and the Central Administration for Meteorological Services of the Red Army Air Force improved the operations efficiency and quality of weather services in the air force. In spite of the difficult situation and the presence of a number of inadequacies, the meteorological services of the air force were able to support air operations and obtained much experience in the organization of their services. Many specialists in the service were granted orders and medals for the high level of their work.

Rear support for military operations was much improved. In August–September 1941 there was a reorganization of the units and institutions in the rear, which resulted in more flexibility and mobility.

The office of Head of Rear Operations of the Air Force was introduced and the central control of air force rear units was reorganized. Measures were taken for the precise planning of the services of the rear and their supervision, for the organization of supplies to the air units, the organization of transportation, and the in-depth placement of supplies; advance and rear zones for the basing of aircraft were set up at a distance of up to 400 kilometers (248 miles) from the front lines. Supplies were brought in to the airfields in each of these zones, which aided in the support of military operations and the flexibility of air units.

One of the most important tasks for the rear services of the air force was providing air bases. The loss of a significant part of the airfields in the Western military districts caused a sharp need for the construction of a large number of fields in the eastern districts of the Ukraine and the central regions of the Russian Soviet Federated Socialist Republic. Later on, as our troops retreated, construction began deep within our country, and by the end of 1941 about 70 percent of all airfields were located on the territory of the internal military districts.

In 1941–42 the question of the construction of airfields was considered by the Central Committee of the Bolshevik party and by *Stavka*. Local Soviet governments gave great help in their construction, mobilizing much of the population and local transport to support the engineering–air-base battalions. The measures taken for the construction of airfields helped in the in-depth assignment of aircraft and improved the conditions for their operations, contributing to a sharp reduction of aircraft losses on the ground.

In the first period of the war, the engineering–air-base battalions obtained much experience in the construction of airfields at all seasons of the year and in both defensive and offensive operations. To prepare field air bases in a short period, they were usually constructed in areas with only a small amount of earth-moving necessary. Landing strips were constructed, as a rule, in dimensions of 1200 by 200 meters (3936 by 656 feet).

The first period of the war showed that the new air force organizational structure behind the lines—the air army rear, the region for aircraft bases, the battalion for airfield service—completely justified itself. The supply services to air units were better organized, and technical support for air operations was improved. The units of the air force rear gained some experience in the construction of airstrips during an offensive operation, and particularly during the counterattack near Moscow.

Medical workers met their responsibilities with honor. Under the most difficult conditions they gave medical aid to wounded fliers and saw to their evacuation. Many of them performed deeds of valor for which they received medals.

The personal staff of the Air Force Engineering Air Service dealt with the problem of maintaining air equipment in ready condition and acquired much experience in the organization of maintenance and repair of aircraft and in aircraft armament and equipment.

Air force engineering personnel acquired more skill in handling equipment. Investigation of the causes of every flying accident and the study of defects, their analysis, and generalizations therefrom contributed to the identification of the most common flaws in aircraft parts that might endanger a flight and toward measures for the elimination of such flaws. In such questions concerning the development and adaptation of air technology much help was given by the air force's scientific-experimental organization, by the Zhukovsky Military Academy, and also by the factories of the People's Commissariat for the Aircraft Industry.

Part Two

THE AIR FORCE IN THE PERIOD
OF REVERSING THE WAR'S COURSE
(November 19, 1942, to December 1943)

V

COUNTERATTACK AT STALINGRAD

The Red Army had been fighting for almost eighteen months against the fascist bloc armies. The difficult situation in the first part of the war did not break the Soviet people and its armed forces. Red Army resistance was growing day by day. The enemy could not reach the goals which he had set for summer 1942.

By this time the Soviet Air Force was undergoing great changes. Industry was increasing its production of aircraft, equipment, and supplies. Aircraft were surviving for longer periods of time because of better armor, more efficient equipment, better designed fuel tanks and fire protection equipment. Re-equipment of the air force with new aircraft was nearly complete, contributing to the more efficient fulfillment of military assignments.

The VVS* command structure and the staffs had by now acquired the necessary experience in the organization and conduct of military operations during large campaigns and in a war as a whole. Cooperation between the aircraft of several fronts was improved, as well as the flexibility of aircraft operations on different fronts. The support forces of the rear were stronger, although they still did not have adequate special transport vehicles. Airfield service battalions were more experienced in supporting the air regiments in difficult wartime conditions. Base-shifting operations were better organized, airfields were better defended, and much attention was given to camouflage. Engineering and technical staffs and men from the other services labored unceasingly to prepare aircraft for battle opera-

---

* VVS. This is the commonly used abbreviation for the Soviet Air Force: Voyenno-Vozdushnye Sily. ED.

tions. Many air regiments had received battle awards or had been designated as guards regiments.

The party-political organs had been completely reorganized. After the concept of one-man authority had been introduced, they gave more attention to strengthening the authority of commanding officers, better educational work, and the daily problems of air force personnel. There was a great increase in the size of party and Comsomol organizations in units and groups. They were filled out by young aviators, most of whom had been hardened in recent battles. Thus, the Soviet Air Force was much stronger by the fall of 1942.

Soviet Air Strength Surpasses the Germans. The Luftwaffe and the air forces of its allies at this time had 3300 aircraft on the Soviet-German front. As before, a decisive role was given to bomber aircraft, but German industry was increasing fighter production. In 1941 the production of fighter planes was 11 percent higher than bombers, but by 1942 this had increased to 27 percent. The modified aircraft, the Bf 109G-2, and the new Fw 190, whose flight and tactical capabilities were better than any earlier fighters', arrived at the front.

The productive capabilities of the German aircraft industry remained high. German industry produced 15,400 aircraft in 1942, but this was not enough to replace losses.

The situation in the air in the middle of November 1942 was characterized by the increased effectiveness and higher operational level of our air force, which now had a numerical supremacy over the Luftwaffe.

The Soviet Supreme Command decided during the offensive operations in the winter of 1942–43 to deprive the enemy of his initiative and to achieve a fundamental reversal in the course of the war. The major blow was to fall on the Southwestern Front against one of the strongest and most active enemy concentrations. Subsequently, there was to be a decisive offensive on the southern wing of the Soviet-German front, and a number of operations simultaneously to improve the situation of our troops on the Northwestern and Western Fronts and to break the blockade of Leningrad.

Troops of the Southwestern, Don, and Stalingrad Fronts were to be involved in the counteroffensive. The 17th, 16th, and 8th Air Armies were to be engaged with them, respectively. By *Stavka* order, two composite air corps and seven separate divisions were designated as reinforcements for the air armies of the three fronts. In addition, the 2nd Air Army of the Voronezh Front was assigned to the Southwestern Front. The command over all air power was held by the representative of the *Stavka,* VVS Commander General A. A. Novikov, who was located with a small operational group in the Stalingrad region.

Taking into account all the reserve aircraft assigned to the units, there were 1414 aircraft concentrated for the opening of the counter-offensive, of which 426 (Po-2, R-5, SB) operated at night only. The enemy had 1216 aircraft in this sector.

Special attention was given to strengthening the ground-attack air-craft of the fronts. The two-seat Il-2 had especially distinguished itself in battle operations, successfully operating with infantry and tanks in both offensive and defensive operations. In the four air armies there were 575 Il-2s.

Bases of the 17th and 16th Air Armies were moved closer to the areas where the enemy's defense zone had been penetrated. Air units of the 8th Air Army were assigned to the western bank of the Volga at a distance of 100–150 kilometers (62–93 miles) from the breakthrough area. Because of the absence of a transportation network and the small number of trucks available, these bases were not completely equipped and had very limited amounts of aviation fuel and supplies. Just as the counterattack in autumn began, thin ice formed on the rivers, which complicated communications with the right bank of the Volga.

According to *Stavka*'s plan, troops of the three fronts were to strike two powerful blows at the enemy flanks from northwest and south of Stalingrad, which were to join at Kalach and Sovetsky in order to surround and then annihilate his forces.

Air units of the fronts were given the assignment of protecting and supporting the strike groups during the counteroffensive, es-pecially tanks and mechanized units, and of carrying out aerial reconnaissance. Much emphasis was given to the battle against enemy aircraft. Gaining control of the air was one of the major assignments of the air armies.

On the basis of these assignments the air staffs worked out plan-ning documents for air operations. The 8th Air Army (commanded by General T. T. Khryukin) concentrated its efforts on the support of the strike group of the 57th and 51st Ground Armies. The night before the offensive began, Po-2 light night bombers and ground-attack planes were to attack staff headquarters and communication lines.

To support the drive into the enemy's rear by the 13th and 4th Mechanized and 4th Cavalry Corps, ground-attack planes were to strike enemy artillery and reserves, and fighter patrols were to protect our troops from enemy aircraft. To facilitate cooperation with the mechanized corps, once they were deep in enemy territory, each of them was given one ground-attack and one fighter air regiment.

One bomber division was given the special assignment of attacking enemy reserves. Part of our air power was assigned to the support of the 62nd Army in case the enemy might begin an offensive against its defense zone.

The first military operations of the 8th Air Army during this attack were planned as an air offensive, which was seen as continued action during the preparatory period before the attack, during the attack itself, and when the infantry and tanks were operating in the rear of the enemy.

Fighter and ground-attack divisions of the 17th Air Army (commanded by General S. A. Krasovsky) were operationally subordinated to the commanders of the infantry and tank armies. On the instructions of the commander of the Southwestern Front, General N. F. Vatutin, massed air power was to be used for strikes against enemy reserves, tanks, and motorized divisions.

Military operations for the 16th Air Army (commanded by General S. I. Rudenko) were planned with definite targets to be attacked at the time when the enemy's tactical defense zone had been penetrated.

The AFLRO was given the task of bombing in the area of the Southwestern Front to destroy enemy airfields, railroad lines, railroad stations, and the interdiction of enemy reserves moving up toward the front.

In accordance with these assignments and plans for the application of air power, there was a change in the organizational structure. To strengthen the support of the strike group of the Southwestern Front, three air divisions of the 2nd Air Army of the Voronezh Front (commanded by General K. N. Smirnov) were to be based on the right wing of the Southeastern Front. Part of the air divisions of the

2nd, 17th, and 8th Air Armies were to be brought up to advanced airfields one or two days before the counterattack began.

To conceal the shift of aircraft, mock air bases were built. In the 8th Air Army, 19 false airfields were built in addition to 25 real ones, and on 14 of these mock night operations were conducted.

Much was done by political and party-Comsomol organizations. In order to educate personnel in the military tradition of the heroic past of the Red Army there was broad discussion of the appeal made in the Tsaritsyn campaign to the defenders of the hero-city.†

Encirclement of the German Army. On the morning of November 19, 1942, after a great artillery barrage, the troops of the Southwestern Front began the counteroffensive. Fog and low clouds made it impossible to carry out air operations as had been planned. Only a few ground-attack planes supported the 5th Tank Army in the major attack against the northern flank of the German salient.

After the 1st and 26th Tank Corps were introduced into battle, the troops of the front broke through the enemy defense zone on the very first day of battle and advanced 30–35 kilometers (18–21 miles). On the fifth day of the operation our troops had advanced, fighting continuously, 150 kilometers (93 miles), liberating Kalach and seizing several enemy airfields. This compelled the enemy to shift his aircraft to airfields in the rear and limited his operations against our troops. Because of the bad weather our air power continued to operate with limited forces.

Troops of the Stalingrad Front began their counterattack on the southern side of the German salient on November 20. Because of the fog and limited visibility, the 8th Air Army could send up only isolated aircraft, but they were successful in destroying a number of enemy tanks while flying cover for units of the 13th and 4th Mechanized Corps. During a four-day period the troops of the front moved forward successfully 115 kilometers (71 miles), capturing the city of Sovetsky, and on November 23 closed the trap around the enemy troops, meeting the tank corps of the Southwestern Front near Kalach. During this period the 8th Air Army flew 340 sorties in spite of very bad weather conditions.

---

† Tsaritsyn was the old (prerevolutionary) name for Stalingrad, and at a crucial moment during the Civil War in 1918, the population was mobilized against the White Guards by an appeal made to the city by the Red Army. ED.

The 16th Air Army, supporting the offensive of the 65th and 24th Armies of the Don Front, was not very active because of the bad weather. During the first five days of the offensive, it flew 238 sorties against troops and equipment on the battlefield, and against armored columns and airfields.

During the encirclement of the enemy forces, our aircraft flew about 1000 sorties. Soviet fliers, fulfilling their assignments in bad weather conditions, showed themselves as models of heroism and military skill. For example, on November 21 six Il-2s, led by Hero of the Soviet Union, Captain V. M. Golubev, flew a sortie against the airfield on the sovkhoz‡ "October Victory." As they approached the target they were raked by antiaircraft fire. After they had destroyed the antiaircraft guns, the fliers attacked the field and destroyed eight enemy aircraft. As they returned home, they were attacked by enemy fighters. During the course of this battle the fliers shot down two Bf 109s and returned to their airfield without losses.

Victor Golubev received the title Hero of the Soviet Union at Stalingrad on August 12, 1942; and a year later, August 24, 1943, he was given a second "Gold Star," for outstanding bravery in the battle for Kursk.

The weather improved somewhat after November 24, allowing our aircraft to be more active. Every day they made about 800 sorties to protect our advancing mobile forces, destroy enemy troops and materiel on the battlefield, carry out aerial reconnaissance, strike against enemy airfields, and transport supplies to the 62nd Army men inside Stalingrad who were cut off from their rear by the increasing ice on the Volga.

The swift advance of our troops forced the enemy to move his aircraft back to rear airfields. As a result of this and because of losses, enemy air activity decreased greatly. From November 19 to November 30, his aircraft averaged about 115 sorties every twenty-four hours.

The air armies of the fronts and the AFLRO concentrated their efforts on the encircled enemy troops. At the end of November our aircraft were given a new assignment: attacking enemy transport planes, which were trying to supply their encircled troops by air. During these weeks as many as 600 enemy Ju 52s, Fw 200s, and other aircraft were used for supply assignments. Later on, because of great

‡ State farm.

losses, the enemy was forced to use He 111 bombers for this purpose. At the beginning of December, the enemy began making flights in groups of twenty to forty aircraft with fighter cover.

The 17th, 16th, and 8th Air Armies, and AFLRO were used to blockade the encircled enemy troops from the air in the Stalingrad region; this was to continue until the troops surrendered.

Breakthrough Attempt Fails. The offensive to liquidate the encircled enemy concentration was not yet successful. The enemy continued his stubborn resistance. On December 12, a strong enemy tank (4th Panzer) army began an offensive from the Kotelnikovo region, trying to reach the encircled Germans by breaking through.

Beginning on December 15, when the weather improved, our aircraft attacked advancing tanks and infantry, and also railroad trains. As the result of the efforts of our troops and aircraft, the enemy could not break through to his encircled troops. On December 24 the tank concentration at Kotelnikovo went on the defensive and then began to withdraw.

During the period from December 20 to December 23 the 8th Air Army flew 758 sorties against tanks and infantry. The enemy lost many men, and real help was given to the 51st Army in repelling the 4th Panzer Army offensive.

At the same time that the enemy strike group was retreating to the Myshkova River, the encircled troops were increasing their activities, concentrating a large number of men and tanks near Karpovka for an offensive to join up with a tank group that was located 40–50 kilometers (25–31 miles) beyond the encirclement. Aircraft from the 8th and 16th Air Armies during this period systematically attacked the encircled troops, preventing them from breaking out. The most severe battle was on the banks of the Aksay River on the morning of December 18, when more than 100 16th Air Army aircraft struck at the enemy concentration near Karpovka. The enemy suffered great losses and had to refrain from further attempts at breaking out of the trap.

When the enemy concentration at Kotelnikovo went on the offensive on December 12, the Soviet Supreme Command decided to accelerate the offensive of the Southwestern Front with the intent of disrupting the enemy's plan for liberating the encircled troops. The Front troops had as their major assignment an offensive from the region of Verkhni Mamon toward Nizhny Astakhov and Morozovsk in order to strike at the rear of the Kotelnikovo concentration and then, in cooperation with the 3rd Guard and 5th Tank Armies, which were attacking from the east, to destroy it. In the west, the troops engaged in the offensive were supported by the 6th Army of the Voronezh Front, which was based at Kantemirovka.

To support these troops, 455 aircraft of the 2nd and 17th Air Armies were assigned to the area. The enemy also had 450 aircraft in this area. But during the very first days of the operation, the balance between the two sides shifted somewhat in our favor when the newly formed 3rd Composite Air Corps joined the 17th Air Army.

The troops of the Southwestern Front took the offensive on December 16. Because the weather was bad during the first hours of the operation, aircraft could not support the troops, who, having met stubborn resistance, could only advance slowly. But at mid-day the weather improved and our aircraft were able to fly more than 200 sorties in the area of the offensive. Our fliers dropped bombs and made ground attacks on defensive lines and troop concentrations in the regions of Tverdokhlebovka, Radchenskoye, and Boguchar, and airfields at Tatsinskaya and Morozovsk. The advance of our troops accelerated. By the end of the day on December 18 our infantry, together with tank and mechanized columns with the support of air power, broke through the enemy's reinforced defense zone.

At this time Sergeant Nurken Adbirov, flying a ground-attack plane damaged by antiaircraft fire, imitating the gallant deed of Captain Gastello, flew his aircraft into a group of enemy tanks. Adbirov was posthumously titled Hero of the Soviet Union.

During the first five days of the offensive our aircraft flew 2067 sorties in support of the Southwestern Front troops, including 407 at night. This effective support made it possible for our troops to expand their offensive, and by the end of the day on December 21, they had closed all the escape routes for most of the Italian 8th Army. The most active unit in the offensive was the 24th Tank Corps. During these five days some of its units advanced 240 kilometers (150 miles). On December 24, this tank unit suddenly overwhelmed the airfield and railroad line at Tatsinskaya where they damaged 350 enemy aircraft and destroyed five equipment dumps and seven warehouses full of food and other materials. When the motorized troops reached this region, they seized the railroad main line supplying the enemy troop concentration at Tormosino.

The Italian 8th Army and the left wing of Army Group Don were destroyed as a result of the successful operations of the Southwestern Front. Our troops, with the help of air power, advanced 100–150 kilometers (62–93 miles) to the west. From December 16 to 31, 1942, the 2nd and 17th Air Armies flew 4177 sorties, of which more than 80 percent were flown in direct support of ground troops.

The 8th Air Army actively supported our troops' destruction of the enemy Kotelnikovo concentration. During the first days of the offensive, our fliers helped the ground forces to wear down and exhaust the enemy tank concentration in bitter fighting from the Kotelnikovo area to the Myshkova River, and then supported the advance of our troops. When the 2nd Guards and 51st Armies began to advance swiftly toward the south, the 8th Air Army concentrated most of its efforts on attacks against the retreating foe. Part of this unit, along with the 16th Air Army and AFLRO, operated effectively against the encircled concentration and significantly aided our troops to disrupt the enemy plan for breaking out of the inner defensive line that surrounded them.

First Lt. V. S. Yefremov, commander of a squadron of the 10th Guards Short-range Air Regiment, displayed great courage and genuine heroism in difficult and stubborn fighting near Stalingrad. He was born in this city, completed studies there, worked as an electrician, and there he completed a school for military aviators.

His squadron in their SBs constantly bombed enemy aircraft on the ground, and tanks and infantry on the battlefield both in the region of Kotelnikovo and Tormosino. In the Battle of the Volga alone, V. S. Yefremov flew around 100 sorties. On May 1, 1943, V. S. Yefremov was given the title of Hero of the Soviet Union, and on August 24, 1943, he was given a second "Gold Star," for courage and heroism in battle.

In addition to supporting our troops, the AFLRO struck at enemy reserves, railroad lines, and airfields. From November 19 to December 31, 1942, their planes flew 962 sorties, dropping more than 900 tons of bombs and carrying supplies to troops of the fronts. The Comsomol crew commanded by the illustrious flier and Hero of the Soviet Union, Captain A. I. Molodchy, became famous during the Battle of Stalingrad.

The bombs dropped by Molodchy destroyed scores of Hitler's officers and men, blew up supply dumps and gasoline storage areas, set fire to railroad cars and stations, and destroyed temporary and permanent bridges and other military targets. During the Battle of the Volga, he often flew two sorties a night. At the end of 1942, flight statistics were drawn up for his regiment. They were astonishing: Molodchy's crew had flown 190,000 kilometers (118,060 miles) over enemy territory and had dropped more than 200 tons of bombs on various military and industrial targets and on enemy troops. A. I. Molodchy was given a second "Gold Star," on December 21, 1942, for his outstanding services in the struggle with the fascist invaders and the valor and heroism he displayed in that struggle. He was the first man in the AFLRO to be a Hero of the Soviet Union two times. The crew's navigator, S. I. Kulikov, was also given the title of Hero of the Soviet Union.

Air Blockade. After destruction of the Tormosino and Kotelnikovo troop concentrations, the one and only hope the enemy had for maintaining his encircled troops was by air. Enemy aviation had sustained serious losses. There was now a greater distance between the internal and external lines of encirclement. In spite of this, the German command did not hesitate to supply their troops encircled in the Stalingrad region by air.

The battle against enemy aircraft became the major task for our air force. Most of the airfields from which the enemy operated were 250–350 kilometers (157–217 miles) from the area of encirclement; because of this it was impossible for the enemy to fly fighter cover for his bombers and transport aircraft. He resorted to night flights and flew by day only in bad weather. Part of the aircraft, knowing that the front was discontinuous on the south and we had no airfields there, followed a southerly route to the eastern bank of the Volga, turned to the north, and entered the Stalingrad region from the east. Therefore our command ordered the organization of a continuous aerial blockade around the encircled troops. The campaign against enemy planes became especially acute.

Behind the external front of the encirclement, our bombers and ground-attack planes annihilated enemy aircraft on the ground. The air regiments of the 17th and 8th Air Armies and the AFLRO were used for this purpose. A strike made against Salsk on January 9, where some 150 transport aircraft were based, was especially successful. Seven Il-2s, commanded by I. P. Baktin, with fighter escorts, were sent to destroy them. The first attack on the airfield was made without warning from out of the clouds. The ground-attack planes made six runs on the target. With bombs, rockets, machine gun, and cannon fire, they put out of commission more than 70 Ju 52s.

Fighter planes patrolled in each of the five sectors between the external and internal fronts of encirclement along the probable enemy flight routes, and teams were organized on fighter and ground-attack bases that could be summoned by control stations or visual observers. Antiaircraft artillery shot down enemy planes in a band 8 to 10 kilometers (5 to 6 miles) wide directly on the line of encirclement.

Our planes destroyed enemy aircraft in the air and at airfields in the regions of Bolshaya Rossoshka, Karpovka, and Gumrak both by day and by night. At night Po-2s dropped bombs on enemy transport planes that were being unloaded.

This campaign against enemy transport planes was successful. Eighteen aircraft of the 235th Fighter Air Division headed by its commander, Colonel I. D. Podgorny, attacked sixteen transport planes flying with cargoes toward the encircled army. In the initial attack they shot down nine Ju 52s, five of which burst into flames, and the rest of which made emergency landings. Eight enemy fliers were taken prisoner. The remaining seven Ju 52s tried to turn back, but our fighters overtook them and shot down six more planes. Only one German plane succeeded in returning across the front lines. Ground-attack planes destroyed transport planes on the ground and in the air, both behind the external front and in the area of encirclement. Since they had such powerful armament, the fliers in the Il-2s could approach very close to the transport planes and shoot them down with machine-gun fire, cannon fire, or rockets.

On the whole, the aerial blockade of the encircled troop concentration attained its goals. About 1200 enemy planes were shot down or destroyed on the ground, of which 80 percent were transport planes or bombers.* The troops who were surrounded were put on short rations and were kept critically short of supplies and fuel. This all lowered their battle capabilities and their morale. The German attempt to organize an aerial supply service for the large number of surrounded troops was a complete failure. Favorable conditions were created for the destruction of the entire troop concentration.

Units from the AFLRO were effective during the aerial blockade. The navigator, Second Lt. V. V. Senko, showed himself to be a model

---

* German sources admit the loss, not including fighters, of 490: 266 Ju 52s, 165 He 111s, 42 Ju 86s, 9 Fw 200s, 7 He 177s, and 1 Ju 290.[1] ED.

of courage and skill in bad-weather operations at this time. At night with unbroken cloud cover, he faultlessly guided his plane over railroad lines, troop concentrations, and airfields, and made accurate drops on the targets. Navigator Senko gave great help to his comrades in the interpretation and analysis of targets when they were successfully fulfilling their military assignments.

Second Lt. V. V. Senko was given the title of Hero of the Soviet Union on March 25, 1943, for courage and daring in carrying out military assignments. Subsequently, he guided numerous groups of long-range bombers deep into the rear of the enemy where he made precise strikes at railroad lines, bridges, fuel and supply dumps, and other important targets. During the war V. V. Senko flew 430 sorties. The Motherland had great regard for his exploits and he was given a second "Gold Star."

Destroying the Enemy Force. When the Stalingrad Front was reorganized into the Southern Front on December 30, 1942, and went on the offensive toward Rostov, the task of destroying the encircled troop concentration was given to the Don Front and the aerial blockade was carried out by the 16th Air Army. Having disrupted the enemy plans to break the ring around his troops, the Soviet command decided to eliminate the enemy concentration decisively.

The air situation in January 1943 had definitely changed in our favor. The enemy airfields were located deep in the rear and his fighters could not operate in the area of encirclement. The total number of aircraft at the 16th Air Army's disposal was increased to 610. All of its forces were to support the 65th Army alone, which was to make the major attack.

To provide close coordination with the ground forces two secondary control points were organized and four radio stations were set up along the front lines.

When the enemy rejected the Soviet demand for capitulation, the troops on the Don Front went on the offensive at dawn on January 10, 1943, after a great artillery barrage and bombing attack. The 16th Air Army, giving active support to our troops as they broke through the tactical defense zone, flew 676 sorties in twenty-four hours. It attacked troops, staff headquarters, and centers of enemy resistance. The airfields at Bolshaya Rossoshka and Pitomnik were tightly blockaded from the air. The 2nd Bomber Air Corps fliers (commanded by General I. L. Turkel) were very active, making 172 sorties on the first day of the operation.

The encircled enemy fought furiously and often made counterattacks, which were even more firmly resisted by the troops of the front with the aid of air power. By the end of January 12, our troops had occupied the western part of the territory formerly held by the encircled troops. Military operations went well also in the southern sector. Under pressure from our armies the enemy 57th Army began to retreat in disorder toward Stalingrad on the morning of January 15, and within six days was annihilated.

For a second time the Soviet command offered the Germans the opportunity to capitulate. But this offer was also rejected. On January 22, Soviet troops began cutting up and destroying the enemy concentration. By the end of the day on January 24, our troops came up to the southwestern and western edge of the city, and on January 26 they met the 62nd Army troops located in the city itself. The enemy concentration had been cut into two parts and entire units of enemy troops began to surrender. On January 31, the southern group of troops commanded by General-Field Marshal Paulus capitulated, and on February 2, the northern group.

The 16th Air Army and the AFLRO actively supported our troops, striking against the enemy concentrations of men and equipment and destroying his aircraft both on the ground and in the air.

Control of the air, which was acquired when the counterattack began, favorably affected the operations of our troops and our bomber and ground-attack aircraft. In the first half of January, our bombers and ground-attack planes flew in groups of three to nine planes with one or two approaches to the target, but in the second half of January, they made four to six runs on the target, dropping one or two bombs on each run and strafing the enemy with machine-gun and cannon fire. Bombers flew in groups consisting of as many as forty aircraft.

Aviation technicians also displayed daring and courage during battle operations. On January 15 the control mechanism was smashed and fire broke out on a bomber under attack by enemy fighters. First Technical Lt. V. P. Opolev, an air technician, who was seriously wounded, fought the fire singlehanded. With great effort, he extinguished the fire and repaired the damage, which made it possible for the aircraft to complete its mission and to return to its airfield.

The 16th Air Army and the AFLRO flew more than 10,000 sorties from January 1 to February 2. Real support was given to our ground forces.

Results.   One of the largest enemy strategic concentrations was annihilated during the Red Army counterattack on the southern wing of the Soviet-German front. From November 19, 1942, to February 2, 1943, the 2nd, 17th, 16th, and 8th Air Armies and the AFLRO flew 35,929 sorties. Enemy aircraft flew about 18,500 sorties. Soviet planes dropped 141,000 bombs, incendiary containers, and fired 30,000 rockets. Enemy troops suffered considerable losses and the enemy lost 3000 aircraft from November 19 to January 31, 1943.

The 220th and 268th Fighter Divisions, the 228th and 26th Ground-Attack Divisions, the 263rd Bomber Division, the 272nd Night Bomber Division, the 3rd, 17th, and 24th Air Divisions of the AFLRO, and the 102nd Fighter Air Division of ADF were given the designation of guards units for daring, persistence, and effectiveness in the battle with the German invaders. Seventeen fliers in the 8th Air Army were given the title of Hero of the Soviet Union and 3000 fliers were given orders and medals. Honorary designations were granted to 2 air corps, 12 air divisions, and 21 air regiments for their participation in the battle for Stalingrad.

Maneuvering and massing of air power in the areas where ground troops were making their major attacks were better done during the counteroffensive than had been done earlier. The VVS commander, Air Marshal A. A. Novikov, was almost constantly located in the area of military operations to organize coordination between the different aircraft types. As the representative for the air force from the *Stavka,* he participated in working out plans for the counterattack, set the level of air activity, distributed reserves, and concerned himself with maintaining supplies for the air force.

The VVS gained experience in the organization and conduct of operations involving the surrounding and annihilation of a large group of troops.

For the most part, the control of the air armies during the counterattack was centralized. Secondary posts were organized in the major offensive areas. Experience in operating these posts was reflected in the instructions issued by the air force in May 1943. The major method for air control both on the ground and in the air was by radio.

Hundreds of aircraft from the Civil Air Fleet, which fulfilled assignments in transporting cargoes, maintaining communications between staffs and forward units, and evacuating the wounded, took part in operations alongside military aircraft. During the Battle of the Volga, they flew more than 46,000 sorties, carrying 31,000 soldiers and officers and 2587 tons of military cargo, which was highly appreciated. Hundreds of fliers, navigators, engineers, and mechanics were given orders and medals.

The maintenance services gained much experience in the rear. During the operation they learned how to support air operations in winter during a period of rapid offensive ground operations. Aerial transportation was also utilized to transfer air units and to provide them with equipment and supplies.

The victories achieved by the Red Army in the Battle of the Volga caused a fundamental reversal in the situation in the other sectors of the Soviet-German front and created favorable conditions for the mass eviction of the invaders from our land.

VI

BATTLE FOR THE KUBAN BRIDGEHEAD

By the end of March 1943 the southern front, with the exception of the Kuban region, had stabilized. After the German defeat at Stalingrad, Hitler's command hoped to improve its shaky position and planned a new offensive on the Soviet-German front. The realization of this plan was dependent particularly on the German troops on the Taman Peninsula, who were ordered to hold a bridgehead for a new offensive into the Caucasus and to draw off as many Soviet troops as possible from the western area.

With the purpose of disrupting this enemy scheme, the *Stavka* gave the troops of the Northern Caucasus Front the task of annihilating the enemy concentration in the northern Caucasus. At the beginning of April 1943 the situation on the ground was very difficult. Our troops, who were meeting increased resistance, could not break through the enemy defenses based on the advantageous natural features of the area: the deltas of the Kuban, Adagum, and Vtoraya rivers on the

Sea of Azov. The sector of the front along the hill country from the coast of the Black Sea near Novorossiysk to the village of Krymskaya was especially well-defended. Almost all the heights and populated areas had been turned into defense points and centers of resistance. The enemy resisted most stubbornly of all on the approaches to the village of Krymskaya. Resisting at every intermediate point, he often counterattacked with the support of his strong air power.

The German 17th Army had sixteen divisions. The armies of the Northern Caucasus Front had a 1.5 times advantage over the enemy in infantry and tanks, but a somewhat smaller amount of artillery.

The air situation was characterized by heightened activity on both sides and an increase in the intensity of the struggle for control of the air. Realizing that he had a disadvantage in ground troops, the enemy counted on the aid of his air forces to disrupt the Soviet offensive and to destroy our parachute troops at Myskhako.* In the middle of April the enemy concentrated most of the aircraft of the 4th Air Fleet, about 820 aircraft, in the Taman region and the Crimea. In addition, he could also draw on not less than 200 bombers from airfields in the southern Ukraine for operations in the Kuban region.

The Germans had few fighter units, but they included in their number select, battle-hardened units, including JG 3 "Udet," JG 51 "Moelders," and a group of fighter aces. All enemy air units were equipped with Bf 109s or the newer Fw 190s.†

Preparations. The Northern Caucasus Front Air Force at the beginning of April consisted of 250 aircraft of the 4th Air Army (commanded by General N. F. Naumenko), 200 aircraft of the 5th Air Army (commanded by General S. K. Goryunov), 70 air-

---

* A surprise landing behind the German lines in February 1943 lodged Soviet marines on the coast at Mt. Myskhako, south of Novorossiysk. This position threatened enemy control of the Kuban, so German forces tried unsuccessfully for seven months to dislodge the Soviet troops, whose political officer was the now well-known Leonid Brezhnev.[2] ED.

† On March 10, 1943, Luftwaffe forces in action against the USSR included 15 fighter or fighter-bomber groups, 1 twin-engined fighter group, 15 bomber and 8 dive-bomber groups, and 27 short-range and 18 long-range recon squadrons. Of these, 24 combat groups and 17 recon squadrons were in the south with the 4th Air Fleet.[3]

craft from the Black Sea Fleet, and 60 aircraft from the AFLRO.
The Front air forces had a total of about 600 aircraft. By April
20, the *Stavka* had recruited for the 4th Air Army: the 2nd Bomber
Air Corps (commanded by General V. A. Ushakov), and the 3rd
Fighter Air Corps (commanded by General Ye. Ya. Savitsky); and the
5th Air Army: for the 2nd Composite Air Corps (commanded by
General N. T. Yereminko) and the 282nd Fighter Air Division (com-
manded by Colonel S. P. Danilov), all from out of the reserves.

The AFLRO group was also strengthened under the command of
the deputy commanding general, General N. S. Skripko. The 62nd
Division arrived in April to join the 50th Bomber Air Division,
which was active in this area. In May, both became part of the
newly formed 6th Air Corps (commanded by General G. N.
Tupikov).

By April 20, the Northern Caucasus Front Air Force together
with the group from the Black Sea Fleet, the AFLRO aircraft, and
the additional planes from the Supreme Command reserves had about
900 military aircraft, of which 800 were attached to the front:
370 fighters, 170 ground-attack aircraft, 165 day bombers, and 195
night bombers. This removed the disadvantage which we had had in
air power.

However, because active military operations began when the enemy
attacked the Myskhako region‡ on April 17, the first three days,
until April 20, saw a difficult situation for us in the air. Because
there was such a large concentration of aircraft from both sides in
such a small area, there were intense and stubborn air battles.

An air force staff for the Northern Caucasus Front was created at
the beginning of April to insure dependable and centralized control
over the aircraft of the two air armies. General K. A. Vershinin was
appointed as the Front air force commander. Air Marshal A. A.
Novikov, the *Stavka* representative and the VVS commander, controlled and coordinated the air forces of the Northern Caucasus,
Southern, and Southwestern Fronts.

The battle capability of the Front air force was high. There were
many well-trained units in the air armies, and aircraft quality was
noticeably higher than it had been previously. New types of planes
made up 65 percent of the bomber forces, while during the previous

‡ South of Novorossiysk. ED.

winter offensive in the northern Caucasus they made up not more than 25–30 percent of the units. Interceptor units had almost entirely new aircraft, the Yak-1, Yak-7B, and La-5. There was also a small number (11 percent) of American and English planes in the air armies: A-20 bombers, and the "Airacobra" and "Spitfire" fighters.

As far as air bases were concerned, there were different situations on the two sides. The spring thaw in the northern Caucasus, which had rendered unusable most of the field air bases, limited the activity of our aircraft, but the hard-surfaced airfields in the Crimea and the southern Ukraine could be used intensively by the enemy. Our bases were congested because of the thaw, and also because it was difficult to build airfields along the Black Sea coast. The dirt roads leading to the airfields were impassable in the spring.

It is apparent that both sides had advantages in the aircraft types available. We had an advantage in fighter forces. But the enemy had a significant advantage in bombers, better bases, and maneuverability for his air power.

Preparations for the operation began in the middle of March 1943. The commander of the Northern Caucasus Front decided to deal his major blow toward Krymskaya and Anapa in order to divide and then destroy in separate parts the enemy concentration, so he could seize the Taman Peninsula. The major assignment for breaking the enemy's defense line was given to the 56th Army. The 37th Army troops were to attack and destroy the enemy troops in the regions of Kievskaya and Varenikovskaya. Subsequently both armies were to extend their offensive toward the Kerch Strait.

The Front air force was given the following task: gain control of the air, protect ground troops, cooperate with them in the 56th Army offensive, defend our parachute troops southwest of Novorossiysk, and carry out aerial reconnaissance.

The air force staff worked out a plan for an aerial offensive. The efforts of aviation were to be concentrated near Krymskaya and Novorossiysk. It was also planned to concentrate all aircraft to support the 56th Army, if the enemy remained quiescent near Myskhako.

Great attention was devoted to organizing coordinated activities between different types of aircraft and different units. It was planned that the 4th Air Army commander was to be given several fighter air regiments from the 5th Army for his disposal. Coordination between the air force of the front and the Black Sea Fleet was planned by assigning certain regions and operational periods to each, and also by assigning several fighter units of the 5th Air Army to the Fleet Air Force commander.

In order to control all aircraft, a secondary command point, in addition to the front command point, was set up near Abinskaya village, and the secondary command points of the 4th and 5th Air Armies were moved up closer to the front lines. Air representatives were assigned to the infantry divisions.

Five radio stations were set up near the front lines, three of them in the offensive zone of the 56th Army, for guiding fighter planes and directing them during air battles. (These were control radio stations of the 4th Air Army.) One of these, the main radio station, was located 4 kilometers (2½ miles) from the front lines, and was in fact the command point for controlling all of the fighter planes of the 4th Air Army.

Among the preparations for the campaign, division conferences were held in April, in which the flying personnel studied preceding operations, and where the best fliers shared their experiences with the younger fliers. "This was not done without fiery quarrels," K. A. Vershinin, Chief Marshal for Aviation, recalls. "Sometimes one or another tactical method was tested in the air, but finally a single idea was worked out. We accepted many useful recommendations which were later codified and were accepted in all air organizations."

In this period great publicity was given to the exploits of out-standing masters of air combat: A. I. Pokryshkin, the brothers D. B. Glinka and B. B. Glinka, V. I. Fadeyer, V. G. Semenishin, G. A. Rechkalov, and others. Squadron Commander Captain A. I. Pokryshkin was rightly considered the leader in the invention of the most progressive air combat techniques. By the time of the air battles over the northern Caucasus he was already an experienced, mature commander and a remarkable fighter pilot, who had completed more than 350 sorties and shot down nearly twenty enemy aircraft, beginning on the second day of the war when he shot down his first Fascist near Jassy. In the sky over the Caucasus, Pokryshkin demonstrated by his personal example all the advantages of an echeloned formation at different altitudes, both within a group of fighters as well as between groups of fighters.

The 16th Guards Fighter Air Regiment (commanded by Hero of

the Soviet Union Lt. Col. N. V. Isayev, in which the future Hero of the Soviet Union Pokryshkin was a novice, was rightly considered one of the finest air regiments.*

The 4th Air Army command and staff gave great service in the analysis and propagation of combat techniques among their personnel. During March and April all the air units were given detailed instructions about the most effective tactical procedures and battle formations for fighter planes: improving the coordination of pairs of planes, retaining the advantages of altitude in combat, utilizing driving attacks in air combat, and the necessity of constantly seeking out enemy planes in the air and initiating combat.

Much attention was given to teaching combat techniques to the air corps which had come from the *Stavka*. Mock aerial battles were arranged and the young fighter pilots were introduced to the Glinka brothers, who had shot down more than thirty enemy planes by this time. A group of experienced fliers from the 216th Fighter Air Division instructed 3rd Fighter Air Corps flying personnel about fighter warfare characteristics over the northern Caucasus and flew several sorties with them as a lead group. The commanders of air divisions and regiments were taken on visits to the central control radio station where they could follow the course of air battles in which their subordinates were involved and therefore observe the positive and negative aspects of their actions.

An important part of the party-political work at the time consisted of short meetings, or as they were called then, military shoptalks. From time to time among the air regiments, lectures were given on "a good weapon in good repair guarantees the success of aerial combat," and "every effort to defeat the enemy." Informational lectures were given in fighter squadrons on "heroes of today's battles," and military bulletins were distributed once or twice a day to aircraft on airfields, to command posts, and to living quarters, in which exploits of fliers and ground crews were described. The army and divisional press also devoted much space to exceptional accomplishments. All of this improved flight techniques and mobilized personnel to fulfill the tasks of the air army.

German Attack on Myskhako. The base our troops occupied near Novorossiysk at Myskhako was an irritation to the enemy and many

---

* This unit flew lend-lease P-39s in 1943–44. ED.

of his troops were diverted there. Therefore the German command, in the middle of April, decided to liquidate it and created Army Group Wetzel, which included more than three infantry divisions with tank and air support for this purpose.

On April 17, after a heavy artillery barrage and preliminary bombing, the enemy went on the offensive supported by 450 bombers and 200 fighter planes. We had on our side up to 500 aircraft, including about 100 bombers in the Myskhako region. Moreover, most of our airfields were to the west and northeast of Krasnodar at a distance of 150–200 kilometers (93–124 miles) from Myskhako and the approach route for the 4th Air Army's planes passed over extensions of the central massif of the Caucasus mountains, which at that time were often veiled in clouds. The major enemy airfields were located on level land on the Taman Peninsula 50–100 kilometers (31–62 miles) from Myskhako. Utilizing these favorable conditions, enemy aircraft in groups of 30 to 40 began to bomb our troops on our bridgehead. The Soviet troops besieged in this area were in a difficult position. There were intense air battles with varying success on our side from April 17 to April 19.† Soviet fliers caused considerable losses to enemy aircraft, lowering the effectiveness of their attacks, but could not stop the enemy strikes because of inadequate forces. The troops courageously held their lines with the help of our air power. The Germans succeeded, only at the price of great losses, in penetrating our defensive lines for the distance of 1 kilometer (.62 mile).

Aerial warfare near Myskhako reached its peak on April 20. Having recruited his reserves, the enemy prepared for a "general" attack in order to split our beachhead into two separate parts and then to wipe out all our troops. On our side, the air corps of the Supreme Command reserve moved into action this day, which made it possible to carry out two massed strikes against enemy infantry and artillery directly in front of the lines of our troops.

Our air operations on that day were very successful and in fact decided in advance the collapse of the enemy offensive. Evaluating the success of the air operation, General K. N. Leselidze, 18th Army commander, wrote: "Massed raids made by our aircraft against the enemy trying to annihilate our troops in the Myskhako region dis-

† On these three days, 494, 511, and then 294 Ju 87 dive-bomber sorties were flown by the Luftwaffe.[4] ED.

rupted his battle plans. The men on the bridgehead were greatly encouraged."

As three air corps of the Supreme Command reserves continued their entry into air operations, our aircraft were able to increase the power of their strikes against the enemy, which made it possible to shift the balance of air power in the Myskhako region in our favor. A crucial period had been reached in the aerial situation. German aircraft were noticeably less active. During the period of April 21–22 the number of German flights was cut in half. Our aircraft continued yet more actively to bomb and strafe enemy troops along the front lines of the 18th Army near Novorossiysk and Fedotovka.

Soviet fliers showed themselves to be exemplary fliers as they carried out their military assignments. On April 21 an Il-2 from the 805th Ground-Attack Regiment, flown by Second Lt. N. V. Rykhlin, along with his machine-gunner Sergeant I. S. Yefremov, was attacked by four enemy fighter planes near their target area. In this unequal battle the ground-attack plane shot down two enemy fighters. Although he was seriously wounded, Rykhlin, the pilot, successfully brought his plane back and landed his damaged plane at its base. For daring and bravery in battle, Second Lt. Rykhlin was promoted to first lieutenant and Sergeant Yefremov to second lieutenant.

Meeting increased resistance from Soviet aircraft, the German troops were compelled to cease their offensive and take a defensive position, and their fighter aircraft went over to defensive operations. During eight days of bitter fighting, the enemy lost 182 aircraft and our forces half of that. The commander of the Northern Caucasus Front, evaluating our air operations in the Myskhako region, noted in his report that ". . . as the result of the constant air battles from April 20 to 22 enemy aircraft, having suffered great losses, were compelled to abandon the battlefield. Control of the air passed to our hands."

The attacks made by our bombers against enemy airfields in the second half of April were very important in lowering the level of enemy air activity. During one night an average of thirty to forty bombers would attack one airfield, knocking out of action five to ten aircraft. The AFLRO was especially successful in its attacks on the large airfields at Sarabuz and Saki in the Crimea where more than 100 German bombers were destroyed or damaged.

Aerial photos and subsequently the testimony of captured enemy fliers confirmed the fact that from April 17 to 29 about 260 enemy aircraft were destroyed or damaged on the ground. The enemy was forced to withdraw his aircraft from those airfields that were subjected to the most intensive bombardment.

Krymskaya Offensive. After the enemy plans for the Myskhako region had been disrupted, our aircraft renewed their preparation for battles near the village of Krymskaya. Marshaling their forces, our fighter planes protected the 56th Army, and at night our bombers struck against enemy airfields. Organizational changes were also made at this time: the administrative structure of the 5th Air Army was transferred to the Kursk salient of the Steppe Front, leaving its air groups to the 4th Air Army.

After three days of calm, once more great air battles broke out in the skies over the Kuban. Beginning on April 28, German bombers in groups of 10 to 15 planes, or even more, dropped bombs on our troops, who on the following day were to take the offensive near Krymskaya. During that day 850 flyovers were made by enemy planes. Our fighters flew 310 sorties to combat enemy attacks, destroying 25 enemy aircraft. Beginning on that day aerial battles began over the village of Krymskaya, which except for brief intervals were to continue for many days.

The Northern Caucasus Front Air Force with the addition of forces from the Supreme Command reserves (in accordance with the air offensive plan, confirmed by the *Stavka* representatives, Marshal G. K. Zhukov and Air Marshal A. A. Novikov) began initial air operations April 28 in the area of the 56th Army's future offensive. Twenty bombers appeared in the twilight skies over the enemy positions near Krymskaya. They ignited several fires with incendiary bombs to serve as beacons to facilitate the approaches to the target for later planes. When it became dark, bombers of the 4th Air Army and the AFLRO began to attack the enemy artillery positions.

Women Combat Pilots. For two hours the enemy antiaircraft artillery attempted to fight off our bombers, but it was silenced and ceased firing. Our aircraft suffered no losses. During that night they flew 379 sorties and dropped 210 tons of bombs. The saturation of bombs averaged almost 21 tons per square kilometer. From aerial observation and photos, 160 fires were noted and 25 large explosions. The daring women pilots of the 46th Guards Night Bomber Regiment (commanded by Major Yevdokia D. Bershanskaya) were especially active.‡ Its crews in Po-2s made effective strikes against artillery positions on the northern edge of Krymskaya.

The enemy, taking advantage of the natural defense points of the region, withstood the offensive of our troops. In spite of the softening up from bombing attacks and the support from our not inconsiderable air forces, as well as a powerful artillery barrage, the 56th Army troops had penetrated the enemy defenses only 1 or 2 kilometers (.62 or 1.24 miles) at isolated points by the end of the day. On April 29 we flew 1308 sorties, shot down 74 enemy aircraft in aerial battles and 7 by antiaircraft fire. Enemy flights were cut in half, which testifies to the fact that the initiative in the air had definitely passed into our hands on the first day of the operation.

In the following days air battles became even more intense. Some of them lasted for hours. On a relatively narrow segment of the front (25 to 30 kilometers, or 15½ to 18½ miles) as many as forty aerial battles took place on one day, with each side sending fifty to eighty aircraft into action.

‡ Soviet women pilots were organized in three combat regiments in October 1941 by Marina Roskova, an aviatrice famous for her 1938 long-distance flight. Originally, they composed the 122nd Composite Air Division made up of the 586th Fighter Air Regiment, the 587th Bomber Air Regiment, and the 588th Night Bomber Regiment.

The fighter regiment went into action during the Stalingrad battle. Commanded by Tamara Kazarinova, it flew the Yak-7B in first battles, totaled 4419 operational sorties, and was credited with 38 victories. Squadron Commander Olga Yamshchikova flew 93 sorties, scored three confirmed victories, and after the war became the first Soviet woman to fly jet aircraft when she became a test pilot.

The bomber regiments were honored by being redesignated guards units, the 588th becoming the 46th Guards Night Bomber Regiment, which had first arrived on the Southern Front in May 1942, commanded by Yevdokia Bershanskaya. Fighting from the Kuban to Berlin, this all-women's regiment flew 24,000 combat missions and dropped 23,000 tons of bombs from the then battle-weary Po-2 (originally U-2) biplanes. Twenty-three of its fliers and navigators became Heroes of the Soviet Union for their dangerous work, including flights on the night of July 31, 1943, when four of their two-seaters were shot down over the Blue Line (fortifications in the Novorossiysk-Varenikovskaya-Krymskaya sector. ED.) by a German fighter.

Other Russian women flew with men's units, including Lt. Ekaterina Budanova, credited with eleven victories, and Lt. Lydia Litvak, who scored twelve official victories in her year with the 73rd Fighter Air Regiment before her Yak was lost on August 1, 1943.[5] ED.

Our aircraft gave effective support to the ground troops, concentrating their efforts on the narrow segment adjacent to the breakthrough on the front. On May 3, eighteen groups of Pe-2 bombers from the 2nd Bomber Air Corps, following one another at intervals of ten to twenty minutes, smashed the artillery positions on the western edge of Verkhni Adagum and Neberdzhayevskaya, guaranteeing the advance of our infantry and tanks which had broken through the enemy defenses south of Krymskaya. At the same time ground-attack planes of the 2nd Composite Air Corps prepared the way for the successful entry of a tank group into the gap in the enemy lines.

Air operations during this offensive were carried out in close cooperation with ground troops. During a four-day period, when the breakthrough was being made through the enemy's first defense zone, the bombers and ground-attack planes alone flew 2243 sorties. On May 3 and the morning of May 4, the 56th Army liberated the village of Krymskaya and in the next few days advanced 10 kilometers, (6 miles) into the enemy defense lines in bitter fighting.

Our aircraft, after they had given support to our ground troops in the penetration of the enemy's strongly defended defense zone, and maintaining control of the air, began on May 4 to divert their efforts to the destruction of enemy targets in the rear, striking day and night at rear installations and communications near Kievskaya, Moldavskaya, Nizhnyaya Bokanskaya, and southwest of Neberdzhayevskaya, while simultaneously part of our forces continued to attack enemy troops on the battlefield.

Our aerial tactics during the breakthrough near Krymskaya were clearly offensive in nature. Coordination was successfully organized between different types of aircraft. First three or four pairs of fighters would appear over the battlefield in order to elucidate the air situation and to transmit information about it to the central control radio station. Then, ten or fifteen minutes later, larger groups of bombers and ground-attack planes with fighter escorts would appear over the target. If they met no serious opposition from antiaircraft fire they would make several passes at the target. Such coordination almost precluded losses from enemy fighters, even when there were many in the operational area.

Enemy bombers attempting to strike at our troops met active resistance from our interceptors and had to drop their bombs from altitudes of not less than 3000–5000 meters (9840–16,400 feet), with only one approach to the target, and in most cases without employing bombsights.

In spite of the fact that ground operations did not have the expected results, the war in the air increased in intensity and scope. On the whole the aerial situation on most of the front developed to our advantage. Once our aircraft had an advantage in air power they not only continued to fight actively against German aircraft, but also continued to attack ground troops, tanks, and artillery.

Our fighter planes showed great skill in the struggle with German aircraft. Their success was aided by efficiently organized radio communications with ground stations. On April 29, the 216th Fighter Air Division commander, General A. V. Borman, who was located at a command post near the front lines, received the news that twelve German fighters were approaching. At that moment a squadron of fighters commanded by A. I. Pokryshkin was directly over the battlefield. They received information from the radio station; fulfilling the command post instructions, our fliers took an advantageous position and attacked the enemy in unison. In a brief skirmish they destroyed eight German fighters. Then eight bombers following the interceptors were also destroyed, with the help of instructions from the radio station, by fighter planes commanded by Captain D. B. Glinka.

Beginning with the first day of the operation and also in its most crucial days, our aircraft flew twice as many sorties as the enemy. From April 29 to May 10 the 4th Air Army, the Black Sea Fleet air units, and the AFLRO flew 12,000 sorties, of which 50 percent were against enemy troops and equipment on the battlefield. During this period our fliers fought 285 air battles and shot down 368 enemy aircraft, i.e., more than one-third of his original air group.

Flying in great numbers, our aircraft effectively supported troops as they penetrated strongly-defended enemy lines across natural barriers. After Krymskaya had been liberated, many German soldiers killed or wounded by our air attacks were found, as well as smashed equipment.

However, for a number of reasons unconnected with air operations, the troops of the 56th Army could not expand their breakthrough and penetrate to the enemy's operational rear. One of these reasons was the slowness of the units in the first wave of the offensive and the tardy entry of the second wave into combat. The troops who had broken through the enemy's first defense zone and overwhelmed the enemy's center of resistance at Krymskaya advanced only 10 kilometers (6 miles). When they met enemy resistance at the basic defense position of the Blue Line, they could go no farther.

When the battle was over around Krymskaya, some changes were made in the organizational structure of the Front air force. Because there was only one air army in the air force of the Front, there was no need for a separate air force staff. It was abolished and General K. A. Vershinin, commander of the Front air force, became the commander of the 4th Air Army. General N. F. Naumenko, who had formerly commanded this air army, was given another post.

The May Offensive Fails. Now that the village of Krymskaya was liberated, our air forces prepared for another offensive operation.

During the preparatory period for this new operation our bombers systematically attacked enemy airfields on the Taman Peninsula and in the Crimea. From May 11 to 26, the AFLRO flew 152 sorties against enemy airfields in the Crimea. The ships and aircraft of the Black Sea Fleet made many attacks on the airfield at Anapa. All of this had the effect of weakening enemy air power.

In this new offensive operation the troops of the Front had the task of penetrating the defense line, the Blue Line, defeating the enemy concentration and liberating the Taman Peninsula. It was understood that the major blow was to be delivered by the 37th Army to the north of Krymskaya. The 56th Army was to protect the left flank on the south.

Enemy air power in the Kuban area had been weakened in the preceding battles, but taking into account the reinforcements it had received, the Germans had 700 aircraft on May 25. The 4th Air Army had 924 aircraft.

On the morning of May 26, the troops of the Front went on the offensive after a forty-minute air attack. A few minutes before the attack, ground-attack planes laid down a smoke screen in the sector of the front to be attacked. This air attack was made as a mass strike in which 338 aircraft participated, including 84 bombers, 104 ground-attack planes, and 150 fighters. The attack was well organized and there were no losses.

As the result of an effective artillery and aerial preparation, our troops were able to advance in the attack area 3 to 5 kilometers (1.8 to 3.1 miles) into the enemy's rear, capturing their first and second positions. They created the groundwork for a swift capture of the enemy's major defense zone and the expansion of the offensive.

The German command decided to concentrate all its aircraft over the battlefield to stop the advance of our troops. At the end of the day the enemy made a twenty-minute attack involving 600 aircraft.

The enemy called on his bombers stationed in the southern Ukraine. Therefore he was able to concentrate 1400 aircraft in operations against the troops of the Northern Caucasus Front. Now that the enemy had a 50-percent advantage in air power over us, he temporarily seized the initiative in the air, although he had suffered great losses. Some days he flew 1500–1700 sorties, which was twice as high as the number of sorties flown by the 4th Air Army.

Our interceptors fought heroically against enemy aircraft. They prevented his bombers from making accurate bombing raids and prevented many groups of aircraft from reaching our troops. But they could not completely disrupt enemy air operations. We did not have enough fighter planes nor antiaircraft guns for this task.

The situation on the ground and in the air was a difficult one for us. The offensive operation and movement of our troops on the battlefield was much hampered by constant enemy air attacks during the daylight hours. Therefore the troops' commanders decided to limit offensive operations to the periods immediately before darkness and at dawn.

The first day of the operations also revealed some inadequacies in our fighter operations against massed flights of enemy aircraft. It was not unusual for our fighters to engage enemy fighters in aerial combat and thereby allow bombers to penetrate to our rear. Bombers were often intercepted not before they approached their targets, but directly over them, and sometimes even after they had dropped their bombs.

Great skill was required to eliminate these deficiencies and to discover a means for altering the situation to our favor. Appropriate measures were taken. Interceptors were sent to attack bombers before they approached the front lines. The number of fighter planes assigned as escorts for other types of aircraft was radically reduced. The technique of employing fighter patrols where bombers and ground-attack planes were active was used more extensively. This made it possible to increase the number of fighters over the battlefield and thus, with the same aircraft, more reliably protect our strike forces on the ground and repel mass enemy air attacks. It also became possible to designate fighter "hunters" for intercepting and destroying enemy bombers on the approaches to the front lines. In order to avoid losses when the number of fighter escorts was reduced, our bombers began to operate in groups of not less than fifty to sixty aircraft.

The crews of ground-attack aircraft and bombers were given more responsibility for their own defense. It was recommended that ground-attack aircraft retain as much as 15 percent of their ammunition in case they were attacked by enemy fighters. In order to increase the defensibility of groups of bombers and ground-attack planes, a more effective fire pattern and an echeloned battle formation at different altitudes were worked out, making it possible for more than one aircraft to respond to enemy fighter attacks.

The results of these measures were immediately noticeable. On June 2, nine Pe-2s of the 125th Guards Bomber Air Regiment, flown by women pilots led by squadron commander Captain Ye. D. Timofeyeva, were attacked by eight enemy fighters near Kievskaya, just as they began to drop their bombs. At that point, the six fighters flying escort for them were separated from them by clouds. In this difficult situation the women of the crews showed great courage and self-possession. Maintaining their battle formation they met the fighter attack with concentrated machine-gun fire, at the same time making appropriate flight maneuvers. During the battle they shot down four enemy fighters and returned to their base without losses.

In order to reduce the level of enemy air activity, the number of night attacks against enemy airfields was increased. From May 25 to June 7, 845 sorties were flown against enemy airfields, which was almost 50 percent of all the sorties flown for this purpose during the Kuban campaign.

These measures enabled our aircraft to regain the initiative in the air in a relatively short period of time. By the first of June there was a decline in the level of enemy air activity. Once more Soviet fighters became the masters of the sky over the northern Caucasus. Ground-attack planes and bombers again flew in large groups to fulfill their assignments with only negligible resistance from enemy interceptors.

During the operation, the 4th Air Army fliers flew 10,250 sorties and in 364 air battles shot down 315 enemy aircraft. Our losses were less than one-half of those of the enemy. When the enemy had lost a significant number of aircraft in the culminating stage of the air battle over the Kuban and met with increased resistance he ceased his mass air raids against our troops.

But the offensive operation of the 37th and 56th Armies was not successful, and one of the reasons was the temporary loss of the control of the air by our aircraft. In addition the reasons for the unsuccessful operation were as follows: the stubborn resistance of the enemy at advantageous and well-prepared positions on the Blue Line, inadequacies in the military training of our ground troops and in ground reconnaissance, and the lack of a second echelon in the armies' strike groups.

Results. Summarizing the results of the air operations over the northern Caucasus, the Military Council of the Northern Caucasus Front noted in their dispatch dated June 21, 1943: "There is no doubt that we achieved a victory as the result of the air battles. The enemy did not achieve his goal. Our aircraft not only successfully repelled the enemy, but also compelled the Germans to abandon combat and to withdraw his aircraft."

The Kuban air battles in which Soviet aircraft significantly broke the enemy's power in the air played a positive role in the over-all battle for control of the air over the Soviet-German front. From April 17 to June 7, Soviet aircraft made around 35,000 flights, of which 77 percent were made by aircraft from the Front, 9 percent by aircraft from the AFLRO, and 14 percent by the planes of the Black Sea Fleet. The enemy lost 1100 aircraft, including 900 lost in aerial combat.

The Kuban air operations had a positive influence on the further development of the operational skill of the air force and the tactical use of different kinds of aircraft. There was development and improvement in tactics for all kinds of aircraft, but especially for interceptors. The basic maneuver in aerial combat became the vertical attack. The arrival of new high-speed fighter planes at the front and the widespread use of new battle formations both at the front and the rear, the basic unit of which was a pair of fighters, contributed to this development.

Ground-attack aircraft were employed in close cooperation with ground forces. Strikes were made by groups of fifty to sixty aircraft. This made it possible to crush enemy defenses and major troop concentrations. New in the tactical use of bombers was the transition to concentrated raids made by large numbers of aircraft, including the full complement of an air corps.

Air operations over the Kuban showed that the battle for control of the air could be successful only when it was not limited to one front, but was rather carried out by several air armies encompassing broad territory, so that the enemy was deprived of the opportunity of maneuvering his air power freely.

Effective air operations often depended on the control of aircraft in the air by ground radio stations erected close to the command observation posts of the commanders of general armies.

There were deficiencies also in the Kuban air operations. For example, the commands and staffs of several air groups and units had not been adequately trained in the control of fighter air units involved in the repelling of mass enemy attacks. In the initial period of the air battles, most of our fighters were often diverted to the destruction of enemy fighters in the air, and not enemy bombers. In favor of commanding officers and fliers, it must be noted that they quickly noted these inadequacies and corrected them in future operations.

Summarizing the results of air operations in the Kuban, the commander of the air force said in his directive dated July 7, 1943, that the VVS had become significantly larger and stronger in the period just past. The air force units had begun to operate more skillfully and effectively with the utilization of their basic forces on the solution of the most important problems as dictated by the situation. In the bitter air warfare over the Kuban our aircraft caused serious losses among enemy aircraft and seized control of the air.

The air battles over the Kuban, because of their great extent, numbers involved, and the results achieved, were important far beyond the immediate boundaries of the operation on the Northern Caucasus Front. They provided a school for the Soviet Air Force to perfect its skills.*

* Although the Kuban offensives had failed to eliminate the German bridgehead that summer, in September 1943 the German 17th Army evacuated the area, which after the failure of the German Kursk offensive had become too difficult to maintain. ED.

VII

THE BATTLE FOR KURSK

The victories won by Soviet forces in the Battle of the Volga and the subsequent winter 1943 offensive significantly altered the situation on the Soviet-German front. The Red Army had firmly seized the initiative.

Germans Concentrate for Their Last Offensive. Trying to weaken the political consequences of their major defeats, the German command in spring 1943 prepared a new offensive, calculating to regain the strategic initiative once more and to alter the course of the war in their favor. The central section of the front was selected as the offensive area. Hitler's command calculated on utilizing a favorable configuration of the front line to make two converging strikes, from south of Orel and north of Kharkov, toward Kursk with the goal of trapping the Soviet troops in the Kursk salient. The planned offensive was given the code name "Citadel."

The enemy concentrated on his base of operations 900,000 men, about 10,000 guns and mortars, and 2700 tanks and self-propelled guns.[6] The German command had great hopes for mass utilization of their newest weapons with excellent armor.

As he prepared for the offensive, the enemy sought to create a favorable situation in the air. He shifted his best air squadrons from other sections of the front and other theaters of the war to airfields near Orel, Belgorod, and Kharkov. To strengthen the 4th and 6th Air Fleets operating in the region of the Kursk salient, thirteen air groups were brought from Germany, France, and Norway in the period from March 15 to July 1. German air units near Kursk included seventeen *Geschwader* with 1850 aircraft. In addition it was planned to bring more than 200 bombers from airfields deep in the rear. The Luftwaffe then had 2050 aircraft in this area (1200 bombers, 600 fighters, 100 ground-attack bombers, and 150 reconnaissance aircraft), which was almost 70 percent of the entire Luftwaffe operating at the time on the Soviet-German front.*

The Soviet High Command, which in good time became aware of the enemy's plans, decided to wear down and weaken the enemy as he advanced by means of a stubborn and active defense, and then go over to the offensive and to crush his strike groups. Troops of the Central and Voronezh Fronts occupied the defensive positions on each side of the Kursk salient.

The 16th Air Army from the Central Front, the 2nd Air Army below them on the Voronezh Front, the 17th Air Army on the neighboring Southwestern Front, and major forces from the AFLRO participated in the support and protection of the defensive troops. When the defense operation began, the air armies were significantly strengthened by air groups from the Stavka reserves. Soviet air power, amounting to 2900 aircraft, had more than twice as many fighters as the enemy, but the enemy had 2.4 times the day bombers that we had. This advantage, however, was more than compensated for by our ground-attack bombers and night bombers. The proportion between the two air forces, including the AFLRO, was 1.5 to 1 in our favor.

---

* At this time, June 1943, the Luftwaffe had about half of its first-line strength facing the Soviet Union. Of these 2980 aircraft, the 2050 concentrated against the Kursk salient reduced Air Fleet 1 in the north to one group each of bombers, fighter-bombers and light night-bombers, while in the Arctic, Air Fleet 5 could still draw upon KG 30, JG 5, and I St.G 5. The Black Sea areas in the south were guarded by Rumanian air units, along with the small German I Air Corps.[7]

Against the Kursk salient, the Germans could strike from Belgorod and Kharkov with Air Fleet 4, consisting of: JG 3 and JG 52 with six BF 109G fighter groups; KG 3, KG 27, and KG 55 with two Ju 88A and six He 111H bomber groups; St.G 2 and St.G 77 with six Ju 87D dive-bomber groups; SG 1 with two Hs 123A and Fw 190F fighter-bomber groups; four Hs 129B and one Ju 87G antitank squadrons; one light night bomber group with old biplanes; ten Bf 109 and Fw 189 recon squadrons; the Hungarian Air Division with one group each of Bf 109s and Ju 87s, and two Ju 88 and one Fw 189 squadrons.

Threatening Kursk from Orel in the north was Air Fleet 6, including: JG 51 and JG 54 with six Fw 190A fighter groups; I/ZG 1, a Bf 110F twin-engined night-fighter group; an unidentified twin-engined night-fighter group; KG 4, KG 51, and KG 53 with three Ju 88A and four He 111H bomber groups; St.G 1 with three Ju 87D dive-bomber groups; one squadron each of Hs 129B, Ju 87G, and Bf 110G antitank aircraft; several recon squadrons. ED.

The defense operation at Kursk was preceded by a three-month quiescent period utilized by both sides to prepare for the coming operation. The air army and air groups worked out battle plans that clarified questions of coordination. Training was vigorous in the air regiments. During the course of these training flights, pilots were given additional experience and there was an improvement in group flying techniques; bomb-dropping accuracy and aerial gunnery techniques were also improved.

Units in the rear worked very hard. During a three-month period, the engineering battalions of the 16th and 2nd Air Armies built or renovated 154 airfields with the help of the local population. A reserve of five or six airfield service battalions was created among the air armies to insure flexibility. Much attention was given to improving the camouflage on airfields. In addition to camouflaging actual airfields, fifty false airfields were built by both the armies and a number of these fields were attacked by the enemy. Enough supplies were stockpiled for ten to fifteen days of combat operations.

Several days before the Battle for Kursk began, transport aircraft and ground-attack regiments brought up antitank bombs, invented by our scientists and produced by our industry in a short period. The break in military operations was also utilized for renovating and repairing military equipment. The percentage of aircraft out of commission decreased from 12 percent to 5 percent between May 1 and July 1.

Preliminary Air Battles. Our aircraft did not abandon their operations while preparing for the coming battles. They struck at enemy reserves, fought for control of the air, protected our troops, and carried out aerial reconnaissance.

The Soviet command struggled to weaken the Luftwaffe, so far as it was possible on the central part of the front, and to create favorable conditions for the control of the air. With this in mind, in accordance with the *Stavka* plan two air operations were carried out to destroy enemy aircraft on their airfields.

The first of these lasted from May 6 to May 8, 1943. Six air armies participated in it, from north to south; the 1st, 15th, 16th, 2nd, 17th, and 8th. The first raid against seventeen German airfields was made May 6, simultaneously on a front stretching 1200 kilometers (745 miles), by 112 bombers, 156 ground-attack planes, and 166 fighters. Some of the airfields where German interceptors were based were blockaded from the air. Caught unawares, the enemy could not render any organized resistance, and lost 194 aircraft on the ground and 21 in air battles. Our losses amounted to 21 aircraft. The effectiveness of this operation was insured to a significant degree by aerial reconnaissance, which had discovered the location and composition of enemy air units.

More attacks were made against these airfields in the daytime on May 6 and the morning of May 7. In order to overcome the increasing resistance of the enemy's air defense, large groups of bombers and ground-attack planes were employed with an escort consisting of large numbers of fighters. Special groups of aircraft were assigned the task of eliminating antiaircraft guns. These measures gave excellent results. Making 777 sorties, our fliers on the second and third raids damaged or destroyed 285 aircraft, including 53 shot down in the air. The high effectiveness of our air operations was confirmed by aerial photos, the testimony of captured German soldiers, and reports from partisans.

On May 8 Hitler's command moved many of its air units to the rear. Aircraft were dispersed and carefully camouflaged. A considerable number of fighters were given the task of attacking Soviet aircraft. In order more effectively to identify our aircraft and to warn their air units of impending danger, not only were radar stations set up, but also small fighter units were organized which patrolled along the front lines.

That day our fliers flew 181 sorties. They destroyed only six German aircraft, and lost eight. During the three days of the operation 506 enemy aircraft were destroyed or put out of commission, while our losses amounted to 122 aircraft. The operation was characterized by its large size, well-defined targets, and favorable results. On the average one enemy aircraft was destroyed for every three sorties.

A month later, from June 8 through June 10, there was a second air operation. On this occasion the *Stavka* employed three air armies (1st, 15th, and 2nd) and groups from the AFLRO, which attacked twenty-eight enemy airfields. The purpose of the operation was to destroy enemy bomber concentrations which were making night raids on important industrial centers: Gorki, Saratov, and Yaroslavl.† As

† These were the first serious German efforts at strategic bombing since 1941. Almost nightly raids were aimed at the tank works in Gorki, Saratov oil refineries, and Yaroslavl rubber works. ED.

the result of this operation and subsequent raids, the Germans lost 580 aircraft in June and ceased their attacks against our industrial centers.

During these operations against enemy airfields Soviet fliers performed their military assignments in exemplary fashion. On June 8, ground-attack planes commanded by Hero of the Soviet Union, Major M. Z. Bondarenko, destroyed or damaged as many as 35 enemy aircraft and blew up a hangar and warehouse with military supplies on a raid against the airfield at Seshcha. Squadron commander Major Bondarenko took a very active part in the battle for Kursk, and for his deeds was given a second "Gold Star" of a Hero of the Soviet Union.

Simultaneously our fighters fought enemy aircraft in the air, repelling their attacks on our airfields and railroad targets. There was especially bitter fighting on June 2, when a mass enemy flight was driven away from their attack on the Kursk railroad junction. On that day German bombers with fighter cover flew toward the city in several waves. To intercept them were sent 280 fighters of the 16th and 2nd Air Armies and 106 fighters of the 101st Fighter Air Division of ADF. The first wave of German planes, a group of 137 bombers and 30 fighters, was met by the fliers of the 16th Air Army at 4:45 A.M. while they were still on the distant approaches to the city. Combat with the enemy fighters was begun immediately, but most of our efforts, along with those of ADF's 101st Fighter Air Division, were directed against enemy bombers, and 58 aircraft were shot down.

The attacks against the succeeding waves of enemy aircraft were not so successful. Out of 287 German bombers, about 160 broke through to the city and dropped their bombs, which put the rail lines in the city out of commission for twelve hours. The enemy lost 145 aircraft during the June 2 raids.

When the bombing raids preliminary to the offensive were being made, great attention was given to disrupting the enemy's rail and truck lines. The major communication lines of the enemy along a broad front and to a depth of 200–250 kilometers (125–155 miles) behind the line were attacked for a period of almost three months. The AFLRO was employed mainly for this purpose as well as the air armies. The enemy's transportation network was systematically weakened. The fliers of the 16th and 2nd Air Armies, who made 1909 sorties, alone destroyed 6 railroad trains, as many as 260 railroad cars with their cargoes, 7 locomotives, more than 120 vehicles, made more than 90 major hits on railroad stations, and started as many as 220 fires.

The Soviet Air Force operated against enemy troops in areas where they were concentrated, and against staff headquarters, communication lines, and warehouses. To carry out these missions, 7987 sorties were flown. These very effective raids were made after detailed reconnaissance flights. At the beginning of May a group of fifty bombers, Pe-2s of the 16th Air Army, blew up a large stock of military supplies, destroyed several tanks and armored cars, and smashed a train with military supplies near the Brasovo railroad station and the settlement of Lokot.

Aerial reconnaissance operations were intense, seeking out concentrations of major enemy forces, the bases and composition of German air forces, air defense systems on enemy air bases, defensive positions, strong points, artillery concentrations, and enemy reserves. This helped the Soviet command to analyze enemy intentions, take measures to organize strong defense, and prepare effectively for the coming offensive.

During this period before the offensive, much attention was given to the organization of coordinated operations with the ground troops. Operating on the basis of the fronts' plans for defensive operations and the air armies' operational plans, the air staffs carefully coordinated air force operations with all the general armies and the tank armies. To solve special problems which might arise, the air armies sent responsible representatives to the general and tank armies.

Air Marshal A. A. Novikov and his deputies, Generals G. A. Vorozhyekin and S. A. Khudyakov, located with small staffs at the fronts' command posts, coordinated the air combinations according to the *Stavka* decisions. Plans were worked out for coordinated operations north of the Kursk salient between the 16th and 2nd Air Armies and south of the salient between the 2nd and 17th Air Armies.

Party and Comsomol organizations were very active, as well as the air force political organs, which directed their efforts, above all, to increasing the battle capabilities of air units. Much attention was given to strengthening the friendship between fliers and the personnel of the general and tank armies. Battle-hardened fliers were sent to visit the ground forces. They spoke at meetings and gatherings. In turn, the general and tank armies sent their representatives to the air units.

The Kursk Battle Opens in the North.   The enemy offensive began on the morning of July 5. It came as no surprise to the Soviet troops. On July 2, the *Stavka* warned the commanders of the Central and Voronezh Fronts that the enemy might well take the offensive in the immediate future. Therefore, ground and air forces were put on full alert and on July 5 made a powerful artillery counterattack.

From his base at Orel, the enemy sent his major forces down toward Olkhovatka with secondary drives against Maloarkhangelsk and Gnilets. The German troops were supported by powerful groups of aircraft, which concentrated their efforts on the battlefield in a band that was 25–30 kilometers (15–18 miles) long and not more than 10–15 kilometers (6–9 miles) deep. Each raid was made by 100–150 bombers with cover provided by as many as 60 fighters.

When the enemy planes appeared over the front the 6th Fighter Air Corps (commanded by General N. Ye. Yerlykin) and the 1st Guards Fighter Air Division (commanded by Lt. Colonel I. V. Krupenin) rose to meet them. When it was established that the major forces of the enemy were advancing toward Olkhovatka, ground-attack planes and bombers were assigned the task of destroying tanks, guns, and men during the daylight hours.

When the major forces of the 16th Air Army (commanded by General S. I. Rudenko) entered the battle, air activity increased greatly. Fliers of the 3rd Bomber Air Corps (commanded by General A. Z. Karavatsky), 6th Composite Air Corps (commanded by General I. D. Antoshkin), 2nd Guards Air Division (commanded by Col. G. I. Komarov), and 299th Ground-Attack Air Division (commanded by Colonel I. V. Krupsky), flying in groups of six to eight planes, attacked tanks and troops on the battlefield near Yasnaya Polyana, Ozerok, and Arkhangelskoye. Here for the first time, our fliers dropped very effective antitank bombs which were cumulative in nature. They burned through the armor plate on enemy tanks and put them out of action.‡

With the effective air force support our troops successfully repelled the enemy attack. By the end of July 5, the enemy had broken through our lines for 6 to 8 kilometers (4 to 5 miles) only on the Olkhovatka sector. Nonetheless, the first day of the defense operation showed that our air force had dissipated its efforts in the attack and destruction of a large number of targets.

‡ Apparently refers to PTAB hollow-charge bombs. ED.

The war in the air was intense from the very first day. Providing protection for our troops on the battlefield, our fighter pilots heroically repelled German bombing strikes and shot down 106 aircraft in 76 mass air battles. Our losses amounted to 98 aircraft. Soviet fliers displayed daring and great skill in these aerial battles. Second Lt. Polyakov (1st Guards Fighter Air Division) especially distinguished himself when he shot down one plane with machine-gun fire and rammed a second. First Lt. S. K. Kolesnichenko shot down three German planes on the first day of the battle.

However, there were serious deficiencies in our fighter operations. Our fighters were diverted to fight with enemy interceptors and thus had no effect on enemy bomber operations. Some fighter patrols did not take formations at different heights when they were protecting their areas. Procedures for warning of the approach of enemy planes were not well organized. This made it necessary to cover our troops with constant air patrols at great cost to our forces.

On the second day of battle, our troops counterattacked in order to regain their position and to eliminate the enemy wedge. Therefore, the command of the 16th Air Army decided to make a concentrated attack with 140 planes on the major enemy troops near Podolyan, Saborovka, and Butirki at 5:00 A.M. on July 6.

As soon as it was light, fliers of the reconnaissance groups located areas where tanks, motorized infantry, and artillery were concentrated and sent word by radio. Groups of bombers and ground-attack planes rose immediately into the air and attacked at five o'clock, utilizing antitank, fragmentation, and delayed-action bombs. The effect was stunning. Soviet ground troops, seeing how our fliers had set fire to more than ten tanks, charged, shouting "Forward!" Two more strikes like this were made on the same day.

The success of our bomber and ground-attack raids was guaranteed by reliable support from our fighter planes. Fliers of the 127th Fighter Air Regiment, headed by Captain F. V. Khimich, were especially successful in carrying out these assignments. The bombers under their protection completed their missions without any losses.

By July 6 the air commands had eliminated the fighter operation inadequacies noted on the first day of battle. Commanders of the 6th Fighter Air Corps and the 1st Guards Fighter Air Division personally organized air control for interceptors from advance command posts located in the counterattack area close to the front lines. They carefully followed the air situation and when necessary strengthened the number of patrolling fighter planes from the ranks of units on alert at the airfields. The patrol zones were advanced beyond the line of the front, thanks to which German aircraft were intercepted before they reached the battlefield. The efforts of our fighter units increased sharply, which was apparent immediately in the air situation.

Meeting with stubborn resistance, the Luftwaffe raised the level of its operations. In the meantime our air force increased its efforts, doubling the number of the strikes it had made on July 5. One hundred and thirteen German planes were shot down in 92 air battles.

As the result of the counterattack made by our troops and the effective actions of our air force, the enemy suffered serious losses in men and materials. The momentum of his advance was noticeably slowed. However, the German command tried to rectify the situation. Infantry and tank divisions, as well as new interceptor units from other sectors of the front, were rushed to the Orel base. But these measures could not avert the crisis. On July 7–8, in spite of all his efforts to break through to Kursk through Ponyri, the enemy had to admit defeat.

At the same time there was a decisive shift in the struggle for the control of the air. Beginning on July 7, our fighters firmly claimed the initiative in the air. Most of the German bombers were intercepted before they reached the battlefield. The level of German air activities declined noticeably. On July 7, 1162 enemy flights were noted, but on July 9, only 350.

By July 10, enemy offensive capabilities were completely exhausted. After July 12, when the Western and Bryansk Fronts went on the offensive in the Orel region, the German troops north of Kursk clearly were on the defensive.

During the defense operation in the Kursk-Orel region the 16th Air Army flew more than 7600 sorties and the AFLRO around 800. Soviet fliers destroyed 517 fascist aircraft, captured control of the air, and gave great help to our ground forces in their efforts to break the enemy offensive.

The Southern Side of the Kursk Salient. Meanwhile, on the Kursk salient's southern side, air operations also began on the morning of July 5 in the Belgorod sector. The 17th Air Army made mass strikes at 4:30 A.M. against the enemy airfields at Mikoyanovka, Sokolniki,

Pomerki, Osnova, Rogan, Barvenkovo, and Kramatorskaya. To obtain significant results, 132 ground-attack planes and 285 fighters were used. But at the time of the strike there were not many aircraft on all of these airfields. At 4:00 A.M. the German command had some of its air groups into the air as part of a softening-up operation for the coming offensive. Therefore, the effectiveness of our air operations was not high everywhere. Our crews reported that about 60 enemy aircraft were put out of action.

Since they had devoted a large part of their forces to strikes against airfields, our air armies were somewhat late in striking against the advancing enemy troops. Troops of the Voronezh Front began their defensive operations without adequate air support. But by 9:00 A.M. the situation had changed. The air units that had just returned from their assignments were sent to attack tanks, artillery, and infantry on the battlefield.

The fiercest battles broke out in the Oboyan sector. Having concentrated as many as 700 tanks and major infantry and artillery forces, the enemy struck his heaviest blow here, trying to break through to Kursk on the shortest route. Simultaneously his troops advanced toward Korocha hoping to divert our troops to a secondary area. The enemy troops were supported by almost all the 4th Air Fleet aircraft.

In order to break the enemy offensive as soon as possible, the command of the Voronezh Front concentrated most of its forces near Oboyan; almost all of the 2nd Air Army (commanded by General S. A. Krasovsky). Near Korocha air support was given by the 17th Air Army (commanded by General V. A. Sudets).

Most of the ground-attack and bomber missions were directed toward annihilation of the enemy tank concentration trying to break through in the zone of the 6th Guards Army. During the first days of the defense operation ground-attack planes and bombers operated in groups of six or eight, but then began to make concentrated strikes in groups of thirty to forty, which both increased the effectiveness of the strikes as well as lowered aircraft losses. Large groups of ground-attack planes and bombers turned out to be easier to defend, because it was simpler for fighter planes to fly cover for them. In addition, part of such a group could be diverted in order to suppress antiaircraft defenses near the target. Concentrated strikes against enemy troops also had a great effect on enemy morale, and they not rarely disrupted enemy attacks. On July 7, two concentrated strikes made by the 1st Ground-Attack Air Corps (commanded by General V. G. Ryazanov) broke the attack of the German force of tanks and infantry near Syrtsevo and Yakovlevo.

The *Stavka* representative, VVS Chief of Staff General S. A. Khudyakov, reported on July 8 to the VVS commander: "The recent decision to move to larger groups of aircraft has turned out to be completely correct. The Voronezh Front command confirms that the effectiveness of our air force is much higher than formerly."

From the very beginning of the enemy offensive in the Belgorod-Kursk area, there was a fierce struggle for control of the air. More than 2000 aircraft from both sides were operating over an area measuring 20 by 60 kilometers (12 by 37 miles). Often there were battles involving 100–150 aircraft. All in all, from July 5 through July 10, 2nd Air Army fighters were involved in 205 air battles, shot down more than 330 enemy aircraft, and lost 153 planes. The fliers of the 8th Guards Fighter Air Division, under the command of General D. P. Galunov, shot down around 76 planes on the first day of the battle, and especially distinguished themselves. However, in these operations Soviet fighters, as in the Orel-Kursk sector, showed serious inadequacies, which led to the loss of control over the air during the first days of the operation. It was only after these in-adequacies had been eradicated that our fliers were able to become the complete masters of the situation in the air.

During five days of bitter fighting, Soviet troops, with active air force support, caused great losses to the enemy, especially his tanks. Enemy attempts to reach Kursk through Oboyan were disrupted, and by July 10 his offensive in that part of the front had been arrested. But the German command did not wish to accept this. After regrouping their forces, enemy tank and motorized divisions with air support shifted their major efforts eastward toward Prokhorovka in order to break through to Kursk by an indirect route.

Attempting to disrupt this new enemy plan, the Voronezh Front commander decided to continue to wear down the enemy troops with a stubborn and active defense, and on July 12 made a powerful counterattack aimed at decisively smashing the enemy concentration attacking toward Prokhorovka.*

During the nights of July 10 and July 11, the AFLRO and the night bombers of the 2nd and 17th Air Armies struck against trains

---

* This became the largest tank vs. tank battle of World War II. ED.

and smashed troop columns on major and secondary roads trying to prevent fresh reserves from reaching the area where future battles were to take place. Strikes were also made against troops on the battlefield.

On the morning of July 12, forty minutes before the beginning of the counterattack, the 2nd Air Army conducted a preparatory operation in which more than 200 aircraft participated. Because of bad weather, the fliers had to operate against tanks and artillery positions in small groups.

The counterattack near Prokhorovka became a general tank battle in which the enemy suffered great losses in men and materials. Thus, joint efforts of ground troops and the air force disrupted the enemy's last attempt to break through to Kursk.

The enemy offensive south of Kursk, therefore, also ended in failure. From July 17 through July 23, our troops regained the position that they occupied before July 5. During the defensive operation in the Belgorod-Kursk section, our air force flew 19,263 sorties. The Military Council of the Voronezh Front in its report to the *Stavka* noted that "on the testimony of prisoners, the enemy suffered especially great losses in tanks and men from our air attacks and artillery barrages."

In these days of bitter fighting Soviet fliers displayed daring and high skill. First Lt. A. K. Gorovets, a flight commander, especially distinguished himself. When returning on July 6 from his assignment, he noted a large group of bombers flying toward our positions. The daring flier decided to attack them. Approaching them in cloud cover he knocked down nine German bombers and he himself died the death of the brave. The Soviet government awarded Gorovets the title of Hero of the Soviet Union posthumously.

At this time Major M. S. Tokarev, Captain S. D. Lugansky, Second Lt. V. I. Andrianov, and many other pilots, navigators, aerial gunners, sergeants, and officers of air force units and groups distinguished themselves. It was here that Ivan Kozhedub, now a general and three times Hero of the Soviet Union, received his baptism of fire and began his count of downed German aircraft.†

Thus, the defense operation in the Orel-Kursk region lasted until July 12 and in the Belgorod-Kursk region until July 23. During the

† Flying the La-5 and later models, Kozhedub became the most successful Soviet fighter pilot, with 62 victories on 520 sorties. ED.

course of these few days Soviet troops, with VVS active support, wore down and exhausted the enemy and subverted his offensive.

Soviet air operations over Kursk were conducted on a significantly larger scale than in the defense of Moscow or Stalingrad. In the defense operations on the two fronts, three air armies were involved (16th, 2nd, and 17th) and a considerable number of AFLRO units.

Toward the end of the operation on the Voronezh Front (from July 17 to July 24) the 5th Air Army of the Steppe Front (commanded by General S. K. Goryunov) also took an active part in the fighting.

The major efforts of the Fronts' air forces were directed toward destruction of the most important troop concentrations and were massed decisively in the most important areas. Air force operations were conducted in close cooperation with ground troops, especially during counterattacks and in the struggle to retain the major defense zones.

Skirmishes were often transformed into air battles, providing an opportunity for improving the fighter pilots' skill. About 4000 planes from both sides operated over the major targets. It was not unusual for 200–300 interceptors to be flying over the battlefield. On July 5 alone, there were 175 large-scale air fights in which more than 239 enemy aircraft were shot down. What was characteristic about this struggle for the control of the air was its aggressive nature on both sides. All in all, during the defense operation the Soviet Air Force destroyed in the air and on the ground more than 1500 aircraft, and lost about 1000 aircraft itself.

The Soviet Counteroffensive. When planning the counterattack at Kursk, the *Stavka* intended to smash the enemy concentrations at Orel and Belgorod-Kharkov, liquidate the enemy salients, and create favorable conditions for a general offensive that was to follow. It was planned to break through the enemy defenses at several points and then to make further converging strikes toward Orel to surround and destroy the enemy concentrations one by one. A series of attacks was planned in the Belgorod-Kharkov region west and southwest of Kharkov to split the enemy concentration and destroy it in separate operations.

Groups of the 6th German Air Fleet continued their operations in the Orel region, operating from airfields near Orel, Bryansk, and Seshcha.

Among the Soviet air units operating in the Orel region were the 1st Air Army of the Western Front, the 15th Air Army of the Bryansk Front, and the 16th Air Army of the Central Front. Thanks to the fact that the air armies had been strengthened by units from the *Stavka* reserve, we had nearly a threefold advantage over the enemy. Moreover, from time to time groups from the AFLRO also participated in this operation.

The German 4th Air Fleet and the 2nd Hungarian Air Corps were based in the Belgorod-Kharkov salient. The Soviet concentration included the 2nd Air Army of the Voronezh Front, the 5th Air Army of the Steppe Front, and some elements from the AFLRO. After reserves had been supplied by the *Stavka,* our aerial forces were twice as strong as the enemy's.

The Soviet Air Force had the following assignments: maintain firm control of the air and protect our strike troops from enemy air attacks, cooperate with the ground troops to break through the enemy defenses and to expand the breakthrough, resist any enemy attempts to take up intermediate defense lines, destroy enemy communications, hinder the movement of reserves, and carry out aerial reconaissance. In accordance with these assignments and the plans for offensive operations, the air armies' commanders made plans upon which operations were carefully developed for an air offensive.

The Drive to Orel. The counterattack in the Orel region began on July 12. Fifteen minutes before the ground attack of the Western Front's 11th Guards Army, 70 Pe-2 bombers and 48 ground-attack planes of the 1st Air Army (commanded by General M. M. Gromov) struck against enemy artillery and troop concentrations. All night, groups from the AFLRO had flown against these same targets, as well as units of the 213th Night Bomber Air Division of the Air Army, which flew 362 sorties and dropped 210 tons of bombs on the enemy. Only night flights were made in the attack area of the Bryansk Front's 61st Army. The crews of the AFLRO and the 313th Night Bomber Air Division of the 15th Air Army (commanded by General N. F. Naumenko) attacked artillery and mortar positions, wiped out centers of resistance, and destroyed troops in areas of concentration. As the result of the artillery and aerial attacks the enemy's defense was significantly weakened.

At dawn on July 12, the strike groups of the fronts went on the offensive with air support and under a smoke screen laid down by ground-attack planes. Ground-attack planes, in flights of ten to twelve planes with fighter protection were constantly over the battlefield, striking at fire points and destroying enemy tanks and personnel.

The Fascist troops defended their positions stubbornly. They were aided by their Luftwaffe, which was especially active in the 61st Army area. An hour after the attack began, groups of enemy bombers began to appear over the battlefield, attempting to strike at our troops. However, the fighters of the 1st Guards Fighter Air Corps (commanded by General Ye. M. Beletsky) were ready both in the air and on their bases. They broke up the enemy bomber formation, knocking some out and not allowing them to make accurate drops against our troops.

The Normandy Squadron.   On July 12, planes of our three air armies made 2174 sorties, were involved in 72 air battles, and destroyed 86 enemy planes, losing 59 planes. The fighter pilots A. P. Maresyev, B. V. Panin, P. I. Muravyev, I. P. Vitkovsky, and A. Ye. Borovykh, who were all later given the title of Hero of the Soviet Union, especially distinguished themselves in these battles. French fighter pilots from the "Normandy" squadron fought in these battles along with Soviet pilots.‡

During eight days of the operation, troops of the Western Front advanced 70 kilometers (43 miles) and the 61st Army of the Bryansk Front advanced 20 kilometers (12 miles). Favorable conditions were created for surrounding an enemy troop concentration at Bolkhov.

In order to hold Bolkhov and to save their troop concentration from destruction, the German generals from July 13 to 19 rushed as many as ten divisions to this area from other sectors of the front and the rear, including six tank and motorized divisions. Enemy troops made powerful counterattacks against the soldiers of the Western and Bryansk Fronts. The situation was altered sharply in favor of the enemy. Hit-

‡ The Normandy unit was composed of Free French pilots who arrived in Moscow in November 1942, and entered combat in the Smolensk region in March 1943, flying Yak-1s as part of the 303rd Fighter Division of the 1st Air Army. During July 1943 they changed to the Yak-9, and in 1944 they shifted to the Yak-3, which they flew until April 1945.

In three years, these French pilots flew 5240 missions, fought 869 air battles, and were credited with 273 victories. Forty-two pilots were killed or missing, and four were honored as Heroes of the Soviet Union, including Captain Marcel Albert, with 23 victories.[8] ED.

ler's forces, now that they had an advantage in forces, retarded our offensive.

Under these conditions it was essential that reserves be brought into the battle immediately. Therefore the Soviet command, from July 16 to July 25, brought the 25th Tank Corps, the 11th Army, the 4th Tank Army, and the 2nd Guards Cavalry Corps, all taken from the *Stavka* reserves. Almost all of the 1st and 15th Air Armies were brought into the battle.

Our planes made effective strikes against the counterattacking enemy. On July 25 alone, the 1st Air Army destroyed around 25 tanks, as many as 150 vehicles, 5 artillery batteries, and many foot soldiers.

Our planes were active in support of the 4th Tank Army, both when it came into battle and as it advanced into enemy-held territory. In spite of bad weather, bomber and ground-attack pilots made precise strikes against the antitank artillery of the enemy as well as his troops in areas where our tank groups were attacking, and fighters in constant patrols flew cover for our tank formations. With active air support our tank groups advanced rapidly toward Khotynets, in an attempt to cut off the enemy from his base at Orel.

By July 29, ground troops and planes of the Western and the Bryansk Fronts completed their rout of the enemy concentration at Bolkhov. Remnants of the enemy divisions began to withdraw to the west.

Before the offensive of the Bryansk Front's 3rd and 63rd Armies, which began west of Novosil, there were even more intensive air preparations than there had been near Bolkhov. The night of July 11 bombers of AFLRO and the bombers of the 15th Air Army flew more than 600 sorties and dropped around 550 tons of bombs in the major defense areas. In the morning, planes of the 3rd Ground-Attack Air Corps (commanded by General M. I. Gorlachenko) attacked the enemy. Operating in large groups, they destroyed many artillery pieces and enemy troops in the breakthrough area. Five minutes before the attack began, 89 bombers dropped 500 high-explosive and 3000 fragmentation bombs on the major enemy troop concentrations and his artillery positions.

These mass bomber and ground attacks, as well as mass artillery attacks, demobilized the enemy, and for a time he could offer no serious resistance. Soviet troops overran two defense lines and began to advance further. Those enemy fire points and areas of resistance still effective were destroyed by small flights of ground-attack planes. The

Chief of Staff of the 3rd Army, General M. V. Ivashechkin, wrote: "The operations of the ground-attack planes on the battlefield made it possible for the ground forces to advance rapidly and to capture enemy areas of resistance and defense points."

Hitler's command quickly began to throw his reserves and units from areas not under attack into the battle. The enemy's major air forces were also shifted to this area, and began to attack our infantry, tanks, and crossings over the Zusha River in groups of 40 to 50 planes. But the fighters of the 1st Guards Fighter Air Corps were alert, and in 48 mass air battles they shot down 67 enemy aircraft.

Expanding their operations, our infantry and tank forces continued to press the enemy with air force help, and by July 16 emerged onto the banks of the Oleshnya River, where the German army had constructed a defense line on the western bank. In order to accelerate the offensive, the front commander introduced the 3rd Guards Tank Army into the battle. General N. F. Naumenko assigned the basic forces of the 15th Air Army—120 ground-attack planes, 112 bombers, and 200 fighters—to support it and to provide protection in the air.

Orel Is Recovered.   At 8:00 A.M. on July 19, 63 bombers struck at enemy artillery positions, troops concentrations, and tanks at the point where our tanks were to enter the battle. At the same time, ground-attack planes struck at enemy targets in the flanking areas. Three hours later, our tank units began to enter the battle under cover provided by our fighter planes. The German command sent groups of 8 to 35 bombers with accompanying fighter planes in an attempt to halt the advance of our troops. Bitter air battles began in which our fighters shot down 23 enemy aircraft and compelled most of the bombers to turn back.

With active air support, the Bryansk Front troops broke through the German intermediate defense line and reached the Oka and Optukha rivers where a battle began at the point where the last defense line was pierced. The enemy, afraid of encirclement, quickly began to withdraw his troops from Orel. On the morning of August 1, aerial reconnaissance revealed a movement of as many as 300 vehicles out of the city toward the west, and the 15th and 16th Air Armies immediately attacked it. Because we had complete control of the air, our ground-attack planes and bombers carried out attacks at low altitude or at ground level, making several passes at the enemy columns. Simultaneously, our bombers struck at trains, bridges, and river crossings on the escape routes of the enemy and at night Po-2s dropped fragmentation bombs on the enemy troops.

During five days the 15th Air Army flew around 4800 sorties, and the 16th Air Army more than 5000, of which more than 50 percent were against the retreating troops. The roads against which our aircraft were operating were strewn with the corpses of German soldiers and littered with burnt-out vehicles, tanks, and other military equipment.

At dawn on August 4, troops of the 63rd and 3rd Armies broke through to Orel with air support and fighting began in the streets of the city. By the morning of August 5 the entire city was cleared of German troops. On the evening of August 5, in honor of the Soviet soldiers who had liberated Orel and Belgorod, an artillery salute was fired in the capital city of our Motherland, Moscow, for the first time in the Great Patriotic War.

The Western and Bryansk Fronts' offensive operations forced the enemy to reinforce his 2nd Tank Army with part of a division drawn from the southern sector of the Orel salient. Taking advantage of this, the troops of the Central Front counterattacked on July 15. Three days later they had recaptured the positions that they occupied on July 5, and on August 6 they liberated the city of Kromy.

The units of the 16th Air Army gave effective support to the ground forces. Since they had met only relatively weak resistance in the air, they flew as many as 1000 flights or more every day, and caused serious losses to the enemy in men and materiel.

When the cities of Bolkhov, Orel, and Kromy had been liberated, Soviet troops began pursuit of the remnants of the enemy concentration. The *Stavka* ordered the 15th and 16th Air Armies and the AFLRO to concentrate their efforts on destruction of the retreating troops. Carrying out this assignment, the ground-attack planes and bombers flew their missions, when they were summoned by reconnaissance aircraft, to attack motorized columns on the road from Kromy to Karachev, or the railroad through Orel-Khotynets-Karachev-Bryansk. From time to time fighter planes attacked these targets, along with aircraft from the fronts or long-range bombers at night. As the result of these high-level operations as many as sixty trains were destroyed, as well as many tanks and vehicles, from August 6 to August 11.

By August 18 the Orel operation was completed. Our troops, with the help of air power, destroyed 21 German divisions and liquidated the Orel salient, creating thereby the conditions for the subsequent offensive operations. During a thirty-six-day period, the front aircraft and the AFLRO flew 60,995 sorties and dropped 15,000 tons of bombs. The Luftwaffe lost more than 1400 aircraft in that period, of which more than 1320 were destroyed in the air and 80 on the ground. All attempts by the German command to regain the initiative which they had lost ended in failure. The Soviet Air Force retained complete control of the air.

Belgorod and Kharkov Are Liberated.   Troops of the Voronezh and Steppe Fronts went on the offensive on August 3. The night before the attack, AFLRO bombers flew 370 sorties, striking the areas to be attacked. In the morning, two hours before the offensive began, bombers and ground-attack planes from the 2nd Air Army in groups of six to twelve planes with fighter cover flew against enemy targets in the sectors assigned to the 5th and 6th Guards Armies of the Voronezh Front. Just before the attack, 36 bombers, 76 ground-attack planes, and 45 fighter planes struck at targets in the major defense zone. During the course of the raid on the attack zone assigned to the Steppe Front, the fliers of the 1st Bomber Air Corps (commanded by Colonel I. S. Polbin) made two concentrated strikes on centers of resistance in the first and second positions in the major defense zone, flying a total of 150 sorties.

As the result of the effective strikes from the air and the artillery barrage, the firing capabilities of the enemy artillery were eliminated or limited and the German troops could not offer any real resistance during the first thirty minutes of the offensive. Individual artillery batteries that attempted to open fire were wiped out by ground-attack planes that were over the battlefield. During the first half of the day, troops of the 5th and 6th Guards Armies overwhelmed the enemy's major defense zone.

Struggling to halt our offensive, the German command threw large numbers of aircraft into the critical area. Enemy bombers, flying for the most part in small groups, tried to bomb our advancing infantry and tanks. But these planes were repelled by Soviet fighter planes.

Hoping to quicken the rate of advance through the tactical zone the front commander brought up the 1st and 5th Guards Tank Armies. Most of the aircraft of the 2nd Air Armies were assigned to support them. At the same time, the 5th Ground-Attack Air Corps and the 291st Ground-Attack Air Division attacked enemy artillery and centers of resistance on the battlefield, bombers of the 202nd Bomber Air Division attacked reserves moving up to the front, and fighters flew cover for our tank groups.

With the support of our air force, which had control of the air, the tank armies broke through the tactical defense zone and by the end of August 3, they reached the Tomarovka, Sayenkov, and Dobraya Volya regions, having advanced 26 kilometers (16 miles). At the same time, troops of the Steppe Front had driven 7 to 9 kilometers (4½ to 5½ miles) into enemy territory.

On the first day of the counterattack, front aircraft flew 2670 sorties. These flights were highly regarded. General V. G. Ryazanov received the following telegram from the commander of the 48th Infantry Corps: "The ground troops were able to advance thanks only to the attack planes."

When they had broken through the enemy defense line, troops of the Voronezh and Steppe Fronts advanced rapidly. By August 11, the 1st and 5th Guards Tank Armies, with air support, had split the Belgorod-Kharkov enemy concentration into two parts and cut the railroad line from Kharkov to Poltava. On August 5, troops of the Steppe Front liberated Belgorod and came up to the outer Kharkov defense perimeter.

The German command began quickly to bring up reserves from the Don basin and other areas of the front to Kharkov and Akhtyrka by railroad and road. They decided to concentrate two large forces south of Bogodukhov and Akhtyrka in order to make strong counterattacks against the flank of the Voronezh Front.

The movement of reserves was detected by aerial reconnaissance. The *Stavka* took decisive measures to disrupt the enemy plans. Large numbers of aircraft from the fronts and the AFLRO were employed in attacks on railroads and roads and against the reserves themselves. The Southern Front's 8th Air Army was the unit to move against the enemy reserves. Its bombers and ground-attack units were active against enemy tank and motorized groups that were moving from the Don basin toward Kharkov. From 400 to 500 sorties were flown every twenty-four hours on this assignment. Subsequently, as the reserves moved into areas along the front, bombers and ground-attack planes of the 17th, 5th, and 2nd Air Armies took up the battle, hitting the railroad stations at Gorlovka, Slavyansk, Barvenkovo, Makeyevka, Pavlograd, and others, and destroying trains and motorized columns.

Beginning on August 5, as the enemy tank reserves began to approach the Kharkov region, the aircraft of the AFLRO became involved, striking against trains at railroad stations in Kharkov-Center, Lyubotin, Shpakovka, Merefa, and Osnova. From August 6 to August 17, the AFLRO bombers flew 2300 sorties. As a result, the enemy suffered heavily and his organizational plans were delayed.

Hoping to find our force at Akhtyrka unprepared, three enemy tank divisions counterattacked on August 11 south of Bogodukhov and then seven days later also in the Akhtyrka region. Bitter fighting continued in the air and on the ground until August 21.

The enemy counterattack was not successful, thanks to the coordinated efforts made by Soviet ground and air forces. When the German tank and motorized divisions met organized resistance and suffered great losses they were forced to retreat under the attacks from the ground and from the Voronezh Front's Air Force. Fliers of the 2nd Air Army, in the Akhtyrka area alone, destroyed more than 30 tanks and 400 vehicles and put down several artillery-mortar batteries during three days of battle.

At the same time that the troops of the Voronezh Front were driving back the enemy counterattack, soldiers of the Steppe Front were fighting to liberate Kharkov. By August 18, they pierced the defense perimeter of the city and surrounded it on three sides in an attempt to encircle the enemy. Trying to save their forces from total defeat, Hitler's command began to withdraw their tank and motorized divisions from the city and to haul away booty along the road to Poltava. This maneuver was discovered by aerial reconnaissance and almost all the aircraft of the 5th Air Army were dispatched to attack the enemy columns. On August 21–22 alone our fliers made 1300 sorties and destroyed or damaged many tanks and more than 135 vehicles.

Early in the morning on August 23, Kharkov was cleared of the last German forces after stubborn street fighting.

Thus ended the counterattack in the Belgorod-Kharkov region, which became a Red Army general offensive to free the Don basin and the left bank of the Dnieper.

During the Belgorod-Kharkov operation, the Soviet Air Force flew 28,265 sorties. Soviet fliers made a major contribution to routing the enemy forces. On the ground and in the air 800 enemy planes were destroyed. Retaining control of the air, which they had acquired during the defense period, our fliers created the favorable conditions that made it possible for the ground troops to carry out their assignments.

Results. The counterattack at Kursk ended as a brillant victory for the Red Army.

Many air units were given awards, granted guards status, or awarded the designations "Belgorod," "Orel," or "Kharkov" units because they successfully carried out their assignments and for the heroism of their fliers. Thousands of fliers received government medals and were given the title of Hero of the Soviet Union. Five of the finest fliers—N. P. Dmitriyev, I. P. Laveykin, I. N. Sytov, V. I. Popkov, and I. A. Shardakov—were from one regiment, the 5th Guards Fighter Air Regiment of the 295th Fighter Air Division. These brave pilots were granted the title of Hero of the Soviet Union for courage and daring, and the commander of this regiment, Col. V. A. Zaytsev, was given a second "Gold Star."

During this counterattack the air offensive was developed in its complete form as a further advance in the development of air force operational skill. After an initial period of preparation, strikes of ground-attack planes and bombers began in support of the advancing troops in depth in the territory of the offensive. Air power was concentrated on narrow sectors of the front against the most important targets— tanks and artillery—which hindered the advance of our troops. With these constant attacks against the enemy's forces, the Soviet Air Force lowered their capability to resist and caused them great losses and thus contributed to the successful advance of our troops through the enemy's defense position.

When our tank units entered the battle, our air armies exerted their efforts to put down the enemy antitank forces, to isolate the battle area from any reserves that might be sent up by the enemy, and to protect tank and motorized units from attacks from the air. When the enemy troops began to retreat, our air force took an active part in their pursuit. The air force had a significant influence on the operations at all stages.

There was a further development of coordination between the ground forces and the air force, and in the control system for air units both in defensive and offensive operations. A number of radio networks were organized in order to insure more accurate control over air units. In particular, a separate radio network was organized for controlling ground-attack planes on the battlefield. Experience acquired in air support for troops on the offensive during the counter-attack at Kursk, especially the organization of coordinated efforts with tank armies and the control of ground-attack aircraft over the battle-field with the help of ground radio stations, was subsequently utilized in other operations of the war. Our air force also gained valuable experience in fighting against the enemy's operational reserves.

The battle for Kursk was characterized by an intense struggle for control of the air. As many as 35 percent of the sorties flown were devoted to this task. The struggle against the Luftwaffe, which lasted almost a month and a half, concluded in the destruction of its basic forces. The struggle was decisive on a large scale. When our air force routed the enemy concentration at Kursk, it also gained strategic control of the air. The German command could no longer replace its great losses, especially in flying personnel. This created favorable conditions for our armed forces to organize and conduct extensive offensive operations.

Our air force perfected tactics for different aircraft types in the battle for Kursk.

Great experience was gained in the use of ground-attack aircraft both in large and small groups. In order both to control the ground-attack planes over the battlefield as well as to observe the effectiveness of their flights, the command posts of ground-attack air corps and divisions were located close to the observation posts of the commanders of ground armies. Air representatives were sent to infantry corps and divisions to guide planes to their targets, which insured close cooperation between the ground-attack planes and the ground troops.

Bombers were used to deal concentrated strikes in up to division strength, and great experience was gained in dive-bombing.

Fighter planes gained invaluable experience in conducting mass air battles employing vertical attacks. For fighter groups that were protecting ground troops, zones were established in which they destroyed enemy planes. Because there were no radio-location (radar) facilities in the air armies to locate enemy aircraft at great distances, scout planes patrolled near enemy airfields and on his probable flying routes, and transmitted information if any groups of enemy aircraft were observed. This made it possible to take measures to alert our interceptors who could then cut off enemy planes on the distant approaches to their targets.

On the whole the battle for Kursk provided much new experience in air force operational skills. The air command, the staffs, and the maintenance services displayed their skills and alertness in the control of divisions and corps, and in the planning of military operations and the organization of cooperative activities.

VIII

THE BATTLES TO LIBERATE THE LEFT BANK OF THE DNIEPER AND THE DON BASIN

The successful counterattack made by the Red Army at Kursk created favorable conditions for development of a general offensive on the southern wing of the Soviet-German front. The Supreme Command decided to free the entire left bank of the Dnieper and with this momentum to cross the river and seize a bridgehead on its right bank. This assignment was given to the troops of the Central, Voronezh, and Steppe Fronts, which included the 16th, 2nd, and 5th Air Armies. These air armies had 1450 aircraft against the enemy's 900 aircraft.*

The Central Front Attack.   Going on the offensive August 26, 1943, troops of the Central Front struck their major blow near Novgorod Seversk and with active air force support broke through the enemy lines and on August 27 freed Sevsk.

The 16th Air Army, which had more than 600 aircraft, operated very effectively against enemy soldiers and equipment and their actions

---

* This offensive presented the Germans with a difficult choice: to try to hold on to the region with its rich economic resources, or to retreat westward to the natural defensive line offered by the wide Dnieper. Hitler insisted on holding the region, but his generals were anxious to retreat to the Dnieper and take up defensive positions on the river's right (western) bank before the Soviet forces could reach the Dnieper. Successive blows by the three Soviet fronts were to settle the German's decision for them, and Hitler ordered a general retreat to the Dnieper on September 15. ED.

were highly regarded by the general army command. "In the first heavy battles for the city of Sevsk," the 2nd Tank Army's Military Council wrote to 16th Air Army commander General S. I. Rudenko, "we received great help from the Soviet falcons. . . . In the name of the officers and personnel of the 2nd Tank Army, the Military Council thanks you and your next in command, Chief of Staff General P. I. Brayko, the group commanders, and your flying and technical personnel."

Taking advantage of this success and having regrouped their basic forces onto the left wing, the Central Front troops began an offensive toward Konotop. To stop them, the German command increased its air strength in that area to 400 planes. Enemy fighters began to give more protection for the withdrawal of their troops along the roads and to loading points. But control of the air remained in Soviet hands.

Working closely with ground troops, the 16th Air Army made intensive raids on centers of resistance, enemy columns on the roads, and troops at river crossings. When the enemy attempted a counterattack, mass bombing raids followed in which 100 to 160 aircraft took part. On September 5, in a raid against 2nd German Tank Army units preparing for a counteroffensive near Konotop, the enemy lost 100 vehicles, 3 tanks, 32 guns, 4 supply dumps, and up to a company of infantrymen.

The air force made a major contribution to the liberation of Bakhmach. Attempting to hold this city, an important railroad and highway junction, the enemy resisted stubbornly. Ground-attack planes and bombers summoned to the battlefield bombed enemy strong points and his troop concentrations. Our troops broke through to Bakhmach and freed it.

Air operations were very effective. Captured soldiers and officers related that part of the 45th Infantry Division being transported by truck from Komarichaya to Pavlovsky were heavily bombed twice. As a result only one battalion was left from an entire regiment. Those units concentrated in a wood to the north of Shvedchikova and in ravines near the towns of Galchinsky and Pavlovsky lost nearly 80 percent of their men killed or wounded. In addition to destroying enemy troops, the air force struck at railroad lines, bombed airfields, flew cover for our advancing troops and our river crossings, and carried out aerial reconnaissance.

The battle with the Luftwaffe took place both on the ground and in the air. On September 3, in a raid on the Konotop field, eighteen bombers from the 6th Composite Air Corps set fire to ten enemy aircraft and damaged nine others.

The bitterest air combat took place during the fighting against the German troops at Nezhin. The German command, trying to restrain the sally of our troops toward the Dnieper, exerted all their efforts to hold Nezhin, an important railroad and highway junction, and the last defense point on the road to Kiev. It tried to compensate for a disadvantage in ground forces by using air power. Enemy bombers tried to slow our offensive by raids against our troops and the immediate rear lines, but Soviet fighter planes protected our troops and often broke up their formations.

Advancing still further, the Central Front troops swept past the Desna River, and reaching the Dnieper, crossed this great barrier north of Kiev. The river crossing began at dawn, September 22, with air and artillery support. By the day's end Soviet units had secured a bridgehead and the next day they moved 35 kilometers (22 miles) past the Dnieper. By the end of the day on September 30, a bridgehead was also seized near Dymer and to the north. The enemy drew up parts of four tank divisions to this region and with furious counterattacks tried to throw our troops back onto the left bank of the Dnieper. His Luftwaffe became still more active in its efforts against our troops and our river crossings.

The 16th Air Army was soon involved in the struggle to hold the bridgeheads. Operating at highest capacity, its fliers bombed the counterattacking Germans and successfully repelled enemy raids. With air force help, the ground troops drove off many enemy attacks and held the bridgeheads.

With active air force support our troops advanced as much as 200 kilometers (124 miles) and the left wing advanced toward the Dnieper and the Pripet and then seized bridgeheads on their right banks. Favorable conditions were created now for an offensive by the Voronezh and Steppe Fronts.

Attacks by the Voronezh and Steppe Fronts. In the meantime, having driven off all the enemy counterattacks and destroyed his Zenkov concentration, troops of the Voronezh Front captured eight enemy divisions to the east of Priluki by September 10.

The Steppe Front troops went on the offensive on August 25, striking their major blow in the Poltava-Kremenchug area. The enemy resisted stubbornly. But when his northern flank was seized by Voronezh Front troops, he was compelled to begin his retreat toward the Dnieper. At this time, efforts of the 2nd and 5th Air Armies were concentrated on destruction of retreating troops along roads at crossings and bridges, and also in destroying control centers and points of resistance. Ground-attack pilots and fighter pilots of the 5th Air Army (commanded by General S. K. Goryunov) especially distinguished themselves in the battle for Poltava. The 266th Ground-Attack Air Division (commanded by Col. F. G. Rodyakin) and the 294th Fighter Air Division (commanded by Col. V. V. Sukhoryabov, and after July 27, 1943, by Lt. Col. I. A. Taranenko) were given the names of the "Poltava" divisions for their heroic and daring role in the city's liberation.

When they had lost the battle at Poltava, enemy troops began to retreat in large columns toward Kremenchug and to cross to the right bank of the Dnieper, so the 5th Air Army began to attack the river crossings. On September 24, 60 bombers and ground-attack planes made a raid with 35 fighters flying cover. After they had flown through the screen thrown up by antiaircraft batteries, the aircraft approached the Dnieper and dropped their bombs directly on a bridge and two pontoon crossings, blowing them up. Having no other escape route, the enemy troops congregated at the crossings. Near Kremenchug on the Dnieper's left bank, nearly 2000 vehicles were backed up in several columns, which were attacked by our aircraft during the next two days.

In the second half of September, the tempo of our offensive increased significantly with air force help. On several days the troops advanced 30–40 kilometers (19–25 miles) to the west. By September 21, advance units of the Voronezh Front reached the Dnieper and by September 25 the Steppe Front had reached it also, and then they crossed it and seized several bridgeheads on the right bank south of Kiev and Kremenchug. The resistance provided by the Germans increased greatly. They tried several times to throw our troops back into the Dnieper.

Because there were so few airfields near the Dnieper, our bombers and ground-attack planes during this period flew at extended range and with limited force. Some fighter units based at forward airfields carried out their assignments at a high level and fought against German bombers.

During the entire offensive, our air force maintained its control of the air. The enemy constantly tried to halt our troops' advance with bombing raids, and always met resistance from Soviet interceptors. The Luftwaffe was especially active at the beginning of September in the defense zone at the Merefa River, and in the last days of the month when our forces began to cross the Dnieper. It was during this period that the number of air battles was greatest. They were especially severe near the Bukrino bridgehead. In September the enemy lost 198 aircraft in the air battles in this region.

Our fighter pilots showed great skill and heroism in their operations in support of our ground forces and bombers. The 737th Fighter Air Regiment commander, Hero of the Soviet Union Colonel N. I. Varchuk, provided a brilliant example of daring and skill. As the leader of fighters accompanying ground-attack planes, he noted forty German bombers with an escort of fifteen fighters heading toward our lines. He ordered his deputy to continue with our ground-attack planes. Varchuk and his partner attacked the enemy bombers and shot down one of them with cannon fire. As he came out of his attack Varchuk was in turn attacked by two fighters. He took them on and the daring flier shot them both down in frontal attacks.

In spite of some difficulties, the air forces of the three Fronts met their assignments. Because of our air raids, the Germans could not remove many trains with their military equipment, stolen property, grain, and feed. Thanks to our successful operations, tens of thousands of Soviet citizens were saved from deportation to fascist slavery.†

Liberation of the Don Basin. At the same time that the offensive proceeded toward the Dnieper, battles developed for the liberation of the Don basin. On August 13, troops of the Southwestern Front began their offensive, striking out from the Izyum region toward Barvenkovo and Pavlograd to smash the enemy and to cut him off from the Dnieper by making an advance toward the Zaporozhe region. Five days later, troops of the Southern Front went on the offensive to break the enemy defense line at the Mius River and, together with the Southwestern Front, expand the offensive to the south and southwest.

This offensive was supported by the 17th and 8th Air Armies,

† Marshal Goering's September 7 order had instructed the German Army to carry off all movable livestock, foodstuffs, and machines, as well as manpower, and to leave a "scorched earth" of destroyed property behind. ED.

which had 1400 aircraft against 1100 German aircraft. From the operation's start, the 17th Air Army, commanded by General V. A. Sudets, concentrated its efforts on support of the Southwestern Front, which at the end of August crossed the northern Donets and drove into the enemy defense, capturing several resistance points. During the preparatory period and during the operation itself, the 17th Air Army flew 16,188 sorties.

Troops of the Southern Front, supported by the 8th Air Army, after they had overcome the enemy's strong defense positions, expanded their breakthrough to an area 80 kilometers (50 miles) wide by the end of August and then advanced to the west 50 kilometers (31 miles), liberating Taganrog (August 29). The German command marshaled 650 aircraft in this area in an attempt to stop the advance of our troops.

In spite of increasing resistance from enemy fighters, the 8th Air Army retained control of the air and gave active support to the ground troops. Working with ground forces, they destroyed infantry, artillery, and mortars. After the enemy tactical zone had been pierced, efforts of this air army were devoted to aiding our ground troops to encircle and destroy the enemy concentration at Taganrog and to liberate that city. The air force was also very helpful in repelling the enemy's counterattacks. For example, on August 20, when the enemy had nearly cut off our advance units with a flank attack north of Taganrog, ground-attack planes were summoned to the battlefield. By means of intensive attacks, they dispersed the enemy infantry and dampened his artillery fire, contributing to our further advance.

In addition to meeting their ground-support assignments, our ground-attack planes attacked enemy bombers and disrupted their raids against our troops. On August 20, eleven planes of the 655th Ground-Attack Air Regiment, commanded by First Lt. V. A. Kondakov, who was to become a Hero of the Soviet Union in October 1944, met fifty German bombers with fighter cover as they approached their target north of Taganrog. Noting that these aircraft were flying toward our troops, the ground-attack planes, as well as the four fighter planes that were with them, attacked the bombers and in the ensuing air battle shot down six Ju 87s and one Bf 109, then hit their target and returned to their base without a single loss. On August 30, there was another successful air battle when six

Il-2s of the same regiment under Captain S. V. Grigorenko attacked a large group of German aircraft and shot down seven.

In addition to supporting ground troops, the 8th Air Army hampered the approach of enemy reserves to the region of encirclement and disrupted rail communications. The largest operation was against the Uspenskaya railroad station, where the enemy had concentrated troops, stores, and much rolling stock. Raids were made against this station for several days and nights. Little Po-2 biplanes were especially effective in these strikes. On the night of August 23, the Po-2s blew up five dumps with equipment and fuel, and destroyed thirteen guns and twelve vehicles. After each raid, the local inhabitants said later, there were many German funeral processions.

Including operations during the initial period of the offensive, the 8th Air Army made 15,642 sorties in August. Hundreds of tons of delayed action and antipersonnel bombs were dropped, as well as 55,448 individual antitank bombs and 11,753 rockets. In that period the planes from this air army shot down 280 enemy planes in 285 air battles. In addition, 13 enemy aircraft were destroyed on the ground.

Annihilation of the Taganrog troop concentration played not a small role in the subsequent liberation of the Don basin. Afraid of encirclement, the enemy was compelled early in September to begin to retreat over the Dnieper. The troops of the Southwestern Front followed him deep into the Don basin. Aircraft of the 17th Air Army of the Southwestern Front struck by day and by night against enemy troops on the battlefield as well as against his retreating columns on the roads. Protected by his rear guard, the enemy tried to withdraw his troops in order. To restrain the advance of our troops and to free railroad trains blocked by our raids near Slavyansk and Cherkasskaya, the German command on September 9 brought up two fresh infantry divisions opposite the 34th Infantry Corps near Balabasovka. Our advance was halted. Ground-attack planes were summoned to the field of battle. Together with artillery, they fell onto the enemy and helped our troops to break his resistance. After he had suffered great losses the enemy withdrew, abandoning a great quantity of equipment and vehicles with food and other necessaries.

As he retreated, the enemy tried to remove as much stolen goods as possible from the Don basin. Along with the retreating troops there was a steady flow of railroad cars loaded with factory equipment, grain, feed, and livestock moving to the west. The air force was given the task of stopping these shipments. Units of the 9th Composite Air Corps (commanded by O. V. Tolstikov) began this assignment on September 5. Bombers and ground-attack planes raided the station at Lozovaya and the tracks east of the station at Cherkasskaya, where three loaded trains were destroyed and all the rail bed destroyed for a kilometer (.62 mile). This ended all movement on the line from Slavyansk to Cherkasskaya.

Raids against railroad targets were also made in other sectors. The 305th Ground-Attack Air Division, commanded by Col. N. G. Mikhevichev, was especially successful. Eighteen Il-2s from this division hit a storage area at the Barvenkovo station on August 25. Several fires were started by hits from bombs and rockets. Railroad workers afterwards reported that these storage areas continued to burn and explode for more than two days. As the result of this raid a great quantity of supplies was destroyed, as well as food and other goods. For several days not a single train could pass through the Barvenkovo station.

The enemy took urgent measures to restore railroad traffic on this section of track, but our ground-attack planes in the daytime and our Po-2s at night disrupted the repairs. The enemy was compelled to abandon his equipment and his plunder. Our troops captured forty trains in this area with grain, machine tools, metals, equipment, and medical supplies.

At the end of August and the beginning of September, our long-range bombers also made successful raids against railroad lines being utilized to ship reserve troops into the Ukraine. Fliers of the 240th Bomber Air Regiment destroyed fourteen trains and cut railroad lines in several places. The crew of S. I. Kretov hit a railroad line and destroyed four trains. During the war years, Kretov flew 400 sorties against railroad targets, airfields, and enemy troops and equipment. Together with his crew, he destroyed or damaged nearly sixty aircraft on the ground and shot down ten enemy fighters in the air. Early in 1944, Kretov, a member of the Communist party, was given the title of Hero of the Soviet Union, and after the war he was given a second "Gold Star," for the manner in which he carried out his assignments, his courage, and his heroism.

Successful operations of our air force against rail and road communications limited the enemy's maneuverability and disrupted the planned withdrawal of his troops, who suffered great losses as they retreated. The line of retreat was littered with smashed equipment and the corpses of enemy soldiers. Our fliers prevented the enemy from removing his plunder and deporting nearly 60,000 Soviet citizens.

When they had cleared a good part of the Don basin, troops of the Southwestern Front rushed toward the Dnieper. The 17th Air Army in this period had to contend with difficult conditions on their airfields. As they retreated, the enemy troops put their airfields out of commission, as well as landing strips, exploding bombs on them and placing mines in the buildings and equipment. But our air force, which had been compelled to move its base of operations sometimes three or five times, continued to follow our advancing troops. Even at the end of the operation on the approaches to the Zaporozhe district, it continued its operations with the same vigor, flying 3000 sorties in several days.

Continuing their offensive, the troops of the Southwestern Front over the entire area had achieved considerable successes by the end of September. They reached the Dnieper, seized several beachheads on its right bank, and began battle for the approaches to the Zaporozhe district.

These successful operations were aided by our operations against enemy aircraft. The most effective and instructive strikes were made by the 175th Ground-Attack Air Regiment, commanded by Lt. Col. M. D. Zakharchenko. On September 28, eight Il-2s led by Captain M. A. Shnyrev, with sixteen fighters for cover, emerged at low level over the airfield at Kanterserovka. Then, gaining an altitude of 400 meters (248 feet), the ground-attack planes dropped their bombs on the planes based there. They destroyed or damaged fifteen out of the twenty aircraft on the ground and returned, without losses, to their own airfield. The enemy was completely unprepared for this attack. His antiaircraft guns opened fire only when our ground-attack planes were already past the airfield. The 955th Ground-Attack Air Regiment was also very successful in its attack on the Bliznetsy airfield, where they destroyed eighteen aircraft and damaged eight.

The airfields at Barvenkovo, Kramatorskaya, Bliznetsy, Krasnorarmeyskoye, Dnepropetrovsk, and Kantserovka were also subjected to attack. Later, after these fields had been captured, it was discovered from the evidence there, as well as from the testimony of local inhabitants, that our air force destroyed 167 aircraft and damaged 35 aircraft on these fields.

The offensive of the Southern Front's troops was just as successful. When they had liquidated the enemy concentration at Taganrog and emerged at the region of Ilovaysk, it appeared that our troops might be capable of surrounding the enemy's Don basin concentration. Consequently, at the beginning of September the enemy began a hasty retreat. The major efforts of our air force in this period were concentrated on supporting our troops as they advanced and to destroying the retreating enemy.

With active 8th Air Army support, our troops from the Southern Front crossed all of the Don basin and liberated many cities including Donetsk, Mariupol (Zhdanov), and Osipenko (Berdyansk), and reached the Molochnaya River.

In October the battle for the Dnieper became still fiercer. Because he did not have sufficient reserves, the enemy attempted to gain parity or a superiority in numbers in different sectors by shifting troops from other parts of the front. But the Soviet Air Force, in many cases, limited the maneuverability of the enemy troops by attacking railroad lines and junctions. The 16th Air Army on October 6 hit the railroad station at Gomel where an armored train and ten other loaded trains were located. A total of 250 aircraft, during the attack on this station, set fire to 62 railroad cars, destroyed 3 locomotives, 20 loading docks, 40 vehicles, and damaged the armored train.

In his attempts to dislodge our troops from their bridgeheads on the right bank of the Dnieper, the enemy made constant counterattacks supported by raids from large groups of his aircraft.‡ The struggle for the control of the air became fiercer. Our fighter aircraft increased their efforts to protect our most important troop concentrations and especially those on the bridgeheads. As they fulfilled this assignment our crews displayed courage and daring and caused great enemy losses. During October alone, a squadron commander of the 240th Fighter Air Regiment, Lt. K. A. Yevstigneyev, shot down 12 aircraft in 9 air battles. He was given the title Hero of the Soviet Union in August 1944 for the outstanding manner in which he fulfilled his assignments, for his determination, courage, and heroism, and on February 23, 1945, he was given a second "Gold Star," for

‡ The German 4th Air Fleet committed 867 aircraft on October 10 against the southern bridgeheads, while on the same day the 6th Air Fleet attacked with 960 aircraft.[9] ED.

his new exploits. During the entire war, Yevstigneyev flew 300 sorties, participated in 120 air battles, and shot down 56 enemy aircraft.

The enemy's stubborn resistance did not slow our troops' advance. When they had repelled all the enemy counterattacks they continued to expand their bridgeheads and advanced toward Kiev, Kirovograd, Krivoy Rog, and northern Crimea. On October 14 our troops liberated the Zaporozhe district, and on October 24 and 25, Melitopol, Dnepropetrovsk, and Dneprodzherzhinsk, and seized an important bridgehead on the lower Dnieper. The enemy army in the Crimean Peninsula was cut off. As a result of offensives by the five fronts during August–September 1943, rich agricultural districts in the Ukraine were liberated as well as an important industrial region, the Don basin. Soviet troops dealt a serious defeat to the enemy, advanced along a wide front to the Dnieper and then swept over that obstacle.

Much of the credit for these victories belongs to our air force. Maintaining control of the air and thereby supporting the rapid advance of our troops, the air forces of the five fronts in September alone flew more than 90,000 sorties and dropped 9570 tons of bombs and more than 55,000 rockets on enemy targets.

The enemy suffered great losses, losing about 2000 planes in the air. The stubborn air battles over the left bank of the Dnieper and the Don basin showed once more the superiority of Soviet pilots over the Germans and also testifies to the further increase in air force power.

Liberation of Kiev. After the Dnieper had been reached and bridgeheads had been seized on its right bank, troops of the Voronezh Front (which became the 1st Ukrainian Front on October 20) was given the assignment of destroying the enemy's Kiev troop concentration and liberating that city. At the beginning of the offensive, troops of the Front had a total numerical superiority over the enemy only at the center of the area.

Struggling to limit expansion of our bridgeheads, German troops not only stubbornly defended their positions, but also counterattacked with the support of mass flights of aircraft. Therefore our fighter aircraft were preoccupied with the protection of our troops on the right bank of the Dnieper and the crossings over it.

Our troops' first attempt to pierce the enemy defense line from out of our bridgehead at Bukrino was in the period October 12–15. The night before the offensive, our bombers flew 272 sorties against targets in the area. All 2nd Air Army efforts were dedicated to support of our troops. The air force struck against infantry concentration, artillery, and defense strong points.

With air force help our troops enlarged the bridgehead, but they were unable to develop an offensive. The enemy succeeded in strengthening his defenses and holding his lines around the relatively small bridgehead area by utilizing ten army divisions.

After it became apparent that the difficult situation did not favor an advance from the Bukrino bridgehead, the offensive efforts of the 1st Ukrainian Front were transferred to the bridgehead at Lyutezh (north of Kiev) on *Stavka* orders.

By the beginning of the November offensive, the situation in the air had changed somewhat. Both sides had about the same number of aircraft. The 2nd Air Army had increased its aircraft to 603 while the enemy forces had been reduced to 610 aircraft, of which 70 percent were bombers.

An offensive began on November 1 from the Bukrino bridgehead with air support. In spite of bad weather conditions, the 2nd Air Army flew 640 sorties in a two-day period. On November 3, as soon as the German command reacted to the Bukrino offensive and began to move their reserves to that point, the strike force of the Front took the offensive from the Lyutezh bridgehead.

The offensive was preceded by an artillery and air attack. Ground-attack planes and bombers struck the enemy in the Pushcha Voditsa, Goryanka, and Priorka regions. And although the enemy resisted stubbornly, Soviet fliers, inspired by prospects of liberating Kiev, capital of the Soviet Ukraine, fought bravely and confidently. They disrupted enemy attempts to subvert our offensive. Unable to resist the crushing attacks of our infantry and tanks and blows of our artillery and air power, the enemy began to retreat at the day's end. On the morning of November 6, Soviet troops liberated Kiev and expanded their bridgehead to a width of 230 kilometers (143 miles) and a depth of 150 kilometers (93 miles).

There were many times in the air battles when our fliers defeated the enemy not by force of numbers, but by their skill. On the day enemy resistance collapsed in Kiev and our troops began their pursuit of the retreating troops, seven fighter planes took off to fly cover for them over the Belgorodka, Plesetskoye, and Vasilkov areas, commanded by Captain A. V. Vorozheykin. When they had reached their target region, they were instructed by radio to attack bombers approaching them from the southwest, accompanied by sixteen fighters. Gaining altitude and attacking out of the sun, our fighters suddenly attacked the leading group of nine planes. Stunned by this unified and sudden attack, the German pilots dropped their bombs on their own troops. Taking advantage of the confusion, our fighters shot down nine enemy aircraft and returned without losses.

All air units participating in the Kiev battles received the thanks of the Supreme Command; and the most outstanding air groups— the 4th Guards, the 254th and 291st Ground-Attack Air Divisions, the 8th Guards, and the 256th Fighter Air Division—were given the name of "Kiev divisions." Three air divisions were awarded the Order of the Red Banner for the second time.

Understanding that the capture of Kiev and other cities to the west by our troops was a great threat to them, the German command decided to regain the territory they had lost on the Dnieper's right bank. On November 13 they took the offensive with a great tank concentration directly opposite the point where 1st Ukrainian Front units were advancing to the west, and repulsed our troops, but they were not able to achieve all of their desired goals.

Our air force carried on heavy raids against enemy troops on November 12–15, as the enemy offensive was halted near Fastova. One ground-attack pilot, First Lt. I. M. Semin, provided a brilliant example of self-sacrifice. On November 14, a group of eight Il-2s under his command attacked a column of seventy tanks and other vehicles on the road between Khovtnevo and Kornin. The fliers destroyed seven tanks and eight other vehicles with bombs and rockets. The commander's aircraft was damaged by antiaircraft fire over the target. Preferring death to imprisonment, the brave flier directed his aircraft onto the enemy column. First Lieutenant Semin and his aerial gunner Sergeant Bukhlin died as worthy sons of our Motherland.

The crushing blows from our ground-attack planes often disrupted enemy plans. On November 22, when 150 tanks and about 2 infantry regiments took the offensive near Stravishche and Vysokoye, they were met by the 227th Ground-Attack Air Division (commanded by Colonel A. A. Lozhechnikov). Over a five-day period the enemy suffered great losses and was compelled to terminate his offensive. The 38th Army command defending that area of the front had the highest regard for this ground-attack division and gave their thanks to the fliers.

In December, the 2nd Air Army attacked tanks and motorized infantry and also railroad trains in yards. Our fliers caused particularly heavy losses to the enemy on December 12–15 when improved weather conditions made it possible for the planes to operate in large groups.

When the enemy counterattack had been repulsed, troops of the 1st Ukrainian Front ended the Kiev defensive operation on December 23. During that period the 2nd Air Army had flown more than 20,000 sorties. In addition to causing great losses to the enemy in both men and materiel the air army destroyed more than 300 enemy planes in air battles, which significantly weakened German air power.

The victories of the Soviet Air Force resulted from the increasing military might of our country, which provided the front with a constantly mounting number of new aircraft. The victories were at the same time the fruit of great party and political work.

SUMMARY AND CONCLUSIONS

The second period of the Great Patriotic War was marked by great victories of the Soviet armed forces over Fascist Germany. When it had acquired the strategic initiative, the Red Army in the period from November 1942 to December 1943 advanced from 500 to 1300 kilometers (310 to 800 miles) to the west and liberated almost two-thirds of the territory seized by the enemy. Very important industrial and agricultural regions were returned to the Motherland. Soviet troops routed more than 200 enemy divisions, and destroyed more than 20,000 enemy planes, about 25,000 tanks, and about 40,000 guns.[10] Thanks to the efforts of the Soviet people and their armed forces, conditions were created for the final defeat of the Facist Army.

Air Force Operations. Our air force made a major contribution to the defeat of the German troops. In close cooperation with the ground forces and the navy, it destroyed a great quantity of equipment and enemy personnel, captured the control of the air, and thereby created favorable conditions for the ground forces to conduct broader and more energetic offensive operations. The air force flew about 796,000 sorties in the fulfillment of its assignment.* There was a doubling in the number of raids against railroad targets, bridges, river crossings, ports, and ships when compared with the first period of the war.

In 1943 there was a great increase in the utilization of air transport. Units from AFLRO and the Civil Air Fleet transported more than 390,000 men to the Fronts and to the partisans, and more than 29,000 tons of varied cargo. The 2nd, 6th, and 7th Air Regiments of the Civil Air Fleet were designated as guards units for the courage they displayed in battle. The Soviet Air Force continued to develop in numbers and to improve its aircraft quality, organizational structure, and utilization of air power.†

The number of aircraft in the Fronts increased by 1.7 times. The concentration of air power on the most important strategic targets was more decisive. Thus, about 60 percent of all of the aircraft from the fronts and the AFLRO along the entire German-Soviet line participated in the counterattack at Kursk.

The most important stages in the struggle for the control of the air were as follows: the battle for Stalingrad, the air battles over the Kuban, the air operations conducted in the period from May to June 1943, and the battle for Kursk. The operation for destroying enemy aircraft on the ground was organized according to a directive from the *Stavka*. From three to six air armies from the fronts and also part of the AFLRO were diverted for this purpose. During the course of this operation the enemy lost about 1100 aircraft. The Luftwaffe was much weakened during the winter and spring of 1943, an important precondition for the final seizure of the air control which was obtained by our air force in the summer of 1943. The Luftwaffe no longer could have any real influence on the course of operations conducted by his ground troops and his fleet.

In addition to the Front air forces, other air forces took an active part in the second part of the war. The naval air force struck at enemy vessels, protected the ocean flanks of the ground troops, and cooperated in both offensive and defensive operations. The

* Losses during 1943 were one aircraft for each 72 sorties. ED.

† At the end of 1943, Soviet forces included 6,736,000 men, of which 483,000 were air force and 266,000 navy. There were 8500 military aircraft.[11] ED.

AFLRO fulfilled its own assignments against rail communications and industrial targets deep in the enemy's rear. Cooperating with the ground forces it attacked airfields, staff headquarters, reserve concentrations, fortified points, warehouses, and bridges, and also operated against targets on the battlefield, especially during the preparatory period before offensive operations. Fighter units from ADF, along with aircraft from the fronts, flew protective cover for ground troops and important installations along the front and in the rear. Coordination of the operation of all different air units in support of ground maneuvers was carried out by a *Stavka* representative.

Supporting Ground Operations.   As the result of earlier experience, it was now possible to determine precisely the type and manner of coordinated operations with ground troops.

The air offensive, which was much developed in the offensive operations of 1942–43, received its full development in the counter-attack at Kursk. It involved the constant application of all kinds of air attacks both on the battlefield and in the operational rear for the entire operation. This made it possible for the ground troops to pierce the enemy defense line and to conduct offensive operations at a higher tempo and at a greater depth.

The efforts of the Front air forces during offensive operations were concentrated, as a rule, in the area where the major attack would be made. The air attack on the strike area usually began on the night before the offensive. Both Front and long-range bombers were used for this purpose, and they attacked targets in the enemy's major defense zone with the aim of destroying his defense installations, his artillery, and exhausting and subduing his personnel.

The preparatory air attack before the offensive was carried out by Front aircraft. It nearly always coincided with an artillery barrage. The purpose of this air attack was to dampen the enemy's artillery, his points of resistance and defense lines, and also to disrupt his control over his troops in the tactical defense zone.

This air attack was both in the form of concentrated raids and by waves of bombers and ground-attack planes. One after another, mortar and artillery batteries were silenced, and then separate centers of resistance in the path of the advancing troops were attacked. At the same time aircraft attacked the enemy's tactical reserves and his counterattacking troops.

During the offensive operations in the second period of the war, the air armies gained experience in supporting and protecting tank armies. Before they came into the battle, there would be a short preparatory air attack to smash and subdue enemy resistance points and defense lines, and to destroy his antitank weapons both in front and on the flanks of the point at which our tanks were to enter the battle. As much as an entire ground-attack air division and a fighter air division were assigned to the support of a tank army. Experience showed that the success for air support and cover for tank groups during a rapid offensive depended to a significant degree on the appropriate timing of the use of the air power.

During these operations the Soviet Air Force acquired great experience in coordinated maneuvers for crossing rivers, supplying troops on bridgeheads with materials and fuel, and also in supplying troops who had been surrounded by enemy forces.

Operational planning skills of command personnel and air staffs were much improved. This was assisted to a considerable degree by instructions and manuals on military operations published by the air force, as well as by experience gained in the actual operations.

Experience acquired in ground-air operations was developed theoretically at the end of 1943. Published works defined coordinated operations between ground and air forces in order to assign to each their responsibilities according to the location, the time, and the goals to be obtained, and also for combined action on the battlefield. Responsibility for organizing these coordinated efforts was assigned to the commander of the Fronts, which made it possible to utilize air power most effectively in operations. These published works also defined the responsibilities for the organization of co-ordinated efforts by the staff of the Front for the air army commander and his staff, and also for the ground commanders. The principle of a unified command for air power was considered to be fundamental. Instructions for the use of recognition signals and communications between ground and air forces were very important in the command system for joint operations.

In the second period of the war, the staffs from air armies and ground armies developed plans for coordinated offensive operations. What was exceptional in them was that the assignments for the air force were determined by the stages of the operation, and the air strikes were planned depending on the time of the proposed ground operation. The plan for coordinated efforts also determined the number and kinds of aircraft to be used against various targets and also the method for directing aircraft to the targets. These were to be confirmed by the commanders of the armies involved in the coordinated operation.

One of the positive improvements in organizing coordinated operations with ground troops was the systematic arrangements made by commanders of fighter and ground-attack air corps and divisions to visit the command posts of the ground or tank armies from which they could control their air units. Later secondary control points were organized in regions where the advance units of general army units were located for the same purpose. In September 1943, the first radio location stations were set up in the air armies, which were very successful in combating enemy aircraft.

Thus, the control system improvements greatly improved air power flexibility and encouraged close coordination between the air force and the ground forces close to the battlefield.

In 1943 our air force began to operate more actively against enemy transport and reserves. Efforts in this area doubled from those of 1941–42, which greatly aided the repelling of enemy counterattacks and accelerated the offensives made by our troops.

Improvement of Operational Technique. Aerial reconnaissance took an important place in military operations. The number of reconnaissance planes doubled in 1943 as compared with 1942. The Pe-2 remained the basic aircraft in the reconnaissance air regiments, being utilized for operational reconnaissance as far as 300 kilometers (186 miles) behind the enemy lines. In September 1943, each reconnaissance air regiment acquired one squadron of fighter planes or ground-attack planes, which were successfully utilized for tactical reconnaissance.

During deeply extended offensive operations when our troops were moving rapidly forward, aerial reconnaissance was the major, and sometimes the only, means which the commands had for obtaining information about the enemy. Commanders of the Fronts and armies noted in their reports many times that because of the excellent aerial reconnaissance organization they were always aware of both the ground and air situations—a very important condition for the correct planning and conduct of operations.

Aerial reconnaissance played an important role in supplying the general army and air commands with data about the enemy, and was one of the most important forms of reconnaissance available.

As the size of the offensive operations increased in which aircraft were utilized in great numbers, the role of the air force navigational and meteorological services became more important. In the planning and conduct of operations, it was essential to have close cooperation between these services and the staffs, and in particular with their operational and reconnaissance units. Therefore, in accordance with an order from the Red Army Air Force commander dated December 15, 1943, the Chief Navigator of the Air Force and the navigators of the air armies from the air corps and divisions were subordinated to the commanders of the respective staffs as their deputies.

Much attention was devoted to the improvement of aircraft control and bombing accuracy. Radio navigation was utilized more often for these purposes. Radio compasses were installed in fighter and ground-attack planes, and fighter planes were now guided to their airfields by radio bearings. Radio equipment that had been installed at an earlier date in bombers was now used more effectively. All of these things made it possible to fly in bad weather and to cut in half the number of planes that crashed when lost, as compared with 1942.

There was a great improvement in bombing precision; on a given target of 200 by 200 meters (656 by 656 feet) there were 64 percent hits in 1943, i.e., twice as many as in 1941. This was achieved by dive-bombing and by improving navigational equipment and bombsights. Aerial photography taken after raids had a positive effect on the accuracy and effectiveness of subsequent bombing, and this technique was introduced into both the front air forces and the AFLRO.

In 1943 new guides, instructions, and manuals were worked out for the navigational services. *The Manual for the Navigational Services* (NShS-43) was issued, which to the end of the war was the basic guide for air navigation. Instructional materials on the navigational services began to appear at regular intervals to play an important role in the study of battle experiences. Guides and instructions for bombing from Pe-2s, Il-2s, and Po-2s were produced, as well as standards for bomb saturation and expected hits, which made it possible to evaluate bombing success more adequately. These measures in the area of the navigational services increased the effectiveness of our air force and contributed to the successful fulfillment of its assignments.

Support Services. In 1943, especially in the Kursk battle, the support services mastered the problem of supporting air force operations. More than 1800 airfields were built or restored, contributing to base dispersion and flexibility for the Front air forces. During one year, the air armies issued more than 412,000 tons of aviation fuel and oil and almost 100,000 tons of bombs.

In order that the air force not fall behind the ground troops during offensive operations, units from the air service battalions were assigned to follow the offensive troops to work on airfields seized from the enemy to make them ready for our air operations.

There were occasions during rapid ground offensives deep into enemy territory when fighter and ground-attack plane bases were not adequate. This was because there were not enough engineering-airfield battalions in the air armies, and because of their low maneuverability and an inadequate amount of airfield construction equipment. There were also occasions when bases were not adequate because some were out of action, especially during the muddy period in the spring and fall.

The forces in the rear were much concerned with camouflage. One basic technique was the construction of mock airfields. In the 16th Air Army there were special workshops which constructed imitation aircraft. The preparation of these aircraft was important, because more than 60 percent of all enemy raids were made against these mock fields, lowering our aircraft losses.

The air engineering service, reorganized at the end of 1942, became much stronger in the second period of the war. Specialized knowledge and experience was acquired by the technical personnel. The men of this service worked in a better-organized fashion and through their heroic labors they made a large contribution to the successful completion of the air force assignments.

Much work was devoted to the reorganization and strengthening of the air force repair services. Four mobile air repair shops (PARM-1) for the repair of aircraft were set up, and one for the repair of specialized equipment. They were attached to air divisions and the shops in air regiments were also strengthened. Special mobile air repair bases were set up for the repair of aircraft engines, propellers, and radio and electrical equipment. Production of spare aircraft parts was increased in the front's repair shops.

As the result of these measures a strong repair network was organized. Teams of workers from factories played a major part in this repair service. In 1943, 2303 aircraft were repaired. The percent of disabled aircraft in the Front's air forces decreased constantly.

The quality of the repair services was improved by the works of efficiency experts who developed equipment and worked out various time-saving devices and installations to improve repairs and utilization of machinery.

Tactical Developments. Development of tactics for different kinds of aircraft was very much influenced by the appearance of new aircraft types, by the modification of old aircraft, and also by the widespread use of radio communications.

Enjoying a qualitative superiority over the enemy, our fighter aircraft went over completely to formations that were set by the front at differing altitudes to assure great flexibility in air combat. The battles in the spring and summer of 1943 saw a further development in air formations. Fighter planes were dispersed by altitudes, both when they were on the way to their assignments as well as in their operational areas. When new types of aircraft began to appear (especially the La-5), our fliers began to use vertical attacks more frequently.

Fighter operations were also aided by the improvements in ground and air control as the use of radio became widespread. Now it was possible to transmit timely information to pilots about the situation in the air, direct their flights, change their targets, and warn them of impending enemy attack. Now it was possible to increase the number of aircraft in the air by summoning stand-by aircraft from the ground. Improvements in aircraft and the adoption of radio for controlling aircraft made it possible to move the patrol zone beyond the battle lines, which much increased the probability of intercepting enemy aircraft.

Air battles, as a rule, involved more aircraft and lasted longer. In a number of cases they went on continuously for several days and became general air battles. Fighter air groups were assigned action regions or action zones. This increased the accountability of commanders for intercepting and destroying enemy aircraft and increased the activity of our fighters.

The technique of "free hunting" was utilized more frequently. During the Soviet counterattack in the winter of 1943 it was successfully utilized against enemy transports that were supplying their encircled troop concentrations. "Hunters" in the spring took off for the flight paths of enemy bombers over the northern Caucasus, and in sudden attacks caused them great losses. Often airfields were blockaded. Two or three pairs of fighters were assigned to each airfield at an altitude as high as 2500 meters (8200 feet) to attack enemy aircraft as they attempted to take off.

To protect bombers and ground-attack planes during the daytime, it was usual for fighter planes to accompany them to the target and back. Experience was gained in protecting them in the target region. In this case, fighter planes appeared in the target area two or three minutes before the arrival of the bombers or ground-attack planes, and either joined battle with enemy fighters or drove them from the area. Sometimes our fighters flew to the area where they expected enemy planes to appear and thus shielded the approaches to the region where our bombers and ground-attack planes would be operating.

Ground-attack aircraft in the second period of the war increased the range of their activities. Early in the war the major assignment for ground-attack aircraft was destruction of the advancing enemy tank and mechanized columns, but in the second period of the war their major efforts were directed toward supporting our troops by carrying out defensive and offensive operations to disrupt railroad and highway communications, to aid the battle against enemy aircraft, and also to conduct aerial reconnaissance.

When carrying out their assignments, ground-attack planes employed for the most part two techniques: concentrated attacks in large numbers at air regiment or air division strength, or in waves in groups of six to twelve aircraft. In addition, ground-attack aircraft also did "free hunting." In this case the crews were assigned a region or zone for operations and then allowed freedom to choose targets and the method of attack. Ground-attack "hunters" usually flew in pairs, and sometimes in flights. Sorties were flown at low altitudes, taking advantage of local ground contours and weather conditions.

The basic ground-attack formation was one pair of aircraft. Squadrons flew usually in units of six or eight planes in a "line" formation or a "wedge," and regiments, depending on the target size, in a "snake" or a "column" of squadrons. To utilize the formation's defense potential, a "circle" of individual aircraft, pairs, and flights were used more often to provide dense fire cover, a circular field of vision, and great maneuverability. Individual pairs or groups of ground-attack aircraft were assigned to attack antiaircraft installations in the target area.

Demolition, fragmentation, and incendiary bombs were used more often and also the self-igniting liquids "KS" in "AZh-2" casings. Antitank bombs were first used in the battle for Kursk. The damage to tanks, self-propelled guns, armored trains, and other armored targets became much higher when they were used.

When the two-seat Il-2 ground-attack plane was equipped with a rear machine gun, its defense against enemy fighters was increased. Having more powerful cannons, the Il-2 issued in 1943 often attacked not only bombers and transport aircraft, but also enemy fighters, and in some occasions was used to protect ground troops.

Bomber tactics were improved as the old aircraft were replaced by the new Pe-2s. As they were employed in battle, it was discovered that they had additional capabilities and they were used more and more for dive-bombing at an angle of 50–60 degrees. In the 2nd Guards Bomber Air Corps, squadrons were employed in dive-bombing, which gave especially good results in attacks on bridges, river crossings, and fortified areas. The experience acquired in such areas was studied, and at the end of 1943 special instructions were issued for bombers. In the second half of 1943, bombers began to operate more often in regiments and divisions, and as a result their raids became more effective and their defense capabilities improved.

In many cases, bombs that gave off light were employed in night bombing raids. Searchlights were utilized to guide aircraft to their targets, and also the firing of tracer shells by artillery. Rigid controls were set up for evaluating the results of bombing raids. In the AFLRO, for example, in every regiment and division there were controllers from among the commanding officers, political officers, and staff officers, who remained in the target area and observed the accuracy of the bomb drops made by all the crews. This increased the effectiveness of the raids.

Beginning in summer 1943, air corps and divisions of the AFLRO began to use an improved organization. In addition to the strike group, there were also planes for protective purposes, which were given the task of blockading enemy airfields; putting down his anti-aircraft guns; searching out, illuminating, and designating targets; aerial photography; and weather observation. There was an improvement in coordination with the ground forces and the aircraft of the fronts. The air armies built night emergency airfields for their crews and radio-locating stations for the use of the AFLRO.

Political Work.　The success of the air force operations, to a significant degree, depended on well-organized party and political work whose purpose was above all to aid the commands in the completion of assignments. The bases of this work were the resolutions of the Communist party Central Committee, and the orders and instructions of the Supreme Command and the Supreme Political Department of the Armed Forces of the USSR.

By the order of the Presidium of the Supreme Soviet of the USSR dated November 10, 1942, commanders of units and groups were permitted to grant honors to soldiers who distinguished themselves in battle. This increased the ease of awarding honors. In January 1943, epaulets were introduced as new marks of distinction among personnel.‡ In order to instruct the army to regard their military duty highly, the decision was taken to award designations to units and groups that distinguished themselves in battle.

The profound and extensive clarification of documents and requirements of the party and the government to the air force personnel was the most important problem of all the ideological-political work in the air units. Every day information was disseminated about our battle experiences and the heroism of our men. This was all part of the promotion of a feeling of mutual aid and military comradeship.

The political and party organizations gave great attention to the development of a patriotic movement for the collection of funds for the construction of aircraft, which was begun on the initiative of the collective farm workers of the Saratov region. The men of the air units and groups responded warmly to this call. For example, more than 1,764,000 rubles were collected from the 2nd Air Army by January 8, 1943, for the construction of aircraft. In 1943, 1360 aircraft were constructed from funds collected by workers and soldiers. This patriotic movement reflected the love of Soviet citizens for their

---

‡ Officers now were distinguished from enlisted men by epaulets worn on the shoulders of the dress uniform. ED.

air force and their eagerness to rout the hated enemy the more quickly.

Great attention was given to the propagandization of the heroic past of our people and its army. In connection with this, the Supreme Political Department on May 25, 1943, sent a special directive to the army.

Great attention was given to the reorganization of political groups, and of party and Comsomol organizations in accordance with the Communist party Central Committee decision dated May 24, 1943. The duties of the deputy for political affairs to the commander of each unit was merged with the functions of the chief of the political department. Within air squadrons, companies, and battalions of airfield service, the office of the deputy to the commander for political affairs was abolished. In the AFLRO regiments and also in bomber and transport air units, party and Comsomol bureaus to represent the party committees and local party organizations in the squadrons were created. Many young men became the leaders in the party and Comsomol organizations.

Competently directing various kinds of work, the party and political organs of the air force supported the high morale of the fliers, which, together with battle skills, gave rise to courage, daring, and heroism in combat. Evidence for the combat services of the air force can be seen in the increase in the number of awards and honorable designations. During the second period of the war, 107 air regiments, 34 divisions, and 7 ·corps were designated as guards units. In 1943 the following became guards units: the 1st Fighter Corps (commanded by General V. A. Ushakov), the 1st Composite Air Corps (commanded by General V. I. Aladinsky), the 1st Ground-Attack Air Corps (commanded by General V. G. Ryazanov). The following were designated as guards divisions: the 220th Fighter Air Division (commanded by Col. A. V. Utin), the 226th Ground-Attack Air Division (commanded by Col. F. Z. Boldyrikhin), and 263rd Bomber Air Division (commanded by Col. R. I. Dobysh). During this period, 44 air units received government awards, and 148, honorable designations. A thousand fliers were given government awards.

Great service was provided to Soviet air power by the air forces of the rear military districts and the air training institutes, which under difficult wartime circumstances provided the front with an adequate number of trained cadre and reserves.

The results of the second period of the war showed that the Soviet

Air Force in bitter struggles with fascist Germany had the power to force the Luftwaffe to resort to defensive tactics. The Soviet Air Force deprived the Luftwaffe of the power to influence significantly the outcome of the armed struggle along the entire Soviet-German front. In these battles the air force was enriched by combat experiences and improved its organization. The increasing power of the air force had much to do with the successful continuation of the offensive operations of the Red Army in the next period of the war.

Part Three

THE AIR FORCE IN THE PERIOD
OF DRIVING THE ENEMY FROM THE USSR,
AND FASCIST GERMANY'S FINAL DEFEAT
(January 1944 to May 1945)

IX

AIR OPERATIONS OVER LENINGRAD AND NOVGOROD

During the victorious air battles of 1943 the Soviet Air Force seized control of the air and supported the ground forces as they routed huge enemy troop concentrations, and liberated more than 1,000,000 square kilometers (386,000 square miles) of our territory seized by the enemy, upon which 46,000,000 citizens had lived before the war.

The Soviet Air Force continually grew stronger during the war. In 1943 the workers in the rear produced 35,000 aircraft, which made it possible to compensate for our losses and, by the beginning of 1944, assured a 2.5 times superiority in numbers over the enemy.* The air force also had a full supply of military supplies and equipment.[1]

In spite of the Anglo-American air raids against the German aircraft factories, German industry in 1942 increased its aircraft production by 66 percent, producing 25,000 aircraft in 1943.[2] At the beginning of 1944 the German Air Force had more than 6000 military aircraft out of which 2340 operated against the Red Army, 1800 operated on the Western Front, and 900 were located in Germany.†

Favorable conditions allowed the Soviet Supreme Command to plan and prepare several strategic offensives on the most important

---

* There were 8500 Soviet military aircraft available in January 1944. ED.
† Of these German aircraft, 2462 were fighters, 2205 bombers and ground-attack, and the rest recon or transport types, the latter being concentrated almost entirely on the Eastern Front.[3] ED.

sectors of the front. The basic purpose of these operations was first, to annihilate the flanking groups of enemy troops at Leningrad and in the south of our country, and then in White Russia and other important regions.

At the end of 1944 the troops of the Leningrad Front took defensive positions along the coast and to the southeast of Leningrad, while to the south of them were the troops of the Volkhov and Second Baltic Fronts. They were opposed by the German Army Group North, which had constructed a strong, multizoned defense line 250 kilometers (155 miles) deep.

Troops of the Leningrad and Volkhov Fronts were given the task of smashing the flanking groups of the 18th German Army southwest of Leningrad and in the Novgorod region, breaking the blockade of Leningrad, and then advancing toward Kingisepp and Luga and thereby liberating the Leningrad district and creating the preconditions for driving the enemy from the territory of the Soviet Baltic republics.

Preparations. Before the operation the fronts' units were reinforced and were twice as strong as the enemy in infantry and artillery, and almost 6.2 times stronger in tanks and self-propelled guns. The troops strengthened their operational bases.

The 13th and 14th Air Armies, units from the AFLRO, the 2nd Guards Fighter Corps from ADF, and aircraft from the Baltic Fleet, all in all more than 1200 aircraft, were assigned to support the troops from the fronts. In addition, it was planned to bring up also the 15th Air Army from the 2nd Baltic Front.

The 13th Air Army (commanded by General S. D. Rybalchenko) together with some units from the fleet, and fighter aircraft from the ADF and AFLRO units, were to support the offensive of the 2nd Strike Army and the 42nd Army from the Leningrad Front, with the goal of surrounding and destroying the enemy concentrations in the area of Krasnoye Selo, Ropsha, and Strelna; then they were to join the drive toward Kingisepp and Gatchina.

The 14th Air Army (commanded by General I. P. Zhuravlev) was assigned to the support of the Volkhov Front's 59th Army, which was to advance toward Novgorod. When the offensive developed toward Luga our aircraft were to join in the destruction of the 18th German Army and to support Leningrad Front troops.

The Offensive Begins near Leningrad. The Soviet offensive began on the morning of January 14. The night before the offensive, bombers from the fronts and long-range bombers struck in bad weather against the enemy artillery that was shelling Leningrad.

The troops of the 2nd Strike Army after an artillery barrage and raids from the naval air force (commanded by General M. I. Samokhin) began to advance toward Ropsha. Striking in waves of small groups of planes, or as solitary planes, the aircraft hit at enemy artillery, pillboxes, and at counterattacking tanks. Our troops, after having overcome the enemy's stubborn resistance, had advanced about 4 kilometers (2½ miles) by the end of the day.

The next day the 42nd Army took the offensive. During the preliminary artillery barrage, thirty Il-2s from the 277th Ground-Attack Air Division of the 13th Air Army bombed enemy artillery in bad weather, and just before our infantry attacked, ground-attack planes in small groups attacked enemy fire points and trenches in the major defense zone.

Our offensive was supported by ground-attack planes and bombers, which bombed resistance points and artillery from low altitudes. During the day our air force flew 284 sorties, putting out of commission 47 field artillery and antiaircraft batteries and destroying 3 other artillery and 13 mortar batteries, as well as many foot soldiers. The 275th Fighter Air Division (commanded by Col. A. A. Matveyev) also flew support for the ground troops.

The enemy resisted stubbornly. A fierce battle developed during the next three days. Both armies of the front brought in mobile forces—tank brigades and reserve troops who expanded the offensive with the help of the air force. The 13th Air Army and the fleet air force also gave their support, especially for tank units. Groups of Il-2s from the 9th and 277th Ground-Attack Air Divisions were constantly over the battlefield effectively attacking enemy forces hindering the advance of our armored units.

A group of Il-2s under the command of squadron commander First Lt. G. M. Parshin was extremely effective in this period. These fliers were over the battlefield as long as thirty-five minutes at a time and made as many as six passes against their targets, effectively striking against enemy fire points.

G. M. Parshin was given the title Hero of the Soviet Union for courage and daring displayed in the struggle against the enemy of our Motherland. Parshin, a daring and audacious master of ground-attack techniques, was at the front until the end of the war and in April 1945 he was given a second "Gold Star" of the Hero of the Soviet Union.

The 277th Ground-Attack Air Division commander, Col. F. S. Khatminsky, competently and effectively controlled his fliers from his mobile command point located within the 220th Tank Brigade area. He had constant radio contact with his radio officers, who were in tanks and who opportunely directed groups of ground-attack planes to their targets.

At the same time that our air force was giving direct support to our advancing troops, it was also engaged in bombing the German reserves moving up to the front. Bombers from the fronts, on the nights of January 16 and 17, hit enemy troops on the roads leading to Krasnoye Selo. Long-range bombers struck at enemy resistance centers in the 42nd Army area, and the fleet air force struck against the command post and communication centers of the enemy 9th Air Division. During these two nights long-range bombers dropped 876 tons of bombs and caused considerable losses to the enemy in men and materials.

On January 19, Front and naval air force planes and also ADF fighters flew in small groups against enemy troops and equipment in support of the 42nd and 2nd Strike Armies. After the city of Ropsha had been liberated by our troops, a special commission to evaluate the effectiveness of our air raids found a large number of bomb craters in a town where a German command had been located. A direct hit from a 500 kilogram (1100 pound) demolition bomb had smashed the command point of the 9th Air Division, destroyed a communication center, killed about thirty soldiers and officers, and disrupted the communications within the units of the division.

These operations were carried out under heavy antiaircraft fire. The flying crews undertaking these operations showed great skill, courage, audacity, and heroism. A group of fighters under squadron commander First Lt. M. F. Sharonov from the 191st Fighter Air Regiment especially distinguished themselves.

On January 16, 1944, M. F. Sharonov led his squadron on a ground attack against retreating enemy columns along the highway between Pavlovsk and the station at Stekolny. The fascists sent a shower of antiaircraft fire against our first fighter planes. The squadron commander made eight runs against the enemy column and his fliers followed bravely after him, destroying both men and equipment with their machine-gun fire. The commander's plane was hit and tongues of flame appeared in the cockpit. The daring lover of the Motherland was true to his oath. He guided his burning plane onto a concentration of enemy troops and at the price of his life destroyed a large number of German soldiers and officers. By order of the Presidium of the Supreme Soviet, M. F. Sharonov was post-humously awarded the title Hero of the Soviet Union for his feats in the struggle with the fascist German invaders.

Other fliers—Second Lt. L. I. Sazykin, V. A. Shcherbin, and the deputy commander of a regiment from the 9th Ground-Attack Air Division of the naval air force, Captain A. I. Irzhak and his machine-gunner Seaman V. D. Zhdanov—repeated the immortal feat of First Lt. Sharonov.

During the first six days of the operation, the Soviet Air Force flew more than 2500 sorties. This was a great help for the ground troops as they broke through the strongly defended enemy defense zone and routed his troops. The 9th and 277th Ground-Attack Air Divisions were given, respectively, the designations the "Ropsha" Division and the "Krasnoye Selo" Division for their successful operations. Several air regiments were given the order of the Red Banner; and the 73rd Bomber Air Regiment, Baltic Fleet Air Force, was redesignated as the 12th Guards Bomber Air Regiment.

The Volkhov Front. At this same time there was another fierce battle under way. The troops of the 59th Army of the Volkhov Front went on the offensive on January 14 from their base north of Novgorod. Our aircraft could not fly because of the bad weather. The enemy troops resisted bitterly. South of Novgorod our troops crossed Lake Ilmen on the ice, suddenly attacked the enemy, and seized a bridgehead.

Groups from the 14th Air Army struck at bunkers and artillery at a major resistance point, Podberezye, which blocked the pass between marshes and the Volkhov River. Our fliers flew 200 sorties against this point on January 15 and 16, dropping several hundred bombs and causing considerable damage that helped our troops, who were soon to break through the German defense, overrun this resistance point at Podberezye, and cut the road between Chudovo and Novgorod.

At the same time during the day ground-attack planes and fighters, and at night Po-2s, hindered the enemy retreat along the only route that still remained to him from Novgorod to the west. Fighter planes from the 269th Fighter Air Division under Captain V. P. Sinchuk were especially effective against enemy motorized columns. On January 19, when he discovered a column of vehicles northwest of Novgorod, Communist Sinchuk summoned a group of ground-attack planes. Before they arrived his fighters stopped the advance of the column and caused it great losses. Then a group of Il-2s arrived from the 281st Ground-Attack Air Division. With their combined attacks the fighters and ground-attack planes destroyed or damaged about 75 vehicles and 20 wagons with their cargoes and their personnel.

On the morning of January 20, the 59th Army troops surrounded the enemy east of Lyubolyada and captured Novgorod by storm. The 281st Ground-Attack and 269th Fighter Air Divisions, and the 4th Guards Bomber and 386th Night Bomber Air Regiments, were given the name of "Novgorod" units.

During the seven-day battle the Volkhov Front troops broke through the entrenched enemy lines and with the help of the air force opened a breach about 50 kilometers (31 miles) wide. Advancing 20 kilometers (12½ miles), they routed two enemy infantry divisions and additional units.

On January 12 the 2nd Baltic Front, with the help of 15th Air Army aircraft, went on the offensive at Novosokolniki and on January 19 overran the station at Narva and pinned down the German 16th Army, which contributed to the successful offensives of the Leningrad and Volkhov Fronts.

Leningrad Blockade Broken. The great losses which the flanking German 18th Army had suffered and the fear of encirclement forced the enemy to begin to withdraw out of his Mginsk salient. Beginning on January 21 our line of advance stretched from the Gulf of Finland to Lake Ilmen and was then transformed into a pursuit of the 18th German Army with the goal of annihilating it. Aircraft of the 13th and 14th Air Armies, in spite of low clouds (at 100 to 200 meters, or 330 to 660 feet) and limited visibility, supported the offensive of the 2nd Strike Army and the 42nd and 59th Armies.

During this offensive the enemy gave great attention to defense of his major resistance points, which made it necessary periodically to strike concentrated air blows in order to destroy them. On

January 24 and 25 the 13th Air Army, part of the ADF units, and the naval air force flew in support of the 42nd Army offensive aimed at seizing Gatchina, a major enemy resistance point. During these two days these aircraft flew 432 sorties. Bombers from the 276th Bomber Air Division led by Capts. P. I. Syrchin and N. I. Kuzmenko were especially effective. Flying with fighter cover, they made precise hits on enemy men and materials, dampened his artillery fire, and disorganized his defense. These units received a commendation from the General Army Command.

Simultaneously, the Front and long-range bombers were raiding the enemy reserves and limiting their approach to the cities of Gatchina and Volosovo. Then they dropped bombs on the railroad stations at Siverskaya and Volosovo. During the night of January 26, 227 aircraft dropped 243 tons of bombs on the yards and trains there, causing significant enemy losses and blocking the movement of troops from Narva and Luga.

During the first stage of the offensive (January 14–30, 1944) the aircraft of the 13th and 14th Air Armies in extremely bad weather conditions flew more than 4500 sorties, of which more than 70 percent were in direct support of ground troops. A low level of activity by the Luftwaffe made it possible to utilize fighter planes against the retreating enemy troops and railroad trains, and for aerial reconnaissance.

The Soviet Air Force gave great aid to the troops of the fronts as they broke through the deep enemy defense, pursued the enemy, and caused him great losses. With air force help, the troops advanced from 30 to 100 kilometers (18–62 miles), broke the blockade of Leningrad, and liberated many cities in the Leningrad district as well as the October railroad.

The victory at Leningrad was celebrated on January 27, 1944, with a great artillery salute. The Presidium of the Supreme Soviet of the USSR established the medal "For the defense of Leningrad," and on January 26, 1945, the city was given the order of Lenin, thereby giving it the name of the "Hero City."

The February Offensive. After this victory over the German troops at Leningrad and Novgorod, our aircraft from January 31 to February 15, 1944, took an active role in pursuing the enemy toward Narva, Gdov, and Luga. In this period, the air forces' basic goal was to thwart the enemy attempts to halt our advance and to rescue the remnants of his 18th Army at the rear edge of the defense zone at Narva-Pskov-Ostrov.

Part of the naval air force operated over the Narva region, and the 13th Air Army and 2nd Guards Fighter Air Corps (commanded by General N. D. Antonov), which had 150 aircraft, over Gdov and Luga. In order to increase our air activity, the commanders of air groups were given the right to call down strikes at the request of the commanders of general armies and infantry corps, and also as the result of aerial reconnaissance. When it was necesssary, aircraft were concentrated in one of these regions when the situation demanded more air power.

During the course of the first three days of the pursuit after the enemy troops, the aircraft of the Leningrad Front flew more than 1000 sorties. Aerial observers sent out groups of ground-attack planes, bombers, and fighters, which attacked the retreating enemy troops on roads, river crossings, and in areas of concentration. When our aircraft caused traffic jams and disorganized the enemy retreat, it was a great help for our troops who were liberating the city of Kingisepp and seizing a bridgehead on the west bank of the Narva River.

Our fighter planes were also active against the enemy. On February 1, a flight from the 11th Guards Fighter Air Regiment of the ADF, commanded by Major G. N. Zhidov, Hero of the Soviet Union, discovered two enemy troops columns 30 kilometers (18 miles) north of Luga. The leader reported to his command post what he had seen and ordered his planes to attack these columns. A few minutes later seven fighters from the 26th Guards Fighter Air Regiment arrived. Making several passes, our fliers destroyed about 25 vehicles and killed a considerable number of enemy soldiers and officers with machine-gun fire and rockets.

As our troops advanced toward Pskov, it appeared that they might be a threat to the communication lines of the German concentration at Luga. The enemy began to shift his reserves into that area in order to prepare a counterattack against the 42nd Army. On February 6 and 7, 50 bombers, 60 ground-attack planes, and 79 fighter planes from the 13th Air Army attacked reserves moving from Pskov toward Lyady. Later on, partisans from the village of Demyanovka confirmed that an enemy column had been destroyed that consisted of 300 vehicles with men and equipment, 200 loaded wagons, 20 guns, and a railroad train with military supplies. They watched as the Germans collected the corpses of more than 200 officers and men.

Subsequent strikes from our aircraft against advancing reserves contributed to the disruption of the enemy's counterattack against the 42nd Army troops, who had liberated Lyady, crossed the Plyussa River, and destroyed two regiments of the 58th German Infantry Division northwest of Chernoye Lake, in conjunction with our air power and partisans.

In the Narva area the air force continued to support the offensive of the 2nd Strike Army. On February 1944 with continuous cloud cover at 50–150 meters (165–500 feet), 102 aircraft from the 277th Ground-Attack and 275th Fighter Air Divisions struck in small groups at artillery and mortar batteries and personnel in the trenches along the Narva defense line. This systematic air support helped our troops to expand their bridgehead southwest of Narva.

The enemy, striving to restrain our advance, began to increase his air activity. On January 31 there were about 240 German aircraft opposing the Leningrad Front, instead of the 120 which had been there at the beginning of the operation, and by the end of February there were about 400 in this area.

Great attention was given to the provision of air protection for the river crossings of the 2nd Strike Army bridgehead. The utilization of "hunters," as well as patrolling fighter planes, assured the interception of enemy planes. On February 7, two flights of planes from the 1st Fighter Air Division of the naval air force commanded by Capts. Ye. M. Karpunin and V. M. Dmitriyev were assigned to "free hunting" along the expected routes of enemy bombers, and one flight was assigned to patrol over our river crossings. Two enemy bomber groups were intercepted by our fighters 25–35 kilometers (15–22 miles) from the river crossings. As a result, they jettisoned their bombs before they reached their targets. A third group was attacked by our patrolling fighter planes and did not have the time to employ bombsights as they dropped their bombs. As the result of these air battles, the enemy lost five bombers and one fighter and was not able to complete his assignment. The 159th Fighter Air Regiment, commanded by Major P. A. Pokryshev, two times Hero of the Soviet Union, was also active in repelling enemy aircraft.

Near Luga the 14th Air Army continued to support the Volkhov Front offensive. Taking advantage of the fact that bad weather grounded all aircraft, the enemy brought in fresh reserves and stubbornly resisted the advance of our troops. Our aircraft were most active southwest of Luga. With their accurate bombing raids and ground attacks, our aircraft supported the troops of the front as they repelled enemy counterattacks. Planes from the 269th Fighter Air Division commanded by Captain V. P. Sinchuk was sent against enemy bombers and attacked them courageously. As the result of this battle, four enemy bombers and one fighter were shot down by our fighter planes. On April 13, 1944, Captain V. P. Sinchuk was given the title of Hero of the Soviet Union for his outstanding accomplishments.

The units of the 13th and 14th Air Armies carried on their operations in close cooperation with the troops of the Front. Efforts between the air armies was supported by a constant stream of information about assignments, regions of operations, and post-attack evaluations. The staffs of the armies exchanged information by radio, assuring prompt dissemination of data.

Troops of the 67th Leningrad Front, with the support of our air power, liberated Tolmachevo on February 9, and began to surround Luga and advance toward Strugi Krasnye. From February 6 to 11 our air force flew 700 sorties and destroyed about 200 wagons, 134 railroad cars, and many enemy ground troops.

On February 12, our troops liberated the towns of Batetskaya and Luga. The enemy continued his retreat on the road to Pskov. Our air force disrupted his withdrawal. On February 14, a large enemy column was attacked by ground-attack planes from the 281st Ground-Attack Division and then bombers from the 280th Composite Air Division bombed it. As the result of these air attacks, about 75 vehicles with their crews were destroyed and fuel tanks were blown up.

Troops of the 2nd Baltic Front, with the help of the 15th Air Army, continued their advance to the west of Novosokolniki. From January 31 to February 7 our air force flew around 2000 sorties, half of which were at night. The advance of our troops was insignificant, but they pinned down the German 16th Army and it was not able to give any real aid to the 18th Army as it tried to halt the Soviet advance.

The transport air regiments of the Civil Air Fleet and the 13th Air Army, and AFLRO units during this operation delivered 278 tons of equipment and 383 individuals to partisans; in turn they evacuated about 740 men including 592 who were seriously wounded. Partisans liberated a number of large populated areas: Oredezh, Gdov, and the station at Plyussa, wiped out enemy garrisons in conjunction with the troops of the fronts, and paralyzed movement in the enemy's rear, blowing up 58,563 rails and 300 bridges and derailing 133 German trains with men and supplies.

The rout of the enemy concentration at Luga and the break-through of his defense line at the Luga River ended the second period of the offensive operation. During this period our aircraft flew 4637 sorties. The troops of the Leningrad and the Volkhov Fronts with air support had pursued the retreating enemy 50–100 kilometers (31–62 miles).

After the Leningrad region had been liberated (February 16 to March 1), the major assignment of the Fronts' air force was to cooperate with the troops of the Leningrad and the 2nd Baltic Front to expand the offensive toward Narva and Pskov-Ostrov. (The Volkhov Front was dissolved at this time. The 14th Air Army became part of the Leningrad Front. After February 26, its staff became part of the reserves of the *Stavka* and its air groups became part of the 13th Air Army.)

Our fighter aircraft also took an active part in the campaign against enemy troops in the Narva region. On February 16, eighteen planes from the 191st Fighter Air Regiment commanded by Major A. G. Grinchenko attacked enemy ground troops at low level near the railroad station and road junction at Iykhvi, 45 kilometers (28 miles) west of Narva. When they were in the target region the fliers first dropped their bombs on troop concentrations and equipment and then followed this with several strafing runs in which they killed many enemy soldiers and officers.

As the weather improved, the number of Soviet aircraft flights increased almost threefold. From time to time, mass raids were made against enemy troops. On February 18, 104 ground-attack planes and 120 fighter planes from the fronts and the naval air force attacked artillery batteries and defense positions on the west bank of the Narva River in the area under attack from the 2nd Strike Army, and as a result, enemy artillery fire was dampened and the enemy defensive fortifications were damaged.

From February 22 to February 26, our air force continued to raid the enemy with 400 ground-attack planes and bombers with fighter protection. Aircraft from the AFLRO also supported the offensive.

On the nights of February 24 and 25 three of its corps (the 5th, 6th, and 7th) flew 1043 sorties, and dropped 1155 tons of bombs against enemy centers to the west of Narva causing the enemy great losses.

As the enemy increased the movement of his reserves there was also a great rise in the level of his air activity. There were more attacks against our troops. On February 18, about 160 enemy aircraft attacked our troops on the crossings and the far bank of the Narva and Plyussa rivers, and on February 26 there were 230 enemy aircraft involved in such an attack.

As the enemy raised his level of activity in the air, our fighters also increased their operations. In the last days of February we flew more than 1100 sorties to repel enemy attacks and to protect the 2nd Strike Army troops. In the second half of February, men from that army, with air force help, expanded their bridgehead on the west bank of the river to 35 kilometers (22 miles) in breadth and 15 kilometers (9 miles) in depth, thereby creating conditions for a further offensive to free Soviet Estonia.

The offensive of the 42nd and the 67th Armies toward Pskov was supported by part of the 13th Air Army. By the end of February the ground armies of the Front with the help of air power, approached the outermost limits of the fortified region at Pskov-Ostrov.

The 14th Air Army supported the offensive of the 8th and 54th Armies on the left flank of the Leningrad Front. (On February 26, the air groups of the 14th Air Army were transferred to the 13th Air Army and moved onto advance airfields.) Our aircraft were most active on February 18. That day units of the 280th Composite Air Division (commanded by Lt. Col. P. M. Podmogilny) struck effectively against enemy defensive positions, troops, and equipment along the west bank of the Mshaga River. This contributed to the breakthrough at the enemy's intermediate defense line and the expansion of the offensive at a later period.

In addition to ground support, at times our air force also struck against railroad targets. From February 16 to March 1, the 13th Air Army flew 492 sorties against targets on the line from Narva to Tallin, and from Plyussa to Pskov. On the night of February 18, 380 aircraft from the AFLRO dropped 547 tons of bombs on the railroad yards at Pskov. As a result about fifteen trains were burned as well as several warehouses and station buildings. To prevent German planes from attacking our bombers, the airfields at Pskov, Porkhov, and Dno were blockaded. The fact that the important railroad junc-

The Pe-2 was the most widely used Soviet bomber.

The heaviest wartime Soviet bomber was the Pe-8; the one shown was used to fly V. M. Molotov to Britain in May 1942.

The Tu-2 was used in the last year of the war.

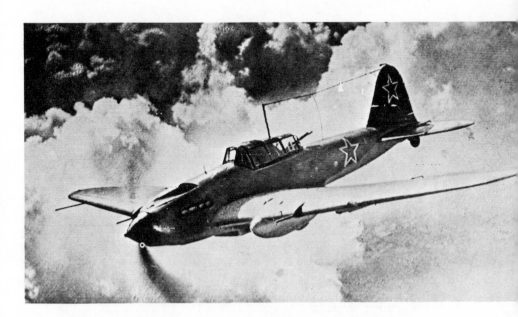

Over 36,000 Il-2 ground-attack planes were built.

Fighter pilots of a guards regiment in typical uniforms, with La-5 in rear.

The Su-2 light bomber was used during the war's first year by the composite divisions.

Designed in 1928, the R-5 still served some light night-bomber units in 1942.

These little U-2 trainers were used for night bombing, and renamed Po-2.

tion at Pskov was out of operation for several days greatly hindered the work in the enemy's operational rear and contributed to the success of our offensive.

Taking advantage of the favorable conditions created by the successful Leningrad front offensive, troops of the 2nd Baltic Front renewed their offensive on February 18. That day the 1st Strike Army liberated the city of Staraya Russa, and with the 54th Army of the Leningrad Front and the help of our air force, captured the railroad junction at Dno and advanced to the line between Novorzhev and Pustoshka.

Air operations were carried out in bad weather. In order to take advantage of brief spells of good weather, the 15th Air Army command concentrated regular groups of reconnaissance aircraft and air regiments of ground-attack planes and fighters on advance airfields. This made it possible to increase the activity level of Soviet aircraft and assured that enemy flights could be promptly repulsed by fighter units, which were always on the alert.

The offensive being carried out by units of the 1st Strike Army was supported only by reconnaissance and Po-2 night bombing raids, and the rest of the aircraft were concentrated in the support of the troops on the left wing of the front. During the second half of February, 2183 sorties were flown.

Over a two-day period bombing raids were conducted against enemy airfields in order to lower the level of enemy aircraft activities and to maintain control of the air. On February 26 there was a raid against one of these airfields by the 13th Air Army in the Tartu region. The first to attack were ground-attack planes at low levels and then these were followed by dive-bombing attacks from an altitude of 2500–2900 meters (8200–9500 feet). Twenty-one out of the 46 aircraft on the ground were destroyed as was later confirmed by aerial photos. Six German fighters were shot down in the air over the airfield without any losses to our air force. On the same day, 19 ground-attack planes and 36 fighters from the 9th Ground-attack Air Division of the Baltic Fleet attacked the airfield at Rakvere, where 8 of the 33 aircraft on the field were destroyed and 1 fighter plane was shot down as it took off.

The next day, 54 aircraft from the 15th Air Army bombed the airfield at Idritsa where 90 aircraft were stationed. The raid was carried out by two waves, the first consisting of six Il-2s flying at low level and the second consisting of two groups of six ground-attack planes which dive-bombed from an elevation of 1200 meters (3900 feet). At the same time fighters blockaded the airfield and participated, together with the ground-attack planes, in destroying enemy aircraft. As the result of this attack 32 planes were destroyed on the ground and 6 in the air. We lost 7 planes.

When our troops reached the enemy's major rear line, our fighter planes were more skilled in repelling enemy bombing raids. When the 275th Fighter Air Division was brought to the Pskov region to fight against enemy aircraft, our fighters became yet more effective as they repelled enemy bombers before they could attack the troops of the Leningrad Front, destroying 156 enemy aircraft in the air during the month of March.

During the offensive, the AFLRO bombed the ports of Kotka and Turku at night on February 10 and 22, disrupting the flow of strategic raw materials from Finland to Germany and reserve troops from Norway and Finland to Estonia. During these nights, 358 aircraft dropped 402 tons of bombs on port facilities and ships.

On the nights of February 6, 16, and 26, aircraft from the AFLRO made three raids on military-industrial targets near Helsinki. In these raids, 1980 aircraft dropped 2386 tons of bombs on military targets. The third raid was especially large, being carried out by 850 aircraft over a twelve-hour period using different approaches at different times from different altitudes.

In addition to supporting the offensive of the Leningrad Front the naval air force attacked transports, dropped mines, and attacked enemy warships, while naval fighter planes fought to control the air over the Gulf of Narva and to drive off enemy bombing raids. The naval air force secured the maritime flank of the Leningrad Front and also protected the flank and rear of the 2nd Strike Army.

During this offensive operation, our aircraft flew more than 6600 sorties and gave great help to the ground forces as they destroyed the 18th and 16th German Armies and liberated the Leningrad region. The ground troops with the support of air power advanced from 50 to 180 kilometers (31 to 112 miles).

Results. The victory gained by Soviet troops at Leningrad and Novgorod had great military and political significance. During the course of this offensive operation the enemy's northern strategic flank was destroyed, the blockade of Leningrad was broken, the city freed from any danger from artillery fire, the Leningrad and part of the Kalinin districts were liberated, a base was provided for the Red Banner Baltic fleet, and conditions were created for the liberation of Vyborg and the Soviet Baltic regions.

The Soviet Air Force, in spite of bad weather conditions, gave great assistance to the ground forces and the fleet as they fulfilled their assignments. Day and night it supported the offensive of our troops, fought enemy aircraft in the air, carried out aerial reconnaissance, bombed targets deep in the enemy rear, and supported partisans. As it carried out these tasks, the air force flew about 30,000 sorties and dropped 4500 tons of bombs. Two hundred and ninety enemy aircraft were destroyed on the ground or in the air. The arrival of units from the AFLRO, the naval air force, and fighters from the ADF, made it possible for the air command to increase its support of the ground forces, especially at the beginning and the end of the offensive operation. Experience was gained in the organization of coordinated efforts between different kinds of aircraft during the offensive operations carried out by the fronts.

During the offensive in bad weather, over an area which is both marshy and wooded, aerial reconnaissance became very important. It discovered troop concentrations and defense lines and followed enemy movements during an offensive. During the daytime, such assignments were carried out by fighters, and at night, Po-2 bombers continually observed enemy operations.

Before an operation began, and when it was being carried out, great attention was devoted to the air support services. Personnel of the rear units of the 13th Air Army supported military operations flown by the front aircraft and several corps of the AFLRO because there was a significant shortage in transportation facilities.

Ten air units were given guard status and were designated as Krasnoye Selo, Ropsha, Pushkin, Gatchina, and Novgorod units. Hundreds of fliers were given medals and many others were given the title Hero of the Soviet Union.

X

OVER THE RIGHT BANK OF THE DNIEPER

One of the major assignments given to the Red Army in the winter campaign of 1944 was the liberation of the right bank of the Dnieper, which was to have great military-political and economic significance. Preparations for this campaign began in autumn of 1943. At that time, troops of four fronts with the cooperation of both front aircraft and the AFLRO struck several powerful blows at German troops, liberated the Dnieper left bank, crossed the wide river barrier, seized several strategic bridgeheads, and brought back to the Motherland hundreds of population centers and cities, including the Ukrainian capital, Kiev.

The German command had not expected the powerful offensive made by Soviet troops in spring 1944 in the Ukraine. As they continued to prepare their defensive positions and to concentrate their men and aircraft, they planned on recapturing our bridgeheads on the right bank of the Dnieper and establishing communications with their forces cut off in the Crimea.

At the end of 1943, the Soviet Supreme Command planned a strategic offensive operation on the southern wing of the Soviet-German front. Its basic aim was to break the enemy defense line, rout the enemy's troops one unit after another, and liberate the right bank of the Dnieper. To this task were assigned the 1st, 2nd, 3rd, and 4th Ukrainian Fronts and, respectively, the 2nd, 5th, 17th, and 8th Air Armies, which had 2360 aircraft.

The Soviet armies were opposed by three German army groups and the 4th Air Fleet which, with more than 1460 aircraft, had 54 percent of the German aircraft based on the Soviet-German front.

At the beginning of the offensive, the Soviet Army had an advantage in men, guns, and mortars of 1.7 to 1, in aircraft 1.6 to 1, and was somewhat inferior to the enemy in tanks and self-propelled artillery. These armies were to become involved in stubborn battles in which more than 4,000,000 men, 4400 tanks and self-propelled guns, 44,800 cannons and mortars, and more than 3800 aircraft participated.

The 1st Ukrainian Front's Offensive. The operation for the liberation of the right bank of the Ukraine began on the morning of December 24, 1943. After an artillery barrage and air attack, troops of the 1st Ukrainian Front went on the offensive and in three days, together with Soviet air power, routed the opposing enemy forces and overran the strong point at Radomishlem. By December 30 the front had been pierced in an area 300 kilometers (186 miles) wide and as much as 100 kilometers (62 miles) deep.

Air groups from the 2nd Air Army (commanded by General S. A. Krasovsky) struck systematically at resistance points and retreating enemy troops as they supported the successful offensive of the 1st, 18th, and 38th Armies in the Zhitomir and Berdichev regions. Simultaneously the air force attacked railroad targets and enemy airfields. The most successful raid was on January 7 against the railroad junction at Shepetovka, by Il-2s from the 525th Ground-Attack Air Regiment commanded by I. M. Dolgov. In spite of heavy antiaircraft fire, the Soviet fliers broke through to the railroad junction jammed with trains, and on the command of their leader, dropped their bombs. As the result of this successful operation by seven daring crews, twelve enemy trains with their personnel, tanks, fuel, and supplies were destroyed and the railroad yard at Shepetovka put out of action for a long period. The fliers were given state medals for this successful operation. Twelve enemy aircraft were destroyed and a fuel dump was blown up in a later surprise raid made by the ground-attack regiment against the airfield at Vinnitsa.

The right wing of the 1st Ukrainian Front by the end of January had advanced about 200 kilometers (124 miles). When our troops advanced toward Vinnitsa and broke through in the Khristinovka region, the enemy group in the Korsun-Shevchenkovsky area appeared to be in danger of encirclement. Therefore the enemy was compelled to take a number of measures. At the beginning of January, there was a major shift of German troops and aircraft to the area of the 1st Ukrainian Front offensive. After he had concentrated his air power and had almost a double superiority in aircraft, the enemy began intensive operations. On January 10, he counterattacked in the Vinnitsa region and subsequently northwest of Uman.

Bitter fighting continued in the air and on the ground for two weeks. Units of the 2nd Air Army struck for the most part at enemy tank concentrations, and fought air battles, thus aiding our troops as they repulsed the enemy counterattack. In order to fulfill these tasks 4200 sorties were flown, including 2500 against enemy tanks. The Germans succeeded by January 24 in throwing back the troops of the 40th, 38th, and 1st Tank Armies 25–30 kilometers (15–18 miles), but only at the price of great losses.

The 2nd Ukrainian Front.   Men of the 2nd Ukrainian Front with the help of aircraft from the 5th Air Army (commanded by General S. K. Goryunov) went on the offensive on January 5, 1944. After an initial artillery barrage they broke the enemy's defenses and then, expanding their offensive with air support, three days later liberated Kirovograd. The Soviet Air Force flew 1100 sorties in the operation to free Kirovograd in three days. The troops were given great support, as a large number of aircraft were concentrated in a small area. The 1st Guards Bomber Division, the 205th and the 302nd Fighter Air Divisions, and the 1st Ground-Attack Air Corps were designated Kirovograd units for their successful operations.

At the same time that they supported ground troops, Soviet fliers were fighting the Luftwaffe in the air as it tried to stop the advance of our troops. On January 8, four fighters commanded by Hero of the Soviet Union First Lt. N. D. Gulayev, while flying cover for ground troops, attacked fifty German bombers and fighters. Taking advantage of the clouds, our fliers shot down four enemy planes in a sudden attack. In this brief battle, N. D. Gulayev shot down two German planes.

Troops from the 3rd and 4th Ukrainian Fronts with the support of the 17th and 8th Air Armies succeeded in driving only 5–10 kilometers (3–6 miles) into the enemy defenses from January 10 to January 16. The major reason for this was the lack of equipment, especially tanks, and other military gear, which was difficult to bring up because of the thaw that resulted in muddy roads.

Encirclement of the Enemy at Korsun.   At the middle of January, the enemy still held large areas in the regions of Korsun-Shevchenkovsky and Nikopol. Therefore, the *Stavka* made the following assignments: The 1st and 2nd Ukrainian Fronts were to surround and destroy the enemy in the region of Korsun-Shevchenkovsky, and the 3rd and 4th Ukrainian Fronts were to expand the subsequent offensive. Troops from the Fronts were given instructions from January 12 to January 25, while the 2nd and 5th Air Armies concentrated their efforts on the major enemy concentration.

When the operation at Korsun-Shevchenkovsky began, the 2nd and 5th Air Armies had 768 military aircraft. The enemy had about 1000 aircraft in the area.

The German command tried to halt our offensive, laying great hopes on the Luftwaffe. Our fliers supported ground operations. On January 24, fighter planes of the 4th Fighter Air Corps successfully fought off several large groups of German aircraft, thus disrupting enemy plans.

The offensive of the 2nd Ukrainian Front against the enemy troops in the Korsun-Shevchenkovsky region began on January 25, and that of the 1st Ukrainian Front on January 26. These ground and air operations were carried out in bad weather (clouds at 100–150 meters [328–490 feet], fog, snow). Our planes flew in groups of four or eight in support of ground troops.

Aerial reconnaissance was very important for ground operations. This was done by the most experienced ground-attack and fighter crews to assure immediate information for both ground and air commands. A constant flow of information contributed toward the most effective use of the small number of sorties that could be flown in the bad weather.

Later, as the enemy troops at Korsun-Shevchenkovsky were being surrounded, the spring thaw put our field airports out of action. Some days the air armies had only one or two open airfields, but the need for air power was very great. Therefore the command was compelled to concentrate several air regiments with different kinds of aircraft on one field in order to assure constant operations against the enemy.

In addition to attacking enemy troops on the battlefield, our aircraft also attacked reserves as they neared the battle area. On January 31, thanks to a reconnaissance report made by Captain G. T. Krasota, a raid was made against a column of tanks and other vehicles approaching the village at Shpola. The next day, Krasota, together with First Lt. I. Kh. Mikhaylichenko, discovered about seventy enemy tanks advancing toward Shpola from the south, attacked the head of the column, and stopped its advance. For the entire day, crews of the 1st Guards Ground-Attack Air Corps attacked this column, causing great losses to the enemy. During the entire operation Captain Krasota continued his reconnaissance operations in bad weather, and also struck against the enemy, displaying daring and heroism for which he was given the title Hero of the Soviet Union.

These air attacks stopped the movement of German tanks toward the battlefield, contributing toward the success of the 5th Guard Tank Army, the 4th Guard Army, and the 53rd Army in repelling the enemy counterattack, and by Jauary 28, troops of the 1st and 2nd Ukrainian Fronts completed the encirclement of the enemy's Korsun-Shevchenkovsky troop concentration.

On the morning of February 2 the enemy began massive counter-attacks in order to provide an escape route for his encircled troops. A very difficult situation developed for our troops because we had so few reserves in this region. The air force came to their aid. The commander of the 5th Air Army sent units of the 1st Guards Ground-Attack Corps to destroy the enemy's counterattacking tank units. In a short period the ground-attack planes flew 127 sorties. They caused great losses to the enemy and gave timely aid to the 5th Tank Army and the 53rd Army in repelling the enemy counterattacks.

Our fighter aircraft were also very active, retaining control of the air as the enemy troops were being surrounded, and protecting our troops. From January 29 to February 3, more than 120 air battles were fought and 130 enemy aircraft shot down.

In spite of difficult circumstances, the 2nd and 5th Air Armies flew more than 2800 sorties from January 29 to February 3, while enemy planes flew only half as many. Such a high level of sorties, in spite of bad weather and the spring thaw, was the result of the initiative and persistence of all the men of the air units in carrying out their military assignments, and the excellent air crew training and their eagerness to give the greatest possible help to our troops surrounding the enemy.

When the enemy had been surrounded the German command tried to supply them from the air, and also to break through our lines. Therefore a large number of tanks and infantry were concentrated west of Zvenigorodka and a large number of aircraft were recruited for their support.

In order to insure the successful destruction of the encircled enemy concentration, the authority over all our forces was given to the commander of the 2nd Ukrainian Front. Support of the ground troops was entrusted to the 5th Air Army and the air blockade was assigned to the 2nd Air Army and the 10th Fighter Air Corps of the ADF.

After regrouping their forces, our troops moved to annihilate the enemy on February 3.

In spite of bad weather, our air force flew day and night, supporting ground troops, fighting enemy planes in the air, transporting supplies to our troops, and carrying out aerial reconnaissance. Because artillery and tank units could advance only slowly and because it was difficult to supply them with military supplies and fuel by truck during the spring thaw, air power played a very important role in the operation against the enemy concentration at Korsun-Shevchenkovsky.

At the same time our air force took an active role in repelling German counterattacks against our outer lines in the Tolmach and Lisyanka regions.

The most critical situation developed on February 4 in the area held by the 53rd Army. Enemy tank units drove into our lines. Emergency help was needed from the air force. General I. I. Vorobyev, Chief of Staff of the 53rd Army, sent the following radio message: "Smash the tanks and armored vehicles in the regions of Sobolevka and Tolmach—they are the enemy's. Don't touch the artillery—it is ours."

The encircled enemy troops were under constant attack from our aircraft. On February 8, a raid of our ground-attack planes and bombers against enemy troops forced them to abandon their strong point at Gorodishche. From February 4 to February 18, 5th Air Army planes flew more than 1400 sorties.

When the encirclement of the enemy troops was being completed, about 3000 Germans collected in the village of Shandorovka where they set up a defense point. The night of February 16, the 392nd Night Bomber Air Regiment was given the assignment of raiding the enemy in Shandorovka and starting fires as an aid for our troops. In spite of falling snow and a strong gusty wind, Captain V. A. Zayevsky and his navigator V. P. Lokotosh successfully started several fires which served as targets for precise drops made by other crews from the regiment. The German-held village burned. The Korsun-Shevchenkovsky enemy concentration was wiped out by ground and air attacks.

Simultaneously with supporting ground troops, the air force attacked enemy airfields and landing strips on the territory held by the encircled troops and attacked his planes in the air, thus blockading his troops from the air.

On February 3, the air regiments of the 10th Composite Air Corps and the 264th Ground-Attack Air Division made surprise raids against airfields in the Vinnitsa region, destroying about eighty transport aircraft. This had a significant influence in reducing the flights of German aircraft supplying encircled German troops from the air. In a telegram the commander of the Front sent to the commanders of the air groups it was said that "the military council of the 1st Ukrainian Front is pleased with your fliers' operations against the German transports on February 3, 1944. We congratulate you on your victory, and give our thanks to the men who participated in the foe's defeat. The Military Council wishes great success to the fliers in exterminating the German invaders."

Our air operation against enemy air bases and the destruction of German aircraft in the air disrupted the flow of materials to the encircled troops. From January 31 to February 18, our air force flew 210 sorties against enemy airfields and fought 75 air battles, as the result of which about 200 enemy planes were destroyed, approximately 125 of which were on the ground.

When the thaw began, the air transportation of supplies and fuel to the advance units of the 2nd and 6th Tank Armies became very important. A sudden warm spell with frequent heavy rain made dirt roads almost impassable for all kinds of vehicles.

Tank units that had advanced far from their supply bases needed help. The 326th Night Bomber Air Division was given this assignment by the commander of the 2nd Air Army. Its air regiments, equipped with Po-2s, were moved to the air bases at Fursy and Yanushevka, located not far from a railroad. This made it possible to accelerate the shipment of goods from the railroad line and increase the level of air shipments. From February 8 to 16, in extremely bad weather, 822 flights were made both by day and night in which 49 tons of gasoline, 65 tons of supplies, and 525 rockets were delivered to ground forces.

In the South with the 3rd and 4th Ukrainian Fronts. When the men and aircraft of the 1st and 2nd Ukrainian Fronts were routing the encircled enemy troops at Korsun-Shevchenkovsky on the morning of January 31, the 3rd and 4th Ukrainian Fronts, with the support of the 17th Air Army (commanded by General V. A. Sudets) and the 8th Air Army (commanded by General T. T. Khryukin) took the offensive from their base near Nikopol.

During this initial period, when the enemy lines were being pierced and the offensive was being expanded, about 67 percent of the Front aircraft was concentrated on the direct support of ground troops, which contributed to their rapid advance. On February 2 the advancing troops, with air force cooperation, threatened to encircle the enemy troops at Nikopol. The German command began to remove its troops and equipment by rail and on highways. In addition to supporting our troops, our air force gave part of its efforts to attacking enemy supply lines.

The air regiments of the 9th Composite Air Corps (commanded by General O. V. Tolstikov) were most active in fulfilling this assignment. They attacked in small groups of ground-attack planes, disrupting German communications on the railroad from Nikopol to Apostolovo. Then the Air Corps units struck at enemy troops on the roads from Nikopol to the west and southwest. On February 4 alone, 117 sorties were flown and about 100 vehicles and carts were destroyed along with men and materials.

With air force help, Soviet troops liberated Apostolovo and Nikopol on February 9, and by the end of February they had reached Krivoy Rog and the Ingulets River. The enemy defenses collapsed under the blows of our ground and air forces. Soviet fliers—the best friends of the infantry, tank crews, and artillery forces—did not spare their efforts or their lives to aid them from the air. Aircraft from the 17th and 8th Air Armies attacked the enemy on the battlefield, his reserves, and his retreating columns, and thus joined with the ground forces in the rout of the Nikopol and Krivoy Rog enemy troop concentrations.

The German command increased its flow of reserves during these battles. The Soviet Air Force struck several powerful blows at railroad lines in order to halt these movements. The 306th Ground-Attack Air Division was especially active in fulfilling this assignment. Ground-attack planes commanded by the deputy squadron commander of the 672nd Ground-Attack Air Regiment, First Lt. N. Ye. Platonov, were especially successful in raids against railroad targets. On one sortie in bad weather he led his ground-attack planes against a railroad junction. After several accurate attacks, a fuel tank burst into flame, railroad cars loaded with supplies began to blow up, and the Germans fled in panic. N. Ye. Platonov was given the title Hero of the Soviet Union for the manner in which he successfully completed his military assignments during the liberation of the right bank of the Dnieper.

During January and February, Soviet troops, with air force help, annihilated major German troop concentrations and liberated the Kiev, Dnepropetrovsk, and Zaporozhe districts, and drove the German invaders from the Zhitomir and almost all of the Rovensky and Kirovograd districts and also some regions in the Vinnitsa, Nikolayev, Kamenets Podolski, and Volynsk districts. The enemy was thrown back along much of the length of the Dnieper. Favorable conditions were created for a further offensive along the entire Soviet-German front.

In spite of bad weather and the spring thaw, Soviet fliers constantly supported the Soviet ground troops. During a two-month period, the units of the 2nd, 5th, 17th, and 8th Air Armies flew 31,836 sorties, 13,176 of which were against enemy troops.

Driving the Enemy Back to the Southern Frontier. After he had lost the great battles in the winter of 1944, the enemy took all possible measures to hold his remaining regions on the right bank of the Dnieper. In March his southern armies had 83 divisions, of which about 27 percent were tank and motorized units, and about 1475 aircraft.

In the second stage of the offensive operation in the Ukraine, the ground and air forces of the 1st, 2nd, and 3rd Ukrainian Fronts had the assignment of destroying the enemy forces with offensives toward Chernovtsy, Uman-Jassy, and Nikolayev-Odessa, and then completing the liberation of the right bank of the Dnieper and advancing to the Carpathians. After they had regrouped their forces, the men of the three fronts renewed the offensive early in March.

On the morning of March 4, the groups of the 2nd Air Army began their air support for the just-begun 1st Ukrainian Front Proskurov-Chernovtsy operation. Because the weather was so bad, ground-attack planes flew alone or in pairs, which struck at enemy resistance points, artillery, and mortar batteries. After three days had passed and the weather had improved, our planes flew in groups of six or eight aircraft.

As they carried out their assignments in this bad weather, the flying personnel displayed courage and resourcefulness. On March 7, five Il-2s commanded by Second Lt. S. V. Kamensky with fighter cover were directed to attack enemy troops and equipment situated north of Starokonstantinov. Before they reached their target, our fliers discovered two large columns approaching the city. Lieutenant Kamensky attacked one of these immediately. The attack was so sudden that the Germans could not fire in defense. As the result of this unexpected attack, the enemy column was stopped. Our ground-attack planes then continued their strikes. The enemy suffered great losses.

Our raids against railroad targets were also very successful. Ground-attack planes and bombers, directed by aerial reconnaissance, systematically attacked railroad yards, stations, and open tracks, limiting enemy mobility and hindering the export of valuables and food.

Eight Il-2s commanded by Captain V. M. Bochkarev attacked the Klemashovka railroad station where there was a large concentration of military trains. The first attack blew up a train leaving the station, thus blocking the line for a long time. Their subsequent attacks caused considerable losses to the enemy. The railroad station was swept by flames. Cars burned and exploded, along with equipment and fuel.

By March 11, troops of the Front had advanced 100 kilometers (62 miles) with air force help and cut the main railroad line between Odessa and Lvov.

The 1st Ukrainian Front troops, after an artillery barrage and air attack, renewed their offensive on March 21. Our air force struck in two groups of 60–100 aircraft, which contributed toward the successful break-through.

On the offensive's second day the basic efforts of the 2nd Air Army were devoted to the support of the 1st and 4th Tank Armies in hot pursuit of the enemy. When the German troops had been driven from their defensive positions, they found themselves cut off from the main roads. Since they feared encirclement, they retreated rapidly, but Soviet reconnaissance planes followed them closely. The veteran reconnaissance pilot Captain N. P. Bykov discovered a column of enemy tanks and reported this by radio to his regiment's command post. A few minutes later our ground-attack planes struck at the column. After the pilots had returned to their airfields, the staff of the air regiments received the following telegram from the ground troops: "Give our thanks to the ground-attack planes. Hits against enemy tanks were accurate. Request an attack against the infantry."

And once more the tireless ground-attack planes took off. Their precise strikes caused the retreating enemy great losses and helped the successful tank army offensive.

The field airports went out of operation as the result of the spring thaw and it was impossible to build new ones. Impassable dirt roads also created great difficulties for transporting materials, which disrupted the supply system. But in spite of these bad conditions our flights continued ceaselessly, especially those of ground-attack planes and bombers. Much credit for this belongs to the workers on the airfields and especially the truck drivers, who ignored the bad roads and delivered supplies, fuel, and other materials to the advance airfields.

In this period the spring thaw made the roads almost impassable, and the delivery of supplies and gasoline to the tank groups by air was one of the most important assignments given to our air force. In spite of bad weather, the 2nd Air Army aircraft flew 400 sorties a day until April 17; 15 percent of these sorties were to transport military supplies and fuel to tank groups.

During the 4th Tank Army's offensive the city of Kamenets Podolski was liberated and on March 29 the 1st Tank Army liberated Chernovtsy. In the next few days, both ground and air forces fought bitter battles with approaching enemy reserves. Enemy resistance stiffened as reserves were brought from France, Denmark, Greece, and other regions. As a consequence, on April 17 the 1st Ukrainian Front on the orders of the *Stavka* ceased their offensive and temporarily went on the defensive.

Almost the same time that the Proskurov-Chernovtsy operation began (March 5) the troops of the 2nd Ukrainian Front began their operation at Uman-Botoshan. Bad weather, difficulties in preparing airfields, and problems with supplies significantly limited the operational level of the 5th Air Army. Because of this, part of the air regiments were moved to advanced airfields, from which they continued to support the ground forces, flying as many as eighty sorties per day. In order to protect our troops, the fighter planes flew at their maximum range. Under these conditions the planes led by Major N. D. Gulayev, Hero of the Soviet Union, were especially active and effective. Six fighters he commanded took off to fly cover for our ground troops. As they patrolled beyond the front lines, the fliers discovered 27 German bombers, with 8 fighter planes for protection, flying toward our lines. The Soviet fliers attacked them and in brief battle shot down 11 planes, 5 of them by N. D. Gulayev. He had already shot down 50 enemy aircraft before this.

G. A. Rechkalov, Hero of the Soviet Union, fought bravely in the sky over the right bank of the Dnieper. Captain S. D. Lugansky, Hero of the Soviet Union, also made his contribution toward the region's liberation. He flew a fighter plane given to him by his fellow Young Communists and other young people of Alma-Ata. He shot down more than thirty enemy planes in aerial combats. The Motherland held high the military exploits of her sons. By the order of the Supreme Soviet Presidium of the USSR, dated July 1, 1944, Captains N. D. Gulayev, G. A. Rechkalov, and S. D. Lugansky were given second "Gold Stars" of a Hero of the Soviet Union.

Second Ukrainian Front troops, with air support, on March 26 reached a point 85 kilometers (53 miles) from the Prut River—the border of the USSR.

On March 6, after an artillery barrage and air attack, the concentrated and regrouped forces of the 3rd Ukrainian Front took the offensive in the direction of Novy Bug. The same day the mechanized cavalry group commanded by General I. A. Pliyev entered the battle. Support for the ground forces was provided by the 17th Air Army, whose basic efforts were directed to putting down the enemy fire points and concentrations and also disrupting the regrouping of his troops and his communications. With the active support of air power the mechanized cavalry group, in two days, liberated the city of Novy Bug. Continuing to expand their offensive toward Bereznigovatoye and Snegirevka, they posed a threat, along with the other troops of the front, to the German 6th Army.

Therefore, the German troops began to retreat beyond the southern Bug toward Nikolayev. Our air force efforts were dedicated to the destruction of the enemy's retreating columns.

In spite of the difficulties resulting from the thaw and the large number of dirt airfields that were out of action, our planes flew about 300 sorties every twenty-four hours. During these battles to liberate the right bank of the Dnieper the fliers and commanders at all levels showed resourcefulness, courage, and daring in the struggle against the German invaders.

Colonel Isupov's Heroism. At dawn on March 24 the commander of the 306th Ground-Attack Air Division, Col. A. F. Isupov, arrived at his plane. His ground-attack planes were to attack an enemy concentration that was preparing for a counterattack. Low clouds made it impossible to send a fighter plane escort along with the Il-2s. Taking into consideration the fact that this was an important assignment under difficult conditions, Colonel Isupov decided to personally lead the attack. At 10:15 A.M. the ground-attack planes approached the village of Bezuvarovo, found their target, and attacked it.

The fliers made many daring strikes at the enemy. The division commander thanked the flying crews over the radio for the successful manner in which they had fulfilled their task and instructed them to return to the airfield. At that point German fighter planes appeared, but the gunners repelled their first attack. An enemy fighter seriously wounded both Isupov and his gunner Krivko in a second attack. The damaged ground-attack plane burst into flame and began to drop. Over the village of Kovalevka the damaged engine failed and then their plane made a forced landing on enemy territory.

Isupov, who was seriously wounded, was captured and sent to Germany. The Germans asked the colonel to appear before his fellow prisoners with the request that they participate in the war against their Motherland. A few days later, the Soviet prisoners were drawn up in formation in their camp. Isupov appeared on the speaker's platform to address his comrades-in-arms. He quickly exposed the lie they had been told about the situation on the Soviet-German front and exhorted the prisoners to be true sons of the Motherland to their last breath. His speech was interrupted. Once more on July 15, 1944, all the prisoners of the camp were lined up. Isupov was summoned from the ranks as well as five other Soviet fliers, handcuffs were put on them, they were pushed into a police car and taken away. Isupov and the other patriots had time to shout out in farewell, "Long live our Soviet Motherland!" Air Division Commander Col. A. F. Isupov honorably carried out his duty and died defending his Motherland.

Odessa Is Liberated. Under the blows of the men and planes of the 2nd and 3rd Ukrainian Fronts the 6th German Army retreated toward the west. On April 4, the 37th Army and the mechanized cavalry group commanded by General I. A. Pliyev with air support from the 17th Air Army liberated the railroad station at Razdelnaya, splitting the enemy army into two parts. On April 10, Soviet troops liberated Odessa and four days later emerged at the Dniester and immediately seized a number of bridgeheads on its right bank. The 17th Air Army gave great support for the ground troops in this operation, and the 9th Composite Air Corps and the 288th Fighter Air Division fliers especially distinguished themselves.

The transport operations of the air force were a great aid to the advancing ground troops. When the roads were impassable in the spring the air force hauled military supplies and fuel. In seventeen days alone, it flew 4817 sorties and transported 670 tons of fuel, supplies, and more than 5000 reinforcements and wounded men. The flight commanded by Second Lt. L. P. Postupayev was especially successful in this task and also a group of fliers from the 866th Fighter Air Regiment commanded by Capt. A. I. Koldunov.

The mechanized cavalry group under General I. A. Pliyev broke through deep into the enemy's rear and appeared to be cut off from our lines. It was essential to give it immediate aid. Six transports, Li-2s,* with six fighters for escorts had to locate our cavalry units in the enemy's rear and drop supplies for them. Directly over the front, twelve German fighter planes attacked our aircraft. The situation was developing in the enemy's favor.

Over his aircraft's radio, Captain Koldunov gave his fighter planes the command to attack and flew straight at the lead plane. It seemed as though a collision was inevitable, but the German fliers could not stand the tension, and turned sharply aside and up. A short burst of machine-gun and cannon fire triggered by Koldunov knocked down the enemy and he plunged into the earth. Then Koldunov shot down a second enemy plane at close range. After covering our Li-2s at long range, the fighter planes left the battle. The transport planes dropped their precious cargo at the right place and returned to their airfield without any losses. At that time Captain Koldunov had already shot down twenty-two enemy aircraft. By the order of the Presidium of the Supreme Soviet of the USSR dated August 2, 1944, he was given the title Hero of the Soviet Union, and by the end of the war he had shot down forty-six aircraft and was granted a second "Gold Star" of a Hero.

In March and April of 1944, the AFLRO groups began to operate in this area. The 2nd Guards Air Corps, commanded by General Ye. F. Loginov, was especially active. They struck at railroads,

* Soviet-built Douglas DC-3s. ED.

bridges, and enemy reserves and gave great aid to the troops as they pursued the enemy and completed the liberation of the right bank of the Dnieper.

Results of the Offensive. In the winter and spring of 1944, Soviet troops, with the active support of the air force, inflicted a serious defeat on the German armies, liberated the right bank of the Dnieper, and advanced onto Rumanian territory. The Front air forces took an active part in nine offensive operations and flew more than 66,000 sorties, while the Luftwaffe flew about 31,000. During this period about 7000 tons of bombs were dropped on enemy troops and other targets and about 1000 air battles were fought. In addition to causing great losses to enemy men and materials, the Soviet Air Force shot down or destroyed on the ground more than 1400 German aircraft.

As the result of competent direction and the persistent efforts of the personnel in the air regiments and the rear units in fulfilling their tasks, more than 2000 sorties were flown on some days in good weather. The organization of ready teams on the airfields, the utilization of the briefest periods of good weather for air operations, the high morale and skills of the flying crews, and the flights made by small groups of planes or single planes all contributed to the successful fulfillment of the air force assignments.

In the conditions of the spring thaw and the very limited number of airfields available, the ground-attack planes and the fighter planes were most important in ground-support operations. Basing a large number of units on different airfields with careful camouflage and concern for a high level of operations were some of the most important conditions for improving the operations of the air force.

In addition to supporting ground forces and fighting German aircraft in the air, great service was provided by the air force in transporting supplies and fuel, especially to tank units. About 14 percent of all sorties were expended for this purpose.

During the bitter struggles for the liberation of the western Ukraine, the flying crews in the air armies displayed courage and dedication to the Communist party and the socialist Motherland. Soviet fliers successfully completed their military assignments to rout the fascist invaders, for which eighteen of them were given the title Hero of the Soviet Union.

The air force operations in the liberation of the right bank of the Dnieper were highly regarded by the Supreme Command. Many fliers were given orders and medals. Several air groups and units were designated as guards units and received names of honor, such as the Berdichev, Vinnitsa, Kamenets Podolski, Kirovograd, Nikolayev, Nikopol, Odessa, Proskurov, and Uman units.

XI

THE BATTLE TO LIBERATE THE CRIMEA

Although cut off by land from the rest of the German Army, the Crimean peninsula was still considered vital to German plans. Hitler insisted that control of Crimea was decisive to the attitude of Rumania and Turkey, and ordered his 17th Army, including six German and six Rumanian divisions supported by the First Air Corps, to hold their position. Three Soviet attacks over the shallow Sivash Sea, the Perekop Isthmus, and west from the Kerch Peninsula threatened the Axis forces.[4] ED.

The campaign to liberate the Crimea began in the first half of April 1944. Expecting an offensive from the Red Army, the enemy built a defense system that was 20–70 kilometers (12–43 miles) deep and which utilized the mountains that intersect the area.

The task of liberating the Crimea was given to the troops of the 4th Ukrainian Front, the Independent Coastal Army, the Black Fleet, and the Azov Flotilla. The following units were to support the ground forces: the 4th Air Army (commanded by General K. A. Vershinin), the 8th Air Army (commanded by General T. T. Khryukin), groups from the AFLRO, and the naval air force. The operations of these units were coordinated by a *Stavka* representative, General F. Ya. Falaleyev.

The campaign plan called for simultaneous strikes by the 4th Ukrainian Front from the northern part of the Crimea, and the Independent Coastal Army from the eastern end of the Kerch Peninsula, toward Simferopol and Sevastopol to annihilate the enemy force and to interdict any evacuation from the Crimea. The 4th

Ukrainian Front was to strike from its base south of the Sivash with the men of the 51st Army and the 19th Tank Corps leading the attack.

In order to assure that all assignments would be successfully carried out, extensive preparations were made, including the delivery of adequate supplies, the construction of new airfields, and the training of personnel for their future assignments. Conferences were held for the commands of units and training sessions were held to prepare units for the future operation. About 72 percent of all aircraft were assigned to the support of the offensive units, and especially to the support of tank units.

At the same time that these preparatory actions were being taken, both air armies were protecting our troops as they were regrouped and concentrated in certain areas; they attacked the enemy's maritime transport; they drove off enemy bombers as they tried to bomb the crossings between the Sivash and the Kerch Strait; and they systematically carried out aerial reconnaissance, which provided essential information about troop concentrations, defensive installations, and the location of artillery.

From November 1943 to April 1944, the 4th and 8th Air Armies flew more than 50,000 sorties as they carried out their assignments.

Attack from the North. Troops of the 4th Ukrainian Front began their offensive on April 8. In accordance with the plan, the 8th Air Army gave its total support to the 51st Army troops at their base south of the Sivash. One or two minutes before the offensive began, 108 ground-attack planes struck against the outermost enemy defense line. Then the aircraft began operations in support of ground troops. Groups of four to six aircraft, constantly over the battlefield, smashed enemy troops and put down artillery and mortar fire. The German troops offered stubborn resistance, especially in the area of Karankin and Tomashevka. The 51st Army commander requested that several groups of ground-attack planes be sent to this area to put down enemy strong points, dampen enemy artillery fire, and destroy their troops on the ground. After the air attack the troops renewed their offensive and occupied several enemy trenches.

As they fulfilled their assignments the flying crews showed exceptional bravery, courage, daring, and high skill.

On April 9, ground-attack planes commanded by Captain A. I. Svertilov were attacking enemy artillery in the Tarkhan region when they observed bombers with the Fascist swastika flying toward our area. The Soviet fliers attacked the German aircraft head on, broke up their formation, and shot down five bombers with machine-gun and cannon fire. After he had exhausted his ammunition, N. N. Pechenov rammed an enemy bomber, which fell out of control and plowed into the earth. But the Soviet patriot's aircraft was seriously damaged, and N. N. Pechenov died a hero's death.

Communist party members displayed exceptional courage and skill in air combat. Second Lt. M. Ye. Pivovarov, a flier from the 402nd Fighter Air Regiment, became a Communist party member on the eve of the decisive battles. On April 6, as he received a government award, he said that he would destroy the enemy in the battle for the Crimea without sparing his own life. His words were true to the deed. The next day he shot down two enemy fighter planes.

The Il-2 of flight commander First Lt. L. I. Beda was badly damaged by antiaircraft fire on an attack on the airfield at Kurman-Kemelchi. He made a forced landing behind the enemy lines. He was rescued by his second-in-command, Second Lt. A. A. Beresnev, who landed his plane near the downed aircraft, picked up his commander and his gunner, and returned safely to his airfield. For his courage and resourcefulness in saving his commander, the daring ground-attack pilot A. A. Beresnev and his commanders were given the highest government award by their command—the title of Hero of the Soviet Union.

Troops of the 51st Army, with air support, continued to expand their offensive. To the north of Tomashevka at Hill 30.3 they met stubborn enemy resistance that blocked the advance of our troops at the center. The storming of the hill was fruitless. Bitter fighting developed. Before an infantry and tank attack, a bombing raid was made by 100 ground-attack planes and 36 dive bombers, after which our troops took the hill. The road to Tomashevka was open and our troops occupied it the same day.

Taking advantage of the favorable situation, the 19th Tank Corps entered the battle on April 11, and with the help of air power broke through the enemy's secondary defense line and the same day occupied the important road junction and town of Dzankoy.

At the time of the advance south of the Sivash, troops of the 2nd Guards Army with the help of the naval air force broke through the enemy defense line on the Perekop Isthmus and on April 10 reached the lines at Ishun. The successful operations of the 51st Army and the 19th Tank Army in the Dzhankoy region appeared to threaten the enemy entrenched at Ishun and he was compelled to retreat deep into the Crimea.

Attack from the East.   The success of our operation in the northern part of the Crimea created favorable conditions for a Soviet offensive on the Kerch Peninsula. Late on April 10 aerial reconnaissance revealed a shift of enemy troops from their positions. The Independent Coastal Army commander gave the order for an offensive early on April 11.

Because of the changing situation the 4th Air Army commander increased the number of flights to be flown by night bombers to silence the enemy artillery covering the retreat of his troops. To ascertain when the enemy troops would begin to withdraw from their positions, our aircraft dropped flares to light the enemy's major defense zones. At dawn on April 11, ground-attack planes were instructed to attack enemy troops on the roads leading to the west. Bomber units were alerted to be ready for raids against concentrations of men and materials.

Late on the night of April 10 and early on April 11 our troops, with air support, liberated Kerch. The enemy troops on the Kerch Peninsula began to retreat rapidly to the west. At dawn on April 11 aerial reconnaissiance planes reported that the roads leading west from Kerch toward the Akmonaysk positions* were jammed with retreating troops. And most of the railroad yards of the Kerch Peninsula were discovered to be filled with enemy trains, indicating that the enemy intended to use rail facilities to evacuate his troops and equipment. The 4th Air Army commander ordered all his aircraft to destroy the retreating enemy troops. All that day, ground-attack planes and bombers struck in waves of four or five aircraft against men and materials on roads. Bombers, in groups of twelve to eighteen or more, struck effectively against railroad yards, bridges, and troop concentrations.

These bomber and ground-attack raids caused great enemy losses and disrupted his plans for evacuating his troops from the Kerch Peninsula.

Groups from the 4th Air Army and the naval air force maintained a high level of support that assured the successful advance of our

* This probably refers to the enemy's fall-back line around Sevastopol. ED.

troops, who by April 11 had advanced as much as 40 kilometers (25 miles) and by the end of the day on April 11 had liberated the city and port of Feodosiya with the help of partisans. All of the Kerch Peninsula, in a short period of time, was liberated from the German invaders.

After the enemy's defense line had been broken in the northern part of the Crimea and on the Kerch Peninsula, the next task of our ground and air forces was to complete the rout of the German troops and to liberate the Crimea.

The troops of the 4th Ukrainian Front, supported by the 8th Air Army, began their pursuit of the enemy. Soviet ground-attack planes, bombers, and fighters destroyed his troops along the roads or in villages. Night bombers were very active in this period in harassing the enemy as he was trying to evacuate his troops under the cover of night. The 2nd Guard Army, with air support, routed the enemy's rear guard on the Chatyrlyk River and pressed on in pursuit of the retreating enemy.

The pursuit of the German troops toward Simferopol and Sevastopol was carried out by a mobile group from the strengthened 19th Tank Corps. The 1st Guards Ground-Attack Division and the 3rd Fighter Air Corps provided support for the tank units, constantly attacking retreating enemy troops and intermediate defense lines, thus contributing to the success of the offensive. On April 14 the enemy stiffened his resistance in the region of the railroad station at Syuren. Ground-attack planes were called in to support our troops, and after their attack the infantry and tanks went on the offensive and drove the enemy from his positions.

During the pursuit of the enemy the fliers from the Fronts, in addition to supporting the ground forces day and night, struck considerable blows at the airfields in the Crimea, and at ships and the transportation system at the harbor at Sevastopol.

The Luftwaffe, from April 12 to 18, flew a total of 530 sorties in the area of the 4th Ukrainian Front. It was active on April 14, making on that day 150 sorties. In the remaining days it flew about 40–60 sorties, and, certainly, offered no serious resistance to the operations of our advancing troops and air force.

As they expanded their offensive, the troops of the 4th Ukrainian Front with air support advanced from 150 to 200 kilometers (93–150 miles) and on April 15 reached Sevastopol, where they met stubborn enemy resistance.

The Independent Coastal Army's pursuit after the retreating enemy toward Sevastopol was made in two directions—most of the troops advanced through Stary Krym and Simferopol and a smaller number of men through Sudak and Alushta along the southern coast of the Crimea. Ground-attack planes and bombers in groups of four to eight flew against retreating troops on the roads, intermediate lines, and populated centers to support the advance of our troops. On April 13, our advance units reached the Karasubazar region where they joined with the troops of the 4th Ukrainian Front.

Then the enemy fled along the only road which was still open to him, which went along the Black Sea shore and ended at a number of ports. Aircraft of the 4th Air Army routed his troops in this mountainous region and in these harbors. Aerial reconnaissance revealed a great concentration of troops along the coast in the Sudak region, where there was a constant flow of retreating units from the Kerch Peninsula. On April 13 they were attacked from the air by the 4th Air Army and the naval air force. As a result of this raid, several barges were sunk with men and equipment. Enemy troops could not be evacuated by sea.

In spite of the rapid advance, coordinated operation between the ground and air forces continued. This was achieved by locating the commanders of ground-attack air divisions in the command posts of the ground units who controlled his aircraft directly on the battlefield. Operations against the retreating troops did not cease at night. The discovery of the retreating troops was made easier because the German vehicles had to use their headlights at night in the mountainous terrain. In order to halt the enemy troops, and destroy men and materials, landslides were started by the bombers.

In the mountainous regions of the Crimea's southern coast, ground-attack planes flew in small groups, since maneuverability was limited in the mountains. Attacks on a target were made in a deeply-extended formation. In most cases waves, of two planes or flights of planes, at a distance of 300 to 500 meters (984 to 1640 feet) were utilized. Approaches to the target were made down gorges, valleys, or ravines from the mountains toward the sea. The approach to the target was made at an altitude somewhat higher than the highest point in a given region. Repeated passes were made difficult because of the badly cut-up terrain.

Bombs were dropped, in accordance with the character of the region, either from a dive-bombing attack or in horizontal flight.

The pursuit of the retreating Germans continued. The Independent Coastal Army reached the Sevastopol Fortified Region on April 17. (On April 18 the Independent Coastal Army was merged into the 4th Ukrainian Front and renamed the Coastal Army.)

In the six-day period in which it was pursuing the enemy, the 4th Air Army flew more than 1000 sorties. As our armies advanced to the west, the level of our air operations somewhat decreased because the support units were left behind. But the German Air Force, even as our troops left the Kerch Peninsula, could not really offer any effective resistance.

As the front air forces operated in cooperation with the ground forces to pursue a retreating enemy, the AFLRO raided ports and bays, and the naval air force operated against ships and transports, which were mostly out to sea. In the course of two nights on April 15 and 16, 233 aircraft dropped bombs on ships and transports in the bays at Sevastopol, sinking several barges with men and materials.

From April 12 to 18, our air force flew 4666 sorties. The rapid rate of the offensive, and the lag in rebasing ground facilities in the Crimea caused by the bodies of water that had to be crossed, created great difficulties in supply services and led to a decrease in the intensity of air operations.

Assault on Sevastopol.   When it had lost the battles in the northern and eastern parts of the Crimea, the German command strove at any price to hold Sevastopol, to which it had evacuated the remainder of its army. About 6000 officers and men were shipped there by sea and air to strengthen its defenses. The Germans created a powerful defense system in the region of the city, which included three zones with many permanent installations. The strongest point was at Sapun hill, which was surrounded by several arcs of continuous trenches protected by anti-infantry and antitank mine fields and several rows of barbed wire. There were also strong points at the Mekenziyevy mountains, Inkerman, and the Sakharnaya Golovka hill. There were about 72,000 men and soldiers and about 100 aircraft on the bridgehead held by the enemy, which was 29 kilometers long and about 17 kilometers deep (18 by 11 miles). All this area was protected by three or four rows of antiaircraft artillery.

On April 19, the 4th Ukrainian Front began to prepare for the assault on the Sevastapol Fortified Region. The major attack was to be made by the left wing of the 51st Army and the Coastal Army in the area of Sapun hill and Karan, and then on to the major docks at Sevastopol which the enemy could use to evacuate his troops. A secondary attack was to be made by the 2nd Guards Army from the east and northeast somewhat earlier to distract the enemy from the area of the major attack.

The nights before May 5 and May 6, the air army was given the task of supporting the 2nd Guards Army; they were to attack enemy artillery, mortars, and troops with ground-attack planes and bombers; they were to protect our troops from enemy air attacks and to destroy enemy planes in the air and on the ground; they were not to allow enemy reserves to come up to the battlefield; and they were to destroy ships and transports in the bays and in the approaches to them. On May 7, and in the following days of the assault, most aircraft were to be devoted to supporting the offensive launched by the Coastal and 51st Armies.

The battle plan for the air army was devised for a three-day period at a level of about 2900 sorties. Great attention was given to close coordination of efforts between the air and ground forces, and to close strikes from ground-attack planes and bombers to destroy the enemy's fire capabilities directly in front of the advancing troops. Experienced air officers were sent to the ground units, and attention was given to the timely and precise marking of the forward line of advance. All of these measures contributed to the effectiveness of our aircraft against targets located very close to our own troops.

As the result of energetic measures taken by the 8th Air Army command before the assault of the fortified region began, air units were shifted to forward airfields and essential quantities of fuel, supplies, and other equipment brought up; the enemy defense system studied; air operations worked out; and coordinated efforts planned with the troops from the front. At the end of April the command of the 4th Air Army became part of the 2nd White Russian Front, and its units were transferred to the 8th Air Army, as the result of which the latter now had more than 1000 aircraft.

When these preparations for the assault were under way the air force did not abandon its high level of operations. In the six days before the assault began, the AFLRO and the 8th Air Army dropped more than 2000 tons of bombs and about 24,000 antitank bombs. The enemy's great losses in men and materials contributed to the successful advance of our ground forces.

On May 5, the 2nd Guards Army took the offensive. Bombers and ground-attack planes struck at artillery and mortar positions, destroyed permanent defense installations, and annihilated men and materials.

A group of Il-2s commanded by Captain A. I. Svertilov was outstanding. On May 6, near the Mekenziyevy mountains, in spite of the strong opposition of enemy fighter planes and antiaircraft fire, his ground-attack planes attacked their target three times. As the result, artillery and mortar fire was put down and our ground forces attacked and occupied a series of trenches. A *Stavka* representative, Marshal of the Soviet Union A. M. Vasilevsky, who watched the skilled operation of the pilots, expressed his thanks to them. P. F. Nadezhdin of the 307th Ground-Attack Air Regiment performed an immortal feat in the sky over Sevastopol. As he attacked enemy troops his plane was hit by antiaircraft fire. Reared in the spirit of boundless love and dedication to the Motherland, he preferred death to shameful captivity and directed his burning plane on an enemy fuel dump. For this exploit, P. F. Nadezhdin was posthumously granted the title Hero of the Soviet Union.

Supporting these operations, the technical staff gave all their efforts and skills so that aircraft equipment and engines might work faultlessly. On May 8, four aircraft from the 136th Guards Ground-Attack Regiment were damaged when they attacked enemy troops. The mechanics, Comsomols Novikov, Kozenko, Komarov, and Rumyantsev, worked all night to repair the damaged aircraft so that they could be flown on more missions in the morning.

The fliers of the 1st Guards Ground-Attack Air Division (commanded by Hero of the Soviet Union, Lt. Col. S. D. Prutkov) were especially effective. In rugged mountain terrain, they skillfully located and destroyed enemy fire points, which were hindering the advance of our troops. The Military Council of the 2nd Guards Army gave them its thanks for their exceptional activities.

After a two-day battle the troops of the 2nd Guards Army with air support moved forward in difficult mountain and wooded territory.

The night of May 6, before the offensive of the 51st and Coastal Armies began, the AFLRO and the front air force hit the enemy defense line. The next day as the offensive began, eighteen Il-2s for a fifteen-minute period made ground attacks against enemy artillery on the rear slope of Sapun hill, and the men and artillery in the trenches. Eighteen ground-attack planes hit the same targets in three groups of six in the period from 10:45 to 11:30 A.M.

Utilizing effective air support, the infantry captured the Puzyr hill and approached the foot of Sapun hill. The enemy met our infantry with organized fire from the secondary trench line, and advance was stopped. At this critical moment, three groups of six ground-attack planes under the command of Capts. M. T. Stepanishchev and N. P. Anisimov and Second Lt. V. G. Kozenkov were sent into the battle. Following radio instructions, the ground-attack planes made precise strikes against the upper trenches of Sapun hill, making several passes at the target. As the result of this firm and courageous operation the ground-attack planes of the 1st Guards Ground-Attack Air Divisions caused the enemy great losses and silenced his guns.

A monument was later erected to the fliers of the 8th Air Army on Malakhov mound commemorating the manner in which they supported the troops on the ground and for their fearlessness, courage, and heroism in battle.

The air force also supported our advancing troops as they captured Sakharnaya Golovka hill and other points of resistance protecting the approaches to Sevastopol. The night of May 7 the AFLRO and front night bombers made about 1000 sorties against enemy defenses.

The front's troops with air support continued to expand their offensive. Ground-attack planes and bombers struck against enemy strong points and artillery and supporting the infantry who were fighting for Karan, Kaya-Bash hill, Height No. 10, and other points. Simultaneously the air force struck at transports and other ships in the harbors and also against enemy airfields.

At the end of the day on May 8, our troops with air support broke through the enemy's first defense line, and on the second day they overwhelmed the inner defense line around Sevastopol and liberated the city. The remnants of the enemy forces withdrew to Khersonesky Cape.

Captain P. M. Kamozin, Hero of the Soviet Union, especially distinguished himself in the battle for the liberation of Sevastopol. The fliers of his squadron shot down 63 enemy aircraft. During the war he shot down 35 enemy planes. For his new exploits he was given a second "Gold Star," by order of the Presidium of the Supreme Soviet of the USSR dated July 1, 1944.

On these two last days, the Front's troops brought up their reserves and prepared to break through the last German defense line. Our air force kept up its active operations. Because the enemy was attempting to evacuate the remnants of his troops from the Crimea, most of the efforts of our ground-attack planes and bombers were expended against transports in the harbors at Kamyshovaya and Kazachya and the approaches to them.

On May 11, the German commander attempted to evacuate his remaining troops by night from Khersonesky Cape. But at 3:00 A.M. our troops renewed their offensive and broke through the final defense positions; by noon the last enemy troop concentration in the Crimea was routed.

A convoy of ships approaching from the west to evacuate the German troops was driven off by air attacks and by artillery. That day our air force and ships of the Black Sea Fleet sank thirteen German transports with their men and cargoes in the harbors, at approaches to the harbors, and at the docks.† The evacuation of enemy troops was disrupted. A large number of officers and men were killed or wounded and 25,000 prisoners were taken.

Thus, the troops of the 4th Ukrainian Front with the support of air power in a short period captured the Sevastopol Fortified Region. The air force played a major role in the solution of this problem, flying more than 13,000 sorties in eight days, of which about 2000 were expended against enemy convoys. The Luftwaffe flew only about 700 sorties in this period.

Results. The Crimean offensive operation has gone down in military history as one of the most successful operations of the Great Patriotic War conducted by ground troops in cooperation with the Soviet Navy and the air force. During this operation the 17th German Army was completely destroyed and the Crimean Peninsula was liberated together with the major base of the Black Sea Fleet, Sevastopol.

In 1941–42 the German troops required 250 days to enter Sevastopol, but in 1944 the troops of the Red Army broke through the strong fortifications in the Crimea, destroyed the 200,000-man German troop concentration, and captured the city in thirty-five days.

The victory achieved by the Soviet armed forces in the Crimea contributed to the further strengthening of the military-political situation of our country. The Black Sea Fleet occupied more advanta-

† The largest ships sunk by the Soviet aircraft were the transports *Teja* and *Totela,* and 8000 evacuating troops were drowned.[5] ED.

geous positions and could now actively participate in the defeat of the German troops in the Balkans.

Two air armies and the air force of the Black Sea Fleet with a total of more than 1250 aircraft participated in the operation.

In addition, the AFLRO also participated in the operation. The presence of sufficient air power made it possible to use it en masse. Thus during the assault on the Sevastopol Fortified Region more than 1000 Front aircraft and more than 500 aircraft from the AFLRO were active in a small area.

The Soviet Air Force gave major support to our ground forces. It struck against the enemy on the ground, in the air, and on the sea. During these operations our air force flew more than 36,000 sorties (this includes 1865 flown by the AFLRO against troops, railroad targets, airfields, and ships), of which about 60 percent were in support of ground troops. The Luftwaffe in this period flew 3000 sorties.

During the operation efforts were continued to retain control of the air. There were 599 air battles, in which 297 German aircraft were shot down and about 200 German aircraft were destroyed on the ground. Thus, the Soviet Air Force caused great losses to the enemy in the Crimean operation.

The heroic accomplishment of the Soviet warriors was highly regarded by the Motherland. Moscow fired a five-gun salute in honor of the troops and fliers who liberated the Crimea from the German invaders. Thirty-six air groups and units received honorary titles: Crimean, Sevastopol, Kerch, or Feodosiya. Many fliers were given orders or medals, and the most outstanding of them, including General Ye. Ya. Savitsky, were given the title of Hero of the Soviet Union.

XII

THE BATTLES FOR THE KARELIAN ISTHMUS AND THE ARCTIC

After 1942, the Finnish Army north of Leningrad, and the German 20th Mountain Army in the Arctic, had remained relatively quiet. Disappointed in their expectation of a short war, the Finns concentrated on fortifying the narrow Karelian Isthmus, while the Germans, whose efforts to take Murmansk had been frustrated, held the valuable nickel mines in Petsamo. ED.

During the winter and spring of 1944 the Soviet armed forces had achieved great victories at Leningrad and Novgorod, on the right bank of the Dnieper, and in the Crimea. Favorable conditions were created now for carrying out new large offensive operations in other areas of the front.

In the northern sector of the front, Finnish troops were located 25 kilometers (15 miles) from Leningrad. During three years of war, the enemy turned the Karelian Isthmus into a powerful fortified region. The defense system consisted of three defense zones with various reinforced-concrete installations, the walls of which were 2 or 2.5 meters (6.6 or 8.2 feet) thick with caps as much as 3 meters (9.8 feet) thick. In the second defense zone, which was 12–25 kilometers (7–15 miles) from the front line, there were about 1300 different fortifications. The total depth of the defense zone exceeded 100 kilometers (62 miles). On June 1, the enemy group named "Karelian Isthmus" consisted of more than six divisions. The greatest concentration of troops was in the heavily defended Vyborg area.

The ground troops were supported by part of the 1st German Air

Fleet and 300 aircraft of the Finnish Air Force.* In addition the enemy could utilize as many as 100 aircraft from the Petrozavodsk region. His system of airfields made it possible to base his fighter planes 20–30 kilometers (12–18 miles) from the front lines, giving his aircraft great mobility.

Preparations. The 21st and 23rd Armies of the Leningrad Front were assigned to the Karelian Isthmus. At the beginning of the offensive, we had twice as many men as the enemy and nearly six times as many guns and tanks. These groups were supported from the air by the 13th Air Army and the 2nd Guards Fighter Air Corps of ADF, a total of 757 aircraft. In addition some aircraft from the Red Banner Baltic Fleet were also available under the operational control of the commander of the air army.

In accordance with the *Stavka* decision, men of the 21st and 23rd Armies, together with the Red Banner Baltic Fleet and the 13th Air Army, were given the task of breaking through this powerful fortified region with the goal of crushing the enemy's opposing army and liberating the Karelian Isthmus and the city of Vyborg† from the Finnish invaders.

The training period for air units and groups for the coming operation began on May 3. The 13th Air Army protected ground troops and the city of Leningrad, carried out aerial reconnaissance, and struck at fortifications, men, and equipment in the first and second defense zones. From May 1 to June 9, 1944, the air force flew about 1800 sorties. Naval aircraft attacked enemy convoys and sea transportation, planted mines, conducted reconnaissance at sea, and protected the bases and ships of the fleet.

The command, staffs, and support services of the air army and the air groups devoted much labor to organizing operations for the coming campaign. The problems of coordination between air and ground units were carefully studied. Command points for ground-attack, bomber, and fighter divisions were set up close to the front lines, which made it possible to control air operations at all times.

The staffs of the air army and the naval air force agreed on the place and time of air operations over the battlefield, and decided in

---

* In January 1944, the Finns had 223 fighters, 106 bombers, and 31 recon aircraft on active duty.[6] ED.

† Before 1940, this city was Vipuri, and part of Finland. ED.

advance the question of targets, and devised plans for supporting demonstration parachute landings in the region of Cape Ino and to the north of Sestroretsk, and repelling enemy air raids over Leningrad.

Aerial reconnaissance was very important in this period. To photograph the defense zones 610 sorties were flown and about 87,000 square kilometers (33,620 square miles) of land were photographed. Aerial reconnaissance revealed the nature of the defense system and the type and location of enemy ground and air units. Ground armies, groups, and units were given photographs in advance of the defense zones and enemy resistance centers.

Much attention was given to the question of camouflage. A network of mock airfields was constructed within the air army, amounting to 65 percent of the actual bases. On these fields, 252 mock aircraft and 176 mock buildings were built. The soldiers and airmen of the front conducted an operation similar to the one under way in the Narva region where the 13th Air Army was conducting intensive aerial reconnaissance operations. The naval air force struck systematically at enemy ships in the Gulf of Narva. The AFLRO bombed rail communications in Estonia and hit the men and equipment of the enemy where they were concentrated to the west of the city of Narva. In May these planes flew 572 sorties and dropped 4260 bombs.

In this training period for the coming operation, the commanders of the political organizations of groups and units increased their educational work. Lectures and reports were given, and meetings and party conferences were called. Many gatherings were held in order to study our break-through of the Mannerheim Line in 1939–40. Party and political work played an important role in the mobilization of personnel to fulfill their battle assignments.

There was a detailed plan for air operations in the first three days of the offensive. The basic efforts of the 13th Air Army were devoted to the support of the 21st Army at the center of the region. Twenty-four hours before the offensive began, it was planned to destroy permanent fortifications, disrupt the enemy's artillery network, and to wipe out his reserves. Around 1500 sorties were to be devoted to these assignments.

During this preparatory period, large groups of bombers and ground-attack planes were to be employed with fighter cover. Ground support was to be carried out by concentrated strikes and waves of small groups of bombers and ground-attack planes.

It was planned to expend about 6000 bomber and ground-attack sorties in the preparatory period and in the first three days of the operation. Of these sorties, 65 percent were to be against permanent fortifications and 26 percent against enemy reserves. In addition, more than 5400 sorties were to be made by fighter aircraft to protect our ground troops, the city of Leningrad, and as cover for bombers and ground-attack planes.

Breaking Through the Fortified Line.   As was planned, on June 9, a day before the offensive began, artillery and aircraft heavily attacked permanent fortifications in the enemy's first defense zone. Early in the morning, 215 bombers and 155 ground-attack planes with fighter cover made a mass raid at defense points in the regions of Stary Beloostrov, Lake Svetloye, and the station at Raijajoki.

The bomber groups proceeded to their target in a column by regiments, and the regiments in a column by squadrons, with respective intervals of 750–1000 meters (2460–3280 feet) and 300–500 meters (984–1640 feet). Bombs were dropped from an altitude of 1800–2500 meters (5900–8200 feet) at a signal from the lead plane. Ground-attack planes struck in regiment strength on a single approach, five to ten minutes after the bombing raid. These attacks were effective. Their density reached 80–100 tons per square kilometer (.386 square mile) of target area.

At noon, 95 bombers in groups of nine to twelve planes struck in several waves against railroad yards and stations at Vyborg, Rautu, Rayvola, and Kiviniemi. At 1:30 P.M., bombers in regiment-sized groups attacked reserves concentrated in the region of Kiviniemi, Valk-yarvi, and Kivennapa, and bombers in pairs attacked railroad and highway bridges at Kiviniemi.

On June 9, Soviet fliers flew around 1150 sorties; of these 510 were made by bombers, 235 by ground-attack planes, and 406 by fighter planes. As the result of these operations, as Finnish historians wrote, "Many defense installations and barriers were destroyed and mine fields blown up." Nine enemy planes were shot down in the air.

The next day, during the preliminary artillery barrage thirty minutes before the offensive started, the Front air force and the naval air force sent 172 bombers and 168 ground-attack planes with fighter protection in a mass raid against strong points near Stary Beloostrov, Svetloye Lake, and the station of Raijajoki. According to aerial photographs and ground reports, our fliers destroyed or damaged

70 percent of the ground installations. The effectiveness of these raids and their timing just before the opening of the offensive contributed significantly to breaking the enemy defense line.

Support for ground troops in the offensive was made in the form of concentrated attacks and waves of aircraft against enemy artillery, men, and equipment. From 11:40 A.M. to 12:00 noon, 244 bombers and ground-attack planes with fighter cover raided artillery positions near Kallelovo, Zabolotye, Novy Alakul and Stary Alakul. As a result of this raid, eight artillery and mortar batteries were destroyed, fourteen damaged, and many bunkers destroyed. In the same period, 54 ground-attack planes from the naval air force attacked artillery and mortar positions near Stary Beloostrov.

Troops of the 21st Army‡ crossed the Sestra River and by the end of the first day of the offensive had penetrated the enemy defenses to a depth of 14 kilometers (9 miles) on a front about 20 kilometers (12½ miles) wide. With the aim of expanding their advance, the commander of the front reinforced the 21st Army by sending in the 108th Infantry Corps. When enemy resistance had been overcome, our troops, with air support on June 11, overwhelmed a series of strong points near Rayvola, Terijoki, and Kellomaki. By the end of the day our troops had advanced as much as 30 kilometers (19 miles) and reached the second zone of the fortified region, but they were not able to break through it.

To support the efforts to break the second defensive zone, 274 bombers and ground-attack planes from the 13th Air Army struck at strong points at Liikula, Kuterselka, and Metsyakyula on the morning of June 13. During that day, bombers hit reserves that the enemy was moving up from the Karelian Front. The 334th Bomber Air Division in groups of seven to nine aircraft raided railroad yards and stations at Vyborg, Perkjarvi, Leipasuo, and Sajnie, destroying 47 railroad cars and disrupting the railroad network. On June 13 the front air force flew 631 sorties.

The next morning before the attack, 347 bombers and ground-attack planes from the 13th Air Army and the naval air force made preliminary strikes. Strong points at Mustamaki, Rasvattu, and Vuotta were attacked. The area at Rasvattu was hit at a very high level, with 324 tons of bombs on one square kilometer (.386 mile) of land. As a result, trenches and bunkers were destroyed, 22 pillboxes

‡ On the left of the isthmus, next to the Gulf of Finland. ED.

and 4 storehouses were blown up, and 5 artillery-mortar batteries were silenced. Later 280 bombers and ground-attack planes with fighter protection struck effectively against strong points at Neuvola and Mustamaki.

The attacking troops, taking advantage of the effective air force blows, moved forward to capture these strong points. "Air operations in the area of the 108th Infantry Corps," as its commander reported, "were well carried out. The infantry units advancing in the corps area had strong air support."

The Finnish command brought up reserves in order to stem the Soviet advance. Our air force, in groups of eight to twelve aircraft, attacked the Mesterjarvi and Taivola sectors and also the railroad stations at Vyborg, Kiviniemi, Hiitola, Antrea, and Keksgolm. Since the enemy did not have sufficient forces to deliver any powerful air counterattacks, he was forced to utilize his bombers in pairs and groups of four against our troops. But these attacks were repelled by our fighters.

As the result of stubborn battles, the ground troops with air support broke through the second defensive line, which was fundamental to the entire defense of the Karelian Isthmus, at the end of the day on June 17. From June 13 through June 17, the Front air force flew 5623 sorties against strong points, men, equipment, and reserves, and in the battle against enemy aircraft and in aerial reconaissance. The naval air force flew 1082 sorties while fulfilling various assignments at sea. During this period our fliers fought 33 air battles in which they shot down 43 enemy planes.

Beginning on June 18 our troops continued to expand their offensive with the goal of capturing the third defensive zone and the city of Vyborg. The air force, attacking the enemy defensive positions, disrupted the orderly retreat of his troops to the third defensive zone, hindered defensive efforts, and disorganized his rail transportation. On the night of June 18, when the AFLRO bombed the railroad yard at Vyborg, 76 aircraft dropped 450 bombs.

Vyborg Is Captured. As the enemy retreated to the Vyborg region, he resisted stubbornly. On June 19, troops of the 21st Army broke through the third defensive zone and overran the well-defended stations at Leipasuo, Summa, and Karhula. The troops of the neighboring 23rd Army in the Keksgolm region cleared the enemy from the southern shores of Suvanto-Jarvi and Vuoksi-Jarvi lakes.

To stop the advance of the Soviet troops, the enemy shifted more than 100 aircraft to this area from the 54th German Fighter *Geschwader,* the 1st Dive-bomber *Geschwader,* and other units based in Karelia.

Our aircraft bases became rather distant from the front line as our troops advanced. Because of this the fighters of the 275th Air Division could not give constant support to our troops on the battlefield, while the 2nd Guards Fighter Air Corps of the ADF was protecting Leningrad and could not be used for ground support.

Because of these conditions, fighter aircraft located on advance airfields had to operate at maximum levels. Fighter pilots flew five or six sorties every day. Intense fighting flamed in the sky. For example, on June 19, Front fighter planes were involved in 24 air battles and shot down 35 enemy aircraft. The next day, there were 28 air battles in which 200 aircraft from both sides participated. That day Major A. V. Chirkov, Hero of the Soviet Union, commander of the 196th Fighter Air Regiment, and a remarkable master of air combat, especially distinguished himself. He engaged three enemy fighters in battle, shot one down, and forced the other two to flee.

In these days of intense battle the best pilots, navigators, aerial gunners, technicians, and mechanics entered the ranks of the Communist party. Within the 13th Air Army, 344 men were taken into the party in June as members or candidates. Second Lt. D. V. Yermakov was taken into the party from the 159th Fighter Regiment and in several days shot down 8 enemy aircraft. The fighter pilot and Communist V. G. Serov displayed his skill and daring. He shot down 8 enemy planes and destroyed 26 enemy planes in all. Fliers and Communists A. I. Gorbachevsky, V. A. Zotov, S. G. Litavrin, and I. P. Neustruyev each shot down 3 to 6 aircraft in the month of June. They were all given the title Hero of the Soviet Union. Twenty-six fliers were given that title in the 275th Fighter Air Division commanded by Col. A. A. Matveyev. Major P. A. Pokryshev, two times Hero of the Soviet Union, fought with extraordinary fearlessness. By this time he had already shot down more than 20 aircraft. As the commander of a fighter regiment, he showed by his personal example how to fight against the enemy and shared his rich experience with his subordinates.

As they expanded their offensive, troops of the Leningrad Front, together with the fleet and the air force, were compelled to fight in wooded and swampy country with many rivers and lakes but, nonetheless, within eleven days they had pierced a powerfully fortified region, and on June 20 they captured by storm the fortress city of Vyborg. The enemy suffered great losses but his resistance was not completely broken. He quickly regrouped his forces, and brought in fresh units from the Medvezhyegorsk and Svir regions into the region northwest of Vyborg. Heavy fighting broke out once more. Our ground troops advanced slowly.

The air force continued to operate at a high level. Second Lt. V. F. Kovalev was involved in many air battles. On July 9, a group of our fighters were returning to their airfield after they had completed their assignment. The last one in the formation was Kovalev. Near Vuoksi he noticed twelve enemy bombers flying in the direction of our troops. The daring flier attacked them and shot down two planes.

The ground-attack pilot G. M. Parshin became famous all over the Karelian Isthmus. On the eve of the operation he received a new Il-2 built by funds collected by two Leningrad patriots—Praskovya Vasilyevna Barinova and her daughter Yevgeniya Petrovna Barinova, medical workers in a polyclinic. The daring Soviet ground-attack pilot destroyed many enemy tanks, guns, aircraft, and men. Subsequently he was given the title of Hero of the Soviet Union for a second time.

First Lt. V. I. Mykhlik led many groups of Il-2s in ground attacks against fortification and artillery. He always used the fearful armament of his plane with great skill. Twice he was later given the medal "the Gold Star."

After the liberation of Vyborg, military operations continued for three weeks on the Karelian Isthmus. In order to take advantage of the success of the offensive, the Red Banner Baltic Fleet sent troops ashore on the islands of Teikarsaari and Suonionsaari. Cover for the landing was provided for the naval air force and the 13th Air Army. A day earlier the air force struck at the artillery batteries on the island of Teikarsaari, and fifty minutes before the landing craft came to the islands, 45 bombers and 102 ground-attack planes with fighter cover attacked the fortifications and artillery positions where the landing was to be made, as well as adjacent regions.

Fighter planes flew protection for the landing. Ground-attack planes in groups of four to eight attacked enemy troops and silenced his artillery. Within two days the landing force in cooperation with the navy and the air force fulfilled their assignment, sweeping several islands in the Gulf of Vyborg. Aircraft flew 1800 sorties in support of the landings.

Strikes were made against enemy airfields with the goal of support-ing our troop landings and also weakening enemy air capabilities. On June 23, 28 ground-attack planes and 16 fighters raided the air-field at Lappenranta where ten enemy aircraft were destroyed, a fuel dump and two hangars ignited, two antiaircraft batteries silenced, and the landing strip damaged.

The heaviest raids on the airfields at Lappenranta and Immalam-jarvi were made on the evening of July 2. Careful aerial reconnais-sance preceded these strikes. There were 188 aircraft that participated in the raids: 44 bombers and 28 ground-attack planes over the field at Immalan-jarvi and 16 bombers and 36 ground-attack planes at Lappenranta. The bombers and ground-attack planes made their at-tacks under fighter cover.

Before the bombers and ground-attack planes took off, fighter planes on special assignment blockaded the enemy airfields. Seven groups of four fighter planes flying in three waves patrolling over the airfields prevented enemy aircraft from taking off and impeding our bomber operation. After the bombers had struck, ground-attack planes attacked the airfields. As the result the enemy lost 49 aircraft, 37 of which were destroyed on the ground and 12 shot down in the air. We lost 6 aircraft.

The ground-attack pilots commanded by flight commander Ye. M. Kungurtsev especially distinguished themselves as they attacked the airfield at Immalan-jarvi. His group destroyed or damaged as many as fifteen enemy aircraft, blew up a dump with supplies and fuel, and shot down one enemy fighter. Subsequently, First Lt. Kungurtsev was twice designated a Hero of the Soviet Union.

At the beginning of July, troops of the Leningrad Front swept the islands in the Gulf of Vyborg free of enemy troops, and having com-pleted their basic assignments, took defensive positions in a line from Lake Ladoga along the southern bank of the Vuoksi string of lakes and then through Vuoksalmi, past Lapinlahti, Repola, and Tikkala. At this stage of the operation, our aircraft supporting ground troops flew about 19,000 sorties (June 18 to July 11).

The men of the 21st and 23rd Armies of the Leningrad Front to-gether with the Red Banner Baltic Fleet, the Ladoga Military Flo-tilla, with air support, had dealt a severe defeat to the Finnish Army; the fortified area had been broken, the enemy had been cleared from the Karelian Isthmus, our army had advanced from 110 to 130 kilometers (68 to 81 miles) and captured Vyborg.* Leningrad was free from danger from the northwest and the Baltic Fleet had freedom of movement in the Gulf of Finland.

The operation for liberation of the Karelian Isthmus and Vyborg along the coast had been carried out through the efforts of ground troops, the navy, and the air force. During its course experience was gained in the organization and conduct of coordinated operation between the air force, the naval air force, the AFLRO, and ADF fighters.

The Soviet Air Force, in spite of bad weather, gave much help to the ground forces in breaking through the fortified region, in the destruction of permanent installations, and in combating enemy reserves. During the operation Soviet fliers flew around 28,000 sorties and dropped more than 4700 tons of bombs on the enemy. In the operation many men and much equipment were destroyed and many bunkers and pillboxes smashed.

During the preparatory period and during the operation the 40th and 52nd Transport Regiments of the Civil Air Fleet played an important role. Fliers from these units made 5700 sorties; transported more than 6100 soldiers and officers, a great quantity of equipment, and other cargoes; and evacuated 2503 wounded.

The operation to liberate the Karelian Isthmus was unlike all other operations in the war in that the air force took an active part in destroying the enemy's permanent defensive fortifications. Other important assignments for the air force were air support for our ground forces and attacks on reserves. About 19 percent of all of the sorties of the 13th Air Army were flown against enemy reserves. The struggle for control of the air was fought by destroying enemy aircraft on the ground and in the air. About 45 percent of all sorties were flown for this purpose. More than 400 enemy aircraft were destroyed in the air or on airfields by our fliers.

The Offensive Between Lakes Ladoga and Onega.   During the Leningrad Front's offensive on the Karelian Isthmus, in which units also of the Karelian Front participated, preparations were made for an assault against the enemy on a line along the Svir River and north of Lake Onega to be made by 32nd and 7th Army units. On the morning of June 21, after a powerful artillery and air attack, they took the offensive, delivering the major attack near Olonets. When they had

---

* June 20, 1944. ED.

broken the enemy resistance, Soviet troops advanced 200–250 kilometers (124–155 miles) by the end of July and reached the Finnish border. A great part of the Karelian-Finnish Soviet Socialist Republic was cleared of enemy troops.

Flying in coordination with ground forces, the units of the 7th Air Army (commanded by General I. M. Sokolov) flew 12,000 sorties and dropped 1500 tons of bombs on the enemy, causing him great losses.

Soviet fliers gave firm protection for our ground forces against enemy aircraft. They struck at strong points, and concentrations of men and materials.

The 257th Independent Composite Red Banner Air Division under the command of Colonel A. V. Minayev was very effective. Two groups of dive bombers under the command of V. P. Petrov and A. V. Akvilyanov distinguished themselves. They made accurate bomb drops, clearing the way for advancing infantry and tanks.

The young fighter pilot B. N. Karamyshev, who along with his partner N. P. Kaper took on 26 enemy aircraft, became famous all along the front. In a brief but intense battle, our fighter planes shot down 3 enemy aircraft and forced the rest to flee from the area. Captain Nikolay Bely performed an immortal feat when he directed his damaged aircraft into a concentration of enemy tanks and other vehicles. Many fliers were given high government awards for their courage and daring in the operation to free Soviet Karelia.

The Arctic Offensive. The defeat of the Finnish Army on the Karelian Isthmus and in southern Karelia had a significant influence on the northern sector of the Soviet-German front.† Favorable conditions were created for driving the enemy out of the Soviet Arctic. For three years the Fascist invaders had built and perfected powerful fortifications there. The severe climate of the Arctic strengthened the enemy's defensive position.

The men of the Karelian Front, in cooperation with the Northern

† Finland asked the Soviet Union for peace terms on August 25, and a cease-fire went into effect on September 4, with the requirement that all German forces leave the country by September 15. The Germans failed to do so, and fighting broke out with the Finns, as the Germans slowly withdrew toward Norway, destroying Finnish property as they went. In this situation, Soviet Arctic forces advanced against the Germans to capture Petsamo and the Norwegian port of Kirkenes. ED.

Fleet and the air force, carried out the Petsamo-Kirkenes operation from October 7 to November 9. During this operation the enemy was driven from the areas he held in the Murmansk district, the economically important region of Petsamo, and the warm-water ports on the Barents Sea. The enemy lost a number of airfields from which he had sent bombers against targets in our rear areas.

Ground operations and ships were given air support by the 7th Air Army and the Air Force of the Northern Fleet, with more than 1000 aircraft.

The operational area was a coastal zone of Arctic high tundra. The mountains, multitudes of rivers, marshes and lakes, poor road system, and severe climate complicated the construction of airfields and the maintenance of air operations. Extremely bad weather conditions limited the use of air power.

The Soviet Air Force, in spite of bad weather and the difficulties in ground services, played an important role in the successful conduct of the operation. Early in the campaign aerial reconnaissance revealed the enemy defense system, important points of resistance, troop concentrations, air bases, availability of roads and crossings in the major offensive area, areas suitable for landing troops from ships, and areas that could be used for landing strips. Much useful information about the enemy was obtained by the crews of the Heroes of the Soviet Union A. V. Anokhin, V. I. Donchuk, and A. R. Slivka.

The Soviet Air Force, supporting ground forces and ships from the fleet, attacked the enemy, destroying his strong points and communications centers. On October 9, two groups of six ground-attack aircraft from the 261st Ground-Attack Air Division destroyed four artillery-mortar batteries and blew up three bunkers and a supply dump to the north of Lake Chapr. The 131st Infantry Corps commander held this ground-attack operation in high regard.

On October 11, nineteen Il-2s from the Northern Fleet sank two large transports and damaged two barges, three patrol boats, two submarine chasers, and several other small ships in the harbor at Kirkenes and the approaches to it.

As the offensive developed in an area without roads and the artillery and tanks fell behind the infantry, the only kind of support available was from the air.

Many times the enemy tried to limit our air operations. There were intense air battles over the battlefield. For example, on October 9 our fliers shot down 37 aircraft in 32 air battles. The enemy also lost planes on the ground. On October 11, 56 aircraft from the 261st Ground-Attack and 1st Guards Composite Air Division (commanded by Col. F. S. Pushkarev) destroyed 15 and damaged 18 enemy aircraft on an airfield in the region of Pechenga.

Fliers displayed courage and great skill in the battles for the Soviet Arctic. The names of many of them became known all over our country. B. F. Safonov, a naval aviator who personally shot down 41 enemy aircraft, received the title of Hero of the Soviet Union for the second time for his feats in defense of the far north. Among the fliers in the Arctic were patriots who bravely rammed enemy aircraft: Lt. M. P. Krasnolutsky and Capts. A. P. Pozdnyakov and A. S. Khlobystov.

During the operation Front aircraft flew around 6700 sorties. Soviet fliers dropped hundreds of tons of bombs on the enemy, destroying men and materiel. The enemy lost 125 aircraft in the air. The fliers from the naval air force sank 136 ships, which was 85 percent of enemy fleet losses.

Four times the Supreme Commander thanked the fliers of the 7th Air Army for their effective actions. The 113th Bomber Air Division and the 112th Fighter Air Division from the ADF were given the name of "Pechenga" units, and the 80th, 114th, 121st, and 716th Bomber Air Regiments the "Kirkenes" units. Fourteen of the best fliers of the Front were given the title of Hero of the Soviet Union, and many were given orders and medals, including the medal "For the Defense of the Soviet Arctic."

XIII

IN THE SKIES OVER WHITE RUSSIA

After the successful Allied landing in Normandy on June 6, 1944, Nazi Germany found itself between the jaws of a vise. In the east, 164 German divisions, plus their allies, faced the Soviet Union, while 54 others were in the west, 27 in Italy, and 40 guarded the Balkans and Norway.[7]

Since German Army Groups North and South had been driven nearly out of Russia and the Ukraine, Army Group Center headquartered at Minsk held an exposed salient from Vitebsk down to the Pripet Marshes. This German force was to suffer 1944's worst defeat, shattered both by an overpowering ground offensive and Soviet air domination.

German air strength, due to shifts westward had dropped to 2796 aircraft in the east, according to a Soviet authority that gives Red Army strength at 13,428 aircraft.[8] ED.

At the middle of June 1944, Soviet troops on the central front were located on a line from Lake Neshcherdo, east of Vitebsk, Orsha, Zhlobin, Kovel, Brody, Chernovitsy, Jassy.

The enemy had built a deep defense system in White Russia in three zones. Taking advantage of natural geographic features and a system of defense installations, the enemy calculated on holding his White Russian salient.

Four Fronts Prepare. After the enemy's defeat on both flanks of the Soviet-German front, the Supreme Command decided to open an offensive in White Russia utilizing the forces of four fronts; each with its own air army. From north to south, they were: 1st Baltic Front with 3rd Air Army commanded by General N. F. Papivin, 3rd White Russian Front with 1st Air Army commanded by General T. T. Khryukin, 2nd White Russian Front with 4th Air Army commanded by General K. A. Vershinin, 1st White Russian Front with 16th Air Army commanded by S. I. Rudenko. In addition, groups from the 6th Air Army commanded by F. P. Polynin also participated.

The Supreme Command's plan for the White Russian operation called for simultaneous drives through the enemy's defenses in several areas; then a rapid offensive involving the encirclement and destruction of the major enemy troop concentrations, and the liberation of the capital of White Russia, Minsk.

At that time we had control of the air and a significant superiority in both aircraft quality and quantity over the enemy.

The German troops from Army Group Center were supported by 1342 aircraft of the 6th Air Fleet. We had in our air armies around 6000 aircraft (about 50 percent of these arrived just before the operation from the Supreme Command reserves) including more than 1100 day and night bombers and 2000 fighter planes.

For raids against the enemy's operational rear, some units were summoned from the AFLRO. Communication lines of the 1st Baltic and three White Russian Fronts were protected by fighter aircraft from the Northern Front of the ADF.

As the offensive operation was being carried out, the air force was given the following assignments: maintain control of the air, support and protect the ground forces as they cut through the tactical defense zone and expanded the offensive; interdict the advance of enemy reserves and hinder planned retreat of his forces; constantly conduct aerial reconnaissance and observation of enemy movements.

A great bombing raid, planned for the night before the assault began, was to include 2730 sorties flown by the AFLRO and the Front night bombers. During the initial preparatory artillery barrage, a mass strike was planned with 548 Pe-2s participating on the southern sector of the 3rd White Russian Front attack area where the enemy's defense was particularly strong.

Great attention was given to organization of air support at the time when tanks and mechanized cavalry came into the battle. Beginning with the 1st Baltic Front and the 1st White Russian Front, the air armies' basic efforts were to be devoted to the support of tank and mechanized cavalry units. Some Po-2s from the 213rd Night Bomber Air Division were assigned to lighting the routes at night for the tank groups.

A number of measures were to be taken to limit Luftwaffe activities. Regiments of bombers and ground-attack planes within the 1st and 16th Air Armies were assigned to operate against enemy airfields. One fighter air division in both the 3rd and 4th Air Armies and three or four divisions in the 1st and 16th Air Armies were assigned the special duty of protecting our troops and destroying fascist aircraft in the air. A considerable part of our fighter aircraft were to be used to accompany day bombers and ground-attack planes.

Over-all control and coordination of air operations was in the hands of *Stavka* representatives Chief Air Marshal A. A. Novikov and General F. Ya. Falaleyev.

For a twenty-two-day period there were intense preparatory and training activities in all air units and groups. Questions of coordinated action were carefully planned by air and general commanders: plans for coordinated action were worked out, and five to seven days before the operation's beginning there was special instruction for staffs from both general army and air units.

In those areas where the two attacks were to be made—in the areas of the 1st and 3rd White Russian Fronts—two secondary control points were set up. At each of these there was an air army operational group consisting of six to eight officers and three to five radio transmitters. The air army commander, or else his deputy or a corps commander, had control over these groups. Air officers with radio transmitters were assigned to infantry corps, cavalry divisions, and tank and motorized brigades.

In order to insure surprise and concealment in the preparations for the operations, the number of responsible personnel was very limited. Telegraph and telephone conversations concerning the coming operations were forbidden. Assignments were made only to those directly concerned. Air corps and division commanders were introduced to their assignments five or seven days in advance and regiment personnel only several hours in advance.

New air units and groups were not brought in until the beginning of the operation. They were based 100–120 kilometers (62–75 miles) from the front lines and a day or two before the offensive they flew into their advance airfields in small groups at low altitudes.

There was intensive aerial reconnaissance. Much valuable information was obtained about the enemy's front lines from aerial photography.

Employment of so many aircraft within the air armies required organization of precise navigational control over air operations. In addition to ground control (radio beacons, lights, radio stations, and radio homing stations) orientation markers, letters and numbers, were placed on the ground by the 4th and 16th Air Armies, which aided visual orientation at altitudes from 2000 to 3000 meters (6460 to 9840 feet).

In order to insure a precise approach to the target, the 16th Army used colored markers, smoke pots, and flares at night. In the 1st Air Army the basic orientation mark was a tethered balloon at a height of 120 meters in the center of the break-through area. Light-weight platforms 10 meters (32.8 feet) high were constructed upon which smoke pots were burned in wooded country.

Many temporary dirt airfields were prepared. Thus, by the time the operation began, almost every air regiment in the four air armies was based on its own airfield. About 50 percent of these were built just before the operation began. The local population was used to build these bases. In addition, the military councils of the fronts assigned about 5000 or 6000 soldiers and officers from the infantry groups to each air army. Each dump and airfield had from four to eight days' supply of fuel and oil, and eight to ten days' supply of bombs, shells, and bullets.

Plans were developed for basing and equipping air groups during the operation, and search parties were designated with the assignment of seeking out areas that might be used for airfields. Each army had in its reserves from four to eight air service battalions to work on the problems of shifting bases during the offensive.

The political and party organizations continued their work to inculcate the highest moral and military qualities among our personnel. Before the first flights took off from their fields, short meetings were held and the guards banners were displayed under which the fliers swore to drive the fascist vultures from the Soviet sky. Thus, before the White Russian campaign began there was careful and broad preparation among the air units.

The Offensive's First Stage. The White Russian operation began on June 23, 1944.

Twenty-four hours before the operation, advance units of the 1st Baltic Front and the 3rd White Russian Front attacked the enemy in a number of areas and advanced from 3 to 5 kilometers (2 to 3 miles). Aircraft from the 3rd and 1st Air Armies flew over these areas in single planes or in small groups. Our fliers not only acquainted themselves with the future targets and orientation marks on the critical areas, but also attacked fire points, thus helping the advance units to overcome enemy resistance.

The night of June 22, divisions of the AFLRO and front bombers flew around 1000 sorties, striking at defense centers and artillery in those areas where the 3rd and 2nd White Russian Fronts were to attack. Women fliers of the 46th Guard "Taman" Night Bomber Air Regiment were very active. The crews of Captain Serafima Amosova, First Lt. Larisa Rozanova, and Second Lts. Zoya Parfenova and Yekaterina Ryabova flew three or four sorties during the short summer night.

Long-range bombers and night bombers from the 16th Air Army flew 550 sorties in the 1st White Russian Front assault areas on the night of June 23.

On the morning of June 23 and 24, fog both in the areas of the air bases and over the battlefield greatly complicated air operations, and the day bombers were able to attack only the southern sector of the 3rd White Russian Front assault area with a force of 160 Pe-2s. As the asault began, Il-2s made precise strikes in small groups to support advancing ground forces. They approached the battlefield at intervals of eight to twelve minutes, thus delivering constant blows on the enemy. Their targets were artillery points and tactical reserves. Radio control of these groups from the ground and the availability of data from aerial reconnaissance flights increased the effectiveness of their strikes.

Later in the day as the weather improved our aircraft increased their activity.

The enemy center of resistance toward Orsha in the Gormany and Kireyevo region was bombed by 162 Pe-2s from the 1st Air Army. Bombers of the 16th Air Army on June 24 made two raids in groups of 224 and 163 aircraft on enemy strong points in the Rogachev and Bobruisk area. Some small, important targets were hit by dive-bombing attacks from six to nine Pe-2s.

The crew of Second Lt. V. V. Zakharchenko (124th Guards Bomber Air Regiment) distinguished themselves in battles near Orsha. As they were dive-bombing a bridge across the Adrov River near Zabolotye (6 kilometers [4 miles] west of Orsha) the crew commander was hit in the leg by an antiaircraft shell fragment. In spite of his wound and loss of much blood he continued his assignment. With the help of his navigator, Second Lt. N. N. Tenuyev, the pilot completed the raid, hit his target, and then brought his plane back to his field and landed it. Second Lts. Zakharchenko and Tenuyev were given the Order of the Red Banner for the great courage with which they completed their assignment.

Effective air support contributed to the speed with which our troops overran the enemy's tactical defense zone. Beginning on June 24, tank corps, mechanized cavalry groups, and tank armies entered the battle. The major efforts of all the air armies were devoted to their support. It was only in the Orsha region, where enemy defenses were very strong, that the battles became stationary.

At the 1st White Russian Front area where units of the tank corps were operating, close air force cooperation was attained by assigning ground-attack air divisions to the commanders of these tank groups. The high effectiveness of ground-attack aircraft strikes was assured by having air officers with radio transmitters located at the observation points of the commanders of mobile groups.

At the 3rd White Russian Front area, mechanized cavalry groups and then the 5th Guard Tank Army entered the battle on June 25. The basic efforts of the 1st Air Army were directed to the destruction of approaching reserves and German antitank weapons in the area the tank army was attacking. Control of aircraft assigned to the support of tank groups was in the hands of the 1st Guards Bomber Air Corps commander from his command post, which moved together with the command post of the tank army commander. Profiting from the results of our air raids, the mobile units expanded their rapid offensive.

Supporting the break-through in the defense zone and the entry of mobile units into the battle, the air force operated with maximum effort. During these first four days, it flew around 28,000 sorties.

During the first two days of the battle the Luftwaffe was based at rear airfields. Fascist aircraft rarely appeared in the air. Later enemy aircraft increased their activities, especially in the battles for the cities of Orsha and Bobruisk. Therefore, the command organized a series of raids against enemy airfields. Pe-2s of the 1st Air Army on June 25 and 26 bombed the airfields at Borisov and Dokudovo several times. The raid of the 6th Guards Bomber Air Division against the Orsha airfield was very effective. The staff report of the German fighter unit "Moelders" (JG 51) stated: ". . . 25/6/44. The airfield at Orsha was subjected to a heavy raid. In spite of the fact that the enemy aircraft were expected not one plane could take off. Our pilots were far from their aircraft and arrived at their planes when the enemy planes were over the field. The squadron command post burned down as the result of a direct bomb hit and control over the units was lost for some time."

During the first five days of the operation, troops of the Fronts with vigorous air support routed the largest German troop concentrations and surrounded several German divisions at Vitebsk and southeast of Bobruisk.

Units of the four divisions* at Vitebsk made desperate efforts to escape encirclement, but our troops, supported by the 1st Air Army groups, forced them to surrender on June 27.

The air force played a major role in the defeat of the other German troops surrounded near Bobruisk. The commander of the 1st White Russian Front, Marshal of the Soviet Union K. K. Rokossovsky, and

* Of the 53rd Corps. ED.

the *Stavka* representative, Chief Air Marshal A. A. Novikov, decided on a mass raid against the encircled troops to be carried out by most of the 16th Air Army's aircraft. The 16th Air Army commander, General S. I. Rudenko, assigned this task to two bomber air corps and four ground-attack air divisions.

On June 27 at 7:15 P.M. the first groups of bombers and ground-attack planes began the raid. The mass attack lasted one and one-half hours. The 526 planes in the group dropped 159 tons of bombs. As a result, many tanks and vehicles were destroyed and burned. German soldiers and officers who escaped destruction fled in panic into nearby woods. The enemy lost about 1000 men and officers.

When the large troop concentrations in the Vitebsk and Bobruisk regions were surrounded and liquidated, and the troops in the Orsha and Mogilev areas were routed, the Army Group Center found themselves on the brink of catastrophe. The German command was compelled to withdraw its exhausted divisions quickly to the west. To take their place troops were brought from other sectors of the front and from other countries occupied by Germany. Therefore, the major task of the air force at the end of June became the destruction of approaching reserves and retreating columns of troops and equipment.

From June 25 to July 4, the AFLRO bombed the enemy's major rail communications in White Russia, flying 3200 sorties. On July 1, during daylight hours, ground-attack planes and bombers from the air armies operated against railroad stations and trains on the lines from Polotsk, Daugavpils; and Molodechno, Minsk, Negoreloye, Baranovichi, Luninets. In a four-day period, 790 sorties were flown on this assignment. Our air force significantly hampered the movement of enemy troops, who arrived at the front in disarray and with great delays.

The major assignment of the front air forces was the destruction of retreating enemy troops, beginning on June 26. The enemy attempts to withdraw his troops from Orsha on railroads and by road to Minsk were disrupted. The night of June 25, Po-2s of the 213th Night Bomber Air Division, and the AFLRO bombed the roads west of Orsha. In the morning, the bombers put the railroad station at Tolochin out of commission, where there were a number of trains with men and equipment. During the day, waves of planes from the 1st Guards Ground-Attack Air Division, commanded by Col. S. D. Prutkov, attacked trains. They flew 138 sorties, destroying ten locomotives and fifteen trains. As a result, traffic on the railroad line between Orsha and Tolochin was paralyzed.

Nor were enemy troops able to retreat in an organized fashion from Orsha along the roads to Minsk. Ground-attack planes were active here. Thus, on July 26 a column located 10 kilometers (6.2 miles) west of Tolochin was attacked by eight Il-2s, forced to stop, and then in a two-hour attack completely annihilated.

On the evening of June 26, Tolochin was liberated by the 5th Guards Tank Army. The remains of the German troops had to abandon Orsha and leave to the southwest on dirt roads through forests controlled by partisans. This was a great operational victory achieved by coordinated action on the part of tank and air groups.

Troops of the 2nd White Russian Front pressed their pursuit of 4th German Army units. Ground-attack pilots from the 4th Air Army constantly attacked the retreating columns. The rout of the enemy from the air was carried out in close coordination with the White Russian partisans. On June 26, a column retreating from Orsha was suddenly ambushed by partisans in the region of Staroselya (10 kilometers [6.2 miles] west of Kopys). Not wishing to penetrate further into the forest and fight the partisans, the enemy turned south to the village of Troitsa. Our fliers found him in this region. Our ground-attack planes made a precise strike against this column as it crossed the Berezovka River. The enemy abandoned about 500 vehicles at the crossing and tried to hide in the woods, but there he was crushed by partisans.

When he characterized the situation in the offensive zone of the 2nd White Russian Front, the 4th Air Army commander, General K. A. Vershinin, on July 27 reported to the air force commander as follows: ". . . the air force has been employed in direct support of the ground forces. Everything is proceeding normally. The men and the Military Council are satisfied. Except good reports and thanks, we have nothing to report. But, Comrade Chief Marshal, my heart aches—the Germans are escaping in continuous columns, there are road jams and crowds, and we have nothing to hit them with as we should. We have not had targets like this since the Crimea, but there the enemy offered no resistance, and therefore the air force could be used in all its power. If it is possible, I ask that the neighboring air armies of Comrades Rudenko and Khryukin send part of their forces in order to destroy these columns. . . ."

Considering the great operational significance of the disorganization of the 4th German Army retreat, *Stavka*'s representative for the air force assigned the 16th Air Army the task of destroying the enemy in the zone of the neighboring 2nd White Russian Front. From

June 28 to June 30, bombers of that army made several effective strikes against enemy troops and crossings in the region of Berezino. The troop concentrations east of the Berezina River were attacked by ground-attack planes. On June 29 alone, forty groups of ground-attack planes from the 4th Air Army struck at the retreating troops on the road from Belynichi to Berezino, and in all about 2000 sorties were flown in six days to attack the retreating troops. Not less than 3000 vehicles were destroyed by air attacks in the road between Mogilev and Minsk.

The memoirs of the 4th German Army commander, General Tippelskirch, testify to the difficult situation of the retreating troops and the great effectiveness of the Soviet Air Force. "An endless stream of heavy artillery, antiaircraft batteries, and all kinds of vehicles advanced with great effort along a road long since badly damaged, but the only road available for retreat, which crossed the Berezina River at the town of Berezino. Continuous enemy air raids caused heavy losses (including two corps commanders and one division commander killed), and also caused continuous stoppages among the retreating columns. Russian ground-attack planes from time to time destroyed the bridge at Berezino, after which great accumulations of vehicles formed on the river's eastern bank."[9]

Thus, the Soviet Air Force caused great losses to the enemy and disrupted his orderly retreat, thereby contributing to our successful offensive. These effective air operations were one of the most important factors that brought about the subsequent encirclement of the enemy troops in the forests east of Minsk.

Beginning June 27, our air regiments began to move to bases abandoned by the enemy, or built on newly liberated territory. Units of the 3rd Air Army occupied airfields near Ulla and Beshenkovichi; the 1st Air Army occupied bases near Orsha, Tolochin, and Lepel; the 4th Air Army occupied bases near Mogilev; and the 16th near Bobruysk. The first to arrive were the fighter and ground-attack air groups, which were supporting tanks corps and mechanized cavalry groups.

At the time that aircraft of the 4th and 16th Air Armies were attacking retreating columns, tanks of the 3rd and 1st White Russian Fronts were pressing their rapid offensive toward Minsk and Slutsk.

On July 3, the capital of the White Russian Soviet Socialist Republic, Minsk, was liberated from its German captors. In the woods east of the city, an exhausted group of enemy soldiers and officers numbering about 100,000 men was surrounded. Troops of the 1st Baltic, 3rd White Russian, and 1st White Russian Fronts, with air support, advanced rapidly toward Daugavpils, Molodechno, and Baranovichi.

At this time, ground-attack planes and fighters commanded by the Heroes of the Soviet Union A. Ya. Brandys, A. N. Yefimov, I. F. Pavlov, and A. S. Smirnov were very effective in destroying enemy men and materials. For their exploits accomplished as they fulfilled their command assignments, these brave fliers were given second "Gold Stars."

And so, in the first stage of the White Russian Campaign, which continued from June 23 to July 4, 1944, Soviet troops with air support routed the largest enemy concentrations at Vitebsk, Orsha, Mogilev, and Bobruysk. They liberated Minsk and to the east of the city surrounded the largest part of the German 4th Army. The German Army Group Center was dealt a major defeat.

The Soviet Air Force was very active, and annihilated the squadrons of the 6th Air Fleet. It maintained control of the air and destroyed about 300 German planes in the air and on the ground. Its powerful blows aided the piercing of the enemy's tactical defense zone and in surrounding and liquidating large troop concentrations. It disorganized the enemy's plans for an orderly retreat and regrouping its forces. The four air armies and the AFLRO flew more than 55,000 sorties.

The Offensive's Second Stage. The second stage of the White Russian operation began on July 5. The *Stavka* gave new assignments to the 1st Baltic Front and the 3rd White Russian Front to expand their offensive. The air force was to support the ground force's offensive toward Daugavpils and Vilnius (in Lithuania). Part of the 1st and 4th Air Armies aircraft were assigned to the task of liquidating the encircled enemy group in the Minsk region.

The air force was also given the very important task of conducting aerial reconnaissance over these surrounded troops. This was done by the most experienced fighter and ground-attack crews, and at times, by Po-2s.

Information obtained by aerial observers and transmitted by radio was immediately utilized by the ground troops, and also to organize air strikes against the encircled enemy.

Strikes were made, as a rule, from low altitudes. The encircled troops suffered great losses. After a ground-attack raid, some of the Germans emerged from the forest and surrendered. The great effectiveness of our air operations was confirmed by the secretary of the White Russian Communist party, P. K. Ponomarenko, who informed the *Stavka* representative: ". . . Several days ago we discovered and inspected a huge German fortified region east of Minsk which had been completely destroyed by our ground-attack planes. This region gives a shattering impression of mass destruction and a demonstration of our air fleet's power."

Then he went on to say that the German troop concentration, 11,000 soldiers and officers and much equipment, was smashed by the 1st Guards Ground-Attack Air Division. Squadron commander of the 74th Guards Ground-Attack Air Regiment, First Lt. B. S. Okrestin, Hero of the Soviet Union, attacked the enemy with great courage. When his aircraft was hit and began to burn, he guided it into an enemy troop concentration. After the liberation of the region, the hero's remains were transported to Minsk, where his funeral was held with military honors. The White Russian people hold sacred the memory of the brave flier.

The shift of the air regiments and squadrons close to the encircled concentration increased the effectiveness of air operations. However, in a number of cases, a difficult situation developed on our airfields. fascist soldiers, attempting to break through to the west, appeared at our airfields or at air staffs (the staff of the 1st Air Army in the Rudni region). One enemy group tried to seize the airfield at Ozero, so that their transport planes might land there and evacuate German troops by air. Personnel of the air and support units, and staffs in several cases, fought with German troops utilizing ground-attack and fighter plane support, and sometimes our planes were given the alarm and flew back to airfields at the rear. Personnel of the 4th Air Army support units, when defending their airfields, killed 974 Germans and wounded or captured 1833 others.

On July 11, Soviet troops, with air support, completed the liquidation of the entire enemy troop concentration.

In July and August, in addition to supporting the rout of the encircled enemy troops at Minsk, our air force actively continued to support the Soviet offensive along a broad front.

The AFLRO was most active in raids against approaching enemy reserves, striking against railroad yards in western White Russia, Lithuania, and eastern Poland. The groups from the air armies raided enemy strong points.

From July 7 to 13, 1st Air Army fliers took an active part in the battles for Vilnius, where enemy troops were surrounded. Immediately before the assault on the city, 103 Pe-2s and 51 Il-2s made ground-attack and bombing raids against the major enemy strong points. Shortly after this, our troops, within a period of a few hours, liquidated the encircled group. In the days that followed, our aircraft cooperated with the ground troops as they forced the Niemen River. Ceaseless patrolling of our fighter planes over the crossing and raids of our ground-attack planes at the enemy airfields at Kaunas and Suvalki sharply limited the level of enemy aircraft. The 3rd White Russian Front troops, without any real enemy air resistance, succeeded in crossing still another major river obstacle.

The 1st French Fighter Air Regiment, "Normandy," was part of the 303rd Fighter Air Division of the 1st Air Army and took part in the battles to liberate White Russia and Lithuania. Fliers from this regiment distinguished themselves in the battle for the Niemen River. By the order of the Supreme Commander, this regiment was given the name of the "Niemen Regiment" and thanks were expressed to the men of the unit. The Supreme Soviet Presidium of the USSR granted the "Normandy-Niemen" Regiment the Order of the Red Banner. Forty-two French fliers received medals, and two of them, First Lts. Marcel Albert and Roland de La Poype, were titled Hero of the Soviet Union.

As the offensive continued at high speed, deep in enemy territory, the air force command skillfully directed its aircraft on the front. Often air groups from one air army were utilized to support a neighboring air army.

The air units were especially active when an enemy counterattack was repelled by the 1st Baltic Front in the Sauliai district. The German command secretly managed to bring up selected air units to support the troops who were engaged in the counterattack. Our air force at the time was low on fuel and our aircraft were based far from the front lines. Taking advantage of this advantageous situation, the fascist air force seized the initiative and was very active in its efforts against our troops.

By the order of the *Stavka* representative, 1st Air Army units were sent to the aid of the 3rd Air Army for operation in the Sauliai region. This made it possible to regain the control of the air, which had been lost for a short time.

The 4th Air Army gave support to the ground troops as they fought to liberate Grodno and helped to defeat the enemy troops defending themselves bitterly on the approaches to Bialystok. In August, the 4th Air Army was strengthened by addition of the 4th Ground-Attack Air Corps and the 8th Fighter Air Corps brought from the 16th Air Army. This air army actively supported the offensive of the front's troops toward Avgustov and Lomzha.

Aircraft of the 16th Air Army, at the beginning of July, cooperated with the 1st White Russian Front troops as they liberated the city of Baranovichi and repulsed the enemy counterattack in the direction of Brest. Then they supported the ground forces as they forced the Vistula and advanced toward Pułtusk.

The 6th Air Army, commanded by General F. P. Polynin, was active near Kovel. In the middle of July it was strengthened by the arrival of units from the Supreme Command's reserves. To it also were added several air divisions from the 16th Air Army. Beginning in July 18 it supported the offensive of the 1st White Russian Front (the 47th, 8th Guard, and 69th Armies) in the Brest-Lublin operation. The air units supported the offensive of our troops as they forced the western Bug and contributed to the rapid movement of the 2nd Guard Tank Army in their advance toward Warsaw. At the end of July, the 6th and 16th Air Army concentrated their efforts on the support of the 8th Guards and 69th Army as they forced the Vistula at Magnushev and Pulawi. From July 18 to July 31, 6th Air Army units flew about 12,000 sorties.

The 6th Air Army units were shifted to new airfields. As they moved, every technician had the responsibility for several aircraft, which were flying three or four sorties per day. The mechanics Bovat, Klimentyev, Ignatov, and Tkachenko, as well as gunnery specialist Master Sergeant Loginov and Private Khvorovoy, were especially effective in maintaining ground-attack aircraft. Their achievements were given wide publicity in the army newspaper.

Battles with enemy aircraft became very intense during the struggles for the bridgehead over the Vistula at the beginning of August. Increased protection for river crossings, improved control, and the use of radar made it possible to successfully repel the Luftwaffe, which lost 69 aircraft over the Vistula from August 11 to August 15 alone and was compelled to abandon its resistance in this area.

Thus, in the second stage of the operation, in spite of a number of difficulties and inadequacies, the Soviet Air Force gave active support to our ground forces, who developed their offensive at great depth.

Under difficult circumstances it helped our ground forces to overrun enemy intermediate defense lines, to cross major rivers, and to fight off enemy counterattacks. From July 5 to August 29, the Soviet Air Force flew 98,534 sorties and destroyed about 1500 Fascist aircraft.

Under conditions imposed by a rapid ground offensive and a poorly developed system of airfields and roads, the air groups suffered from difficulties in supplies and in the maintenance of air operations.

Transport aircraft were widely used to deliver supplies to air units, tank corps, and mechanized cavalry groups. The Civil Air Fleet transport regiments flew about 35,000 sorties and transported more than 43,000 men, and Li-2s of the AFLRO transported 11,000 men and around 3500 tons of cargo.

Results. In the White Russian operation, Soviet troops dealt a serious defeat to the Army Group Center and liberated the White Russian Soviet Socialist Republic, most of the Lithuanian Soviet Socialist Republic, part of the Latvian Soviet Socialist Republic, and the eastern part of Poland. By employing large numbers of front aircraft and the AFLRO, the airmen made a great contribution to the enemy defeat on the central section of the Soviet-German front. During the offensive operation the air force flew 153,000 sorties. This was the largest operation of the entire war.

One of the major assignments of the air force was the battle against enemy aircraft, for which 42 percent of the sorties were expended. Two thousand German aircraft were destroyed in the air or on airfields. The German generals testified to these great losses. In the collection of essays entitled *The World War of 1939–1945,* it was noted that "in the winter of 1941 the German bomber force suffered its first major blow, and in 1944 it was destroyed in Russia."[10] It was also noted that Germany lost 11,074 aircraft from June 1 to August 31, 1944, including 1874 bombers, 1345 ground-attack planes, and 7855 fighter planes.[11]

The successful use of air power, especially when the enemy was in flight, depended to a large extent upon flexible control and close coordination between ground armies, especially tank armies, and the air force. The designation of operational groups with radio communications, advanced assignment of targets, and directing groups of aircraft to their targets, insured the most effective and rational application of air power as it carried out its major assignments.

Air operations when enemy troops were surrounded and then

liquidated became an important part of the air armies' work. Air strikes against retreating troops made a significant contribution toward encirclement of enemy units in the operation near Minsk and in other regions. Aircraft became an effective method of destroying retreating enemy troop columns and encircled troop concentrations. Especially great results were obtained when the encircled group was in a limited area with few antiaircraft weapons.†

Aerial reconnaissance was important in air operations. It provided front commands and army commands with data about the enemy during a preparatory period and during an offensive. Since espionage could not provide information on a large scale, aerial reconnaissance conducted by a large number of bombers, ground-attack planes, and fighter planes was widely utilized.

The air force succcess was assured by careful training for the operation, and rational planning during the offensive. The secret massing of aircraft on airfields far from the front, and then their shift in small groups to advance airfields, with total radio silence two or three days before the operation began, was worthwhile.

XIV

THE LVOV-SANDOMIR OPERATION

Even as the battle in White Russia went on, the Red Army prepared an offensive against Army Group North Ukraine, whose 31 German and 12 Hungarian divisions occupied the Lvov area. During this offensive, the Nazi situation was further shaken by the attempt to assassinate Hitler on July 20, and by uprisings begun in Warsaw and in Slovakia. ED.

Preparations. In the spring of 1944, troops of the 1st Ukrainian Front liberated a number of areas along the right bank of the

---

† The extent of German losses is shown by this: of 47 generals commanding the divisions and corps, 10 were killed and 21 captured.[12] ED.

Dnieper and emerged on the approaches to Lvov. The successful summer offensives of the other fronts in Karelia and White Russia created favorable conditions for conducting a large offensive operation with the goal of annihilating the enemy troops who remained within the Ukraine.

The German Army Group of northern Ukraine defended the Rava Russkaya, Lvov, and Stanislavsk areas. In the air, it was supported by groups from the 4th Air Fleet with 750 aircraft. In addition, the German command could bring units with 300–400 aircraft from the nearby 6th Air Fleet into the offensive zone of the 1st Ukrainian Front.

Stavka gave the 1st Ukrainian Front the following assignment: break through the enemy defenses in two major assaults in the Rava Russkaya and Lvov areas, divide and annihilate the opposing armies one after another, and advance to the Grubeszów-Tomaszów-Yavorov-Galich line.

Included as part of the Front was the 2nd Air Army, commanded by General S. A. Krasovsky. To strengthen it, four air corps and two separate divisions were added to its ranks. At the beginning of the operation the army had nine air corps, three separate divisions, and four separate regiments that had a total of more than 3000 aircraft. In the rear there were 65 airfield service battalions, 10 engineering-airfield battalions, and 10 truck transportation battalions.

Thanks to these additions, the air army had a threefold superiority over the enemy in aircraft.

On June 24 the air units began comprehensive preparation for the coming operation. Taking into account the over-all plan for the operation, the 2nd Air Army commander established two air groups. He designated four air corps with 1200 aircraft to support and protect the armies attacking in the Rava Russkaya sector. Control over them was given to the operational group of the army staff headed by the deputy to the commander, General S. V. Slyusarev. In addition, the *Stavka* sent the field control group of the 8th Air Army, which shortly after the beginning of the operation shifted its operations out of the Crimea, and on July 17 began its work of controlling the air units in the Rava Russkaya area.

In the Lvov area, there were five air corps with 1500 aircraft. They were controlled by the commander of the air army. In addition, in the central sector of the front there were three separate air divisions with 400 aircraft. They were the reserves of the air army commander.

During the preparatory period, the most important problem was distribution of the numerous air units in accordance with the over-all plan. Construction of airfields along the front began on June 25.

The regrouping of air units was carried out with measures which insured that preparations for the offensive remained secret. There were limitations in radio use when aircraft were shifted from one base to another. Air regiments were concentrated on airfields 100–150 kilometers (62–93 miles) from the front, and then were moved to advance bases a day or two before the offensive began.

In the Kolomya, Chernovitsy, and Buchach districts, false aircraft and tank concentrations were set up. A network of false airfields was established on which radio stations transmitted and mock aircraft and other air equipment was built. From time to time, small groups of fighter planes would patrol over this region with its false concentrations. When the operation began there were 33 false airfields, of which 9 were supposedly for night use. German reconnaissance was unable to discover our genuine aircraft concentrations. In June and the first half of July, fascist aircraft made 87 percent of their raids against false airfields and only thirteen percent against genuine air bases.

The air army staff carefully planned the operations of the air groups in the offensive's first days. The plan called for massive bombing raids on both sectors of the front which were to be attacked. Then large groups of ground-attack planes were to appear over the battlefield. When the offensive began, 2000 aircraft were to make a mass strike. The result of such a strike, it was assumed, would be to disorganize the enemy's fire power and his communications and thus significantly weaken enemy resistance in the major defense zone. The plan called for pinning down the enemy reserves by means of repeated mass attacks, and between the attacks small groups of ground-attack planes were to silence enemy fire points and centers of resistance.

Thus, at the beginning of the operation, the major enemy troop concentrations throughout the entire tactical defense zone were to be attacked.

Realizing how important were support and protection for tank armies and mechanized cavalry, the air commanders and staff officers devoted much attention to the questions of coordinated efforts with the tank groups. As soon as mobile units entered the battle, it was planned that sixteen divisions of ground-attack planes and fighters would be devoted to their support, which was 60 percent of all the 2nd Air Army aircraft. In addition, if it were necessary, all the remaining reserves of the air army commander could be brought into action to support the tank units.

The Attack Begins Ahead of Schedule. The offensive operation began on July 13, 1944, two days before the projected beginning of the campaign. That day all types of reconnaissance established that the German command in the Rava Russkaya area was attempting to withdraw their troops to a new defensive zone to the rear. Therefore, the Front commander ordered the 3rd Guards Army and the 13th Army with air support to attack the enemy immediately, disrupt his planned retreat, defeat his troops near Gorochow, and expand the offensive in the direction of Sokal and Rava Russkaya.

As a consequence the aircraft of the northern group began operations in the Rava Russkaya area on July 13. The ground-attack planes of the 1st Guards Composite Corps and the 5th Ground-Attack Corps struck at columns of retreating enemy troops, and also enemy centers of resistance. Bombers raided enemy troops at the crossings on the western Bug.

Bitter fighting began in the air. Our fighter pilots from the 7th Fighter Air Corps commanded by General A. V. Utin entered the action. The 9th Guards Fighter Division commanded by the famous flier, Col. A. I. Pokryshkin, fought with special skill and courage.

Once, three groups of four fighter aircraft flew out to protect ground troops near Radziejów. The leader of the first flight was Captain G. A. Rechkalov. The second flight was led by A. I. Pokryshkin, and the third by First Lt. A. I. Trud.*

In their assigned area, the patrolling fliers found about forty enemy bombers and eight fighters. Pokryshkin gave a brief order: "The flight of First Lieutenant Trud is to engage and pin down the enemy fighters; all other aircraft are to attack the leading enemy bombers." Twice our fliers attacked the enemy bombers. Five German planes fell in flames. The enemy fliers were compelled to drop their bombs without reaching their targets, and losing altitude they fled to the west. The Soviet fighter planes pursued the German planes

---

* They flew P-39 fighters. ED.

until their ammunition was exhausted. In this battle they shot down nine fascist aircraft, without losing one themselves.

Other officers of this division fought as bravely. Here is a brief list of their victories. Early in the operation, Second Lt. I. I. Babak shot down six fascist aircraft; Second Lt. V. Ye. Bondarenko, four; Lt. Col. L. I. Goreglyad, four; Lt. Col. V. I. Bobrov, three aircraft.

On July 16, twelve fighters commanded by Hero of the Soviet Union, Captain A. F. Klubov, protecting ground troops in the Radziejów-Stojanów and Suszno regions, fought off a large group of enemy bombers. In the battle which developed, Klubov destroyed two enemy aircraft. A. F. Klubov flew 457 sorties from August 10, 1942, to November 1944, participating in many successful air battles in which he personally shot down 31 enemy aircraft. By order of the Supreme Soviet Presidium of the USSR dated June 27, 1945, he was posthumously granted a second "Gold Star."†

Devyatayev's Escape. The second-in-command to Bobrov, First Lt. M. P. Devyatayev, flew more than 100 sorties by summer 1944. He participated in 35 air battles, shot down 9 German aircraft, and was given several medals. He abandoned his burning plane by parachute near Gorochow. Badly wounded, he was captured by the enemy when he reached the ground. But here also, he found the courage and strength to continue his battle with the enemy. Mikhail Devyatayev bore himself well at his interrogations and gave the Germans no military secrets entrusted to him. When he organized an escape from his camp, he was sentenced to death. His friends substituted his identification number and thus saved his life.

On February 8, 1945, he organized the escape of nine Soviet war prisoners in a Heinkel He 111 which they commandeered. Devyatayev and his comrades successfully returned to our lines. For this exploit Devyatayev was given the high honor of Hero of the Soviet Union in August 1957.‡

In the first four days of the offensive in the Rava Russkaya area, our fighter planes destroyed 115 enemy aircraft and forced the enemy

---

† Alexander Klubov was accidentally killed during the 9th Guards Division's transition from the P-39 to the La-7 in November. ED.

‡ Devyatayev was imprisoned after his return under a strict Stalin regulation that anyone who surrendered was a traitor. After nine years, he was released in 1953 and "rehabilitated" in 1957.[13] ED.

to restrict his activities. German aircraft could no longer fly in large groups. They began to appear along the front only in pairs and flights.

Our ground-attack pilots were very active. Groups of eight to twelve Il-2s constantly attacked artillery, tanks, and troop concentrations, clearing the road for our advancing troops. A good example of their effectiveness were the strikes of several groups of Il-2s against enemy troops defending Radziejów.

Troops of the 13th Army approached this city on July 16 and found stiff resistance. Meeting the requests of the ground troops, the 5th Ground-Attack Air Corps' chief of staff, Lt. Col. T. I. Yarotsky, summoned two Il-2 groups from the airfields by radio. Fifteen planes from the 90th Guard Ground-attack Air Regiment approached the battlefield, led by Major A. G. Kuzin. They attacked enemy positions four times, putting down artillery and mortar fire. Immediately behind Kuzin's group, eight more Il-2s approached the target to bomb and strafe German troops concealed in trenches. Our infantry immediately attacked the enemy and captured Radziejów without much resistance.

On July 16 enemy resistance was broken in the Rava Russkaya area. A tank army and mechanized cavalry entered the battle. During four days of intense battle, our fliers flew 3200 sorties. Their efforts were one factor leading to the successes achieved by the ground troops.

The Battle near Lvov. Our air operations in the Lvov area were on an even larger scale. Here ground troops took the offensive at 8:00 P.M. on July 14. Ten minutes before the attack, bombers of the 2nd Guards Air Corps and the 4th Bomber Air Corps bombed the area in which the ground assault was to be made. There were 252 aircraft that dropped bombs on the troops and enemy fire points. This preparatory period continued as air support for ground troops. In one and a half hours from the moment the attack began, 366 Il-2s struck at enemy artillery, tanks, and troops. In this first mass strike, around 1300 bombers, ground-attack planes, and fighters participated. This blow from the air significantly weakened the enemy's entire defense system. Within a few hours, troops of the 60th and 38th Armies drove 8 kilometers (5 miles) through the enemy's defense positions.

As had been planned, the second mass raid was made against

enemy reserves near Sasov and Zolochev. More than 1400 planes participated in the raid. The raid caused great losses to the enemy's tank divisions, which were part of the Army Group Northern Ukraine reserves. In addition, the raid discouraged their movement into the region in which the Germans planned their counterattack.

On the morning of July 15, enemy tanks counterattacked near Plugow, forcing the 38th Army to take defensive positions. The front commander ordered most of the air army to make a mass raid against the enemy tank unit. Units from the central air group, all the commander's reserves divisions, and part of the forces from the northern air group were called in to support the 38th Army.

The mass attack began at 2:00 P.M. The first planes to pass over the control point in the village of Zalozhtse at an altitude of 1500 meters (4920 feet) were groups of aircraft from the 4th Bomber Air Corps. They passed the control point exactly at the designated time at intervals of one or two minutes. The interval between corps was five to eight minutes.

Then 135 Pe-2s of the 4th Bomber Air Corps advanced toward the target followed by three groups of five dive bombers. The first group of five was led by a master of bombing technique, the 2nd Guards Bomber Air Corps commander, General I. S. Polbin. The second group of five planes was led by the 8th Guards Bomber Air Division commander, Col. G. V. Gribakin. The third group was led by the 162nd Guards Bomber Regiment commander, Lt. Col. A. A. Novikov. The dive-bomber groups were accompanied by eighteen fighter planes led by Captain N. D. Gulayev. At the commander's order, the bombers formed a circle over the target while the fighter planes flew cover for them in two groups: one at an altitude from which dive-bombing began (1500 meters, or 4920 feet) and the other at the altitude at which aircraft completed their attacks (700 meters, or 2300 feet).

The first to attack the tanks at the settlement of Tustoglova was General Polbin. The remaining aircraft followed his example, dive-bombing behind him. Every aircraft made four passes.

Following the dive bombers came the rest of the 117 aircraft from the 2nd Guards Bomber Air Corps. Dropping their bombs from horizontal flight, they also caused serious losses to the enemy. The remainder of the mass raid was carried out by the ground-attack planes of the 1st Guards and 8th Ground-Attack Air Corps and the 10th Guards Ground-Attack Air Division.

Fighter planes supported the bombers and ground-attack planes by maintaining a constant patrol over the battlefield. They repelled all enemy attempts to break through to the Plugow region, shooting down thirty German aircraft.

The mass raid continued for four hours. But our attacks against the enemy tank concentration continued even after this period. More airplanes continued to enter the battle from the commander's reserves. They bombed the enemy again and again. Il-2s also came from the north, from the 5th Ground-Attack Air Corps, and also attacked the enemy tanks.

Our planes flew 3288 sorties on July 15 against the enemy tank concentration. This was a saturation of 102 tons per square kilometer (.386 square mile). The German troops suffered great losses in the Plugow region.

The enemy was not able to bring up his 8th Panzer Division to participate in the counterattack. Our air force struck against tank columns advancing out of Zolochev. Former German General F. Millentin wrote: "The 8th Panzer Division advancing in long columns was attacked by Russian aircraft and suffered great losses. Many tanks and trucks burned; all hopes for a counterattack collapsed."[14]

In this manner the 2nd Air Army disrupted the carefully prepared German plan for a counterattack and thus assured the continuing success of our advance toward Lvov. It was with reason that the 1st Ukrainian Front commander Marshal I. S. Konev said in his analysis of the Lvov-Sandomir operation: "The air force rescued the 38th Army from its critical situation on July 15."

The ground forces, with secure protection from the air force, continued their advance. On July 16 they broke through the enemy's tactical defense zone. Mobile groups began to participate in the battle near Lvov, as well as on the right flank of the front. At this time the most important air force task was support for the tank armies and motorized cavalry groups.

Ground-attack planes in groups of six or eight planes attacked separate centers of resistance along the route of the tanks and the cavalry, and attacked enemy reserves. Fighter planes patrolled constantly in squadrons in support of the advancing columns.

Small detachments assigned to the command posts of the tank army and the mechanized cavalry group by the staffs of the 5th Ground-Attack Air Corps, the 1st Guards Composite Air Corps, and the 7th Fighter Air Corps, successfully solved the problems of controlling their air units. Being located with the commanders of the ground armies, which had supporting air units, they had reliable radio links with the airfields as well as aircraft in the air. Officers, who were part of the operational groups, transmitted the requests of the ground army commanders, directing aircraft to the most important targets on the battlefield, and were thus the connecting link between the air force and the ground forces.

The 1st Guards Tank Army and the mechanized cavalry group supported by ground-attack planes and protected in the air from enemy aircraft, pushed their offensive at a rapid rate, outrunning the general armies by 50–60 kilometers (31–37 miles), and on July 22 attained and began to cross the San River.

The German command tried at any price to prevent our troops from crossing the San. Their first concern was to send their aircraft to destroy our bridges. Our fighter planes were compelled to fight in very bad weather. But, in spite of these difficult conditions, Soviet airmen bravely defended the tank units from enemy aircraft. Very often six or eight of our fighters engaged a larger force of enemy planes. Nonetheless they achieved victory, forcing the fascist bombers to drop their bombs before they reached their targets. Colonel Pokryshkin's division greatly increased their victories over the San bridges. During four days of battle they shot down 28 enemy aircraft.

The 7th Fighter Air Corps command and the workers in the rear took energetic measures in order to quickly shift fighter regiment bases closer to the front lines. On July 26, they moved the 205th Fighter Air Division, commanded by Lt. Col. Goreglyad, closer to the San. This made it possible to double the number of our fighter planes over the front. German losses sharply increased, and they reduced their operations.

When our tank armies entered the battle near Lvov and our offensive efforts increased, they met bitter resistance from the enemy. This increased the need for more support from the air.

All available bombers were employed in the battle for Lvov, including the 2nd Guards Bomber Air Corps, which had been assigned to the right wing of the front. From time to time, 5th Ground-Attack Air Corps units were brought in from the northern air group. Thus, about 75 percent of all the 2nd Air Army aircraft participated in the decisive battles on the central sector of the front.

The Koltow Corridor. Under these advantageous conditions the tank armies entered the Lvov battle. The enemy's tactical zone was pierced in a small sector, with large concentrations of German troops on both flanks. On July 16 the 3rd Guards Tank Army, advancing in a column, entered the battle in the narrow defile south of Koltow. The "Koltow Corridor," as the armored units called it, was 4 to 6 kilometers (2½ to 3½ miles) wide and open from both sides to enemy fire.

Under these conditions the tank armies' entry into the battle was possible only with active air support and protection. On July 16, six air corps and three separate divisions took the assignment of protecting them while the enemy's flanking units were attacked by two bomber corps. On that day, the 2nd Guards Bomber Air Corps struck a number of effective blows against enemy troop concentrations in the Sasov, Koltow, and Bely Kamen regions. The 4th Bomber Air Corps continued to operate against enemy troops near Plugow and Zolochev.

At the same time the fliers of the 1st Guards Air Corps, the 8th Ground-Attack Air Corps, and the 10th Guards Ground-Attack Air Divisions, flying in waves, attacked enemy fire points on the flanks of our tanks' break-through area. Fighter planes from the two corps and the separate divisions, so to speak, created a solid air barrier that prevented enemy aircraft from entering the Koltow Corridor.

Fliers of the 1st Guards Ground-Attack Corps were especially effective in supporting the tank army. Corps commander V. G. Ryazanov, with an operational group and two radio transmitters, was located in the narrowest part of the Koltow Corridor at the village of Nushche. He could plainly see our tank columns and the enemy fire points.

According to a plan that had been worked out in advance, one group of aircraft after another passed over the command point from their bases. They were directed to those targets that were hindering the advance of our troops. When there were not enough aircraft over the target for an assignment, additional aircraft were summoned from the airfields. Ground-attack planes of the 9th Guards Ground-Attack Division, commanded by General F. A. Agaltsov, were especially effective.

The 4th Tank Army entered the battle behind the 3rd Guards Tank Army. On July 18, 3rd Guards Tank Army units met the Soviet mechanized cavalry group commanded by General V. K. Baranov near Krasne. The enemy group at Brody, the vestiges of the 8th Division, was surrounded.

Soviet aircraft made a significant contribution to the enemy defeat near Lvov as the tank armies came into the battle. In a three-day period from July 16 through July 18 they flew around 4500 sorties.

The basic 1st Ukrainian Front assignment after July 19 was the liberation of Lvov and the liquidation of the encircled enemy troops at Brody. Most of the air army aircraft were also devoted to this assignment.

The fluid, rapidly changing situation caused by large numbers of tanks and aircraft on both sides increased the need for aerial reconnaissance, one of the basic sources of information about the enemy troops' concentration and his plans. In addition to the regular reconnaissance regiments, individual aircraft were used for this purpose, particularly fighter aircraft. Aircraft were assigned to aerial reconnaissance by the 728th Fighter Air Regiment, 91st Fighter Air Regiment, and the 31st Guards Fighter Air Regiment, commanded respectively by Lt. Col. V. S. Vasilyaka, Lt. Col. A. R. Kovalev, and Maj. S. Kh. Kudelya, which had the assignment of gathering essential information about the German troops near Lvov on July 19.

That day, rain, fog, and low clouds made it almost impossible for aircraft to carry out their missions. But in spite of the bad weather, Major F. Ya. Morozov and Second Lt. A. M. Siradze were able to make reconnaissance flights in the Lvov area. When they had returned they reported on the enemy troop concentrations on the approaches to Lvov, and in the city. On the basis of the information they obtained, the front commander decided to assault Lvov. Troops of the 38th and 4th Tank Armies advanced on Lvov from the east and the 3rd Guards Tank Army encircled the city from the north.

At the same time that the 38th Army, the 3rd Guards Tank Army, and the 4th Tank Army were approaching Lvov, attacks were going on behind them to destroy the encircled enemy concentration at Brody, which several times attempted to break out toward the south. The critical situation that developed in the liquidation of this concentration often demanded the use of many aircraft. The need was especially great on July 20 and July 21, when the battles in the Bely Kamen region became extremely fierce.

In this period, major strikes were made by 2nd Guards and 4th Bomber Air Corps units and also by the 1st Guards and 5th Ground-

Attack Air Corps. During a two-day period they flew about 2500 sorties, causing serious losses to the enemy and demoralizing him. On July 22, the remainder of the encircled concentration surrendered.

Lvov Is Liberated. Most of the 2nd Air Army aircraft participated in the battles to liberate Lvov. Groups of thirty to forty bombers raided enemy resistance points on the approaches to the city near Vinnikov, Zhuravka, and Kratoshina. Fliers of the 8th Ground-Attack Air Corps and the 10th Guards Ground-Attack Air Divisions struck at artillery and mortars, contributing to the advance of the 60th Army and the 4th Tank Army.

The 1st Guards Ground-Attack Air Corps continued to cooperate with 3rd Tank Army units during the battle. In this period the corps commander was located with the commander of the tank army, while the commanders of the 8th and 9th Guards Ground-Attack Air Divisions, Col. A. S. Fetisov and General F. A. Agaltsov, together with their operational groups and radio transmitters, were placed together with the tank and mechanized corps commanders.

Ground-attack planes went into operation when they were summoned and directed by mobile command points from the divisions or corps. A good example of the effective utilization of Il-2s coordinated with mobile units can be seen in the bombing and ground-attack raid made by the 9th Guards Ground-Attack Air Division against an enemy troop resistance center in the Zholkeva region. After an attack by 36 Il-2s, 9th Mechanized Corps units quickly and without significant losses captured the important defense point.

With air support the 3rd Guards Tank Army units quickly carried out their maneuver, and on July 23 emerged in the rear of the enemy's Lvov concentration in the Sudavaya Vishnya region. Our troops attacked Lvov simultaneously from the east and the west. The enemy could not withstand the pressure from the Soviet vise and was compelled to withdraw quickly from the city. On July 27 the important industrial and communication center, Lvov, was liberated from the fascist invaders. Five air corps that were outstanding in the operation to liberate the city, as well as three divisions and five regiments, were given the name of "Lvov" units.

On July 30 there was a workers' mass meeting to celebrate the liberation of the city. Fliers of the 5th Fighter Air Corps, commanded by General D. P. Galunov, carried out a distinguished assignment that day. Eight fighter planes with Red Star insignia, with constant replacements, continuously flew on guard over the city, protecting Soviet citizens from air attacks in the hours of their celebration.

The German Army Group Northern Ukraine had suffered a serious defeat by the end of July. Its basic concentrations were defeated in the Rava Russkaya area and on the approaches to Lvov, and remnants of the defeated divisions retreated hastily toward the Vistula and the Carpathians.

The 2nd Air Army flew 30,500 sorties from July 13 through July 27. Our fliers destroyed around 350 German aircraft on the ground and in the air.

At the end of July the front troops proceeded to complete new assignments. They renewed their drive to the Vistula from the Yaroslav, Lvov, and Przemysl districts to harass the retreating enemy and then cross that important military barrier.

The 8th Air Army Reorganized.   The newly formed 4th Ukrainian Front continued its advance in the Carpathian foothills. In its ranks were the 1st Guards and 19th Armies, and also the 8th Air Army, commanded by General V. N. Zhdanov, whose field control had formerly been under the 2nd Air Army commander. The following units were transferred from the 2nd Air Army into the 8th Air Army: the 8th Ground-Attack Air Corps, the 10th Fighter Air Corps, the 321st Bomber Division, and parts of two air base regions.

As they participated in the liberation of the Drogobych Oil District and destroyed enemy troops retreating toward the passes in the Carpathians, the 8th Air Army units in August 1944 flew more than 2000 sorties. After this reorganization, the 2nd Air Army was limited to 2000 aircraft.

Air Battles over the Vistula.   *Winning a bridgehead across the Vistula (Visla) was necessary to expel the Germans from Poland. The uprising began in Warsaw on August 1 by the Polish Home Army was believed in Russia to be an attempt by anti-Soviet Poles to gain control of the capital before it was reached by the Red Army.* ED.

On July 29–30, our advance units arrived at the Vistula and attempted to cross it. The 2nd Air Army could fly support for them only in small groups of fighters. The enemy sought to take advantage of this circumstance. His bombers in groups of forty to fifty raided our crossings near Baranów.

The fighter units based closest to the Vistula were summoned to protect our crossings. These were the 304th Fighter Air Division, commanded by Col. I. S. Khotelev; the 6th Guards Fighter Air Division, headed by Col. I. I. Geybo; and the 12th Guards Fighter Air Division, commanded by General K. G. Barnchuk.

Intense air battles broke out over the Vistula. Utilizing radar, our fighter planes left their fields and intercepted groups of bombers; they caused the enemy serious losses and did not allow him to reach his targets. In the morning and evening hours when the probability of German planes appearing was highest, patrolling fighters were organized over the crossings in groups of four to six aircraft. Enemy losses constantly increased: on August 1, four aircraft were shot down and on August 5, nineteen.

Two more air divisions from the 7th Fighter Air Corps were re-based closer to the front lines. The balance of forces in the air swung to our favor. Because of his great losses, the German command began to send his bombers out only at night, and in general ceased his attacks on our crossings.

Taking decisive action, our troops quickly widened their bridgehead on the far side of the Vistula. The enemy tried with all his force to liquidate the Sandomir bridgehead. Bitter fighting on both the ground and in the air raged in the Sandomir, Opatów, Raków, and Pacanów regions.

The 2nd Air Army, at the beginning of August, had completed its shift to the regions of Razwadów, Zeszów, Mielec, and Przemysl. General Headquarters had allocated 7500 tons of fuel for the 2nd Air Army for the month of August. The capabilities of our air force increased. But the limitation on fuel, which was adequate for only 15,000–17,000 sorties, demanded the strictest economy in men and materials. Therefore, it was decided to support the men on the bridgehead by waves of ground-attack planes in groups of eight to twelve. Bombers for concentrated attacks could be used only in the case of very great need. Control over all air units was centralized, which made it possible to use air power most efficiently in support of ground troops where the situation was most critical.

Ground-attack planes provided an invaluable service to the ground troops in repelling the enemy counterattack. They destroyed enemy artillery and tanks on the battlefield with accurate strikes, which contributed to the disruption of enemy battle plans. On August 17, especially bitter fighting broke out in Stopnica where the enemy attacked 5th Guards Army units with large numbers of tanks. When the enemy tanks cut into our troops, two squadrons of Il-2s commanded by Capts. A. P. Kompaniets and M. P. Odintsov were summoned. In the first attack, Kompaniets' planes set several leading tanks afire. The second group also made a precise strike. Repeated attacks from our planes caused the enemy great losses. About fifteen tanks burned. The enemy attack bogged down. The 5th Guards Army commander thanked the fliers and gave the group commander, Captain Kompaniets, a watch as a gift.

From time to time, attacks were made against the largest enemy troop concentrations. They usually operated in groups of nine to eighteen aircraft after careful reconnaissance of the target. Their strikes caused considerable losses to the enemy and in part led to the disruption of his planned attacks.

By the end of August the battles on the bridgehead began to subside. Soviet troops not only held off the enemy, but also considerably broadened their bridgehead on the banks of the Vistula. On August 29 *Stavka* ordered the 1st Ukrainian Front troops to take up defensive positions.

Czech Fighters behind the Enemy Lines.   During the Lvov-Sandomir operation the 1st Czechoslovak Fighter Air Regiment, flying La-5s, became part of the 2nd Air Army. The regiment commander was Major František Feitl.*

The regiment's fliers had received their baptism of fire during the revolt in Slovakia. They fought from the airfield at Tri Duba. For more than a month the Czechoslovak fliers fought heroically behind the enemy lines, flying around 500 flights, and destroying more than 20 fascist aircraft on the ground and in the air. The pilots I. Steglik,

* The Czech pilots arrived at the front led by Major Feitl, formerly a wing commander in the Royal Air Force, just as the Slovakian national uprising, begun on August 29, gained control of territory in central Slovakia.

To support these partisans, the Czechs flew 21 La-5FNs across the German lines and the Carpathian Mountains on September 21. After five years of exile, the Czechs could land on their own homeland again, and began operations from Tri Duba field near Zvolen. Soviet Li-2 transports flew fuel in at night, enabling operations to continue until October 25, when the fighters returned to Soviet lines, for the partisans had to withdraw to the mountains.

This seems to be the only instance in which a complete fighter unit operated behind enemy lines.[15] ED.

S. Šrom, F. Habera, F. Štyčka, and L. Koza especially distinguished themselves. This regiment later became the 1st Czechoslovak Composite Air Division, which produced the cadre for the air force of the new democratic Czechoslovakia.

Results. Important strategic results occurred as the result of the successful offensive of the 1st Ukrainian Front. The German Army Group Northern Ukraine was routed and ceased to exist. Soviet troops liberated the western districts of the Ukraine and southeastern Poland. They captured a large bridgehead on the Vistula's left bank at Sandomir, which was later to become the base for a new offensive toward Silesia.

Air power played an important role and had a beneficent influence on the entire Lvov-Sandomir operation. We maintained control of the air and our aircraft destroyed more than 550 German planes.

The 2nd and 8th Air Armies flew 48,000 sorties from July 3 through August 29. They dropped 6500 tons of bombs on the enemy and fired 3,300,000 shells and bullets, causing the enemy great losses in men and materials, thereby speeding up our offensive on the ground. The air force not only defeated the enemy on the battlefield, but had a great effect on enemy troops located behind the lines. Enemy reserves and communication lines were important targets against which our bombers and ground-attack planes were very effective.

Valuable experience was gained in this operation in the utilization of large numbers of aircraft for solution of the greatest operational problems. Air commanders concentrated their aircraft on major offensive routes with the goal of fulfilling the most important assignments and striking at targets upon whose destruction or control depended the success of a ground offensive at a given moment.

Strict centralization of control and the timing of air attacks to coincide with ground operations was successful, and opened up the possibility of utilizing air power in accordance with the circumstances, and for the solution of different problems. Assignment of operational groups to the command points of ground army commanders provided the best possible condition for closely coordinated operations with ground troops, and gave the entire control system the necessary flexibility to utilize air power in the ground troops' best interests.

Much experience was gained in the concealed concentration of large numbers of aircraft, the construction of large numbers of airfields in a short period of time, and also in the camouflaging of large air bases.

Mass air raids in which as many as 1000–1500 aircraft participated proved to be a very valuable method for utilizing air power. As the result of such strikes, the air force not only caused the enemy great losses, but also strongly affected the morale of his troops. Such mass raids required much detailed planning. The air army commanders and staff determined the order in which units were to strike, not leaving this question to subordinate units.

Soviet fliers displayed great skill in combat. Dive-bombing was mastered by the crews of the 2nd Guards Bomber Air Corps. They employed a series of approaches to the target from different directions, and as a result greatly reduced the effectiveness of enemy anti-aircraft fire.

In their battles with the hated enemy, Soviet fliers provided numerous examples of courage. Ten air units of the 2nd Air Army were made guards units. Thirty-eight regiments, divisions, and corps were given the name of Lvov, Vladimir-Volynsky, Rava Russkaya, Stanislav, Przemysl, and Sandomir.

Hundreds of fliers were given orders and medals. In August–October 1944, seventeen of the finest pilots and navigators were given the title of Hero of the Soviet Union. The daring fighter pilot Major A. V. Vorozhekin was given the title Hero of the Soviet Union for a second time. A third "Gold Star" was given to the skilled authority on air battles, A. I. Pokryshkin.

The active role played by the air force in the Lvov-Sandomir operation showed the further maturity of our air force, and was brilliant evidence for the creative development of its operational skill and tactics.

XV

THE JASSY-KISHINEV CAMPAIGN

Rumania had been important to Nazi victory hopes, since her oil fields supplied the German war machine, and her manpower over half the 800,000 troops in the Army Group Southern Ukraine. Although Soviet forces now stood close to the Rumanian border, as late as August 5, the dictator Ion Antonescu assured Hitler that Rumania would stay in the war until the end. ED.

In March and April of 1944, Soviet troops reached the Dniester and were now in a flanking position in relation to the German troop concentration in the Jassy (Iaşi) and Kishinev area near the Rumanian border. The enemy had constructed a strong and deeply fortified defense area with men from the Army Group Southern Ukraine which had 47 divisions, 5 brigades, the 4th Air Fleet, and the 1st Rumanian Air Corps with a total of 810 aircraft.

Preparations. On August 19, 1944, the 2nd and 3rd Ukrainian Front had ten infantry armies and one tank army, two tank corps, two mechanized corps, one cavalry corps, and the 5th and 17th Air Armies which had 1759 aircraft, and when the planes of the Black Sea Fleet were added, 2650 aircraft. Thus, the ratio of aircraft was 3.3 to 1 in the Soviet favor.

The operational plan called for troops of the 2nd and 3rd Ukrainian Fronts to break through the enemy's defense zone northwest of Jassy and south of Tiraspol and then to press their offensive with these two forces joining in Rumania as they approached near Huşi and Vaslui with the goal of surrounding and annihilating the major concentration of the Army Group Southern Ukraine.

The troops of the two fronts and the Black Sea Fleet were given the assignment of annihilating the opposing enemy force, liquidating their base in the Jassy-Kishinev area, advancing into the central districts of Rumania, and thus taking her out of the war.

In accordance with the decision of the front commanders the air force was given the following assignments: maintain the control of the air; support the ground forces as they broke through the enemy's tactical defense line and advanced into the enemy's rear; interdict the advance of reserves and disorganize the enemy's planned withdrawal; carry out aerial reconnaissance.

The 5th Air Army command (General S. K. Goryunov) decided to lend most of its aircraft to support the 27th Army, the 52nd Army, and the 6th Tank Army, while the 3rd Guards Fighter Air Corps was to fight the enemy in the sky, and cover for the ground-attack planes and bombers was provided by the 279th Fighter Air Division and one fighter air regiment. There was to be no initial air preparatory attack, but the air operation was to begin the moment that the ground forces began their offensive. The air plan was composed for a three-day period during which more than 4000 sorties were to be flown.

The 17th Air Army commander, General V. A. Sudets, decided to devote most of his forces to support of the 37th and 46th Army as they broke through the enemy defenses in the most crucial area of the front. Later on, as the 4th and 7th Mechanized Corps entered the battle, they were to be supported by ground-attack and fighter aircraft. During this three-day period, 7980 sorties were planned.

During the preparatory period, aerial reconnaissance sought out the enemy's defensive facilities and the probable attack routes of our tank units into his rear. Aerial photographers of the 5th and 17th air armies photographed 104,913 square kilometers (40,507 square miles) of land. From these aerial photographs, maps were prepared and duplicated, which were sent to the tank unit commanders and their subordinates. Data from aerial photos made it possible to evaluate the situation before the operations and to take appropriate measures.

Units constructed new airfields not far behind the lines, rebuilt landing strips on many airfields, and prepared shelters for aircraft. At the beginning of the campaign, more than 200 airfields were provided for the two fronts, of which 40 percent were utilized, while the others were mock airfields or reserved for special uses.

Within the political and party organizations, it was pointed out that the Rumanian people, just as many other European peoples who had fallen under the Fascist yoke, were not guilty of unleashing the war and therefore it was essential to make a distinction between the German and Rumanian troops. This distinction was all the more important since formation of the Tudor Vladimirescu Division, consisting of Rumanian prisoners of war, had already begun within the 2nd Ukrainian Front.

The Offensive Begins. The Jassy-Kishinev operation began on the morning of August 20. The 2nd Ukrainian Front, with 5th Air Army support, took the offensive after an artillery barrage. Two hundred ground-attack planes in regiment-sized groups with fighter cover attacked enemy troops and artillery, which had taken positions in the offensive zone of the 27th and 52nd Armies and along the roads from Tirgu-Frumos-Roman-Jassy. At the same time bombers in groups of 27 aircraft with fighter cover, bombed points of resistance near Jassy and reserves in Vaslui, hindering their approach to the battlefield.

The German and Rumanian troops were paralyzed by our powerful artillery and air strikes. At 12:00 noon, aerial reconnaissance discovered that enemy troops were withdrawing from their defensive position. Front troops with air support broke through the enemy's tactical defense zone and created favorable conditions for the 6th Tank Army and the 18th Tank Corps to enter the battle.

In accordance with the 3rd Ukrainian Front plan, before our troops took the offensive, 198 aircraft from the 17th Air Army made a simultaneous strike with the artillery barrage. Ground-attack planes in groups of 12–24 aircraft with fighter cover attacked from altitudes of 400–600 meters (1310–1960 feet) in the 37th and 57th Army offensive zone, hitting artillery and mortars, destroying tanks, and striking at communications and staff headquarters. Many enemy command and observation points and communication lines were put out of order and their personnel killed. These powerful air blows insured the successful penetration of the enemy's deep defensive positions.

Simultaneously bombers were raiding communication lines, large railroad stations, and reserves, their crews displaying exemplary courage and heroism. The flight commanded by Ye. A. Myasnikov, in spite of heavy antiaircraft fire, made a precise strike against the railroad station at Kainari and put it out of commission for a long time. During the attack on the target, Myasnikov's aircraft was hit by antiaircraft shells, the right motor put out of operation, and the navigator seriously wounded. The daring commander completed his assignment, and with great skill and effort brought his damaged aircraft back to its base.

At the end of the day on August 20, most aircraft from both air armies operated in support of the tank units as they came into the battle. For this purpose, ground-attack aircraft made a mass attack against enemy tanks and artillery in the offensive zone of the 6th Tank Army from the 2nd Ukrainian Front. In the Tirgu-Frumos and Voinesti region they flew in small groups against enemy reserves. In other areas of the front, the 5th Air Army struck against enemy troops supporting the 27th and 52nd Armies as they overran enemy defense lines.

Fighter aircraft from the air armies flew systematic patrols to protect the strike groups. Ten Yak-9s commanded by Lt. Col. A. A. Oboznenko were sent to the Podu-Iloaei and Jassy area by the 3rd Guards Fighter Air Corps command post to attack sixty enemy bombers, escorted by twenty fighters, attempting to raid 27th Army troops near Codjaska-Noua. As the result of a courageous and decisive attack, the German bombers were dispersed and did not reach our troops. Seven enemy planes were shot down, while on that day the fighters commanded by Oboznenko destroyed twelve aircraft, the commander himself shooting down three.

Fighters led by Hero of the Soviet Union, Major K. A. Yevstigneyev and Captain N. N. Kononenko were very successful in an air battle, shooting down 20 enemy aircraft. In one battle with 25 bombers and 20 fighters, the 13th Guards Fighter Air Division fliers forced the bombers to drop their bombs on their own positions near Gomesti, and shot down 5 enemy aircraft.

The Mechanized Cavalry Group commander, General S. I. Gorshkov, regarded the fighter operations of the 5th Air Army highly. He wrote: "When the mobile group entered the battle, and during its operations in the operational rear, fighter planes of General Podgorny provided dependable protection for the mobile troops, making it possible for the cavalry units and tanks to maneuver freely."

Because of this dependable protection provided by our fighter planes, on the first day of the operation German bombers could not drop one bomb on our troops. Forty-three German planes were destroyed in air battles, while the 5th Air Army lost two planes.

Fighter pilots of the 17th Air Army were not less successful. They flew cover for the major troop concentration of the front. Four fighter planes led by First Lt. N. M. Skomorokhov, when protecting troops at 2000 meters (6560 feet) met ten fighters flying with bombs to attack our troops. The Soviet fliers bravely attacked and shot down two of them. N. M. Skomorokhov arrived at the front in December 1942, flew 520 sorties, and engaged in around 120 air battles in which he shot down 35 enemy aircraft. He was given the title Hero of the Soviet Union by the order of the Presidium of the Supreme Soviet on February 23, 1945, and in August he was given a second "Gold Star."

Ground-attack pilots were also effective. A group of Il-2s from the 136th Ground-Attack Air Division of the 17th Air Army, headed by First Lt. Ye. R. Ignatov, was directed by radio to dug-in German tanks holding up the advance of a 37th Army group with their intensive fire. They immediately attacked this resistance center with four passes and put several tanks out of commission. Enemy resistance in the sector of Fintina-Muskului and Cirnaceni was broken, and the 37th Army commander thanked the fliers for their successful operation.

Ground-attack aircraft from the 5th Air Army successfully supported the 6th Tank Army, whose advance units by the end of the operation's first day had reached the enemy's third (rear) defense zone along the Mare ridge, thereby creating favorable conditions to expand the offensive. The 27th Army advance units with air support also successfully maintained their attack. As the result of our effective ground and air operations the enemy suffered great losses. Five of his divisions were routed and 3000 officers and men were captured.

Operations of our ground-attack planes against the enemy fire points and troops aided the rapid advance of our ground forces; and our bombing raids against resistance centers, reserves, and communications limited enemy maneuverability and made it impossible for the enemy to introduce his reserves into the battle when needed.

Air operations did not cease at night. Groups from the AFLRO on two nights of August 20 and 21, flew 143 sorties against the railroad yards at Birlad and Romanesti. The enemy suffered great material losses, the movement of his reserves and military trains was restricted, and the railroad bridge across the Prut at Galati was put out of commission.

In the following days, the air armies' efforts were devoted to supporting our advancing troops, especially tank groups of the 2nd Ukrainian Front. The 5th Air Army bombers and ground-attack planes struck at troop concentrations, reserves, and enemy troops blocking the advance of our tank units. On August 21, two ground-attack regiments from the 2nd Ground-Attack Air Corps struck the enemy in the Fedeleseni region, causing him great losses. His resistance was broken, and the 23rd Tank Corps began to press its advance toward the city of Roman.

Ground-attack planes and bombers from the neighboring 17th Air Army struck against retreating enemy troops in the regions of Manzyr, Chaga, Vozneseni, Clastiti, and Romanesti. Fliers commanded by Hero of the Soviet Union, Captain N. N. Dyakonov were especially effective against artillery batteries in the Opach and Tokuz region. Because of their action artillery fire was dampened in the region, and units of the 37th Army continued their offensive.

The German command took measures to disrupt the successful offensive of the 3rd Ukrainian Front. The enemy 13th Tank Division came from the reserves to attack the flank of the advancing 37th Army. Therefore the front commander, General F. I. Tolbukhin, ordered the 17th Air Army to rout the advancing enemy reserves and forbid their approach to the battlefield.

On August 21, our bombers, ground-attack planes, and fighters attacked the enemy's mobile troops in waves in the regions of Cimislija, Batir, and Tarkalija. Antitank bombs were widely used, as well as machine-gun and cannon fire, to destroy many troops and disrupt his plans. Ground-attack planes commanded by Second Lt. A. P. Yeldyshev, First Lt. Ye. A. Seredkin, Capt. K. A. Demidov and others were very effective. A group of ground-attack planes from the 951st Air Regiment led by Hero of the Soviet Union A. I. Kobelev was especially effective. The group leader set three tanks afire in three attacks. Following their commander's example, Second Lts. I. A. Kolesnichenko, S. T. Korpachev, and B. P. Drobinin each put two tanks out of commission. The air corps commander, General O. V. Tolstikov, thanked the fliers for the exceptional manner in which they carried out their assignment.

Ground-attack planes of the 210th Air Regiment commanded by the remarkable pilot, G. F. Sivkov, were very successful in this period. G. F. Sivkov was titled Hero of the Soviet Union in February 1944, and on August 18, 1945, he was given a second medal, the Gold Star.

Ground-attack operations from the 866th, 897th, and 659th Fighter Air Regiments of the 288th Fighter Air Division were also successful against the enemy.

During August 21, the 17th Air Army flew more than 1000 sorties, destroyed or damaged 25 tanks and about 400 other vehicles, silenced 27 field or antiaircraft batteries, and killed about 1200 enemy soldiers and officers.

The heavy losses the German and Rumanian troops suffered during the operation's first days encouraged them to surrender. Remnants of the enemy forces, pursued by our mobile group and the blows of our air force, retreated to the south, attempting to cross the Prut near Poganesti, Leovo, and Falciu. Intense battles broke out near the river crossings.

At the same time, there were also successful operations to capture Akkerman. Part of the 3rd Ukrainian Front with a force which was sent ashore with the support of the Danube Military Flotilla ships, and aircraft from the 17th Air Army and the Air Force of the Black Sea Fleet, forced the Dniester estuary, routed the 3rd Rumanian Army units, and captured the city and fortress of Akkerman. In the days that followed, our troops surrounded the 3rd Rumanian Army and some German units and compelled them to surrender.

Moldavia Is Liberated. On August 24, the fifth day of the operation, the left flank armies of the 2nd Ukrainian Front and the 3rd Ukrainian Front with air support reached the Prut, thereby surrounding the 6th German Army south of Kishinev and liberating the captial of Moldavia. Air power played a great role in the encircling movement. Operating effectively against enemy troops and river crossings, it created favorable conditions for our advancing units. On August 24 at 3:00 P.M., ground-attack planes commanded by Captain V. M. Samodelkin and Major A. V. Matveyev were sent by radio by the 2nd Ground-Attack Air Corps commander against the enemy troop concentration in the Kotu-Mare, Nemtseni region, which was crossing from the left bank of the Prut and threatening the 2nd Ukrainian Front's rear lines.

As the result of this strike the enemy suffered significant losses, he was held in his positions, and the approaching troops routed his concentrations. The 9th Composite Air Corps was effective in its support of the 37th Army and the 4th and 7th Mechanized Corps. During the day the fliers flew 500 sorties. More than 200 vehicles,

144 loaded wagons, 10 tanks, and significant number of soldiers and officers were destroyed.

Strikes made by ground-attack planes against river crossings in the Leovo, Falciu, and Leuseni regions were especially effective. Their constant attacks destroyed bridges and prevented their reconstruction. In one raid, two flights of ground-attack planes, commanded by Hero of the Soviet Union, First Lt. Ye. A. Seredkin, in spite of heavy smoke in the target area and a continuous wall of antiaircraft fire, destroyed the enemy's wooden bridge near Leuseni on their first attack, and then bombed and strafed the enemy's troop concentration.

Destruction of the Prut crossings and constant attacks from ground-attack aircraft on the enemy troops made it possible for the 7th Mechanized Corps on August 24 to rout the enemy's 10,000-man troop concentration at the city of Leovo and establish control over the left bank of the Prut.

Rumania Leaves the War.   As the result of defeats suffered on the ground and in the air, the Rumanian Army and its air force ceased their activities against Soviet troops on August 24.* At that time German aircraft in groups of two to four aircraft were covering the crossings over the Prut River and their retreating troops and carrying out aerial reconnaissance. The German aircraft avoided combat with our fighters.

Having suffered a major defeat in the Jassy-Kishinev region, deprived of Rumania as an ally, the German command hastily withdrew its still-surviving units deep into Rumania or into Hungary or Bulgaria. At the same time they tried to evacuate their troops to the south, but their plans were disrupted by our troops.

At the same time that most 2nd Ukrainian Front units were advancing rapidly southwest of Kishinev, there was bitter fighting to eliminate the encircled enemy troops. All of the 17th Air Army aircraft and part of the 5th Air Army aircraft were used for supporting our troops. Soviet fliers in constant ground-attack and bombing raids contributed to the rapid destruction of the surrounded enemy troops.

* Opposition elements in Rumania had been in touch with the USSR, and on the evening of August 24, Antonescu was arrested, a new government formed, and anti-Soviet hostilities ceased. German forces then attacked Bucharest on August 25, and Rumania declared war on Germany. ED.

Taking advantage of the favorable situation in the air for attacking the surrounded enemy concentration, the air command ordered most of the 288th Fighter Air Division aircraft to be used for ground attack. On August 25–27, sorties of eight to twenty fighters were flown at the demand of the 17th Air Army's command post. The most effective attacks were made by the 866th Fighter Air Regiment commanded by Lt. Col. S. N. Kuzin.

Fighters commanded by Heroes of the Soviet Union Capts. A. I. Koldunov and A. A. Bondar were very effective in operations against the encircled enemy group. When they arrived in the target region they established contact with the control radio station, and under its direction made five or six approaches to the target, and flying at low-level they strafed the enemy. For their effective actions they were thanked by the command and given medals. During the war years, these daring fliers were in many successful air battles and the two of them shot down more than sixty enemy aircraft.

Operations of the 866th Fighter Air Regiment were highly regarded by the command. By the *Stavka* order dated September 7, 1944, the unit was named the Izmail regiment and eight of its pilots, who shot down more than 160 German aircraft, were titled Hero of the Soviet Union.

The enemy made his last efforts to break out of the trap, concentrating his forces in different areas, attempting to feel out any weak places in the Soviet ranks. Fighting to the Prut through Sarata-Rozes, the enemy drove back 4th Guards Mechanized Corps and reached its command post. A critical situation developed. The corps commander asked for help from air units. Within twenty minutes, the enemy was hit by ground-attack planes directed from the radio direction station by the 306th Ground-Attack Air Division deputy commander, Lt. Col. A. V. Samokhin. Ground-attack planes headed by Heroes of the Soviet Union Captain N. N. Dyakonov, First Lt. Ye. A. Seredkin, and Major V. M. Mikhaylov dispersed and partially destroyed the enemy group that had broken through and then the 4th Guards Mechanized Corps completed their annihilation.

The corps commander, General V. I. Zhdanov, regarded this successful air operation highly. He wrote to the 17th Air Army commander: "I ask you to give my thanks to the 306th Ground-Attack Air Division commander, Lt. Col. A. V. Ivanov, and all his flying personnel for the outstanding support given the 4th Guards Mechanized Corps in the annihilation of the enemy group in the Sarata-Rozes region."

On one day alone, the 37th Army, 3rd Ukrainian Front, took about 10,000 men and officers prisoner. By the end of the day on August 26, the region held by the encircled enemy troops had been compressed and was completely within the range of artillery and machine-gun fire so air operations were ended. The 17th Air Army flew 943 sorties on two days—August 25 and 26—against the encircled troops, causing the enemy serious losses.

Air operations against the surrounded enemy troops southwest of Kishinev and in the Huşi region were very important. With their systematic aerial reconnaissance and constant attacks, Soviet fliers caused the enemy great losses and hindered his mobility, thus rendering invaluable service in the rout of his ground forces.

The AFLRO was also of great service in surrounding and annihilating the 6th German Army, striking against railroad bridges, stations, and crossings over the Prut, hampering the enemy's attempt to regroup his forces, disrupting his planned retreat and river crossings, and disorganizing rail transportation.

Clearing the Enemy from Rumania. Because the Soviet Air Force controlled the air and because of its effective strikes against a retreating or encircled enemy, the ground forces could maintain their rapid offensive, and in the course of ten or eleven days occupied the main population centers of Rumania—Ploeşti and Bucharest—smashed the enemy concentration in the south, and liberated the Moldavian Soviet Socialist Republic and the Izmail district of the Ukraine.

Rumania, which had fought against the USSR for more than three years, now left the war and began military operations against the German troops with the Red Army. This was the beginning of a new historical period in the life of the Rumanian people.

After the enemy concentrations had been liquidated near Kishinev and Huşi, and the large industrial centers of Ploeşti and the capital of Rumania, Bucharest, had been liberated, the *Stavka,* on August 29, ordered the 2nd Ukrainian Front to expand its offensive toward Turnu-Severin and to advance to the Bistrita, Cluj, Sibiu line, and the 3rd Ukrainian Front to cross the Danube, and by September 5 or 6 to advance to the Rumanian-Bulgarian frontier.

The 2nd Ukrainian Front troops continued their offensive with air support. The further they advanced into Rumania the more intense enemy resistance became. There were very severe battles in the passes of central and southern Rumania. In spite of the problems of operating in mountainous regions, the distance from air bases, which was particularly difficult for ground-attack and fighter aircraft, and limitations on the amount of fuel available, the Soviet Air Force provided effective support for the successful ground offensive.

German troops were supported and protected by part of the 4th Air Fleet and the Hungarian Air Force, which had more than 400 aircraft in this area. Enemy aircraft were very active from September 18 to September 22 when the Germans tried to seize the cities of Turda, Cluj, Reghin, Timisoara, and Arad. Groups of 15 to 25 bombers with 8 to 12 fighter escorts attacked Soviet and Rumanian troops. In spite of the high activity of enemy aircraft and their access to permanent bases with adequate supplies, they were not able to seize control of the air.

On September 6, the 2nd Ukrainian Front was given the Rumanian 1st and 4th Armies, and the 4th Army Corps and 1st Air Corps with a total of more than 138,000 men. The 1st Rumanian Air Corps, subordinated to the 5th Air Army, had seven groups with a total of 113 aircraft of various types.

The 5th Air Army gave faithful support to the deployment of our troops, employing for this purpose fliers of the 1st Rumanian Air Corps. Our fliers, supporting ground troops in the most important areas, successfully repelled enemy aircraft. Thus, Il-2s from the 570th Ground-Attack Air Regiment with fighter escort from the 279th Air Division ignored antiaircraft fire and made a large bombing raid against counterattacking enemy troops and then caused them great losses with cannon fire and rockets. As the result of the effective ground-attack and fighter operation, units of the 5th Cavalry Corps occupied the town of Karatna.

Often, Soviet fighters flying support for our ground forces entered battle against a numerically superior foe, but thanks to their flying skill, they emerged as victors. For example, six fighters led by Captain Kononenko attacked eighteen bombers and eight fighters. They disrupted their formation and forced the bombers to drop their bombs over their own territory. In this battle, the fliers shot down six enemy aircraft, of which the leader shot down two, while during the day Captain N. N. Kononenko shot down three.

Fighter and ground-attack strikes were very effective on September 16 when our planes destroyed 16 tanks, 3 self-propelled guns and killed as many as 400 infantrymen. Henceforth the enemy was compelled to cease his counterattacks.

In bitter fighting for the cities of Cluj and Timisoara the 5th Air Army fliers flew 5532 sorties, fought in 74 air battles, destroyed 78 enemy aircraft, and lost 19 of their own planes. After they had crushed the German troops near Cluj and Timisoara, the 2nd Ukrainian Front troops liberated most of central and western Rumania and entered Hungarian territory at the city of Makó.

During the campaign for the liberation of Rumania the martial friendship between the Soviet and Rumanian armies and the Soviet and Rumanian fliers, who for the most part were stationed on the same airfields and who flew together on the same assignments, came into existence and grew stronger. Their operations were especially effective during the offensive of the 27th Soviet Army, the 4th Rumanian Army, and the 6th Soviet Tank Army in the Cluj region.

On September 14, German troops counterattacked, attempting to drive our troops out of the city of Turda. Soviet and Rumanian fliers were sent to support our troops there and dealt the enemy a massive blow to help disrupt the counterattack.

Beginning on September 16, the 5th Air Army, with the participation of Rumanian fliers, actively supported operations of the 1st, 2nd, and 4th Rumanian Armies in the Szeged, Oradea, and Cluj areas. On September 25, it flew 509 sorties while the 1st Rumanian Air Corps flew more than 70 sorties in support of Soviet troops. Fifteen enemy planes were shot down, including three destroyed by Rumanian fliers. Because of the Soviet and Rumanian operations, the Luftwaffe could not provide any real resistance against our advancing troops. The successes of the Rumanian fliers were noted with thanks by the 6th Guards Tank Army commander and those who were outstanding were given Soviet awards and medals.

In September 1944, the AFLRO raided Hungarian airfields, military and industrial centers, and rail and highway junctions. To fulfill these assignments, 2905 sorties were flown and 3100 tons of bombs dropped. As many as 200 enemy planes were destroyed or damaged when the 3rd Guards Bomber Air Corps raided airfields near Budapest on September 14 and 15.

At the same time that troops of the 2nd Ukrainian Front were fighting against German and Hungarian troops in the Carpathian passes, the 3rd Ukrainian Front, with cover and support from the

17th Air Army, attained the Rumanian-Bulgarian border on September 6.

Bulgaria Changes Sides. *Bulgaria had joined the Axis Pact on March 1, 1941, allowed German forces to enter, and declared war on Britain and the U.S. on December 13, 1941. Although Bulgaria officially claimed neutrality in the Soviet-German war, Germany supplied aircraft to the Bulgarian Air Force's eight regiments, and kept a military force there, even after being told to leave on August 27, 1944.*

The USSR formally declared war on Bulgaria on September 5, 1944, but there was no resistance and an armistice was declared with a new Bulgarian government formed on September 9. ED.

Partisans, in several regions of Bulgaria at the time, united in the 1st Division of the People's Liberation Insurrection Army, became very active. The division was equipped with Soviet weapons dropped to them on September 4 by AFLRO crews and fliers of the transport regiment of the 17th Air Army.

On September 8, the 3rd Ukrainian Front troops crossed the Bulgarian border and began their offensive into the center of the country. At the same time the Black Sea Fleet, with air support, sent men ashore and dropped parachute troops at the ports of Varna and Burgas. Border guards and soldiers from their garrisons went out to greet the Soviet troops with welcoming placards expressing their friendly feelings toward them and testifying to their willingness to fight against the German fascists.

The 17th Air Army, in the middle of September, was transferred to airfields in Bulgaria and began operations against the enemy rail and highway communications which extended from Greece and Macedonia along the Morava valley to Belgrade. To completely destroy enemy communications, troops of the 1st and 2nd Bulgarian Armies together with Yugoslav units, and with support from Soviet and Bulgarian aircraft, began operations against the most important rail and road junctions—the cities of Nish and Leskovac.

At the beginning of the operation, Soviet and Bulgarian fliers operated shoulder to shoulder to destroy the German "Prinz Eugen" division near the city of Prokuplje. The advancing Bulgarian troops met stubborn German resistance. The 17th Air Army representative,

Major D. D. Syrtsov, summoned ground-attack aircraft when requested to do so by the Bulgarian command and together with Captain A. A. Zinovyev directed them against a German troop column. Soviet fliers caused them great losses and the approaching Bulgarian troops completed their defeat and occupied Prokuplje. Major D. D. Syrtsov and Captain A. A. Zinovyev were given Bulgarian medals for their skillful control over the ground-attack planes that routed the German column and contributed to the successful Bulgarian offensive.

Because of the effective strikes from Soviet and Bulgarian aircraft against the enemy's artillery, fire points, and men, the 2nd Bulgarian Army units, in spite of stubborn German resistance and unfavorable terrain and weather, completed their offensive. They cut the major communication lines to the enemy's southern troops, caused him great losses, and captured the cities and railroad centers of Nish and Leskovac. In support of the 2nd Bulgarian Army, 17th Air Army regiments flew 605 sorties and the Bulgarian Air Force flew 332 sorties.

During this operation, friendly relations were quickly established between the Soviet and Bulgarian fliers. Soviet-Bulgarian friendship, which extended its roots far into the past, quickly grew and flourished in the united battle with the German invaders. The relationship became especially close when the Bulgarian Air Force began to receive Soviet military aircraft.

Based on Bulgarian air bases, the 17th Air Army supported not only the Bulgarian armies, but also the Yugoslav partisans and the Yugoslav Democratic Liberation Army. At the request of Yugoslav partisans, Major I. I. Dmitrenko, staff officer from the 306th Ground-Attack Air Division, was sent to their detachments fighting in the region of Alakenica (25 kilometers, or 15 miles, northeast of Vranje). At his request, ground-attack aircraft struck at the surrounded German garrison at Alakenica.

The Soviet Air Force gave significant support to the 75th Infantry Corps on the left flank of the 2nd Ukrainian Front when it crossed the Danube on September 22 at Orşova-Slabin and seized a major bridgehead at a bend in the river. In spite of bad weather conditions, fliers of the 9th Composite Air Corps caused the enemy palpable losses. They helped our troops to repel the enemy counterattack, strengthen their defenses, win time, and then together with the 57th Army of the 3rd Ukrainian Front, to defeat the enemy in this region.

The 17th Air Army groups flew support for the troops of the 3rd Ukrainian Front and the 1st, 2nd, and 4th Bulgarian Armies and carried out assignments in support of Yugoslav troops.

Results. During the Jassy-Kishinev offensive operation, troops of the 2nd and 3rd Ukrainian Front with support from the air armies, the AFLRO, and the fleet routed the Army Group South Ukraine. The enemy had 256,000 men either captured or killed. The accomplishment of the operation had enormous political significance. Rumania and Bulgaria left the war as allies of Fascist Germany and declared war against her. Favorable conditions were created for liberating the peoples of Hungary, Czechoslovakia, and Yugoslavia and for supporting the democratic liberation wars in Greece and Albania.

The 5th and 17th Air Armies gave significant support to ground troops as they pressed their rapid offensive and surrounded and destroyed the enemy. During forty days of operation the air armies flew more than 20,000 sorties, caused serious losses to enemy troops and equipment, and destroyed 241 aircraft.

Commands and staffs of the air armies gained much experience in organizing coordinated operations with naval aircraft, long-range aircraft, and also with Rumanian and Bulgarian aircraft. The united efforts of different types of aircraft for coordinated fulfillment of major assignments with the ground forces had a real influence on the course and successful completion of the enemy defeat.

The forces in the rear also met their assignments in support of air operations. Personnel worked with complete dedication and great awareness of their duties. Although air bases were very far from supply centers—sometimes as much as 800 kilometers (497 miles) —the rear units of the 5th and 17th Air Armies with the utilization of air transport provided constant support for air units. During the forty days of the operation, rear units of the two air armies transported 10,500 tons of fuel and 3500 tons of ammunition and other supplies.

The Soviet Air Force was one of the most important factors in the victory of this operation. The commands, political organizations, staffs, and air support units received invaluable experience in successful conduct of air operations, which was a valuable contribution to further development of the air force and operational skills.

XVI

THE EAST PRUSSIAN CAMPAIGN

In January 1945, Germany had to face the end with all of her allies gone except Hungary. Six months of fighting in 1944 alone had cost 840,000 dead and missing in the east, and 393,000 in France.[16]

Her air power was so weakened that in the east only 1960 aircraft, according to Soviet sources, faced 15,540 Soviet aircraft. Thirteen air armies provided the air cover for a Soviet force of 6,800,000, including 55 armies (each of nine infantry divisions plus artillery) and 6 tank armies (each of two tank and one mechanized corps).[17]

German forces in the east included five army groups, three renamed and reorganized on January 26, 1945:

Army Group North (renamed Kurland)—encircled and withering in Latvia.

Army Group Center (renamed North)—East Prussia and northern Poland (Group Vistula added to cover Danzig).

Army Group A (renamed Center)—Poland, from Warsaw to Carpathian Mountains.

Army Group South—Hungary.

Army Group F—Yugoslavia.

Since weather was the key to the effectiveness of air support and the speed of tank movements, upon weather would depend the timing of the attacks on the German army groups in East Prussia and Poland. ED.

Preparations. Red Army offensive operations in the summer and fall of 1944 completely freed Soviet territory from the fascist invaders. The *Stavka* assigned the armed forces the goal of defeating

Fascist Germany and forcing her to surrender unconditionally in the 1945 winter campaign. This goal was to be achieved by a great Soviet offensive toward Koenigsberg, Berlin, Prague, and Vienna.

The troops of the 3rd and 2nd White Russian Fronts in the Koenigsberg area were to annihilate the Army Group Center, reach the sea, and capture East Prussia.

To achieve these goals, the 3rd White Russian Front was to make its major drive from the region north of Stallupönen utilizing four armies and two tanks corps, with the 39th, 5th, and 28th Armies, and the 2nd Guards Tank Corps in the first wave. The 11th Guards Army and the 1st Tank Corps were to form the second wave. The 2nd White Russian Front was to pierce the enemy line in two areas. The major attack was to be from the Rozhan area, to be made by the 3rd, 48th, and 2nd Strike Armies and the 5th Guards Tank Army toward Marienburg. The second attack was to be from the Serots area, to be made by the 65th and 70th Armies toward Płońsk and Cape Belsk. These assignments were to contribute to the offensive of the 1st White Russian and 1st Ukrainian Fronts toward Warsaw and Berlin.

The *Stavka* assigned enough units to support the 3rd and 2nd White Russian Fronts in their attack against the East Prussian enemy concentration to insure that we had a threefold numerical superiority over the enemy.

The Soviet air group consisted of the 1st Air Army, commanded by General T. T. Khryukin, attached to the 3rd White Russian Front; and the 4th Air Army, commanded by General K. A. Vershinin, attached to 2nd White Russian Front. Before the operation began, our air force was strengthened by reserve units and had more than 3000 aircraft. In addition, some aircraft of the 3rd Air Army of the 1st Baltic Front, and the 18th Air Army were also involved (the 18th Army was formerly part of the AFLRO, but on June 12, 1944, was given the designation 18th Air Army).

The German Army Group Center was supported by the 6th Air Fleet with 775 aircraft. The enemy had a strong system of airfields to assure mobility for his aircraft both at the front as well as the rear.

The fronts' commanders assigned important roles for the air force in the coming offensive. Thus, the commander of the 3rd White Russian Front, General I. D. Chernyakhovsky, believed that if the enemy had very strong defensive positions and many tanks, the air force would be very important. It would paralyze the enemy reserves and artillery and destroy traffic on railroads and highways.

During offensive operations the air armies were to support the front strike groups as they broke through the enemy's tactical defense zone and expanded their offensives, support the introduction of tank groups, destroy enemy reserves, protect our troops where they were massed in large numbers and on the move, and carry out aerial reconnaissance. To fill these assignments, the air armies' commanders made decisions concerning air operations, and their staffs worked out plans that called for a preparatory air strike and subsequent support for ground troops. One hour and twenty-five minutes before the attack began, 545 front bombers and ground-attack planes were to deliver mass strikes against strong points in the enemy's front lines in the 3rd White Russian Front area. After the attack began, efforts of both air armies were to be devoted to continuous support for the fronts' strike groups.

Ground-attack planes of the 1st Air Army were to attack the enemy's entire defensive zone simultaneously. Bombers were to support ground-attack planes by bombing strong points and resistance centers. One ground-attack and one fighter division were assigned to strike against enemy reserves as they approached the battlefield on the first day of the battle. On the operation's third day, two bomber divisions were also to be given this assignment.

Four ground-attack air divisions from the 4th Air Army were assigned to support the 48th and 2nd Strike Armies. Eight groups of 40–56 aircraft each were formed from these divisions. They were to make their attack one after the other for twenty-minute periods in the "circle of flights" formation. Targets were located less than 1½ kilometers (1 mile) behind the enemy line, to insure a constant and powerful action on the enemy at the beginning of the offensive. Day bombers were to attack railroad lines and the troops and supplies on them.

Both air armies devoted much attention to organization of air combat against the enemy. Two bomber air divisions, three ground-attack air divisions, and four fighter air divisions from the 1st Air Army and three fighter air divisions and one night bomber air division from the 4th Air Army were to operate against enemy airfields before the offensive began.

Air Marshal F. Ya. Falaleyev, the *Stavka* representative, was to coordinate operations of the air armies.

In order to insure surprise and also to confuse the enemy, the 3rd White Russian Front commander decided to conduct a false air preparatory attack on the left wing of the front in the 31st Army area. From January 1 to January 10, the 1st Air Army was to fly cover for a false troop concentration near Suvalki and aerial reconnaissance was to be active in the area of this army. A system of false airfields was also built in this area and 60 mock fighter planes and 100 mock ground-attack planes were placed on it. Radio stations located in the area of the false airfields imitated the transmissions of a staff from an air army, a ground-attack air corps, and three bomber divisions. Other air armies also took measures to conceal the locations of their air units.

The Attack Begins. The 3rd White Russian Front offensive began the morning of January 13. The night before the offensive, 1st Air Army bombers attacked troops and equipment in the assault area and conducted aerial reconnaissance, flying 740 sorties for this purpose.

The front's troops, as they went on the offensive, met stubborn resistance from the enemy, whose 5th Tank Division was brought up from the reserves on the morning of January 14. The Front strike group had to repel strong enemy counterattacks without air force help because of the low clouds and fog.

In the middle of the day, the enemy counterattacked with two infantry regiments and more than 130 tanks. Now the weather improved somewhat, and 1st Air Army ground-attack aircraft flew 257 sorties against the enemy tanks, helping our troops repulse the enemy's powerful counterattack. But on that day, the troops of the front could not break through the enemy's first defense line.

As the weather improved late in the day of January 15, our aircraft played an important role in breaking through the enemy's major strong points and resistance centers, enabling our troops to occupy the strong points of Tutschen and Pilkallen and advance as much as 10 kilometers (6.2 miles), thus piercing the enemy's major defense zone.

On the fourth day of the operation, most efforts of the 3rd White Russian Front aircraft were concentrated on supporting the entry of the 2nd Guards Tank Corps into the battle and its operation deep in the enemy's defenses. The front commander had assigned this corps, together with the 5th Army, to the penetration of the enemy's second defensive line. On January 16, just before this corps entered the battle, 342 1st and 3rd Air Army bombers made a mass raid against the enemy's major positions in the secondary defense zone at the point where the tanks were to attack. This was to insure that the enemy's major defense installations had been destroyed and to support our troops as they occupied them.

Three hours later, 284 of our bombers raided enemy strong points in the third defensive zone. At the same time the 1st Guards Ground-Attack Air Division gave direct support to the 2nd Guards Tank Corps, destroying enemy troops and equipment in front of the corps and on its right flank. On the left flank, the corps units were given reliable support by the 277th Ground-Attack Air Division, which was simultaneously lending its support to the troops of the 5th Army. In addition, the 182nd Ground-Attack and 130th Fighter Air Divisions destroyed men and equipment in the enemy's third defensive zone.

Air support for the tank corps was provided by five bomber air divisions, three ground-attack divisions, and one fighter air division. On January 16, groups from the air armies flew more than 2800 sorties. The next day the front's strike group, with air support, broke through the enemy's secondary defensive zone.

At the end of January 18, the 3rd White Russian Front troops with air support broke the enemy's defenses along a front 65 kilometers (40 miles) wide and advanced 20–30 kilometers (12–19 miles), creating favorable conditions for the second wave to enter the battle. The 1st and 3rd Air Armies flew 10,350 sorties, 24 percent at night, to support our ground forces.

Attack from the South. Troops of the 2nd White Russian Front took the offensive on January 14. That day and the next, it was almost impossible for aircraft to fly because of the bad weather. It was not until January 16, as the second defensive zone was being broken, that it became possible to give ground troops air support. On January 15, the front commander sent two more tank corps into the battle to increase the offensive pace; and on January 16, he sent in one more mechanized corps, which with the help of our air power, broke the secondary defensive zone, thus enabling the 5th Guards Tank Army to enter the breach in the enemy lines.

The next day, the 5th Guards Tank Army entered the battle in the 48th Army area. During a twenty-hour period, it advanced 60 kilometers (37 miles) with air support. Our troops began an incessant pursuit of the enemy. At this time, more than 85 percent of our aircraft were utilized to support the 5th Guards Tank Army offensive. Simultaneously large raids were carried out against railroad yards, open tracks, and bridges. The 5th Bomber Air Corps, during a two-day period, flew 327 sorties against the yards at Ortelsburg, Willenberg, Allenstein, and Neidenburg.

Concentration of most of our aircraft on the front right wing disrupted the enemy's regrouping and gave effective support to the tank army, which reached the Frisches Haff lagoon on the Danzig Gulf January 25 and the next day captured the town of Tolkemit, thereby cutting the land communications of Army Group Center. The 70th Army reached the city fortress of Thorn and blockaded it. Ground attacks against the retreating enemy contributed to the success of the offensive. They made it impossible for the enemy to retreat according to his own plans and to organize a defense at his rear lines.

The 4th Air Army played an important role in the destruction of the enemy force surrounded at Thorn. On January 31, the 70th Army began the assault of the encircled fortress. The enemy, seeing his impossible situation, undertook a strong counterattack, allowing about 5000 enemy troops to break out of the trap and begin to advance toward the northwest. The only possible way of destroying this group was through air power.

In spite of bad weather, the 260th Ground-Attack Air Division made several accurate strikes against the retreating troops. The first ground-attack groups halted the movement of the enemy columns, and subsequent groups caused great losses to the enemy with their gunfire from low levels. The 70th Army commander said: ". . . the strikes from the ground-attack planes played a decisive role in the defeat of the escaping enemy troops."

In the next few days our aircraft, taking advantage of a brief period of good weather, struck at troops and strong points in the Heilsberg fortified region and fought against German aircraft. On the airfields at Heiligenbeil and Grunau, 24 aircraft were destroyed on February 5 alone. The 4th Air Army flew 8130 sorties from January 19 to February 9, destroying a large number of enemy troops and much equipment.

The Second Wave in the North. The 39th Army was the most successful unit in the 3rd White Russian Front. The 1st Tank Corps entered the area of this army on January 18; and on January 20, the 11th Guards Army entered also; this was the second wave. Most 1st Air Army aircraft were concentrated on the front's right wing to support these units. Before the 11th Guards Army entered the battle, 130 aircraft from two bomber air divisions raided the Insterburg railroad yard within this army's area.

When the second wave of our troops entered the battle, our aircraft constantly supported and escorted it, attacking enemy troops as they retreated along the roads. Fighter and ground-attack planes were active against enemy troops. Attacks against enemy troops were based on aerial reconnaissance. On January 19, Major G. M. Parshin, Hero of the Soviet Union, who was on a reconnaissance mission, discovered a large tank group preparing to counterattack against the flank of the 1st and 2nd Tank Corps. He radioed this information to his command post. A group of ground-attack planes on patrol over their airfield were summoned, and they disrupted the enemy's counterattack.

In addition to supporting the front's second wave, part of the 1st Air Army continued to aid the 5th and 28th Army troops, in whose areas the enemy was stubbornly resisting. On January 20, two bomber and two ground-attack air divisions, with 300 aircraft, struck at the enemy strong point at the city of Gumbinnen. Taking advantage of this strike, the 28th Army took a considerable part of the city by storm.

From January 21 to January 25, the 1st Air Army was not active because of low clouds, fog, and poor visibility. On the next few days, in good weather, they supported the front troops as they broke through the outer defenses of the fortress-city Koenigsberg. Pe-2s bombed the major resistance points. On February 3, sixty-five 6th Guards Bomber Air Division aircraft made a concentrated raid against the strong point at Preussisch Eylau, where they dropped more than 55 tons of FAB-500 and FAB-250 bombs. These raids damaged the enemy defense system and aided our troops as they approached Koenigsberg.

In addition to supporting ground troops, the 1st Air Army devoted part of its resources to attacking enemy sea transports, and warships firing on our troops along the coast, and harbors. On February 5, ground-attack planes from the 1st Guards Ground-Attack Air Division

An MBR-2 patrol seaplane, in the Baltic in 1939, was the usual naval type, but during the war the navy received land-based aircraft of the same types used by the Red Army.

The Yak-9 entered service late in 1942, and continued until the war's end.

The fastest Soviet fighter was the Yak-3, introduced into combat in 1943.

The Li-2 transport was the Soviet-built version of the lend-lease C-47 shown here.

Ivan Kozhedub, the leading Soviet ace, had 62 victories.

The P-39Q Airacobra, waiting in Alaska to be flown to the Soviet Union, was the most widely used U.S. aircraft in Russia.

A P-63A Kingcobra lend-leased to the USSR.

A Junkers Ju 88 of KG 51 represents the leading German bomber used in Russia.

The Messerschmitt Bf 109F fighter.

A twin-engined Messerschmitt Bf 110C-4/b fighter-bomber.

The Ju 87D dive bomber.

Heinkel He 111H bombers showing the yellow band near tail that distinguished German aircraft on the Eastern Front.

The Junkers Ju 52 transport used in attempts to supply encircled German soldiers.

The Henschel Hs 129 ground-attack plane was less successful than the Il-2.

The Focke-Wulf Fw 189 reconnaissance plane was known to Russian fliers as the "frame."

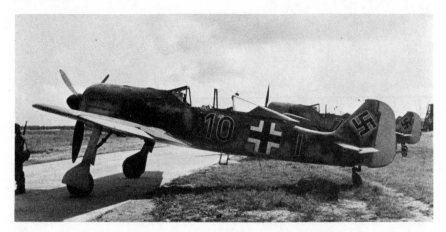

The Focke-Wulf Fw 190 arrived on the Russian Front in 1943.

The Fieseler Fi 156 was the standard German liaison type.

Hitler's invasion forces were supported by allied units, such as an Italian Macchi MC 200 group that arrived in August 1941.

A six-engined Me 323 "Gigant" used to rush supplies to surrounded Nazi forces.

damaged one of the two torpedo boats they were attacking. On the same day, sixty bombers from the 276th Bomber Air Division destroyed troops and equipment in the port of Pillau.

Not less important for the 1st Air Army was the battle against enemy aircraft attacking the 3rd White Russian Front troops. The enemy tried to send 60 planes on a raid. However, the decisive action of our fighter pilots disrupted his plans. On January 18, 6 fighters from the 9th Guards Fighter Air Regiment of the 303rd Fighter Air Division, commanded by squadron commander Hero of the Soviet Union, Capt. P. Ya. Golovachev, entered battle with 25 Fw-190s. The Soviet fliers courageously attacked them and in the ensuing battle destroyed 5 enemy aircraft; the rest, having dropped their bombs off their target, left for the west. Our fliers returned to their base without losses.

Raids were made against German airfields. As many as 250 enemy aircraft were discovered by aerial reconnaissance on airfields near Koenigsberg. The 1st Air Army commander decided to raid this concentration with the 1st Guards Ground-Attack Air Division, the 277th Ground-Attack Air Division, and the 6th Guards Bomber Air Division. As a result, about 65 enemy aircraft were destroyed and 40 damaged.

The 1st Air Army flew 9740 sorties in support of the 3rd White Russian Front from January 19 through February 9. Our troops with air support captured a significant part of the Samland Peninsula, swept past Koenigsberg on three sides, and reached the Heilsberg Fortified Region.

As the result of the coordinated efforts of the ground and air forces of the 3rd and 2nd White Russian Fronts, the enemy's East Prussian concentration suffered great losses and was cut into three parts. Four enemy divisions and other units were blockaded in Koenigsberg and about twenty divisions defended the Heilsberg Fortified Region.

Attack on the Heilsberg Pocket. The task of finally destroying the enemy troop concentration in East Prussia was given to the troops of the 3rd White Russian Front, the Samland Group, created from units of the 1st Baltic Front, and the 1st and 3rd Air Armies.

Destruction of these troops was carried out systematically over a two-and-a-half-month period. First the strongest concentration southwest of Koenigsberg in the Heilsberg Fortified Region was liquidated, then the troops in Koenigsberg, and then those on the Samland Peninsula.

The front troops had to deal with an enemy entrenched in one of the most heavily fortified regions in East Prussia when they turned to the concentration south of Koenigsberg. Therefore the air force was given the task of destroying centers of resistance and strong points at the same time that it attacked artillery concentrations. Moreover, it, along with the navy, was to blockade the enemy from the sea.

The air situation was characterized by the great quantitative and qualitative superiority of our air force. In addition to the two air armies, air units from the Red Banner Baltic Fleet were also deployed.

The 3rd White Russian Front offensive to destroy the enemy southwest of Koenigsberg began on February 10. In spite of bad weather, the 1st Air Army gave considerable support from the air. On February 15, it flew more than 1600 sorties, of which around 1100 were devoted to destroying men and equipment on the battlefield. Troops of the front, aided by air power, advanced 11 kilometers (7 miles) into the enemy defense zone. As they carried out their assignments our fliers showed great tenacity, courage, and daring. On February 17 the 9th Guards Fighter Air Regiment's assistant commander, Major Plotnikov, was hit by antiaircraft fire as he carried out a reconnaissance flight, and his plane burst into flame. He was not able to put out the fire and he directed his burning plane onto an enemy troop concentration.

Rescuing a Downed Pilot.   The next day a flight commander of the 139th Guards Fighter Air Regiment, First Lt. S. S. Dolgalev, was hit as he flew over his target. He made a forced landing in enemy territory. The Fascists tried to seize the Soviet fliers. But his second-in-command came to his rescue. Circling over him, he killed the enemy troops that ran toward Dolgalev's plane with machine-gun and cannon fire. Attacks from other fighter planes confused the ground troops. Dolgalev had time to hide. In the meantime, Second Lt. V. G. Mikheyev, who had returned to his airfield, took off in a Po-2 biplane and a few minutes later landed near his commander's plane. In spite of the danger, Mikheyev, in the sight of enemy soldiers, seated Dolgalev in his plane and returned safely to his base. First Lt. V. G. Mikeyev was given the Order of the Red

Banner for bravery in saving the life of his commander under difficult battle conditions.

By February 18, our troops had advanced as much as 60 kilometers (37 miles) and had reduced the enemy area by half. In order to complete destruction of the enemy in their fortified region, it was necessary to regroup our troops and prepare for a new offensive operation. Under these conditions it was decided to halt the offensive temporarily.

Cutting Off the Baltic Sea Lanes. From February 22 to March 12, the troops of the Front and the air force prepared a new offensive to wipe out the last enemy troops left southwest of Koenigsberg. In this period, in addition to destroying men and equipment on the battlefield, the 1st and 3rd Air Armies along with the naval air force attacked enemy transportation at sea.

This was essential, because the enemy had increased his efforts to supply his troops in East Prussia by sea. In order to interdict this traffic, the 1st and 3rd Air Armies, at the beginning of March, increased their operations against the seaports on the shores of the Frisches Haff lagoon. The 1st Air Army aircraft made a series of strikes against ships in the harbor at Rosenberg, while the 3rd Air Army aircraft raided the naval base at Pillau. The naval air force attacked ships at sea as well as in harbors.

From February 21 through March 12, aircraft of the fronts flew more than 12,000 sorties. They destroyed several strong points and caused the enemy serious losses in men and materials, including losses to his fleet.

On March 13, the new offensive against the enemy troops southwest of Koenigsberg began. Because of the bad weather, air operations could not begin until the fifth day of the operation. The troops from the front had been able to advance only 4 to 10 kilometers (2½ to 6 miles). As the weather improved the widespread use of air power became possible. On March 18, the 1st and 3rd Air Armies flew 2520 sorties. In the opinion of the front commander, Marshal A. M. Vasilevsky, air operations shattered the enemy and weakened his defense.

In the next few days, the air armies were engaged in constant ground support, and together with the AFLRO and naval air force, they struck at the enemy's attempted sea evacuation, destroying troops, equipment, transports, and other targets in the Frisches Haff lagoon, the Bay of Danzig, and in harbors.

Most of the aircraft were concentrated over those harbors where the largest accumulations of men and materials were located. In the period of March 18–25, our bombers dropped 530 tons of bombs on the harbor at Rosenberg. Air strikes were very effective. A prisoner from the 131st Infantry Division stated that it was almost impossible for anyone to be evacuated from Rosenberg in this period because of the air raids. Rosenberg was captured by the 28th Army troops on the night of March 25. That army's military council noted that "the capture of the harbor at Rosenberg was accomplished largely by the use of air power."

At the same time that they were striking against men and materials in civilian harbors, the aircraft from the front and the AFLRO together with naval air force planes raided the enemy base at Pillau. In addition, utilizing information from aerial reconnaissance, our aircraft struck at convoys, lone transports, and warships in the Frisches Haff lagoon and the Bay of Danzig.

From March 13 through March 27, the 1st and 3rd Air Armies flew 20,030 sorties, 4590 of them at night. The support operation and the attacks on the enemy sea evacuation were of significant help to the troops from the front as they liquidated the enemy troop concentration southwest of Koenigsberg.

Units from the air armies operated at a high level in this period. On some days (March 25, 26, and 27) 5000 sorties were flown in a twenty-four-hour period against troops and equipment on the battlefield and ships in the Frisches Haff lagoon and the harbor at Pillau. In March alone, the 1st and 3rd Air Armies flew 30,000 sorties in support of the 3rd White Russian Front, destroying a large number of troops and much equipment, and thereby playing a very important role in the destruction of the enemy troop concentration.

Koenigsberg Is Taken. When the enemy troops southwest of Koenigsberg had been eliminated and after an initial preparatory period, the 3rd White Russian Front troops began their operation to capture the fortress-city of Koenigsberg. Large numbers of aircraft were involved in this operation. Besides the 1st and 3rd Air Armies, which were part of the Front, the 18th Air Army (AFLRO), one bomber corps from the nearby 4th and 15th Air Armies, and air units from the fleet participated in the operation, a total of 2400 aircraft. The *Stavka* representative, Chief Air Marshal A. A. Novikov, coordinated operations of the different air groups.

The use of so many aircraft in this operation is explained by the necessity to destroy the fortifications and strong points in the city and dampen the enemy's artillery batteries so that the front's troops could capture the city rapidly with minimal losses. The importance of air operations in the Koenigsberg attack can be seen from the fact that the assault date was moved from April 5 to April 6 because of bad weather, by a *Stavka* decision.

Before the operation began, the 1st Air Army staff worked out a plan for air operations for both the 1st and 3rd Air Armies in the Koenigsberg operation. The plan called for a preliminary air attack to smash the forts and strong points in the offensive zone of the 43rd and 11th Guards Armies. What was unusual in this operation was that great emphasis was placed upon air strikes to destroy fortified points, pillboxes, and bunkers. Fog made it impossible for the air armies to completely carry out their plans for an initial attack. Instead of the planned 5316 sorties on April 4 and 5, only 766 were flown. This affected the rate of advance achieved by the ground forces who, by the end of the first day's offensive, had moved in different sectors 2 to 4 kilometers (1 to 2½ miles).

In the next three days, the air force was very active, delivering powerful blows against the enemy. One squadron from the 75th Guards Red Banner Ground-Attack Air Regiment, commanded by Captain A. K. Nedbaylo, was especially active in this period. Having arrived at their targets, the ground-attack planes made six or more passes, destroying enemy men and materials. Although A. K. Nedbaylo arrived at the front only in March 1943, he flew 219 sorties before the end of the war. He was titled Hero of the Soviet Union by the Presidium of the Supreme Soviet order dated April 19, 1945, for his heroism, valor, courage, and daring, and on June 29 of the same year he was given a second "Gold Star."

On April 7, from 10:00 A.M. to 1:30 P.M., 246 Tu-2s and Pe-2s delivered three bombing raids on fortifications around Koenigsberg. After this attack by the Front aircraft, 516 18th Air Army bombers made a mass raid during daylight hours. These effective air strikes helped our troops as they quickly drove into the defenses of the fortress. The next day, 456 of our bombers hit reserves west of Koenigsberg.

These mass daytime raids by the 18th Air Army were made possible by our complete control of the air. On April 7, 124 fighters were assigned to escort the bombers. In addition, at the time of the raid,

108 fighter planes patrolled at different altitudes over the city to prevent any enemy fighters from approaching the areas where our bombers were active. Twenty minutes before the bombers arrived, ground-
attack planes and bombers struck at the two largest enemy airfields
to suppress his fighter units. As a result, the 18th Air Army struck a
serious blow at the enemy without losing any planes.

Ground-attack planes and fighters, as they supported our advancing troops, destroyed his men and artillery on the battlefield. In addition to destroying the fortifications in Koenigsberg, the air force attacked enemy troops as they were being shifted from the Samland
Peninsula. On April 7, the 1st and 3rd Air Armies' ground-attack
planes struck at enemy troops in the forests west of Koenigsberg.
These air operations disrupted an enemy counterattack planned to
break the blockade of the Koenigsberg garrison.

The ground-attack group, commanded by Hero of the Soviet Union, Major M. T. Stepanishchev, was very active that day as they attacked enemy troops and artillery on the southern edge of Koenigsberg. In spite of heavy antiaircraft fire, the ground-attack planes he
commanded destroyed several pieces of artillery and blew up three
large supply dumps. M. T. Stepanishchev was given a second "Gold
Star," by the order of the Presidium of the Supreme Soviet dated
June 29, 1945.

During the assault on Koenigsberg, the naval air force, commanded
by General M. I. Samokhin, in cooperation with the Front aircraft
and the AFLRO, continued to attack men and materials in the port of
Pillau, and also the enemy's transports and ships at sea. Thus, on
April 7, more than 240 bombers and ground-attack planes from the
Red Banner Baltic Fleet Air Force attacked ships in the Pillau harbor.

Because of coordinated ground and air force efforts, the enemy
ceased his resistance and on April 10 the Koenigsberg garrison capitulated. During the four days of the operation the air force flew 14,090
sorties and dropped 4440 tons of bombs on the enemy. Its mass attacks significantly accelerated the enemy's surrender. This was indicated by the captured fascist generals. The German commander of
Koenigsberg, General Lasch, said: "Air power played a very important role in the capture of Koenigsberg—the troops were tormented,
driven to the ground, pursued into their bunkers."

The successful defeat of its East Prussian troop concentration seriously weakened the army of Fascist Germany. Now the Soviet com-

mand could employ the troops and aircraft freed from the East Prussian campaign to complete the victory over the enemy.

To commemorate the victory the Supreme Soviet Presidium created the medal "For the capture of Koenigsberg" and awarded it to all personnel of the air units who took part in the assault of this fortress. The 1st Air Army commander, General T. T. Khryukin, was awarded a second "Gold Star," for his skilled supervision of the East Prussian air operation.

French Pilots Decorated. The French Fighter Regiment "Normandy-Niemen" fought bravely alongside the Soviet fliers. During January alone, it flew more than 500 sorties and destroyed about sixty enemy aircraft on the ground or in the air. Twenty-four of its outstanding French officers were given Medals of the Soviet Union.

In the period from March 23, 1943, to May 2, 1945, the French regiment "Normandy-Niemen" advanced from Kaluga to Koenigsberg. The flyers flew 5062 sorties, fought in 869 air battles, and shot down 266 German aircraft. The Soviet government gave the regiment the names "Red Banner" and "Alexander Nevsky." Eight fliers were given Orders of the Soviet Union, and four—Marcel Albert, Roland de La Poype, Jacques André, and Marcel Lefevre were titled Hero of the Soviet Union.

Results. During the East Prussian campaign Soviet troops penetrated the enemy's fortified defense line, annihilated his major troop concentration, captured all of East Prussia with its city-fortress Koenigsberg, and liberated part of Poland. In spite of bad weather during the operation 146,000 sorties were flown, including more than 4100 by the naval air force and around 2400 by the AFLRO.

Most of the air force efforts (61.4 percent of all sorties) were devoted to attacks against men and equipment on the battlefield and in the immediate vicinity, i.e., directly in support of ground forces. In so doing the air force utilized large numbers of aircraft in the decisive areas. This was done by introducing some units from nearby air armies, the AFLRO, and the naval air force to support the front when it was involved in a major offensive. These aircraft were employed in a small area for supporting the front's strike group.

In addition to attacking the enemy on the battlefield, the front aircraft and those from the AFLRO and the naval air force attacked the enemy's fleet. The participation of the front aircraft in such assignments at sea depended on the operational situation. For example, until the end of January 1945, before our troops reached the sea, the 1st and 4th Air Army operated only over land. When the enemy group southwest of Koenigsberg was being liquidated, 20 per cent of all sorties flown by the air armies were for assignments at sea.

During the entire campaign our air force maintained control of the air, one of the most important factors in the successful conduct of the operation. Twenty-six percent of all sorties flown were expended to maintain control in the air.

On the whole, according to the statement of the general army command, air power played an important role in the defeat of the enemy's East Prussian troop concentration.

XVII

FROM THE VISTULA TO THE ODER

At the same time the East Prussian campaign was begun, an even more powerful offensive was launched against the German forces in the center. Two fronts with 2,200,000 men, 163 divisions, and 6400 armored vehicles were in place, the 1st White Russian Front thrusting to Poznań, and the 1st Ukrainian Front to Breslau.[18] ED.

Preparations. After they had successfully completed their White Russian and Lvov-Sandomir campaigns in the summer of 1944, the troops of the 1st White Russian Front and the 1st Ukrainian Front reached the Vistula and seized two bridgeheads on its left bank in the regions of Magnuszew, Puławy, and Sandomir. From November 1944 through January 11, 1945, the troops from this front prepared for a new offensive in which they were to rout the German Army Group A, liberate Poland, and attain the line Bromberg-Poznań-Breslau.

We had the control of the air along the entire front. The 1st White Russian Front included the 16th Air Army, commanded by General S. I. Rudenko, and also the 4th Composite Polish Air Division, while the 1st Ukrainian Front included the 2nd Air Army, commanded by General S. A. Krasovsky. Both armies had a total of 4770 aircraft.

The enemy troops were protected and supported by the 6th Air Fleet, which included the 4th and 8th Air Corps and had more than 500 aircraft.

During the preparatory period before the operation, our aircraft systematically conducted aerial reconnaissance and fought against enemy aircraft protecting their troops from air strikes, and also hit at enemy troops, equipment, and transportation, hindering the movement of enemy reserves and regrouping of his forces. To fulfill these assignments 3500 sorties were flown.

Aerial photographs before the operation began revealed seven fortified zones on the far side of the Vistula extending as much as 500 kilometers (310 miles), six antitank ditches 20 to 60 kilometers (12½ to 37 miles) long, areas in which the enemy had concentrated his reserves and artillery, his defense system in the tactical zone, the rear army zones, his intermediate and extended positions, the defense lines around Warsaw, Radom, and Łódź, and other lines as far as the longitude of Poznań. All of the crossings on the Vistula were photographed on the river section from Modlin to Włocławek, and across the Pilica River from Warka to Tomaszow, and the enemy air base system with the aircraft based on it.

The Vistula-Oder campaign plan called for powerful offensives toward Poznań and Breslau, destruction of the German Army Group A, which defended the Polish territory and protected German population centers, the attainment of the Oder, and the creation of favorable conditions for the final assault on Berlin.

In the offensive along the entire 500-kilometer (310-mile) front between the Vistula and the Oder there were to be simultaneous strikes from tank armies and tank and mechanized corps in coordination with the air armies from the fronts. Two hours before the offensive began there were to be strikes against command and observation posts and communication centers with the goal of disrupting control over enemy units. After this, aircraft were to support and protect ground troops as they broke through the enemy's tactical zone, to support the entry of tank armies into the battle, and to escort and support troops as they operated in the enemy's immediate rear.

All available bombers and part of our ground-attack and fighter aircraft were to strike at enemy reserves. Destruction of the enemy's operational reserves in the first day of the campaign was planned to obstruct enemy plans for a counterattack and to support the rapid advance of our troops through the enemy's defenses.

Mobility for our aircraft as they followed our advancing ground forces through the enemy defenses was to be insured by the creation and utilization of dirt runways. Before the offensive began, seventeen airfields were constructed on the Sandomir bridgehead, 10 to 15 kilometers (6 to 9½ miles) from the front, upon which were stored fuel and ammunition.

The purpose of the preparatory plans was to insure surprise, effective air operations, and precise coordination between aircraft and the tank units as they advanced rapidly into the enemy's rear.

The Attack from Sandomir. The Soviet offensive began earlier than was planned, at the request of our former allies, with the goal of drawing German forces from the Western Front and easing the difficult situation in which the Anglo-American armies found themselves in the Ardennes and Vosges Mountains.*

On the morning of January 12, the 1st Ukrainian Front took the offensive from their bridgehead at Sandomir. Because of the bad weather, the preparatory air attack could not be carried out. The enemy's troops and equipment had been identified for the most part by aerial reconnaissance, and were subjected to a powerful artillery and mortar attack. The ground forces commander wanted to know what fire points remained after the artillery barrage, to what extent resistance centers and fortifications had been damaged, and how enemy reserves were moving in order to successfully break through the enemy's defense zone. These data were provided in adequate detail, in spite of the bad weather, by aerial reconnaissance. Maintaining constant observation over enemy movements, they discovered early in the operation that the enemy was moving large tank columns from the Kielce and Chmielnik regions toward the battlefield.

Late on the first day of the offensive and twenty-four hours before the time planned for it, the front commander brought the 4th and 3rd Guards Tank Armies and the 31st and 4th Guards Tank Corps into the battle. At the same time, groups of ground-attack planes and

---

* Prime Minister Winston Churchill had asked Stalin on January 6 whether the Soviet offensive could be advanced to relieve the pressure from the Ardennes offensive in Belgium. ED.

fighters were transferred to the operational authority of the commanders of tank armies and tank corps.

Our fighter planes, as they patrolled over the strike groups, had the right of "free hunting" in intercepting German aircraft, and constantly escorted our tank troops as they entered the battle. Not one enemy plane was permitted to enter the mobile troop area.

The guard air squadron commanded by the Hero of the Soviet Union, Captain V. I. Popkov, was especially successful. This squadron produced ten Heroes of the Soviet Union during the war. V. I. Popkov was given a second "Gold Star," in June for courage and daring in battle and for the forty enemy planes he shot down.

Before darkness fell, around 400 ground-attack planes and bombers, in small groups or as individual planes, and flying in bad weather with limited visibility, struck at enemy columns moving out of Kielce and Chmielnik. The enemy suffered considerable losses, and many soldiers and officers abandoned their guns, vehicles, and even their tanks in their haste to escape strafing from our planes. By evening, movement of the German tank corps had ceased. The movement of the enemy operational reserves was disorganized.

The morning of the next day, ground-attack pilot and Hero of the Soviet Union, Guards Captain S. G. Chepelyuk discovered the movement and concentration of a large number of enemy on the flank of the 4th Tank Army south of Kielce and north of Chmielnik. Crews of the 4th Bomber and 2nd Ground-Attack Air Corps with fighter escort in groups of nine to eighteen aircraft during daylight hours put about 50 tanks and 400 other vehicles out of commission.

Losses from air attacks and disorganization of his reserves' movement made it impossible for the enemy to carry out his counterattack in the Kielce and Pińczów area. As they tried to stop our offensive, the German command was compelled to bring up reserves as individual units, which made it easier for the 52nd Army to surround and destroy the enemy's scattered units, and then to overwhelm his defenses and force the Czarna and Nida rivers.

At the same time, our ground-attack planes and fighters attacked artillery, mortars, and enemy troops. They supported our tank units in constant patrols or blockaded enemy airfields as the ground forces captured the enemy defense line at the Nida River during the battles for Pińczów and Jędrzejów. Not one enemy planes group was able to strike at our troops. The 106th Guards Fighter Regiment, commanded by Lt. Col. M. V. Kuznetsov, excelled in this assignment.

During one day the 2nd Air Army flew around 700 sorties, of which 400 were against enemy tank columns in the region of Kielce and Chmielnik.

The decisive and effective air operation against enemy reserves, the successful and incessant support for tank troops, and the firm air cover contributed to the rapid advance of our troops to the second defense line, the crossing of the Nida River, and the encirclement and destruction of more than four enemy reserve divisions south of Kielce and north of Chmielnik. As this was being done, the cities of Kielce, Pińczów, and Jędrzejów were liberated and the railway and highway cut between Kielce and Cracow.

After the enemy had suffered great losses, he began to withdraw his troops to the third defense zone in order to create there a defensive line and halt the advance of our troops. Aerial reconnaissance revealed the presence of columns of retreating troops on the roads toward Częstochowa, Sosnowiec, and Cracow. The air force was given the task of preventing the enemy from creating a defensive line in the third zone.

Blows from bombers and ground-attack planes destroyed the bridges and crossings over the Pilica river and destroyed enemy columns retreating in disorder from the major defense line on the Vistula. After they had silenced artillery and mortar fire at strong points in the third defense zone, the air force cooperated with ground forces as they crossed the Warta River and liberated the city of Częstochowa.

Good weather on January 16 and 17 made major air operations possible in support of our tank armies, and about 4000 sorties were flown. Strikes against the columns of the 42nd Army Corps and the 10th Motorized Division retreating from the Skarżysko-Kamienna region toward Radom were especially successful. In groups of thirty bombers and ground-attack planes our aircraft attacked the enemy columns incessantly, giving them no rest by day or night. The scattered and demoralized groups retreated in disorder, trying to avoid air attacks from our advancing troops. But our aircraft struck at the enemy columns, slowing their retreat and causing them great losses while our approaching tank armies surrounded and destroyed them.

During these battles the bomber crew of First Lt. M. Sharabrin showed great skill, initiative, and resourcefulness. Flying as a "free hunter," he discovered a train concentration. Ignoring dense antiaircraft fire, Sharabrin approached the target and dropped his bombs on ammunition cars. The shock wave smashed several trains with their freight and enemy troops.

During the first six days of the campaign, the 2nd Air Army, destroying points of resistance and extinguishing artillery and mortar fire, gave great support to ground troops as they broke enemy defenses along the entire 250 kilometers (115 miles) of the front to a depth of as much as 150 kilometers (93 miles). The air force, in close cooperation with tank units, struck at retreating columns and hampered their retreat to intermediate defense lines, which contributed to the rout of the German 4th Tank Army and their operational reserves stationed opposite the Sandomir bridgehead. Our aircraft actively supported our troops as they crossed the Nida, Pilica, and Warta rivers and their advance units reached a line from Radom, through Częstochowa and Tarnów.

The Attack North of Warsaw. The offensive of the 1st White Russian Front strike group from the bridgeheads at Magnuszew and Puławy began on January 14. An hour before the beginning of the artillery barrage our most experienced night bomber crews bombed the staff headquarters of the 56th Tank Corps, destroying their communication lines. Bad weather made it impossible to implement the planned air attack before the ground offensive began.

In the first days of the offensive, the 16th Air Army carried out aerial reconnaissance, supported our troops as they broke through the enemy's tactical defense zone, and protected the entry of our tank groups into the battle. Because of extremely bad weather, only 276 sorties were flown by the best-trained crews.

On January 16 the weather improved. At dawn aerial reconnaissance established the direction in which German troops were retreating, the location of their advanced units and our mobile groups. After communications had been established with our mobile units, our bombers and ground-attack planes began to fulfill their assignments to support them. On the demand of the ground command and on the basis of information from aerial reconnaissance, our planes attacked columns and concentrations of German troops on highways and railroads on the sectors Sochaczew-Lodz; Skierniewice-Tomaszów-Mazowiecki; Radom-Opoczno.

Planes from the 9th Ground-attack Air Corps and the 11th Guard Air divisions discovered several columns from the enemy's 10th Motorized Division on the road from Mniszek to Opoczno. A group of ground-attack planes struck at the tanks at the head of the column on the bridge over the Zdiezliczka River on the way to Opoczno. The bridge was destroyed. Many men and much equipment accumulated on the bank of the river. Aircraft were sent to destroy this concentration. The enemy suffered great losses as the result of this strike. More than 5000 vehicles, armored cars, and several dozen tanks were abandoned on the roads. About 500 vehicles were destroyed by bomb strikes on the east bank of the Pilica River at Inowlódź. The columns stopped moving. Because of large losses and panic, the enemy could not cross to the west bank of the river to take up defensive positions.

Simultaneously with these attacks against enemy columns, 16th Air Army units attacked railroad yards and stations at Opoczno, Olszewicy, Simanów, and Zyrardów. As the result of successful raids, traffic ceased on the segments from Opoczno to Łódź; and Skierniewice. Tomaszów, and Mazowiecki.

Two Pe-2 groups that raided the railroad yards at Łódź-Vostochnaya under the 301st Bomber Air Division, commanded by Col. F. M. Fedorenko, were very successful. They destroyed 54 cars with freight, platforms with antiaircraft guns, two locomotives, and damaged railroad lines so that rail traffic through the yards was stopped.

Reconnaissance planes reported a troop concentration at strong points at Rawa-Mazowiecka, Strudzianka, Inowlódź, and at river crossings in the Skierniewice region. Aircraft were sent to destroy these troops. The planes dealt serious damage to the enemy's 25th Tank Division as the result of their bombing raids and ground attacks.

These successful air operations supported the irresistible 1st White Russian Front advance into the center and left flank of the Vistula defense line, and the crossing of the Bzura, Rawka, and Pilica rivers as far as the line from Skierniewice to Olszewsk. In three days' advance, the 1st White Russian Front troops reached a point parallel with that of the 1st Ukrainian Front.

Warsaw Is Liberated. Enemy troops in defensive position around Warsaw were now in danger of being surrounded and had to withdraw to the west. Our aircraft hindered their orderly retreat.

Soviet fliers in bombing and ground-attack raids struck at enemy artillery and caused great losses to the reserves of infantry divisions north of Warsaw. Deprived of artillery and part of its reserves, the

German troops defending their bridgehead on the Vistula's right bank and the area between the Vistula and the western Bug could not repel the advancing 47th Army. Its advance units, with protection and support from aircraft, crossed the Vistula on the ice.

As our troops crossed the river, our air force devoted most of its efforts to supporting the major part of our army trying to circle Warsaw from the northwest. Reconnaissance planes in constant flights maintained watch over the battlefield.

South of Warsaw, aircraft destroyed strong points, flew ground attacks against counterattacking units, and put down artillery and mortar fire—all in support of the 61st Army as it broke through enemy defenses on the approaches to Warsaw.

In those areas where the 5th Strike Army and the 2nd Guards Tank Army were advancing, air power sought to disorganize retreating enemy troops and to destroy reserves before they reached Warsaw.

Air operations destroyed the railroad bridge and crossings over the Vistula at Wyszegród, as well as crossings over the Ochnia River at Kutno, and across the Warta at Sierdaz, and the railroad yards at Łódź. Our aircraft broke the ice on the Vistula at Wyszegród and Wulka-Paszbolsk, making it impossible for the enemy to cross over to the river's right bank. The 2nd Guards Tank Army, with air support, struck the enemy flank and rear and wiped out his scattered forces, making it impossible for him to retreat to the west and take defensive positions on the Bzura River. The 47th Army from the northwest, the 61st Army of the 1st White Russian Front and the 1st Polish Army from the southwest, advanced toward Warsaw. Bombers, ground-attack planes, and fighters put down enemy artillery in strong points in the city streets in front of the advancing strike units. After a stubborn battle, at 12:00 noon on January 17, Soviet and Polish troops captured Warsaw, the Polish capital.

The 16th Air Army flew 6656 sorties in the battle for Warsaw including the 1st Composite Air Division of the Polish Army which flew 999. The most outstanding air units were given the honored title of "Warsaw" units.

At the end of the day on January 17, the 1st White Russian Front and the 1st Ukrainian Front with active air support had broken through the major zone of the Vistula defense line on a front 500 kilometers (310 miles) long and to a depth of 160 kilometers (99 miles). The greater part of the German Army Group A had been routed.

The *Stavka*'s assignment to the fronts was to advance in a ten- or twelve-day period to the line through Żichlin, Łódź, Radom, Częstochowa, Miechow; but it was completed in five or six days—only half the time provided in the plan.

From January 12 through January 17 the fliers from the air armies flew 11,748 sorties. In that period the Luftwaffe lost 44 aircraft in air battles and 86 on the ground. The Soviet Air Force without qualification maintained control of the air.

Advance to the Oder.   On January 17 the *Stavka* issued new assignments: the 1st White Russian Front was to continue its advance toward Poznań and no later than February 2–4 advance to a line from Bydgoszcz to Poznań; the 1st Ukrainian Front was to continue its offensive toward Breslau, and no later than January 30 reach the Oder to the south of Leszno, and then seize a bridgehead on the left bank of the river.

As they pressed their offensive the 1st White Russian Front troops advanced toward the great industrial city of Poland and important rail and road junction; Łódź. The German command attempted to hold the rear zone of its Vistula defense line, move up reserves, and thus re-erect a defense line. The enemy was unable to carry out this plan. The 16th Air Army in cooperation with mobile ground units resisted their efforts and assured the unimpeded advance of our troops. The rapid advance of our advance units into the enemy lines was due to the protection and support that they had from the air, which made it impossible for the German troops to utilize their rear areas for a defensive line.

The enemy command quickly began to throw additional forces from its reserves on the Western Front and other sectors of the Soviet-German front against our forces. However, the enemy attempts to mend their broken lines had no success. The reserves as they neared the front were subjected to attacks from our aircraft and tank units and destroyed unit by unit.

Crews from the 3rd Bomber Air Corps destroyed railroad and highway bridges at Płock, Włocław, and Torun; they smashed troop trains and damaged railroad stations at Łódź, Pabianice, and Łask; they hindered the movement of enemy reserves to the Włocławek, Łódź, Piotrków line.

At the same time ground-attack planes and fighters in waves struck decisive blows at retreating enemy columns on the roads through Łódź-Pabianice-Łask; Łódź-Dobra. Before these columns reached the rear defensive line these columns were attacked by the advance elements from our tank units and completely destroyed.

The *Grossdeutschland* tank corps rushed from East Prussia was discovered by aerial reconnaissance planes as it was being unloaded in the Łódź region. Under attack from our air force and tank troops, it had to withdraw with losses even before it could enter the battle. Following up our air strikes, our advance units and tank corps reached the enemy's rear defense line through Żichlin, Łódź, and Radom before the *Grossdeutschland* tank corps units and overwhelmed them.

The German command attempted to remove its troops and equipment out from under our air attacks along the roads and railroads toward Torun, Inowrocław, Koło, and Kalisz. The 16th Air Army was assigned to disrupt their retreat. Small groups of ground-attack planes, bombers and fighters, in waves, struck at the leading units of the columns, hindering their movement toward the intermediate defensive line. In intense raids aircraft attacked resistance centers and destroyed tanks and artillery in concentration areas, as well as tank columns along the roads. In order to advantageously advance our air bases the 66th Tank Brigade seized the Liubien airfield to which immediately moved the 265th Air Fighter Division, so now there were constantly ground-attack and fighter groups over the battlefield to immediately support our advancing forward units.

Our aerial reconnaissance, discovered, in addition to the *Grossdeutschland* tank corps, five infantry divisions moving toward the Warta defensive line. A large number of aircraft were sent to attack them. Bombers and ground-attack planes, in groups of 27–30 aircraft with fighter escorts, attacked and harassed these reserves. Twelve troop trains, 200 vehicles, a locomotive shop, and tracks were destroyed by our bombs and cannon fire at the stations at Skawina, Swieszewice, and in the Łogowniki district. Train movements through these stations ceased. Rail traffic was also disrupted by attacks against trains in the stations at Inowrocław, Kruszwica, Debowiec, and Sierdaz. At the same time, small groups of ground-attack planes and fighters in waves were supporting the advance of our mobile troops by destroying enemy soldiers and equipment on the roads from Szacen to Warta.

The enemy reserve divisions suffered great losses from our tanks and aircraft and could not reach the Warta defensive line in strength. Individual units that took defensive positions along the Warta's western bank were attacked by our aircraft. Our tank units crossed the Warta with air support and continued their advance toward Poznań. The enemy's scheme for creating a continuous defensive line along the Warta, and thereby stopping the advance of our troops, was disrupted by the 1st White Russian Front with active air support.

On January 19, Soviet troops liberated the major Polish industrial center of Łódź. During the next four days most of the front troops advanced 140 kilometers (87 miles).

Under the conditions which developed, the air army plans for maintaining control of the air had to be significantly altered. Instead of devoting their efforts to combating enemy aircraft in the air and on enemy airfields, many fighters were assigned to attack retreating enemy troops. In order not to lag behind the rapidly advancing ground troops, the 16th Air Army command carried out an audacious shift of air bases directly behind the advancing tank units. On January 18, fighters of the 402nd Fighter Air Regiment were moved to the airfield at Sochaczew at the same time that German motorized infantry troops were still on its western edge. On January 24, the 278th Fighter Air Division, commanded by Colonel K. D. Orlov, moved to the Wiednari airfield twenty-four hours before the major forces of the tank army reached the region.

Successfully supporting the troops of the fronts as they broke through the Warta defensive line, the air force directed its basic efforts to supporting our advance to the west. The enemy, who had concentrated large numbers of troops near Poznań, fought furiously. He moved one tank division and six infantry divisions to the Poznań region, attempting to form a defense at the preliminary line and halt the advance of our troops.

The front aircraft destroyed railroad bridges and stations south and west of the cities of Schneidemühl and Poznań and disrupted enemy road and railroad traffic in these regions. Enemy reserves suffered great losses as they moved up and were not able to aid the Poznań garrison or to organize a defense. The 1st and 2nd Guards Armies swept past Poznań on the north and south. Uniting west of the city with the 8th Guards Army on January 23, they completed the encirclement of the 62,000 enemy troops in Poznań.

Leaving part of their forces to destroy the encircled troops, the

1st White Russian Front troops with air support continued their offensive to the west. On January 31, the 5th Strike Army and the 2nd Guards Tank Army reached the Oder, crossed it, and seized a bridgehead northwest of Küstrin (Kostrzyn) in the Kinitc region, which was more than 4 kilometers (2½ miles) wide and about 2 kilometers (1¼ miles) deep.

Advance into Silesia. When they had liberated Częstochowa, the 1st Ukrainian Front troops with air support began bitter fighting for the Upper Silesian industrial region. The enemy tried at any price to hold the metallurgical plants and large coal mines as an economic stronghold for Germany, and as a strategic region. From this area the enemy prepared an attack on the front's left wing. The 2nd Air Army devoted most of its aircraft to supporting ground forces in order to smash the enemy concentration.

Relying on aerial reconnaissance data, the 1st Guards Bomber Air Division destroyed strong points in the Hindenburg and Königshütte regions. The division commander, Col. F. I. Dobysh, often led groups of his planes as they completed their assignments. The fliers silenced artillery, destroyed enemy troops and equipment, and attacked troop trains in stations at Sosnowiec, Katowice, Bejten, and Będzin.

Bad weather once more limited use of air power. Missions were flown by small groups of planes or by single aircraft. However, search-and-attack on likely targets by "hunters" was very widely utilized and was very effective. Our fliers disorganized the enemy's rear, his control over his troops, and hindered orderly movement of reinforcements.

On January 20, a bomber crew consisting of commander Lt. N. A. Grigoryev, navigator First Lt. A. P. Auchenkov, and radio operator and gunner Master Sergeant A. A. Kvachev destroyed several freight trains at the Estenberg station. They were attacked by eight enemy fighters over the target. In this unequal battle, the crew shot down three Fw 190s and then brought their damaged bomber flying on one motor back to their airfield.

Our air force's decisive action made it possible for our troops to advance rapidly, and then, in sweeping movements, by-pass the enemy's Silesian troop concentration on the north and the south. Then on the night of January 21, 4th Tank Army advance units crossed the Oder in the Köben region north of Steinau and seized eighteen pillboxes in the Breslau Fortified Region on the left bank of the river. A squadron of the 81st Guards Ground-Attack Air Regiment led by Hero of the Soviet Union, Captain P. A. Plotnikov, was very effective in its support of ground troops.

As they pursued the retreating enemy, troops of the front occupied the city of Katowice, center of Upper Silesia, on January 28. Hitler's troops had avoided encirclement and defeat in the Upper Silesian industrial region, but were hit by air strikes and finally were crushed by tank units in the forests west of it. The Polish government could immediately open the factories and mines in the Silesian region.

Our ground-attack planes were remarkably effective. Nine Il-2s from the 140th Guards Ground-Attack Air Regiment, led by Major Yakovitsky, escorted by a fighter flight, led by First Lt. I. N. Shumsky, set fire to several trains, destroyed dozens of freight cars, locomotives, and destroyed tracks as they bombed and strafed the Wassowka railroad station. On their second approach to the target the ground-attack planes met twenty enemy bombers escorted by sixteen fighters. The flight commanded by First Lt. Shumsky opened fire immediately. The flight commander shot down two fighter planes, and his second-in-command shot down two more. Then our ground-attack planes attacked the German bombers. Major A. A. Yakovitsky, First Lt. N. P. Pushkin, and Sergeant N. S. Nesterov each shot down one bomber, and Master Sergeant A. P. Naumov shot down a fighter. Second Lt. P. P. Ivannikov, having exhausted all his ammunition, rammed an enemy bomber.

The major units of the fronts advanced simultaneously along the huge, 1000-kilometer (620-mile) front following their advance units. During this pursuit all types of aircraft supported the inexorable advance of the front's troops by day and night. They sought out enemy reserves moving toward the battlefield, located retreating German columns in the rear, found weak segments in enemy defense lines, put down centers of resistance, disorganized rail and truck movements, and successfully repelled enemy air raids.

The ground-attack squadron commanded by Hero of the Soviet Union, Captain V. I. Andrianov made an effective strike against the Tarnowskie Gory railroad station. Approaching from out of the sun, two crews silenced the antiaircraft guns and then others attacked troops and freight trains, setting fire to about fifty cars. Captain V. I. Andrianov was given a second "Gold Star" of the Soviet Union in June 1945 for his successful actions in support of the troops who captured the Silesian industrial region.

When the 1st White Russian Front reached the German-Polish

border and the 1st Ukrainian Front reached the Oder south of Breslau, they had completed the assignments received from the *Stavka*. But the fronts' offensive continued.

The enemy air force, based on permanent airfields near Berlin, increased the level of their operations. Several infantry and motorized divisions from the Army Group Center advanced to the Oder and organized a continuous defense line at that point. Taking advantage of permanent fortifications, German tanks and infantry with significant air support counterattacked against our troops on the bridgeheads in the regions of Küstrin, Breslau, and south of Oppeln.

In spite of bad weather and the distance our airfields were in the rear, the air force continued its operations against the enemy, although with very limited forces. On January 28, the most experienced crews of the 6th Guards Fighter Air Corps flew through a heavy snowstorm to the Breslau region and while protecting our ground forces repelled six raids from a much larger number of enemy aircraft. Hero of the Soviet Union First Lt. P. M. Nikonorov, and Second Lt. S. M. Novichkov especially distinguished themselves in this operation.

In order to restore a high air force operational level, 32 airfields were built and 15 restored with hard-surfaced landing strips from January 26 through February 7. However, air groups could not move to them, because it was impossible to take off from the field airstrips still muddy after a thaw. Under these circumstances, aircraft began to utilize sections of the Autobahns. The intermediate strip between the concrete lanes would be filled with rubble and paved with bricks. As a result, a landing strip 23 meters (75 feet) wide could be constructed. The first units to utilize these landing strips were the 15th Fighter Air Regiment of the 3rd Fighter Air Corps of the 16th Air Army, and the 9th Guards Fighter Air Division of the 2nd Air Army. As our units and groups were moved onto the newly constructed fields, their activities increased in support of the front's troops involved in bitter struggles to hold and expand their bridgeheads on the Oder's west bank.

When summoned by army commanders or by control officers, our aircraft attacked enemy strong points and fire positions. As the result of the powerful and constant Soviet strikes the enemy was forced to abandon his counterattacks.

At the beginning of February the German command, having collected a large number of aircraft, made a desperate attempt to win control of the air in support of the defensive efforts of his ground troops. Severe air battles broke out. But the balance of forces in the air was too uneven. In the first ten days of February, advance posts of the 1st White Russian Front recorded 13,950 enemy overflights. The 16th Air Army flew only 624 sorties against enemy aircraft because their airfields were inoperative because of mud. In 200 air battles, fighter pilots shot down 155 enemy aircraft. Sometimes the initiative in the air passed to enemy aircraft.

In the second ten-day period in February, advance posts noted only 3140 enemy overflights. Having built a number of field landing strips and moved in air units to them, the 16th Air Army in this period flew 5453 sorties to repel enemy raids and to attack enemy advance landing fields. When they suffered extensive losses in air battles the fascist fliers began to avoid meeting our fliers, who once more maintained unlimited control of the air.

Simultaneously the 16th Air Army flew support for the ground troops as they destroyed the enemy encircled in Poznań. Bombers attacked forts and fortress walls, knocking passages through them. Ground attack and fighter aircraft put down fire points, destroying men and equipment. A total of 1834 sorties were flown against the enemy within the city.

From January 26 through February 3, the 1st White Russian Front, with air support, pierced the enemy's border defenses, reached the Oder in force, and expanded the bridgeheads seized by advance units on its western bank near Küstrin. The 1st Ukrainian Front liberated the Silesian industrial region and expanded the bridgeheads that their advance units had seized on the western bank of the Oder in the Breslau region and south of Oppeln.

Results. The Vistula-Oder campaign was one of the largest offensive operations of the Great Patriotic War. During its course Soviet troops with close air force cooperation, in a shorter period of time than was foreseen in the operational plans, rapidly defeated the German Army Group A, liberated a considerable part of Poland, transferred military operations to the central regions of Germany, and reached the approaches to Berlin.

In the twenty days of the offensive, 31 divisions were annihilated and 25 divisions lost from 60 percent to 70 percent of their men. Soviet troops captured 147,400 enemy soldiers and officers, and seized 1377 tanks and other vehicles, 8280 mortars, and 1360 aircraft. Enemy losses in men killed and equipment destroyed were in fact even greater than this.

Operations of the 16th and 2nd Air Armies were unexcelled in their scope, nature, and results achieved, and proved the increasing skill of the staffs, indisputable superiority in equipment and its skillful application. Soviet air power once more showed that it could operate at a depth of 500 kilometers (310 miles) during an entire campaign to provide constant and effective ground support at any time of the year in bad weather, when the tank armies and corps were rapidly advancing. The units of both air armies flew more than 54,000 sorties. Our fighter planes fought 1150 air battles and destroyed 908 enemy aircraft.

The air force acquired much valuable experience in moving its air bases in the wake of advancing troops. During the offensive operation from the Vistula to the Oder, fighter units were moved seven times, and ground-attack units, six times.

XVIII

THE BERLIN CAMPAIGN

Ready for the Last Battle. In winter 1945, the Red Army routed large enemy forces in East Prussia, Poland, and on the southern wing of the Soviet-German front. Soviet troops entered the territory of Fascist Germany and in the first days of February reached the approaches to Berlin.

At the beginning of the Berlin campaign the German command still had at its disposal significant numbers of troops and aircraft as well as material resources. Hitler's government attempted to win time, calculating that serious disputes might arise between the Allies in the anti-Hitler coalition and favorable conditions might arise in which to conclude a separate peace with the governments of the United States and England.

Therefore, the enemy took all measures to increase his resistance on the Soviet-German front with the hope of halting the Red Army advance. The best-trained and best-equipped troops from the Army Groups Vistula and Center with about 1,000,000 men, 10,400 guns and mortars, and 1500 tanks and self-propelled guns were collected to defend the approaches to Berlin. Major defense systems at the Oder-Neisse defense line and the Berlin fortified region extended for a total of about 100 kilometers (62 miles).

The Luftwaffe had about 2000 aircraft near Berlin, of which 70 percent were fighters. This included about 120 Me 262 jets. A well-prepared air-base system assured that the Luftwaffe would be able to concentrate its aircraft in the most important regions.

Antiaircraft guns were also available to protect Berlin, German troops, and the most important targets, in addition to fighter aircraft. Opposite the 1st White Russian and 1st Ukrainian Fronts were 200 antiaircraft batteries, and near Berlin were 600 antiaircraft guns.

The Soviet Supreme Command decided to prepare and carry out the Berlin campaign rapidly so that Soviet forces could defeat the major German armies, capture Berlin, compel Fascist Germany to accept an unconditional surrender, and triumphantly conclude World War II in Europe. The 2nd and 1st White Russian Fronts and the 1st Ukrainian Front were used for this purpose. (The 1st and 2nd Polish Armies were included as part of the 1st Ukrainian Front and the 1st White Russian Front.)

Soviet aircraft were organized into three air armies: 4th Air Army of the 2nd White Russian Front, commanded by General K. A. Vershinin (northeast of Berlin); 16th Air Army of the 1st White Russian Front, commanded by General S. I. Rudenko (east of Berlin); 2nd Air Army of the 1st Ukrainian Front, commanded by General S. A. Krasovsky (southeast of Berlin).

In addition, the 18th Air Army, commanded by Chief Air Marshal A. Ye. Golovanov, was involved in the operation, as well as the air force of the Polish Army, including the 1st Polish Composite Air Corps and the 4th Polish Composite Air Division. The total number of aircraft in the Berlin campaign was 7500, of which 297 were Polish. To support our aircraft, 290 airfields were either built or renovated in a short period.

Preparations. The Supreme Command plan called for a powerful offensive through the enemy's defense lines, the cutting of the enemy Berlin armies into parts and then their encirclement and destruction, the capture of Berlin, and an advance to the Elbe.

A significant role in this plan was given to air power. The follow-ing air force assignments were given by the commanders: maintain control of the air; protect ground troops and targets in the rear from enemy air attacks; carry out a preparatory attack and support ground forces as they cut through the enemy's tactical defense zone; cooperate with troops of the 2nd White Russian and 1st Ukrainian Front as they crossed the Oder, the Neisse, and Spree; support the entry of tank armies into the battle; protect and support them during the entire operation; destroy enemy reserves; carry out aerial reconnais-sance and observation over the battlefield.

In the center, the 1st White Russian Front commander, Marshal G. K. Zhukov, decided that most troops of his front were to begin their attack one and a half or two hours before sunrise. Therefore, the air preparatory attack was to be made by 16th Air Army night bombers.

Ground support for the front's troops as they broke through the enemy's defenses was to be provided by the 18th Air Army, which was to make a mass strike of 800 bombers before sunrise against enemy strong points in the secondary defense zone. At sunrise ground support was to be provided by the 16th Air Army. During the first two hours of the attack there was to be a mass raid of 730 ground-attack planes and 455 bombers. Later, in accordance with the cir-cumstances, there were to be concentrated strikes, and attacks in waves, carried out by small groups of aircraft.

The 1st Ukrainian Front, commanded by Marshal I. S. Konev, were to begin their offensive at dawn, which made it possible to utilize large numbers of aircraft to support the break-through of the enemy's defense lines. This 2nd Air Army battle plan called for four mass attacks on the first day of the attack. The first strike was to be carried out by 800 aircraft as a preparatory attack and as support for the troops of the Front as they crossed the Neisse and cut through the enemy's first defense zone. Two hundred and eight bombers were to make the preparatory strike to destroy enemy strong points, silence artillery, and kill troops in the first defense zone.

The 2nd White Russian Front troops in the north began their offensive by crossing a major obstacle, the Oder River. Our artillery on its eastern bank could not reach the entire depth of the enemy's defense zone. This assignment was given to the air force. Three nights running, night-bombing Po-2s were to fly 1400 sorties against artillery, mortars, and troops and thus weaken the enemy's resistance against the troops of the front as they crossed the Oder.

A two-hour ground-attack preparatory air assault was planned. During its last hour, artillery was to join in.

Air operations in the period when tank armies were being introduced into the battle were very carefully planned. Approximately 75 percent of the 16th and 2nd Air Armies aircraft were to be devoted to this task.

The 16th Air Army flew 2600 reconnaissance sorties in the preparatory period. Aircraft photographed areas of 155,250 square kilometers (59,942 square miles). The enemy's tactical zone into which the fronts' troops were to advance was photographed eight times and the entire territory from the front lines to Berlin was photographed twice. This made it possible to identify the structures in the entire defense zone and the enemy troop concentrations.

Organization of coordinated efforts between the air and ground forces was a very important part of the preparatory period. The air armies commanders told each air group with what ground army and tank army it would be coordinated during the operation. This made it possible for the commands and staffs of the ground forces and the air groups to establish personal contacts, harmonize coordinated operations, organize a plan for studying targets to be attacked, and work out the necessary documentation.

Coordinated operations with tank armies were carefully worked out. The army staffs and the air group representatives worked out joint operational plans. In these plans, assignments were shown for ground and air forces, aircraft were assigned according to the day of the operation and the missions, aircraft controls were worked out, the front line of our troops was identified, and also methods were agreed upon for transmitting and evaluating reconnaissance data and information about the battlefield situation.

To insure that our aircraft would follow closely behind the advancing tank armies, airfields were constructed directly behind the front lines. During the offensive, tank groups were to seize enemy airfields and hold them until the infantry arrived. The 2nd Guards Tank Army of the 1st White Russian Front had the assignment of seizing and defending the airfields at Alt Friedland, Werneuchen, Eberswalde, and Strausberg on the second day of the offensive. Air units were designated for flying cover and support for our mobile forces. It was planned that engineering air-base battalions and air-base service battalions from the 16th Air Army would advance behind the 2nd Guards Tank Army.

The 1st Ukrainian Front artillery staff and the 2nd Air Army staff developed a plan and map for the coordinated employment of artillery and air power on the first day of the operation. Artillery and air power were assigned targets and time of attack during both the preparatory period and time when the operations were under way.

Chief Air Marshal A. A. Novikov was in charge of the over-all coordination of operations of the 2nd, 4th, 16th, and 18th Air Armies and with his operational group was located in the 16th Air Army command post.

The Attack Begins in the Center. The Berlin campaign began on the night of April 15, 1945. The 1st White Russian Front troops took the offensive two hours before dawn. The 4th Air Army of the adjoining front also took part in the preparatory air attacks. All night its bombers raided enemy fire points and troop concentrations. Thirty minutes before the attack, 109 16th Air Army aircraft struck at enemy staffs and communications. Simultaneously, an artillery barrage was under way.

At 5:00 A.M. Moscow time, the troops took the offensive under an artillery barrage. The area in front of the attacking troops and the enemy's forward defense line were lighted by 143 searchlights. At first the enemy was confused by the sudden night attack, the artillery barrage, and the blinding light from the searchlights. Our troops moved ahead, rapidly finding no serious resistance from the enemy. Later on, as our troops moved deeper into the enemy defense, resistance increased and reduced the speed of our advance.

To support the ground troops, the 18th Air Army sent 743 bombers against the enemy's major resistance centers in the secondary defense zone; Letchin, Langsof, Werbig, Seelow, Friedersdorf, and Dolgelin. There were many famous fliers among the bomber crews who had participated in bombing raids against the German capital in 1941–42. Among them were A. I. Molodchy, V. N. Osipov, both twice Heroes of the Soviet Union; the Heroes of the Soviet Union E. K. Pusep, V. F. Romanov; and many others. The raid against the enemy positions lasted forty-two minutes. Every minute, 22 tons of bombs were dropped on targets, most of them large bombs.

The 16th Air Army began operations at dawn. However, a ground fog made it impossible to carry out the planned mass strike. The ground-attack planes were forced to operate in small groups, silencing and destroying artillery centers and troops on the battlefield. Even these efforts helped the advancing troops. As they advanced at the center of the front, units of the 80th Infantry Corps of the 5th Strike Army were subjected to heavy fire from the vicinity of Diedersdorf. The infantry was forced to lie low and tanks had to take cover.

The air representative located at the 80th Infantry Corps command post summoned planes from the 198th Ground-Attack Air Division. The first to arrive were nine aircraft commanded by Captain Sorokin, who attacked the German artillery. The subsequent groups of ground-attack planes took a "circle" formation and silenced the enemy's artillery fire. Taking advantage of this, our troops advanced and completed the break-through of the second position in the first defense zone.

Evaluating the air operation, the 80th Corps commander wrote, "The 198th Ground-Attack Air Division played a large role in guaranteeing the success of the infantry. The ground-attack planes cleared a path for the infantry, destroying and silencing enemy fire points and artillery. They often operated 300 meters (984 feet) from our advancing troops, completely eliminating enemy resistance. The planes appeared at the target quickly and when needed."

To support constant air attacks when there were locally foggy areas, the 16th Air Army commander, General S. I. Rudenko, gave his permission for ground-attack planes returning from their assignments to land at any airfield within the air army that was not closed by fog, there to be refueled and armed to once more attack targets on the ground. In such a case, the air group commanders gave assignments by radio as the groups of ground-attack planes left for their operational areas.

Later in the day the 1st White Russian Front troops cut through the enemy's first defense zone. In the heat of the battle for the enemy defense lines, Soviet fliers supporting the 8th Guards Army dropped four large gate keys like the historical keys to Berlin which the enemy was compelled to give to Russian troops during the Seven Years' War (1756–63). To each of them was attached a message: "Guardsmen and Friends, on to victory! We send you the keys to the gates of Berlin."

The enemy fought desperately at the second defense zone. The commander of the front sent the 1st and 2nd Guards Tank Armies into the battle with air support in order to increase the power and momentum of the drive through the enemy zone. Ground-attack planes destroyed enemy artillery in the assault zone and on the flanks of the tank groups. Bombers from the 16th and 18th Air Armies raided enemy reserves day and night, not allowing them to reach the area where the tank armies were active.

At the end of the day on April 16, aerial reconnaissance revealed a movement of enemy troops from the Berlin region. The night of April 16, 18th Air Army bombers flew more than 200 sorties, destroying enemy columns and hitting roads along which they were moving at Münchenberg, Buckow, Fürstenwalde, and Heinersdorf. The enemy troops suffered losses from the air attack and their advance to the battlefield was disorganized.

Fighter aircraft from the 16th Air Army successfully fulfilled their assignments in support of our advancing troops. The famous Soviet fighter pilot I. N. Kozhedub shot down two more enemy fighters (Fw 190s) on April 19. These were his sixty-first and sixty-second victories in the Great Patriotic War.*

On April 18, hundreds of planes participated in air battles over the major offensive zone. After the Germans had been defeated in the tactical rear of their defense lines, the German command planned to devote its air power to support of its ground troops holding the third defense line. Late in the day a 16th Air Army radar station discovered 35 enemy bombers and ground-attack planes flying toward our tank armies. At that time, three groups of Soviet fighters were in the air, eight in each group. First Lt. I. G. Kuznetsov commanded one of these groups, the 43rd Fighter Air Regiment.

Warned by the 3rd Fighter Air Corps command post that enemy aircraft were approaching, First Lt. Kuznetsov led his planes to intercept the enemy. Hidden in clouds, our fliers attacked, spoiling the enemy's formation and compelling the planes to drop their bombs on their own troops. During the battle I. G. Kuznetsov, I. F. Chernenkov, and N. T. Gribkov shot down four German aircraft.

On April 20, the 1st White Russian Front broke through the Oder defense line. Tank armies together with infantry and air power began to encircle Berlin and to cut up the enemy's army.

---

* The most successful Soviet ace, Kozhedub flew his first combat sortie on March 26, 1943, in an La-5, and shifted to the La-7 in July 1944. In 520 sorties, he shot down 22 Fw 190s, 19 Bf 109s, 18 Ju 87s, two He 111s, and a single Me 262, the latter on February 24, 1945.[19] ED.

Attack Southeast of Berlin.   The 1st Ukrainian Front went on the offensive on the morning of April 16. All of the front bomber and ground-attack aircraft carried out a preparatory strike to support the ground troops. As they supported the crossing of the Neisse and the break-through of the first defense zone, 668 2nd Air Army aircraft struck in a massive raid. From among them, 208 dive bombers from the 4th and 6th Guards Bomber Air Corps struck at resistance points in the first defense zone at Forst, Kaune, and Muskau. Using these strong points the enemy could counterattack on the flank of the front's army and also fire from a flanking position.

Before the attack began, ground-attack planes laid down a smoke screen in the major front offensive areas. To disrupt enemy communications, three bomber groups, each with nine aircraft, raided enemy control centers and communication lines.

The air and artillery preparatory attack killed enemy troops, silenced artillery, and disrupted communications. The smoke screen along front areas confused the German command, so that they did not know where to expect an attack, and it concealed the beginning of the Neisse crossing made by our advance battalions.

Utilizing the great effectiveness of our air strikes and artillery, troops in the center assault area quickly crossed the Neisse and began their successful advance.

At the beginning of the offensive the enemy opened an artillery barrage and counterattack from the Forst, Gross-Tschaksdorf, Kebeln, Jemlitz, and Muskau regions. Our troops had to stop their advance. A situation had developed that might sharply retard our advance and cause the whole plan for breaking through the enemy's tactical defense zone to fail.

But this did not happen. The 2nd Air Army commander summoned air power to aid the ground troops. The 2nd Guards Ground-Attack Air Corps sent 110 Il-2s escorted by 50 fighters to make an intensive strike against artillery and troops at the strong points of Forst and Gross-Tschaksdorf. At the same time, 100 1st Guards Ground-Attack Air Corps aircraft escorted by 65 fighters hit near Kebeln, Jemlitz, and Muskau. As a result, artillery fire was silenced, enemy troops pinned down, and their counterattack disrupted. Taking advantage of these attacks, our troops quickly seized these strong points.

Tank armies entered the battle on the afternoon of April 17. 1st Ukrainian Front commander, Marshal I. S. Konev, instructed the tank personnel to cross the Spree, break through the enemy's third defense zone, and press a rapid advance toward Berlin and Brandenburg. The German command tried to hinder the advance of our tank armies. For this purpose, he introduced three reserve tank divisions and one motorized infantry division, and initiated strong counterattacks from the areas of Cottbus and Spremberg. German aircraft in groups as large as 24 aircraft struck at our tank formations, but the enemy was not successful.

Seventy-five percent of our aircraft were assigned to support our tank armies. Ground-attack planes constantly destroyed strong points, counterattacking tanks and enemy troops. Bombers directed their efforts against reserves. Aerial reconnaissance revealed tank concentrations in the third defense zones and at Cottbus, Neuhausen, Gross-Osnig, and Spremberg. One hundred and fifty bombers struck at tanks. In addition, bombers hit columns of tanks and roads. The enemy suffered great losses and his advance to the battlefield was disorganized.

Cover for our tank armies was provided by constantly patrolling fighter groups and by fighters, directed by radar reports, intercepting enemy aircraft. The 6th Guards Fighter Air Corps alone, flying support for the 4th Guards Tank Army, fought 50 air battles and shot down 56 enemy aircraft. Enemy aircraft were unable to have any significant effect on the advancing tank armies, which with effective air support, repulsed the enemy counterattacks, crossed the Spree, broke through the third defense zone, and began a rapid advance toward Berlin and the area to the west of it.

When the offensive was being expanded, heavy use was made of fighter planes against ground targets, which they attacked with machine-gun and cannon fire and bombs, disorganizing highway and rail traffic and airfields.

After they had lost the battle on the Spree the German command took measures to halt the advance of our tank armies toward Berlin. For this purpose they made a massive flanking counterattack from the Görlitz region aimed at the rear of the 3rd and 4th Guards Tank Armies to prevent them from surrounding their army at Berlin.

Troops of the 52nd Army and the 2nd Polish Army on the left wing of the front began bitter fighting with the German troops at Görlitz. The 5th Fighter and 3rd Ground-Attack Air Corps provided these armies protection and support. During the worst of the fighting, bombers were also brought in to support the ground troops.

Most of our aircraft were devoted to destroying enemy tanks and artillery. On April 21, ground-attack planes destroyed 12 tanks, an armored train, 2 armored cars, and silenced 5 artillery batteries northwest of Görlitz. The next day, aerial reconnaissance discovered 110 tanks, 5 artillery batteries and many troops near Reichenbach. Units of the 4th and 6th Guards Bomber Air Corps were sent. Their strikes destroyed 12 tanks and silenced the artillery. Thanks to air support, the front troops repelled the counterattack from the Görlitz troops and then annihilated it. The threat to the front left wing was abolished. To accomplish this, aircraft flew 4440 sorties, destroyed about 50 tanks, and silenced 10 artillery batteries. Tanks of the 1st Ukrainian Front, with air support, rapidly advanced and by April 21 were at the edge of Berlin.

The Attack from the Northeast.   The 2nd White Russian Front took the offensive April 20. During the night, 4th Air Army bombers flew 1085 sorties, hitting at enemy fire points. At dawn, front troops began to cross the Oder. The enemy tried to throw the Soviet troops back into the river from our bridgeheads on the west bank, and our troops needed artillery support. However, the great width of the river made it impossible to construct bridges that might be utilized by heavy equipment in a short time. Under these circumstances air support played an important role. The success of the Oder crossing and the drive into the enemy's defenses depended upon effective air support.

All air army resources were devoted to support of the ground troops as they crossed the Oder. The air force flew day and night, first of all seeking out, attacking, and destroying enemy tanks and artillery. Because of the bad weather, ground-attack planes and bombers flew in pairs, or alone without fighter escorts. When the weather improved, ground-attack planes flew in groups as large as 36 planes, which attacked in waves. The attack on the targets was made from the "circle" formation, consisting of a line of pairs and four fighter planes. Each group made several approaches and was over the target from twenty to thirty minutes.

The air force gave significant support to the ground forces. As the bridgehead was being expanded, 70th Army units were stopped by artillery fire at the approaches to the strong point of Tantow. The 260th Ground-Attack Air Division commander summoned 22 aircraft from the 839th Ground-Attack Air Regiment, led by First Lt. V. V. Kamushkin. To add to the surprise, the ground-attack planes approached the target from the enemy's rear. The first strike was made from the formation "column of pairs." The subsequent four attacks were made from the "circle" formation and the planes were twenty-five minutes over the target. As a result, the artillery batteries were silenced, a munitions dump was blown up, and the enemy troops pinned down. Taking advantage of the air strike, the 70th Army advanced rapidly and occupied the strong point at Tantow.

In the 65th Army zone, bombers in groups of nine commanded by Major P. G. Yegorov and Captain V. V. Bushnev bombed the Pomerensdorf strong point. After this attack the 4th Air Army commander sent the 5th Bomber Air Corps commander the following telegram: "Inform your flying crews that their bombing raid silenced the enemy artillery. Everything was afire in the target areas. Our ground units left cover and advanced rapidly."

The 65th Army commander in his report to the front staff gave his high opinion of the air operations: "If the ground-attack planes had not hit the counterattacking tanks, self-propelled guns, and enemy troops, we would hardly have been able to hold our bridgehead."

The front troops with great air support crossed the Oder, captured bridgeheads, beat off enemy counterattacks, and fought successfully to penetrate the enemy's defense zone. The 3rd German Army suffered great losses and was pinned down by our troops. The German command could no longer reinforce its troops guarding Berlin. As a consequence, the 2nd White Russian Front offensive had great significance in fulfilling the assignment of capturing Berlin.

Berlin Is Surrounded. Beginning April 21, troops of the 1st White Russian and 1st Ukrainian Front with the support of the 16th, 2nd, and 18th Air Armies were involved in bitter fighting for Berlin. Simultaneously, tank groups operating with infantry armies continued their sweep around the city and the dismemberment of the Berlin army. This assignment was completed by April 25. Two isolated German groups found themselves surrounded: one in Berlin itself and the second in the woods to the southeast of it, which came to be called the Frankfurt-Guben troop concentration. On the same day, American and Soviet troops met on the Elbe near Torgau. The German troops were divided into a northern and a southern army.

The Frankfurt-Guben troop concentration was annihilated by joint ground and air force efforts of the 1st White Russian and 1st Ukrainian Fronts. Bombers and ground-attack planes caused serious enemy losses. Fighter planes blocked the encircled group so that they could not be supplied or reinforced by air. Reconnaissance planes maintained constant observation of the enemy, noting troop movement and concentration.

On the morning of April 26, aerial reconnaissance discovered concentrations of major forces of the Frankfurt-Guben army in the regions of Täupitz, Birkholz, Wendisch Buchholz, and Halbe. The enemy planned to break out of this region through the troops of the 1st Ukrainian Front and join his 12th Army advancing from the west. Then he planned to break the ring around Berlin, utilizing both these groups.

Taking advantage of the brief numerical superiority which he enjoyed on the very narrow segment of the front, the enemy overwhelmed our troops and broke through the Baruth region. But he could not complete his plans. Bombers and ground-attack planes from the 2nd Air Army were sent to attack the enemy and caused him serious losses. First to appear over their targets were seventy Pe-2s summoned by the 4th Bomber Air Corps commander, General P. P. Arkhangelsky. Eight tanks and fifty other vehicles were destroyed in this raid. On April 26 alone, bombers flew more than 200 sorties. At the same time, planes from the 6th Guards Bomber Air Corps dive-bombed the crossings on the Dahm River and thus disrupted the plans of the Frankfurt-Guben army before it could leave its own territory. Ground-attack planes constantly attacked the encircled enemy. Flying in small groups, they displayed initiative and resourcefulness, seeking out and destroying tanks, artillery, and enemy troop concentrations.

Units of the 1st Guards Ground-Attack Air Corps supported the 5th Guards Mechanized Corps and the 13th Army as they repelled the counterattack of the 12th German Army on their external front. Hitler ordered this army to hurry to the rescue of the Frankfurt-Guben troop concentration. Large enemy forces attempted to capture the important road junction at Beelitz. The tank brigade of the 5th Guard Mechanized Corps could not repel the numerically superior enemy forces.

When the tank unit appealed for help, General V. G. Ryazanov summoned ground-attack planes to hit the counterattacking troops. On April 29, they flew 400 sorties for this purpose. The enemy was cowed and pinned down. Ten burned tanks remained on the battlefield and many soldiers and officers were killed. With air support, our troops beat off all counterattacks and held the city of Beelitz.

Having suffered a defeat at the approaches to Beelitz, the 12th German Army attempted to counterattack against our troops in other areas of the front. However, this was not successful and the Soviet troops drove the enemy to the Elbe. The encircled Frankfurt-Guben concentration could not receive any aid from the 12th Army. The 1st Ukrainian and 1st White Russian Front cut it into pieces and by May 1 it was liquidated. While the Frankfurt-Guben concentration was being annihilated and the 12th German Army counterattack repelled on the external front, the 2nd and 16th Air Armies flew 5578 sorties.

Bitter fighting was under way at this time in Berlin. The enemy offered a desperate resistance. During the first days of the battle for the city, our air force made a number of large raids against armed forces communication centers and fortifications.

To control the aircraft operating over Berlin, two control points were set up: northern and eastern. The eastern was the major one, with officers from the staff of the 16th Air Army commanded by Deputy to the Commander of the Army, General A. S. Senatorov. The northern control point was headed by the 6th Ground-Attack Air Corps, commanded by General B. K. Tokarev.

All air units and single planes were required to maintain communications with the control point chief and could attack their targets only with his permission. Air observers stationed on roofs of buildings in the city communicated by radio, lights, or rockets the location of the front, and aided air crews as they hunted out their targets.

The night of April 21, 529 18th Air Army heavy bombers and 184 16th Air Army aircraft made a mass raid against enemy defense systems, troops, and equipment on the eastern and northeastern edges of Berlin. On April 24, 205 6th Guards Bomber Air Corps aircraft of the 2nd Air Army, supporting the 3rd Guards Tank Army in their battle for the southern part of the capital, struck against fascist troops and artillery positions.

The Soviet Air Force made especially strong strikes on the enemy on April 24 and 25. At night on April 24, 111 18th Air Army bombers struck; and in the daytime on April 25 the 16th Air Army, in accordance with its plan, named "Salute," made two massive raids in which 1368 planes were involved. The night of April 25, the 18th Air Army sent 563 planes on a raid. Major P. A. Taran, twice Hero of the Soviet Union, participated.

German troops defending Berlin were subjected to lengthy attacks from the Soviet Air Force using large delayed-action bombs. The enemy suffered large losses in men and materials, and many fortifications were destroyed. A large part of the city was wrapped in flame, and there were dozens of large explosions.

"I can only say that we sat in the basement floors of the Imperial Chancellery and could not emerge into the daylight," said General Bauer in describing the destructive power of the Soviet air raids. "I think," said Lt. Col. Otto Ernst, "that the Soviet Air Force performed its tasks brilliantly. Not only was each bomb materially effective, it was also effective on morale." Nonetheless the enemy continued his resistance. Bitter fighting developed for every building, street, block.

When the assault on the central city began, aircraft operated in waves of small groups. This was because of the difficult situation on the ground. Smoke and dust caused by bomb explosions, artillery shells, and fires severely limited visibility, and made it impossible to ascertain our troops' location from the air.

Soviet fighter planes blocked Berlin from the air and protected our troops fighting in the city. Tank units from the 1st White Russian Front seized several enemy airfields in Berlin, onto which aircraft from the 16th Air Army were immediately shifted.

On April 28, the 193rd Fighter Air Division's 515th Fighter Air Regiment landed at the Tempelhof airfield. Fighting was still going on in the vicinity. The first to land on the field were the regimental commander and Hero of the Soviet Union, Lt. Col. V. G. Gromov and his partner Second Lt. Yu. T. Dyachenko. As they approached the field they were fired on by antiaircraft artillery. But they were not frightened. Coming in at ground level, they landed. Then the German troops began to fire at their planes with mortars. The Soviet artillery silenced the mortars.

On the same day the 347th and 518th Fighter Air Regiments, commanded by Lt. Cols. P. B. Dankevich and N. G. Khudokormov, began to operate out of the Berlin airport at Schoenefeld.

Intense air battle developed over Berlin. Seven 263rd Fighter Air Regiment pilots courageously attacked a large group of enemy aircraft intending to strike at our troops. Second Lt. N. A. Brodsky cut into the enemy formation and shot down one plane. He was attacked by six fighters. With a skillful maneuver he disappeared into the clouds and then suddenly emerged to shoot down another plane. Captain A. I. Chetvertkov shot down two fascist planes in this battle. Polish planes operated in a comradely manner with Soviet aircraft in these battles. During the operation they destroyed seventeen German planes.

Bitter fighting developed for the central parts of the city. German troops set up a hurricane of gunfire and began frenzied counterattacks. On April 30, stubborn battles began for the Reichstag. Late on that day, Soviet troops broke into the building, and early on the morning of May 1, the Red Banner flew over the Reichstag. Sergeants M. A. Yegorov and M. V. Kantariya, daring reconnaissance specialists, raised it by order of the 3rd Strike Army Military Council.

On the international holiday, May Day, fliers of the 2nd Air Army made an unusual flight over Berlin. The guard-fighter pilots prepared two red banners. On one side of one of them was written "Victory" and on its other side "Glory to the Soviet soldiers who raised the Victory Banner over Berlin." On the other was written "Hail the First of May!"

At noon, the daring Guards pilots Capt. V. K. Novoselov and Major N. A. Malinovsky, escorted by 16 fighters commanded by two-time Hero of the Soviet Union Lt. Col. A. V. Vorozheykin, and including the Heroes of the Soviet Union V. N. Buyanov, I. P. Laveykin, P. I. Peskov and others, appeared over the Reichstag and dropped red banners on it by parachute. Spreading out in the smoky Berlin sky, they slowly fell into the hands of Soviet troops. The greetings commemorating May 1 from the fliers were received with great enthusiasm by our ground troops. Patriotic slogans on the banners sounded a call for the final battles.

Remnants of the Berlin garrison, cut into parts, tried to break through to the west. On May 2, about 3000 Germans with tanks and artillery approached the Dalgow airfield where our 265th Fighter Air Division was stationed. When the alarm was given, our planes left the airfield. Personnel of the 3rd Fighter Air Corps control group, the 462nd and 609th Air Service Battalions, and technical personnel of the air units fought against the enemy troops. The enemy's escape route to the west was blocked. Late in the day artillery, infantry, and tanks from the 125th Infantry Corps arrived to help the airmen.

Fliers from the 265th Fighter Air Division made ground attacks in support of their comrades on the ground. The fighting did not end until late at night. In this ground battle, unusual for airmen, 379 Germans were killed and 1450 captured.

At the same time, staff personnel of the 13th Fighter Air Corps, the 283rd Fighter Air Division, the 471st and 481st Air Service Battalions, and technical crews of the 56th, 116th, and 176th Fighter Air Regiments were involved in stubborn fighting with large numbers of the enemy near Stansdorf and Hueterfelde. Aircraft from the 13th Fighter Air Corps helped their comrades with machine-gun and cannon fire and bomb strikes. The airmen continued their battle along with infantry until the end of the day, killing 477 and capturing 1288 German troops. The 3rd and 13th Fighter Air Corps personnel bravely resisted the enemy and made it impossible for him to escape the surrounded city.

Capitulation. The defeated enemy had no other choice but to lay down his arms.† On May 2, the 56th Tank Corps commander General Weidling, who had been in charge of the Berlin defense, surrendered. He asked the city garrison to end their resistance. In his order, Weidling wrote, "In accordance with the Supreme Command of the Soviet troops, I demand an immediate end to the struggle."[20] The same instruction was issued in the name of the German government by Frietsche, Goebbels' next in command. Mass surrenders began.

At the end of the day on May 2, Berlin was completely occupied by Soviet troops. At the middle of the day on May 8, Allied representatives arrived at the Berlin suburb, Karlshorst, to sign the unconditional surrender documents. General of the Army V. D. Sokolovsky and the Commandant of Berlin, General-Colonel N. E. Berzarin, met the Allied command at Tempelhof airport.

That same day, eighteen fliers of the 16th Air Army's 515th Fighter Air Regiment under the command of Major M. N. Tyulkin filled an unusual assignment. They escorted the flight of the English, French, and American delegations from Stendal to Berlin. Among these fliers were famous Soviet aces—Captain V. A. Gubich and others. Representatives from the German command also arrived by plane at Karlshorst from Flensburg—Field Marshal Keitel, Fleet Admiral Friedenburg, and General-Colonel of the Air Force Stumpf, who signed the unconditional surrender agreement for Fascist Germany.

The fall of Berlin and the subsequent unconditional surrender of Fascist Germany were the greatest accomplishments of the Berlin campaign. The long heroic struggle of the Soviet people in the Great

† Hitler had committed suicide April 30. ED.

Patriotic War ended with total defeat of the enemy. The long-awaited peace arrived in Europe. The great sacrifices, immense suffering and privations, exhausting labor in the rear, and the feats of Soviet soldiers at the front had not been in vain and were crowned with total victory over the Fascists.

The Soviet Air Force had a great contribution to make in the attainment of victory over the German armed forces. Flying personnel performed brilliantly and the commanders demonstrated their great skill as they directed the large numbers of air units that made up the four air armies.

During the campaign the Soviet Air Force flew about 92,000 sorties, more than half of them at night and in bad weather.

During the campaign our fighters maintained firm control of the air, fighting 1317 air battles, shooting down 1132 enemy planes, and destroying 100 on the ground. Our air victory over Berlin did not come easily. The air force lost 527 aircraft in air battles or from anti-aircraft fire.[21]

Forty-five air units and groups were given the title of "Berlin" or "Brandenburg" units. All the participants in the campaign were given the medal "For the Capture of Berlin," which was established in honor of the historic victory. Hundreds of fliers, navigators, machine gunners and technicians received medals or honors.

SUMMARY AND CONCLUSIONS OF THE THIRD PERIOD

In the third period of the war the Soviet Air Force fought with more decisive goals. It gave great help to the ground forces as they liberated the Leningrad district, the right bank of the Dnieper, the Crimea, White Russia, the western districts of the Ukraine, the Baltic region, southern Karelia, the Arctic, northern Norway, the eastern part of Poland, Czechoslovakia, Hungary, Rumania, Bulgaria, and Yugoslavia.

The successes achieved by the Red Army, especially at the beginning of 1944, showed the entire world that it could defeat the German armies alone. It was just this which accelerated the opening of the second front by the U.S. and England. But after it had been opened, the situation on the Soviet-German front hardly changed at all, because the major German ground and air forces remained in the east where, in fact, the fate of the war was settled.

In the final stage of the war, the Soviet Air Force gave invaluable help to the ground forces as they captured or destroyed the major enemy troop concentrations and liberated Poland, Czechoslovakia, Hungary, the eastern part of Germany, and a significant part of Austria.

During the last third of the war, our air force flew 1,470,000 sorties and dropped 18,332,000 bombs with a total weight of 286,326 tons, causing significant losses to enemy troops and equipment. Soviet aircraft and antiaircraft artillery destroyed more than 21,000 enemy aircraft. When our pilots became more skilled and the level of our operations increased, it was possible to control the air and sharply reduce our losses in air battles and from the enemy's antiaircraft fire.

Thousands of fliers received orders and medals for successful operations, courage, daring, and heroism; 95 air force units and groups were given guard designations, 840 were given orders, and 547 received the names of large cities for their active part in their liberation.

The constant improvement in the air personnel training and the invaluable experience gained in battle were two major factors that brought victory. The air force command, the commanding officers, and the staffs at all levels came to understand the nature of their operations and could apply their knowledge in the concrete conditions on the battlefield.

The decisive successes of the air force were supported by the heroic endeavors of the workers in the rear. The rapid development of heavy industry and machine construction increased military production. In 1943–44 the aircraft plants produced four times as many aircraft per year as in the prewar years.

During its operations the air force improved its organizational structure, its control and coordination with the ground forces. Later on, new equipment for the air force, improved morale, battle training of commands and staffs at all levels and the flying and engineering-mechanical personnel, all had a beneficial influence on the operational skills of the air force and the use of different kinds of aircraft as it solved its major problems in the third stage of the war.

Control of the air was one of the most important air force assignments. Experience in the two preceding war periods showed that control of the air was one of the most important conditions for successful ground offensive operations.

The Supreme Command gave great importance to air power and concentrated its largest forces in the major offensive zones. In the war's third period Supreme Command reserve units were employed with great mobility and made it possible to have great superiority over the enemy and to achieve major operational and strategic results.

The creation of large aircraft groups was made possible for the most part by the use of the Supreme Command reserves, which increased rapidly in numbers as compared with the second period of the war. At the beginning of the White Russian offensive campaign, the 1st, 3rd, 4th, and 16th Air Armies received eleven air corps with more than 3000 planes from the reserves of the Supreme Command. During the preparatory period before the Lvov-Sandomir campaign, the 2nd Air Army received four air corps and two air divisions with 1440 aircraft. The *Stavka* thus provided flexibility for creating the most favorable situation in the air, which made the air force more effective in destroying the enemy's major troop concentrations.

In all 1944–45 offensive operations, thanks to reliable air cover, the fronts' strike groups could enter the battle and advance rapidly without fear of a reaction from the enemy aircraft. The war's third period demonstrated clearly the superiority of the Soviet Air Force. It captured the initiative in the air, possessed great striking power and large reserves, and was superior to the enemy in maneuverability, control of operations, skill, and in the morale of its personnel.

With the very active support of our air force the German Army Groups North, Center, Northern Ukraine, and Southern Ukraine were annihilated in 1944.

The air force delivered even more crushing blows in the offensive operations of 1945 against all the enemy's strategic troop concentrations active on the Soviet-German front.

During the war's third period, thanks to the constant increase in power possessed by the air force, an air offensive could be carried out with larger forces, making it possible to increase the breadth of offensive operations and to expand the theoretical aspects of the use of air power.

The study of an offensive operation through a stable enemy defensive zone showed that the most effective use of air power, when the defensive line was being cut, was in the form of an air offensive, which would have as its goal control of the air and constant support for ground troops. Such study also provided the principles for a preliminary and an immediate air attack before the assault. It was determined that the preliminary air attack should begin long before the offensive, and should be carried out by concentrated strikes and also by small groups of aircraft and individual aircraft along a wide front during the entire preparatory period. The immediate air preparatory period should be the culminating stage of the first period of the air offensive, and could be carried out on the night before the offensive during an artillery barrage, and should end with a powerful concentrated strike just before the infantry and tank assault, and in the area in which the major assault was to be made.

In 1944–45 the fronts and the AFLRO expanded their efforts against enemy transportation and reserves, which made it possible to broaden offensive operations. From time to time they disrupted enemy transportation (White Russian campaign), destroyed his troops on roads as they approached the battlefield (Lvov-Sandomir campaign), hit and destroyed enemy reserves in areas where they were concentrated (Łódź and Kielce).

Training activities were very important in increasing the efficiency of the air force. Manuals that gave instructions for the use of different kinds of aircraft, were worked out and distributed to air force units.

The staff of the Red Army Air Force regularly issued informational leaflets, bulletins, and other documents. During periods before an offensive operation, much attention was devoted to the utilization of battle experience, and training for the command personnel and flight personnel of the air units.

Before an operation began, much study was devoted to the problems before the air force. The questions of control over units during the operations, coordination of efforts with ground troops, and the use of different aircraft types were very carefully worked out.

Air maintenance was further improved. These units received more men and equipment for service and repairs. Thanks to the great experience in air operations, high morale, and hard work the service personnel were successful in meeting their responsibility for supporting air operations during the largest offensive campaigns.

Much attention was devoted to aerial reconnaissance. The fronts' commanders considered it to be a basic technique for gathering valuable and reliable information about the enemy, and during the campaigns to liberate the right bank of the Dnieper, White Russia, Poland, Rumania, Bulgaria, and other areas it was the most important source of such data. Before every offensive, reconnaissance planes searched and photographed the enemy's major troop locations and his defensive systems, helping us to plan and carry out offensive operations.

Navigational techniques were much improved in the large offensive operations. One of its accomplishments was reduction of lost planes and misdirected planes to a minimum, and also more accurate bomb drops.

To improve our flying staff training and to improve bombing accuracy, the Navigational Service of the Red Army Air Force published new manuals on bombing techniques (PB-44) in 1944 that included information on the use of bombs and bombing calculation, and also other essential information. Aircraft were equipped with bombsights OPB-1D (for bomb drops from horizontal flights) and PBP-4 (for dive-bombing). These made it possible to improve the number of hits in 1944 by 11 percent compared with the previous year.

Great attention was devoted to radio guidance for aircraft and a system of ground control was developed (ZOS). During offensive operations, its mobile units were shifted to where they were needed in order to control aircraft. The ZOS system included radio towers, radio-directing stations, radio-bearing transmitters, and beacons. The number of sorties flown with ZOS support constantly increased. In 1943, ZOS supported 597,212 sorties; and in 1944, 879,559.

The Engineering Air Service greatly improved its work and particularly its field repair duties. Before each major offensive, almost all the mobile repair shops (PARMs) with complete staffs collected a mobile supply of repair materials and parts sufficient for six or seven days of operations, and specialized repair shops enough for twelve to fifteen days. PARMs specialized in the repair of certain types of equipment and followed not far behind the advancing air service battalions.

The repair services greatly increased their production. In 1943 they worked on more than 540 aircraft per day; in 1944, 2155; and in 1945, more than 4000.

The air force rear service worked hard supporting air operations, and in building and repairing airfields during offensive operations. In Poland, Hungary, Czechoslovakia, and other countries, as a rule, there were many airfields but they were often destroyed by the enemy as he retreated, and there were also not enough areas in which to construct new airfields. This added to the difficulties of providing air-fields for the air armies.

Thanks to the strengthening of the air force support services, personnel in the rear were able to deal with their assignments and gained much valuable experience during large extended offensive operations.

In this manner the Soviet Air Force, in cooperation with other branches of the armed forces, successfully fulfilled its assignments in the Great Patriotic War.

XIX

DEFEAT OF THE JAPANESE KWANTUNG ARMY

After Fascist Germany capitulated, peace came to Europe. But in the Far East the Second World War was still blazing. The ally of Hitler's Germany, militarist Japan, in spite of the defeats it had suffered in the Pacific and its complete political isolation, declined the surrender demand by the U.S., England, and China (the Potsdam Declaration), sent on July 26, 1945, and continued the war.

The Soviet Union could not be indifferent to military events occurring close to its Far Eastern borders. All the more that Japanese imperialism for decades had been a constant source of aggression in Asia, and was the bitter enemy of our Motherland.*

* Enmity between imperial Japan and the Soviet Union went back to the surprise attack on Russia in 1904, and increased during 1937–40 with the USSR's aid to China. Several hundred aircraft and volunteers came to fight the Japanese invasion, over 100 Soviet fliers being killed in this struggle.

The incidents at Lake Khasan and the Khalkhin-Gol River increased tensions, and Japan formally joined the Berlin-Rome Axis in September 1940. Japan's forces, including some 1500 army and 1600 navy first-line combat aircraft in late 1941,[22] placed Soviet Siberia in danger of invasion, and even after the German attack, a large part of the Soviet Air Force had to remain in the East to prevent Japanese attack.

However, lured by the rich natural resources of their Pacific possessions,

Preparations. In order to extinguish the last flames of World War II, to guarantee the maintenance of our Far Eastern borders and to aid the peoples of Asia as they struggled for freedom, the Soviet Union declared war against Japan on August 8, 1945. Our country fulfilled punctually its obligations according to the Yalta agreements: within two or three months after the defeat of Germany, it was to aid our allies in the defeat of militarist Japan.†

Our ground and air forces had to operate under unusual conditions in the Far East. The great expanses of land in the theater of war were located in different climatic zones. Before the Soviet troops lay massive mountain ranges, deserts, wide rivers, and wild taiga. The road network was poor. In many regions, there were almost no landmarks that could be used as orientation points for aircraft.

When military operations began, the Japanese Kwantung Army, its finest operational-strategic unit, was located in Manchuria, Korea, and Inner Mongolia. In addition, here were also located troops of the puppet government of Manchukuo and the Mongolian prince De Vana. In this theater of the war, the enemy had 1,200,000 men, 1155 tanks, and 5360 guns.

The enemy had an air force consisting of seven air brigades and nine separate air units that were part of the 2nd and 5th Air Armies located in Manchuria and Korea with about 2000 aircraft, including 600 bombers, 1200 fighters, more than 100 reconnaissance planes, and about 100 accessory aircraft.

The *Stavka* planned operations in the Far East with the goals of defeating the Kwantung Army, forcing the Japanese army to capitulate, and to return southern Sakhalin and the Kurile Islands to the Motherland. The Trans-Baikal Front, the 1st and 2nd Far Eastern Fronts (included in the Trans-Baikal Front with Soviet troops was also the Mongolian People's Army commanded by Marshal Choybalsan), the Pacific Fleet, and the Red Banner Amur River Flotilla were to complete these assignments. Our troops had a 1.2 times advantage in man power, a fourfold advantage in guns, and a sixfold in tanks.

Soviet Air Force units that were to participate in military operations included the 12th Air Army from the Trans-Baikal Front, 9th Air Army from the 1st Far Eastern Front, and 10th Air Army from

---

Japan chose instead to attack the American, British, and Dutch in December 1941 with a temporarily very successful sea and air campaign. ED.

† The Yalta meeting was in February 1945, and the August 8 date was told to the U.S. on May 28, 1945.[23] ED.

the 2nd Far Eastern Front, commanded respectively by Air Marshal S. A. Khudyakov and Generals I. M. Sokolov and P. F. Zhigarev. The Soviet Air Force had 2945 aircraft (1573 fighters, 740 bombers, 479 ground-attack planes, and 153 reconnaissance planes), which was 1.5 times more than the enemy possessed. If you take into account the 1131 aircraft from the naval air force, then our advantage in the air was much greater.

The Soviet Air Force also had a qualitative superiority. The Japanese fighters Type 97 and Type 1 were noticeably inferior to our Yak-9 and La-7 in speed, rate of climb, and armament. The Soviet bombers Pe-2 and Tu-2 were 150–180 kilometers per hour (93–112 miles per hour) faster than the enemy Type 96 and Type 97.‡

Our air force included three bomber corps, three separate air divisions, and two regiments brought from the west with crews experienced in fighting against Fascist Germany. Taking into consideration the difficult terrain, the Soviet command strengthened the air armies by adding to them transport air regiments and divisions. Chief Air Marshal A. A. Novikov, Red Army Air Force commander, coordinated efforts of the air groups.

The Soviet command's plan called for the three fronts to penetrate the enemy's fortified regions at several points, to press their offensives to a common destination at Harbin, Changchun, and Mukden, surround the major enemy forces, cut them into separate pieces, and destroy them one after another. The Pacific Fleet was to disrupt enemy maritime communications, send landing parties ashore, and with the 1st Far Eastern Front troops to occupy the ports of northern Korea (Rashin, Unggi, Seishin) and also to protect our maritime transport in the Sea of Japan and the Tatar Strait.

The air force was given the following assignments: acquire control of the air and protect our troop concentrations; disrupt the movement of enemy reserves by raids against railroad lines, trains, and roads; support our ground troops as they broke through fortified regions and pressed their offensive; operate against staff headquarters and communication centers to destroy enemy control over his troops; and carry out systematic reconnaissance.

‡ These were the Nakajima fighters known to Americans as Nate and Oscar; the inactive Manchurian squadrons had not received the newer Japanese types committed to action in the Pacific theaters. The Mitsubishi bombers mentioned were known here as Nell and Sally. ED.

Air operations were planned to take into account the peculiarities of the situation in which ground and air forces were to operate. Thus, the major 9th Air Army bomber and ground-attack forces were to be utilized to support troops on the battlefield, because the 1st Far Eastern Front had to penetrate a heavily fortified zone toward the coastal areas of Manchuria. Bombers of the 12th Air Army received the assignment of paralyzing rail and road traffic and isolating battle areas from the reserves, and ground-attack divisions were to support ground troops on the battlefield.

The 10th Air Army was to devote most of its resources to support ground troops as they crossed the Amur and advanced toward the Sungari.

Control of the air was to be gained by destroying Japanese aircraft on the ground and in the air. The 12th Air Army assigned two bomber air divisions, two ground-attack air divisions, and one fighter air division to attack enemy airfields on the first day of the operation.

Great attention was devoted to aerial reconnaissance, because our air force could not fly reconnaissance flights over Manchuria before war was declared, and the Soviet command did not have precise data on enemy defenses, troop concentrations, communications, and Japanese air bases.

Intensive training was carried out before the offensive operation began. In summer 1945, the air armies were strengthened by the arrival of new planes and flying and technical crews who had battle experience against the Luftwaffe. The new personnel familiarized themselves with the problems of flight in the Far East.

The staffs from the air armies and the staffs from the ground (tank) armies worked out joint plans for coordinated actions, prepared common coded maps, radio signals and other signals for mutual identification. To work out agreements with ground army commands for joint actions during ground operations, and to inform the air staffs and air army commanders about the ground situation, operational groups of air army officers, who were to summon aircraft and to control them over the battlefields, were sent to the 6th Guards Tank Army of the Trans-Baikal Front and the ground armies. Just before the operation began, the cooperating ground-attack and fighter divisions commanders who organized their command points in the ground units visited the tanks and motorized corps. Air scouts with radios were sent to infantry and tank divisions.

To harmonize efforts of ground and air forces during the break-through of the enemy fortified regions, staffs of the air and ground armies involved worked on the problems of mutual operations during an offensive by participating in war games and group exercises. Bomber and ground-attack units practiced day and night techniques of hitting small targets (pillboxes) on specially prepared ranges.

A series of control-recognition signs were placed along the border and on major roads, and other identification procedures of ZOS (radio-directing equipment, lights, etc.) were established; they were shifted to forward bases just before the offensive began, all for the purpose of improving ground control over aircraft.

One difficult problem to be solved was organization of air base supply and maintenance. In mountain regions, it was difficult to find level areas on which to build airfields, to say nothing of the fact that exceptionally long landing strips were necessary at high altitudes. In the deserts and semideserts of eastern Mongolia, there were few sources of water and fuel for heating, and therefore air service battalions had to transport not only aviation fuel, ammunition, and food, but also supplies of water and firewood.

Realizing the great number of air support difficulties, the Red Army Force commander added air technical groups to the air armies. In addition, the fronts' commanders planned to employ ground troops and their engineering units to construct airfields.

Search groups were set up with transport aircraft to find airfields on territory liberated from the enemy. In order to insure mobility in basing our aircraft behind our advancing troops, commanders of the air armies held in reserve for each air army two or three regional air base units, which were stationed near the border at the beginning of August. As the result of this arduous work the rear units were well prepared for the campaign. They had a fifteen-to-twenty-day supply of materials and had prepared an essential network of airfields.

On the eve of the campaign the air armies regrouped their forces. Their groups were moved to advanced bases, from which they initiated their operations. In order to conceal this move, flights were made in small groups at low altitudes and radio communications were severely limited. All aircraft were dispersed on the airfields and camouflaged. Besides real bases, there was also an extensive network of mock airfields, on which there were mock aircraft; and feigned regimental operational activities were also set up.

The Attack Begins on Three Fronts. Soviet troops went on the offensive the night of August 8. There were no artillery barrages or preliminary air attacks, in order to insure that the attack would be unexpected. Advance units penetrated enemy territory undetected, bypassed and blockaded fortified installations, and began to attack their garrisons. During the night, Soviet troops captured many border points and thus insured the free movement of our major offensive forces.

Our air force also began operations that night. Seventy-six Il-4s from the 19th Bomber Air Corps of the 9th Air Army, commanded by General N. A. Volkov, attacked military targets in Changchun and Harbin. At dawn on August 9, bomber corps and divisions from the 9th and 12th Air Armies and the fleet struck at railroad stations and trains, industrial targets in Harbin and Changchun, airfields at Payansa, Khailar, Ganchurmao, and other places, and harbors at Rashin (Najin), Unggi, and Seishin (Chongjin) in order to paralyze communications, disrupt enemy control over their forces, cause panic in the rear, and destroy aircraft on the ground. Aircraft also supported and protected our strike groups and conducted reconnaissance.

In spite of bad weather, the Soviet Air Force on the first day of operations flew about 2000 sorties and caused great enemy losses. The 12th Air Army alone set more than twenty fires, caused ten large explosions, destroyed nine buildings, and destroyed several freight trains with military equipment.

Constant Soviet attacks against rail targets were very effective. They put the enemy's communication system out of order, limited his troops' mobility, and isolated the front from the areas where fresh reserves were stationed. The Japanese command could not bring up its divisions from the Manchurian plain to occupy defense positions, nor evacuate his troops out from under the blows of the Red Army tank group, nor remove his goods from the border zone.

Enemy aircraft offered hardly any resistance. The Japanese command was stunned by the sudden powerful blow dealt by our ground and air forces and began to withdraw its troops deep into Manchuria, fighting only in fortified regions. Attempting to save his air power for the defense of Japan, it had shifted its best air groups home to city airfields. The Soviet Air Force had an unlimited control of the air.

Reconnaissance flights were made from the beginning of the offensive, not only by reconnaissance regiments and squadrons, but also by bomber, ground-attack, and fighter aircraft. Every day as much as 30 percent of all flights were devoted to reconnaissance within the air armies. Information was immediately sent by radio, which made it possible for the Soviet command to react immediately to any changes in the situation. For example, early in the operation reconnaissance planes established that there was a large Japanese force in the rear of the advancing Trans-Baikal Front, so the Soviet command immediately took energetic measures to destroy them, or to take them prisoner.

Reconnaissance was carried out along a broad front and to considerable depth. Reconnaissance planes of the 12th Air Army were active in a zone 1500 kilometers (930 miles) long and 600–700 kilometers (373–435 miles) deep. At first no one knew what resistance enemy antiaircraft artillery would offer, and reconnaissance flights were carried out at an altitude of 5000–6000 meters (16,400–19,680 feet), but later recon was carried out from intermediate altitudes (1000–1500 meters or 3280–4920 feet).

During the campaign's first five days, Soviet troops in close cooperation with the air force routed the enemy border forces. At the same time, the 1st Far Eastern Front drove 40–100 kilometers (25–62 miles) into enemy territory, liberating the cities of Khutou, Dunin, and Mishan. Bombers and ground-attack planes of the 9th Air Army supported the front's strike groups, hitting at troop concentrations and fire points on the battlefield.

Our fliers operated against fortified areas, as a rule, in groups of ninety to one hundred aircraft. Especially great results were obtained as the result of concentrated attacks. For example, on the second day of the operation the 35th Army came up to the Khutou fortified region and were met by frenzied enemy resistance that stopped its advance. The ground forces turned to air power for assistance. Soon 81 34th Bomber Air Division Pe-2s, commanded by Col. K. A. Mikhaylov, appeared in the air. They struck at targets within the fortified region, destroyed a series of pillboxes, and silenced the Japanese mortar and artillery fire. Taking advantage of enemy confusion, Soviet troops broke through to the fortified region, and two days later, captured it.

In the Mudantszyan region the Japanese command concentrated their reserves and prepared a counterattack against the 5th Army. On the evening of August 10, aerial reconnaissance reported that troop trains had arrived and were unloading men, artillery, and tanks at the railroad station and that there was a large concentration of men and equipment at that point. To disrupt the enemy plans, the 9th Air Army commander organized a raid against the railroad station at Mudantszyan (Mutanchiang) to be carried out by the 34th Bomber Air Division.

The battle for Mudantszyan (Mutanchiang) continued for five days. August 16 was the day of the severest fighting for the 1st Red Banner Army and the 5th Army. The enemy concentrated large forces of infantry and tanks and organized a counterattack. Most of the 252nd Ground-Attack Air Division planes (commanded by Lt. Col. V. Kh. Makarov) were assigned to repel this attack and they attacked in waves against artillery, tanks, and infantry in support of our troops. Due to the joint efforts of our ground and air forces, the enemy was decisively defeated in the Mudantszyan district.

To destroy the resistance center in the Dunin fortified region at the rear of the 25th Army, 108 19th Bomber Air Corps aircraft made a concentrated strike. The effect of this action was very great. After the areas had been occupied, it was established that direct hits from large bombs had destroyed four pillboxes, two bunkers, a munitions dump, killed 130 men, and wounded many soldiers and officers. After this raid, the fortified region was occupied by our troops.

Because Japanese fighters and antiaircraft guns offered no resistance, our bombers and ground-attack planes attacked from intermediate and low levels and remained over the targets for long periods of time and raised the effectiveness of their strikes. As they completed their assignments, the flying crews showed initiative, resourcefulness, courage, and heroism. The 75th Ground-Attack Air Regiment commander, Major Chernykh, together with flight commander Lieutenant Yurchenko, his partner, were "free hunting." They discovered an armored train and attacked it. On the third pass, the aircraft of Major Chernykh was hit by antiaircraft fire and was forced to land on the slope of a mound. Yurchenko landed his plane nearby, picked up Major Chernykh, and returned safely to his airfield.

Troops of the Trans-Baikal Front were even more successful. The 6th Guards Tank Army in the first wave of the offensive bypassed enemy centers of resistance, and by the fourth day of the operation, with 12th Air Army support, swept over the Greater Khingan mountain range and reached the central Manchurian plain, having advanced about 450 kilometers (280 miles).

Ground support for tank units was provided for the most part by bomber groups, because other aircraft (ground-attack planes and fighters) had limited ranges and their bases remained far behind the rapidly advancing tank units. In support of the tanks, bombers struck against fortified regions, centers of resistance, approaching reserves, retreating columns, and railroad stations, and conducted intensive reconnaissance.

Transport divisions and regiments were employed to bring up fuel and ammunition to the tank units, which were far from their supply bases. Transport aircraft flew 1755 sorties and moved more than 2000 tons of fuel and 186 tons of ammunition. Flying conditions were very bad. Air routes passed over the wide Greater Khingan range. There were no areas available for emergency landings. The weather was unfavorable. But Soviet fliers solved these difficulties in transporting supplies to the 6th Guards Tank Army and supported its successful operations. On an average day, ninety to one hundred aircraft were utilized for this purpose.

At the same time that the 1st Far Eastern and Trans-Baikal Fronts took the offensive, the 2nd Far Eastern Front crossed the broad Amur and Ussuri and advanced rapidly toward Sungari and Zhaokhei. Because of torrential rains, which flooded the river valleys and rendered highways impassable, the advancing troops were forced to move on railroads.

In spite of bad weather, the 10th Air Army gave active support to the ground troops. Flying in small groups, bombers and ground-attack planes attacked enemy equipment and troops on the battlefield, struck at centers of resistance, ships from the Sungari flotilla, and trains at Beian (Peian), Keshan, and Tsitsikar (Chichikeah), and carried out reconnaissance.

Fliers of the 253rd Ground-Attack Air Division, commanded by Lt. Col. K. T. Tsedrik, were especially active on the first day of the campaign, attacking and sinking a steamship, a barge, three sailboats, and three armored launches. "Hunters" from the 254th Fighter Air Division, commanded by Lt. Col. N. A. Silayev, set a ship afire in the Sinchuchina region and sank a sailboat with twenty soldiers on the Sungari River.

On August 11, six Il-2s from the 253rd Ground-Attack Air Division, led by squadron commander Major Blinov, were directed to a Japanese artillery battery hindering the advance of the 203rd Tank Brigade. Making several attacks, our fliers silenced the enemy and thus assured that the tanks would have an open path.

On August 12, our troops advancing toward Tsitsikar were stopped by a powerful artillery barrage and enemy counterattacks at Sun-U. Ground-attack planes commanded by Lt. Col. I. A. Kochergin were called to support our infantry and tanks. Our fliers made as many as five passes at the target and compelled the enemy to cease his fire. The Japanese soldiers sustained great losses, raised a white flag, and surrendered. Our troops continued to advance.

During the first day of the campaign, the Pacific Fleet attacked enemy marine transportation, sent troops ashore and captured the north Korean ports of Unggi, Rashin (Najin), and Seishin (Chongjin), although they were well-defended from land, sea, and air. Aircraft made a preliminary attack before the troops were sent ashore, supported them as they landed and captured the harbors, protected them from the air before they landed and afterwards, and carried out reconnaissance.

Paratroop Landings. Soviet troops continued their advance. By the middle of August, they had advanced as much as 500 kilometers (310 miles) deep into Manchuria. As the enemy was being pursued, to hasten the final defeat of the Kwantung Army, the Soviet command sent parachute troops into the largest Manchurian cities of Changchun, Mukden, Kirin, Harbin, and others from August 19 to 22. These groups consisted of 50 to 500 men who seized airfields, railroad junctions, and weapons, and quickly disarmed local garrisons. Aircraft of the three fronts flew more than 5000 sorties to deliver these troops and to supply them with equipment.

While the enemy forces were being rapidly pursued, groups of ground-attack and fighter aircraft fell behind our advancing troops and could not operate. Sometimes transport aircraft were employed to move airfield service battalion command staffs and equipment to forward air bases. But it was impossible to move all the air force bases by utilizing transports, because such aircraft were employed for the most part for supplying advance ground units since there were no roads that could be used for ground transportation.

Japan Surrenders. When the Manchurian administrative, political, and industrial centers were seized by advance ground units and parachute troops, the enemy completely lost control of his troops and reserves. Convinced that further resistance was impossible, the Japanese virtually ceased military operations and began to lay down their arms on August 19.*

As the result of the defeat of its Kwantung Army, imperial Japan lost its effective power and the capability of continuing the war, and on September 2 its government signed an unconditional surrender agreement.†

Therefore, the entry of the Soviet Union into the war against imperial Japan and the decisive action of our armed forces assured the liquidation of the Far Eastern center of aggression and quickly ended World War II. The American general, Claire Chennault, who then commanded the American Air Force in China, told a New York *Times* correspondent, "The entry of the Soviet Union into the war against Japan was a decisive factor in speeding up the end of the war in the Pacific, which would have occurred even if atomic bombs had not been used. The rapid blow dealt by the Red Army against Japan completed its encirclement and brought it to its knees."[25]

Results. Thanks to the victory, our Motherland regained its former territories, southern Sakhalin and the Kurile Islands. The Soviet Fleet obtained assured access to the Pacific Ocean. Conditions were created to organize a sound defense for our Far Eastern territories.

The defeat of imperial Japan contributed to the rise of a national-liberation and democratic movement in Asia and provided favorable conditions for the formation of the Chinese People's Republic, the Korean People's Democratic Republic, and the Democratic People's Republic of Vietnam.

---

* About 594,000 Japanese prisoners surrendered to the Red Army.[24] ED.

† Since this chapter is confined to events in Manchuria and Korea, no mention is made of other factors in the Japanese defeat. American readers may wish to be reminded, at this point, of the dates of certain other related events. On August 6, 1945, the atomic bomb hit Hiroshima, and a second atomic bomb hit Nagasaki on August 9, the day after the USSR entered the war. On August 10, the imperial council was told by the emperor that the war must end, and a message was sent to the four Allied powers. After desperate debate in Tokyo, the government finally announced its acceptance of the Allied surrender terms on August 14, and on August 15 and 16, cease-fire orders went out to the U.S. and then the Japanese forces. Long before that time, of course, many high-ranking Japanese were convinced that the war was lost, but the military clique controlling the government persisted until August in continuing the war. The emperor's order to his armed forces to surrender was not actually issued until after the surrender was signed on the battleship *Missouri* on September 2. ED.

On the evening of August 23, 1945, Moscow saluted the illustrious troops who defeated the Kwantung Army. To honor the victory over imperial Japan, a medal was established which was awarded to all the campaign participants. Many units, including air units, were given honorary titles such as "Mukden," "Khingan," "Amur," "Sakhalin," and "Kurile." Hundreds of thousands of enlisted men and officers were given awards and medals from the USSR.

The Soviet Air Force made a major contribution toward the victory over the Kwantung Army, flying more than 22,000 sorties and dropping about 3000 tons of bombs on the enemy. Air power was a powerful and flexible weapon in the hands of the Soviet command and had a great effect on the outcome of the operations against the enemy's million-man army. As they struck at pillboxes and troop concentrations, our aircraft helped our ground troops quickly cut through fortified areas, disrupted communications, paralyzed enemy movements, and played a major role in repelling enemy counterattacks and then surrounding and annihilating the Kwantung Army. Our aircraft provided most of the intelligence available and was an important means of transportation for troops and equipment.

During the campaign 16,500 soldiers and officers, about 2780 tons of fuel, 563 tons of ammunition, and 1496 tons of miscellaneous cargo were moved by air. When the air force assisted in the dropping of parachute troops in the enemy's rear and also supplied fuel and ammunition to our advancing tank and motorized divisions, it made a major contribution to fragmentation of the enemy army and its final surrender.

During the campaign against the Kwantung Army, the Soviet Air Force received valuable experience in operating in the difficult circumstances of the Far Eastern theater. Highly unstable weather (torrential rains, haze, and fog), uniform topography (great expanses of mountain taiga, deserts, and semideserts), and the absence of orientation points made navigation, the locating of targets, and the carrying out of assignments very difficult. However, these problems were overcome by such methods as constructing artificial points of orientation at the international borders, and along main highways; assignment of Far Eastern veterans as leaders for units newly arrived from Europe; widespread use of locational equipment; and careful study of various scale maps of the areas in which units were based, or to operate; and practice flights along the border areas.

There were a number of peculiarities in air operations against the Japanese Kwantung Army:

First of all, much effort was devoted to disorganizing the enemy's rail traffic and reserves—13 percent of all sorties. In the offensive areas, the Trans-Baikal Front devoted 85 percent of all its sorties to this purpose. This was not accidental, because 75 percent of the Kwantung Army's divisions were located in the central part of Manchuria. The Japanese command for the most part planned on utilizing railroads to move its troops. However, as the result of our air attacks the enemy's plans were thwarted. Our aircraft isolated the battle areas from the flow of reserves. The Japanese command could not evacuate goods from the border areas, nor remove its troops out from under the blows of the advancing units of the Red Army.

Secondly, because Soviet troops took the offensive immediately after the declaration of war and in the absence of precise information about the enemy, it was necessary to expend great numbers of sorties on aerial reconnaissance, two or three times more than in the operations against Fascist Germany. Aerial reconnaissance was carried out by direction and regions (zones), visually and photographically. Thanks to intensive and well-organized reconnaissance, the Soviet command quickly received reliable information about the enemy, which was very important in our later operations.

In the preparatory period in the campaign against the Kwantung Army, the Soviet Air Force obtained practice in the concealed concentration and movement of its air groups. Measures taken to camouflage air bases by constructing a network of false airfields, careful disguise of aircraft on the ground, dispersal of flying units during the preparatory period, and the shift of air regiments to advance air bases at low altitudes in small groups, were all carefully carried out.

Organization of coordinated efforts between the air force and ground troops in mountain and wooded territory, particularly with tank units, received much attention. Detailed plans were worked out, operational groups were sent from the air armies to infantry and tank armies, and air representatives were sent to army groups; command posts were organized by ground-attack air divisions close to the front, special documents were written to facilitate coordinated efforts such as uniform coded maps, standardized radio signals, joint identification signals, etc., and there was a wide use of air transportation for parachute troops and to haul tank group supplies.

Experience gained in the Far Eastern operation was important in developing air force skills and tactics for different kinds of aircraft.

XX

CONCLUSION

Political Results. The Great Patriotic War lasted about four years and ended in complete victory for the Soviet Union over Fascist Germany. During this heroic struggle the Soviet people and its illustrious armed forces under the leadership of the Communist party and the Soviet government defended the honor, freedom, and independence of the world's first socialist state, and freed mankind from the threat of fascist slavery.

As the result of the victory of the Soviet Union there were radical changes in the relationship between the powers in the international arena. A number of states in Eastern and Central Europe fell out of the capitalist system and took the path of building socialism and under Soviet leadership formed a single, powerful, and ever growing socialist camp. Socialism became a worldwide system.

The Soviet Air Force and the other armed forces branches fought stubbornly against the fascist invaders. In spite of unfavorable conditions, which developed because of the sudden German attack against our country, the air force was able to retain its fighting ability. At the beginning of the war, under difficult conditions, it retrained its flying personnel to use the newer planes. It continued to use the older aircraft for many missions, it constantly sought out and employed the latest operational techniques, and finally it dealt a decisive blow to the Luftwaffe.

Operational Results. During the years of the Great Patriotic War the capabilities of our air force as an independent force within our armed forces became apparent. The major efforts of our aircraft were devoted to the completion of three assignments: the battle for control of the air, support for ground troops and the fleet, and reconnaissance. In addition to our operations in support of troops, the air force struck systematically at administrative and political centers and military targets deep in the enemy's rear, and also against rail transportation and the enemy's strategic reserves.

The air force took an active role in both offensive and defensive operations. Front aircraft and the AFLRO flew 3,124,000 sorties in support of ground troops, in air battles, bombing raids in the enemy's rear, aerial reconnaissance, support of partisans, and other assignments. About 30,450,000 bombs were dropped on the enemy with a total weight of more than 660,000 tons.

The Soviet Air Force destroyed or damaged many German tanks, self-propelled guns, guns, mortars; ships, transports, and submarines; many thousand vehicles, wagons, locomotives, a large quantity of military equipment, and enemy personnel. In 1941–45 the air force, the naval air force, and the fighter planes of the ADF destroyed in the air or on the ground 57,000 German aircraft. The total enemy losses in aircraft on the Soviet-German front amounted to 77,000 aircraft, and this was 2.5 times greater than the losses on all other fronts. Therefore, the Luftwaffe was defeated basically on the Soviet-German front.*

Control of the Air. The struggle for the control of the air during the entire war was one of the most difficult and important aspects of our air operations. More than 35 percent of all sorties were flown for this purpose. The war proved that in the absence of control of the air, it was impossible to be assured of the success of the total operation, and the war as a whole. The outcome of the struggle for control of the air to a significant degree determined the success of ground and sea operations, and also the successful completion of other air force assignments.

Beginning on the first day of the war, the struggle for control of the air developed along the entire Soviet-German front and was characterized by an unheard of intensity and persistence. However, in the first period of the war, control of the air in the most important areas was on the Fascist side. This is explained by the fact that the enemy's invasion came as a surprise and that he destroyed a significant quantity of our aircraft on the ground and in the air. In addition, the Luftwaffe was in very good condition in this period. It had many thousands of modern aircraft, experienced, well-trained

---

* Total German aircraft production in 1941–45 was 86,821, not including gliders.[26] ED.

personnel, and was the best and strongest air force of any capitalist country.

But the German command's plan to deal a stunning blow against Soviet Air Force airfields, and thus to assure complete mobility for its tank and motorized units and to win a blitzkrieg, failed. The only serious losses among the Soviet Air Force were in the border districts. But the Long-range Bomber Force of the Supreme Command and aircraft in the internal districts far from the border were hardly hit at all during the first days of the war. The enemy also did not have sufficient forces to strike at aircraft plants, training schools, or other military institutions located deep within the country, which were the sources of replacements and reinforcements. In addition, our air force lost few men from German air attacks against our air bases. Flying personnel deprived of aircraft were incorporated into newly formed air regiments and divisions.

The Soviet Air Force, in spite of these bad conditions, maintained its battle readiness and fought against enemy aircraft, destroying more than 15,000 enemy aircraft and killing many experienced fliers during the first period of the war. Over various important sectors of the front, we were able to seize operational control of the air from time to time, thanks to the skilled use of masses of aircraft—for example, in the counterattack at Moscow. Great enemy losses in both aircraft and fliers in the first period of the war and the increasing might of the Red Army Air Force created the conditions that made it possible to seize control of the air.

The second period of the war was marked by a sharp change in the struggle for the mastery of the air, which was finally acquired in the summer of 1943. In the winter and summer-fall campaigns of 1943, particularly in the counterattack at Stalingrad, the air battles over the northern Caucasus and the battle for Kursk, the Soviet Air Force dealt a series of powerful blows to the Luftwaffe, annihilated its major concentrations on the Soviet-German front, and destroyed its best-trained flying personnel.

As the result of great losses, German air power on the Soviet-German front on July 1, 1943, was decreased by 40 percent compared with the first days of the war. Morale of the German fliers fell rapidly. After the battle for Kursk, when the Luftwaffe lost about 3700 aircraft in one and a half months, control of the air completely and irrevocably passed into our hands along the entire Soviet-German front.

Thanks to this fact, our ground forces and fleet had favorable conditions for carrying out their operations, the air force could now operate more decisively and actively, and the rear was freed from danger of enemy bombing raids. The military capabilities and activities of the Soviet Air Force constantly increased. The average number of sorties per month flown by the Soviet Air Force in 1943 was one and one half times greater than in the summer-fall campaign of 1941, and in 1945 three times greater.

At the same time as the Luftwaffe went over to defensive operations, it decreased its activities and no longer could influence events on the ground or at sea. In 1942, enemy aircraft flew an average of about 41,000 sorties per month on the Soviet-German front, but in 1945 they flew only about 40 percent of this number per month.

When the Luftwaffe began defensive operations, there was also a significant change in the relative numbers of different types of aircraft. At the beginning of the war, bombers made up fifty-two percent of the total aircraft pool and fighters only 32 percent, but by the end of 1944 the proportion of bombers was much lower and the proportion of fighter planes much higher. This is explained by the enemy's transition to a strategic defense, great losses from bomber squadrons, and difficulties in replacements, but most important of all by the increasing activities of the Soviet Air Force and by the fact that we had control of the air.

Soviet Losses.   When we gained mastery of the air the losses among enemy aircraft increased at the same time that ours decreased. In 1941 we lost 1 aircraft for every 32 sorties; in 1943, 1 for every 72; and in 1945, 1 for every 165 sorties. On the enemy side, however, 1 aircraft was lost for every 25.5 sorties in 1942; in 1943, 1 was lost for every 22.5 sorties; and in 1945, 1 was lost for every 11 sorties.[27]

What Really Caused the German Defeat?   Bourgeois falsifiers of World War II history attempt by any means at their disposal to minimize the role of the Soviet Air Force in the defeat of the Luftwaffe. They affirm that the power of the Luftwaffe was undermined by the Anglo-American bombing raids on German aircraft factories. However, historical documents and facts overthrow these unfounded assertions. Before 1943, when the fascist Luftwaffe was still strong and the battle for the control of the air was still in question, the American and English air forces had flown almost no raids against air targets in Germany. In 1943, they dropped only 2 percent of their bombs on aircraft factories and the effect of their raids was not great.

The opening of a second front in Europe in the summer of 1944 had no real influence on the struggle of our air force with Fascist air power. The increased efforts of the Anglo-American air force against industrial targets (including aircraft plants) did not give the desired results. In 1944, Germany increased its aircraft production in comparison with 1943, from 24,365 aircraft to 40,482.[28] The most effective Anglo-American raids were against synthetic fuel plants in 1945, but they occurred when Germany was already on the verge of an unavoidable catastrophe.

In spite of great losses, the Germans were still able to maintain their original air armies on the Soviet-German front, where most of their experienced air units and groups were located even after the opening of the second front. About 30 percent of the German aircraft located on the Western Front and other theaters of the war were in fact the reserves of the German command.

Thus, the loss of the control of the air which the Germans suffered in 1943 can be explained not by the English and American air raids on German aircraft plants, but by the defeat of its best squadrons on the Soviet-German front.

In the first half of 1944 the Soviet Air Force was strengthened by more than 3000 aircraft and had nearly a fourfold advantage over the enemy. This additional growth made it possible for the Soviet Air Force to complete its assignment of defeating the Fascist air forces without Anglo-American help.

Ground Support Missions. During the war the Soviet Air Force also fulfilled its second assignment—to support ground forces. This was accomplished by closely coordinated tactical and operational efforts with the ground forces. Ground support was carried out for the most part by front airmen, who devoted 46.5 percent of all their sorties to this assignment. But the AFLRO was also employed for ground support and, in coastal areas, the naval air force as well. In some cases fighter aircraft from the ADF were also used for this purpose.

In both offensive and defensive operations the basic efforts of the Soviet Air Force were expended on the destruction of enemy troops and equipment on the battlefield and in the operational rear. The small number of front bombers flew 43 percent of all their sorties against enemy troops on the battlefield.

The shallow operational area over which bombers and ground-attack planes flew in support of ground troops was the result of the type of conflict on the Soviet-German front. Enemy troops, both in offense and defense, were never deployed to any depth. The great mass of his troops was concentrated on the battlefield, and the success of our ground troops was dependent on the destruction of these troops.

When it flew in support of ground forces, the Soviet Air Force massed its forces in the major sectors of the front in the hope of carrying out its most important assignments. When the air armies were created in May 1942, a means was found for the most effective use of mass air power, since up to 80–95 percent of all available aircraft could be concentrated in the areas where major assaults were to be made. This was achieved by concentrating in these areas almost all of the aircraft from a front, as well as by involving reserve air groups from other fronts and aircraft from the AFLRO.

As many as 1500–2000 aircraft were employed over relatively small segments of the front into which our ground troops were making their major drives in the second and third periods of the war. This insured the success of the break-through and the expansion of the offensive. An increased level of activity was also achieved by increasing the number of sorties for each aircraft to two or three in every twenty-four-hour period.

Air force operations in the offensive operations in 1943–45 took the form of air offensives, a development that was born at the end of the first period of the war and represented a new advance of air force operational skill. It was accompanied by intense air battles, because both sides concentrated great masses of aircraft over the battlefield, leading to bitter fighting for control of the air.

During the war, the front aircraft gained extensive experience in cooperative efforts with ground troops. Air power developed as a flexible means of supporting general and tank armies, contributing to the rapid piercing of intermediate defense lines, successful repelling of enemy counterattacks, crossing large rivers, enemy pursuit, his encirclement, and the destruction of large troop concentrations.

Reconnaissance. One of the major air force assignments was aerial reconnaissance. It was of great use for the Soviet command as it observed enemy troop concentrations, his ships and aircraft, defense systems, movement of reserves, location of staffs and other control groups, contributing thereby to the most efficient use of troops and aircraft and the determination of the enemy's intentions. More than 11 percent of all sorties were flown for reconnaissance purposes.

During the course of the war there were improvements in the techniques of aerial reconnaissance and it was better organized. In addition to visual observation, photography of defense systems and important targets became common. The proportion of photographic aerial reconnaissance to visual reconnaissance increased from ten to 87 percent between 1941 and 1945. During the war, 6,500,000 square kilometers (2,500,000 square miles) were photographed, which is 1,000,000 square kilometers (386,000 square miles) more than the area of the European part of the Soviet Union.

The skilled use of different types of reconnaissance, wide use of cameras, special radio networks for reconnaissance planes, precise organization of the transmission and reception of data concerning the enemy, increased flying skills—all of these contributed toward the reliability and utility of aerial reconnaissance. During the war its use constantly increased.

Strategic Bombing. During the years 1941–45 the Soviet Air Force obtained some experience in the organization and conduct of operations against the enemy's operational transports and reserves. In several cases the attacks against enemy reserves were made by several air armies and the AFLRO. Because of the problems which the Soviet Air Force had with operations against enemy transport and reserves, because of the limited number of bombers and the emphasis upon utilizing them for direct troop support, these areas were not emphasized. To fulfill this assignment, front aircraft and the AFLRO flew 168,000 sorties in 1941–45, 5.4 percent of the total sorties flown.

During the war, units of the AFLRO and the naval air force systematically struck at administrative-political and military-industrial targets, harbors, naval bases, railroads, reserves, and other targets deep in the enemy's rear.

As early as June and July of 1941, long-range bombers of the Supreme Command, together with aircraft from the Black Sea and Baltic Fleets, struck at targets in the oil fields in Rumania and the western Ukraine, and also attacked military and industrial targets in

Koenigsberg and Danzig. Beginning on August 8, 1941, our bombers made several attacks on the capital of Fascist Germany, Berlin. Later in the war, especially in its third period, our attacks against war industries and administrative centers increased. In a number of cases, they became major air operations.

Our operations against targets deep in the rear caused the enemy material losses, and forced the German command to shift considerable forces and antiaircraft equipment deep to the rear, thereby weakening defenses along the front.

Partisan Support. For the first time in military history, aircraft were widely used to support partisans in the enemy's rear. Front aircraft, long-range aircraft, and Civil Air Fleet units flew more than 109,000 sorties into the enemy's rear, including 13,000 that ended in landings on airfields and landing strips held by partisan units. The AFLRO and the Civil Air Fleet moved 17,000 tons of ammunitions, guns, food, radio transmitters, medicine, mail, and other cargoes. More than 83,000 men were removed from partisan units and then returned by air. The evacuation of badly wounded and sick men from the enemy's rear saved the lives of tens of thousands of brave patriots.

The transportation of various cargoes to the enemy's rear, operations in support of partisans, evacuation of the wounded, the sick, and children, intelligence gathering, the dropping of millions of propaganda leaflets, were ways in which the Soviet Air Force gave invaluable help in the organization and conduct of partisan activities, in the increase of battle capabilities and mobility of partisan units and groups, in strengthening their activities and the effectiveness of their strikes against the enemy, and in improving the morale of the people's avengers and inspiring them for the remorseless battle with the German invaders.

French fliers and patriots from the "Normandy-Niemen" regiment fought next to Soviet fliers against the invaders beginning in 1943. Daring volunteer pilots from Poland and Czechoslovakia joined the battle against the Luftwaffe in summer 1944. After Rumania and Bulgaria had been liberated, Rumanian and Bulgarian air units fought together with Soviet troops against the Germans. The Soviet government had the highest regard for the fliers from these friendly states who distinguished themselves in battle, and granted them USSR awards and medals.

Technical Advances. The concern of the Communist party and the Soviet government for the strengthening and development of its air force was a major factor in their successful operations. Mass production of different types of aircraft, guns, and other weapons, insured that our aircraft could fulfill their most essential assignment in support of ground troops and in the war as a whole.

The fundamental industrial institutions, academies, and scientific-experimental organizations of the air force were very important in the development of air and rocket technology.

The most important aspect in the improvement of different aircraft types was the changes made in fighter planes. At the end of the war, the air force fighter units were equipped with the maneuverable fighters, Yak-3 and La-7. The Yak-3 with a VK-105PF engine had a maximum speed of about 650 kilometers (404 miles) per hour and the La-7 a speed of about 670 kilometers (416 miles) per hour. These aircraft were superior to the German Bf 109 and Fw 190 in speed and maneuverability. The Germans had great hopes for their jet fighter, the Me 262, with a maximum speed of 870 kilometers (540 miles) per hour. However, their use in the Berlin campaign did not come up to expectations.

At the end of the war our air force stood on the threshold of a major advance; the transition to jet fighter with supersonic speeds, rocket weapons, and automatic controls.

During the war the problem of creating large reserve forces was solved. As mass production turned out more planes the Supreme Command was able to increase the size of its reserves. From the autumn of 1942 to the end of 1944, thirty air corps were formed armed with new bombers, ground-attack planes, and fighters. The proportion of aircraft in the reserves increased from thirty-two percent to 43 percent from November 20, 1942, to January 1, 1945. This made great mobility possible and large aircraft concentrations could be shifted to the most important areas on the Soviet-German front.

Twenty-three hundred aircraft participated in the campaign to liberate the right bank of the Dnieper, about 6000 in the White Russian campaign, and about 7500 in the Berlin campaign. Utilization of reserves to create massive concentrations assured that we would have a great superiority over the enemy and contributed to the successful fulfillment of air force assignments.

Personnel. The reserve air brigades and regiments in the internal military districts were also active. Thanks to their daily efforts and labor of the personnel they succeeded in fulfilling their assignments of supplying and training front air regiments. In 1941–45 the reserve air units and groups trained and sent to the front about 2000 air units and subunits.

During the war supplying highly qualified cadres for the Soviet Air Force was a major concern. In 1941–45 the Air Force Red Banner Academy, the Air Force Red Banner Zhukovsky Engineering Academy, the Air Force Mozhaysky Engineering Academy, and other military training schools trained a large number of command, engineering, flying, and technical personnel who met the needs of the air force during the war.

A major factor in the victory in the war was the mass production of aircraft, materials, and equipment, and the rapid training of air cadres and reserves. The Soviet people gave great help in strengthening the air force. The air force received 2565 aircraft built by funds saved and contributed to the defense fund by the Soviet people.

One of the most important aspects of the successful fulfillment of military assignments was the high morale, consciousness, and creative activities of the Air Force personnel. "We believe," said Lenin, "that the state is made strong by the consciousness of the masses. It is strong when the masses know about everything, they can judge everything, and they can go on to everything consciously."

Interpretation of the party and government decisions, interpretation of the situation on the front and their assignments, meetings, discussions, conferences, and publicizing battle experiences and mass heroism—all contributed to the airmen's education and inspired them to heroism.

During the war, 288 air groups, units, and subunits from the fronts and the AFLRO were given guards designations, 897 were given military orders, 708 were given individualized names, 197,849 airmen were given orders or medals, 2420 were given the honored title of Hero of the Soviet Union, 65 two times, and two airmen were given the distinction three times.

Many brave Soviet airmen died in air battles with the German invaders. Their names and heroic deeds are engraved in golden letters in the glorious chronicles of our air force. The Soviet people and the members of the armed forces will hold the memory sacred of those who fell in battles for the socialist Fatherland. As a memorial, many are enrolled forever in the rolls of the air units in which they served. Every day names of these heroes are repeated. Books, articles, songs, and films have been devoted to them and monuments have been erected in their memory. Their names have been given to streets and squares in our cities and to factories and collective farms. Those who died the death of the brave in the struggle with the foe will live forever in the memory of the grateful Soviet people.

The war was a practical school for testing the training of air cadres. During the war they obtained rich experience in the organizational conduct of air operations, learned how to defeat the enemy, utilizing all the principles of Soviet military science, and made a major contribution to development of the theory of air operations and tactics for different aircraft types. Battle experience gained by the air cadres was of great value in developing and strengthening the air force might and in maintenance of military preparedness in the period after the war.

Influence of the War on Today's Air Force. Battle experience acquired by the air force during the war years is still of great value. It helps air force officers and generals to evaluate the organization of air operations, equipment, and to find inadequacies and mistakes which emerged first in the war, to broaden their military point of view, and to develop procedures for solving practical problems. This experience maintains and expands the air force military traditions in the spirit of Soviet patriotism.

Air technology after the war developed at a rapid rate. Re-equipping our air force with new jet aircraft, and introduction of thermonuclear weapons and rocket armaments, contributed to the air force striking power. But it would be dangerous to ignore experience from the Great Patriotic War.

Such questions as the maintenance of battle preparedness in the air force, training of reserve and air cadres, wide use of the flexible resources of air power, coordinated efforts with ground troops, implementation of constant control and coordinated efforts between different aircraft types, and other questions are still of significance today.

At the present time, there are new organizational problems in the conduct and maintenance of air operations that require new theoretical answers. As they answer the new questions concerning the use of air power, air force officers must study and evaluate the experience of the past war, with special attention to the characteristics of air operations under present conditions. This would make it possible to reorganize the means of achieving victory over a strong opponent under conditions different from those at the present time, and might serve as an important basis for the solution of theoretical and practical questions which must be met by the air force. V. I. Lenin showed a rare ability in the application of historical experience for the solution of contemporary practical problems. He pointed out that "it is impossible to solve our problems with new methods today unless yesterday's experience has opened our eyes to the incorrect methods of the past."

The experience of the Great Patriotic War has great significance for teaching high moral attributes and boundless dedication to the socialist Fatherland to air force personnel. Mass heroism, the urge to fulfill one's duty with honor for the Motherland, strict discipline in the most difficult wartime conditions, especially in its initial period, can provide an inexhaustible source of inspiration for many generations of fliers.

One of the most important assignments for party, political, and Comsomol organizations is the daily skilled utilization and dissemination of the glorious air force traditions. Reports, lectures, discussions, the celebration of the anniversaries of air groups and units, meetings between veterans and current members of the air force, visits to museums and historical locations, showings of historical documentary and feature films, and other measures are some of the basic methods for popularizing the experiences of the Great Patriotic War.

After the war, new replacements arrived at the air units and air force institutes. The young airmen are vitally interested in the heroic traditions of the older generation of fliers, revere them, and imitate them. The example of the elder comrades inspires our airmen to fulfill their assignments and calls them to complete their training and to master the new complex jet and rocket air equipment and armament.

Appendix One

SOVIET WORLD WAR II AIRCRAFT

Data on first line is metric, second line is English

FIGHTERS

Type	Year (service)	Engine Type	Engine hp. max./rate	Span m./ft.	Length m./ft.	W. Area 2 m./ft.	Weight Empty kg./lb.	Weight Gross kg./lb.	Fuel lit./gal.	Speed/height max. km./mph	Speed/height max. m./ft.	Ceiling m./ft.	Range km./miles
I-15	1934	M-25	715	9.75	6.1	21.1	964	1,373	260	362	3,000	9,000	725
				32'	20'	227	2,120	3,020	69	225	9,840	29,250	450
I-152	1937	M-25A	750	10.2	6.33	22.5	1,320	1,736	310	375	–	8,000	770
				33'6"	20'9"	242	2,904	3,820	82	233	–	26,240	478
I-153	1939	M-62	1,000	10	6.17	22.14	1,452	1,859	210-410	443	4,600	10,700	695
			(800)	32'10"	20'3"	238	3,202	4,090	55-108	275	15,090	35,100	432
I-16	1936	M-25	715	9	6	14.54	1,200	1,460	255	454	3,000	9,200	820
				26'6"	19'8"	156	2,640	3,218	67	282	9,840	30,175	510
I-16	1939	M-62	1,000	9	6.13	14.54	1,475	1,912	255	489	4,000	11,000	740
				26'6"	20'1"	156	3,252	4,215	67	304	13,120	36,080	460
LaGG-3	1941	VK-105PF	1,110	9.8	8.82	17.51	2,789	3,150	480	570	4,000	9,600	570
			(1,050)	32'1"	29'	188	6,136	6,930	127	354	13,120	31,490	354
La-5	1943	M-82FN	1,850	9.8	8.67	17.59	2,605	3,320	530	648	5,000	9,500	765
			(1,523)	32'1"	28'5"	189	5,731	7,304	140	404	16,400	31,160	475
La-7	1944	M-82FNV	1,850	9.8	8.6	17.59	2,638	3,265	–	665	–	9,900	635
				32'1"	28'2"	189	5,804	7,183	–	413	–	32,470	395

Type	Year (service)	Engine Type	Engine hp. max./rate	Span m./ft.	Length m./ft.	W. Area 2 m./ft.	Weight Empty kg./lb.	Weight Gross kg./lb.	Fuel lit./gal.	Speed/height max. km./mph	m./ft.	Ceiling m./ft.	Range km./miles
MiG-3	1941	AM-35A	1,350 (1,200)	10.3 33'9"	8.15 26'9"	17.44 187	2,595 5,720	3,350 7,386	649 171	640 398	7,800 25,585	12,000 39,360	1,250 776
Yak-1	1941	VK-105PF	1,110 (1,050)	10 32'10"	8.47 27'9"	17.15 185	2,330 5,126	2,895 6,369	408 108	580 360	3,500 11,480	10,050 34,450	850 528
Yak-3	1944	VK-105PF	1,110 (1,050)	9.2 30'2"	8.5 27'11"	14.85 160	2,105 4,631	2,650 5,852	— —	655 407	3,300 10,824	10,800 35,425	900 560
Yak-3U	1945	VK-107A	1,700 (1,650)	9.2 30'2"	8.5	14.85 160	— —	2,984 6,580	— —	720 447	— —	11,800 38,350	1,060 659
Yak-7B	1942	VK-105PF	1,110 (1,050)	10 32'10"	8.47 27'9"	17.15 185	2,480 5,456	3,010 6,222	— —	610 379	— —	10,200 33,460	830 515
Yak-9	1943	VK-105PF	1,110 (1,050)	10 32'10"	8.5 28½"	17.15 185	2,505 5,511	3,060 6,732	650 171	605 376	— —	10,000 32,800	1,420 882
Yak-9U	1945	VK-107	1,700 (1,650)	10 32'10"	8.71 28'7"	17.15 185	2,315 5,093	3,170 6,974	590 155	698 433	— —	12,060 39,550	925 575

Appendix One (continued)

BOMBERS

Type	Year	Engine No. Type	hp.	Span m./ft.	Length m./ft.	W. Area 2 m./ft.	Weight Empty kg./lb.	Weight Gross kg./lb.	Max.	Speed Max. km./mph	Alt. km./mph	Ceiling m./ft.	Range km./m.	Load kg./lb.
DB-3	1937	2xM-86	950	21.4	14.3	65.6	5,270	7,600	9,700	480	4,200	7,300	3,000	500
				70'2"	46'11"	706	11,620	16,758	21,388	253	13,780	23,950	1,860	1,100
IL-4	1940	2xM-88B	1,100	21.44	14.8	66.7	5,490	10,300	—	445	6,400	9,700	3,800	1,000
				70'4"	48'6"	718	12,078	22,660	—	276	21,000	31,800	2,360	2,200
Pe-2	1941	2xM-105R	1,100	17.16	12.66	40.5	5,870	7,680	8,496	540	5,000	8,800	1,200	600
			(1,050)	56'3"	41'6"	436	12,943	16,934	18,738	335	16,400	28,900	745	1,320
Pe-2	1943	2xM-105F	1,210	17.16	12.45	405.	5,950	7,770	8,520	581	5,000	9,000	1,770	600
				56'3"	40'10"	436	13,119	17,733	18,786	361	16,400	29,520	1,100	1,320
Pe-8	1941	4xAM-35A	1,350	39.1	23.59	188.68	16,000	27,000	3,200	441	6,400	9,300	4,700	4,000
				128'3"	77'4"	2030	35,280	59,535	70,560	274	21,000	30,500	2,320	8,800
SB-2	1935	2xM-100	860	20.33	12.27	51.95	4,060	5,732	—	424	4,000	9,560	980	500
			(760)	66'8"	40'3"	589	8,952	12,640	—	263	13,120	31,350	608	1,100

Type	Year	Engine No. Type	hp.	Span m./ft.	Length m./ft.	W. Area 2 m./ft.	Empty kg./lb.	Weight Gross kg./lb.	Max.	Speed Max. km./mph	Alt.	Ceiling m./ft.	Range km./m.	Load kg./lb.
SB-2bis	1939	2xM-103	960	20.33	12.27	51.95	4,300	6,380	—	450	5,000	10,000	1,200	600
			.(860)	66'8"	40'3"	589	9,460	14,036	—	279	16,400	32,800	745	1,320
Su-2	1940	1xM-82	1,330	14.3	10.46	29	3,273	4,700	—	486	5,580	8,400	1,100	400
				46'11"	34'3"	312	7,200	10,340	—	302	19,190	27,550	683	880
TB-3	1932	4xM-17	700	40.5	24.4	230	11,207	17,400	—	215	s.l.	3,800	2,200	3,000
				132'10"	80'	2475	24,720	38,370	—	135	"	12,460	1,360	6,600
TB-3	1936	4xM-34RN	970	40.5	25.3	230	10,956	19,500	21,000	288	3,000	7,740	2,470	4,000
				132'10"	83'	2475	24,158	43,000	46,305	179	9,840	25,390	1,535	8,800
Tu-2	1944	2xM-82FN	1,850	18.86	13.8	48.8	8,260	10,380	13,500	547	5,400	9,500	2,100	1,000
			(1,525)	61'10"	45'3"	525	18,200	22,880	29,760	340	17,700	31,170	1,300	2,200
Yak-4	1941	2xM-105	1,100	14	10.17	32	—	5,200	—	567	4,800	8,800	1,600	400
				45'11"	33'4"	344	—	11,466	—	352	15,740	28,865	995	880

Appendix One (continued)

GROUND-ATTACK AND OTHERS

Type	Year	Engine No. Type	hp.	Span m./ft.	Length m./ft.	W. Area m²/ft.	Weight Empty kg./lb.	Gross kg./lb.	Max.	Speed Max. km./mph	Alt. m./mph	Ceiling m./ft.	Range	Load
IL-2	1941	AM-38	1,600	14.6	11.6	38.5	4,200	5,340	—	470	—	4,000	750	400
			(1,550)	47'11"	38'	414	9,260	11,775	—	292	—	13,120	465	880
IL-2/3M	1942	AM-38F	1,760	14.6	11.65	38.5	4,525	5,873	6,360	420	1,500	3,500	765	400
			(1,550)	47'11"	38'2"	414	9,977	12,950	14,024	261	4,920	11,480	475	880
IL-10	1944	AM-42	2,000	13.4	11.2	30	4,500	6,336	—	507	s.l.	7,500	1,000	400
				43'11"	36'9"	323	9,920	13,979	—	315	s.l.	24,600	620	880
Li-2	1941	2xM-62	900	28.81	19.65	91.33	7,700	10,700	11,280	280	—	5,600	2,500	—
				94'6"	64'6"	983	16,978	23,593	24,872	174	—	—	1,552	—
MBR-2	1935	M-34N	830	19	13.5	55	3,186	4,285	—	275	—	7,900	1,000	200
			(750)	62'4"	44'3"	592	7,025	9,448	—	171	—	25,912	620	440
Po-2	1941	M-11D	115	11.4	8.17	33.15	773	1,400	—	131	s.l.	1,500	450	250
				37'4"	26'10"	357	1,700	3,080	—	81	s.l.	4,920	280	550
R-5	1930	M-17	680	15.45	10.6	502	1,900	2,955	3,347	259	s.l.	6,400	900	250
				50'8"	34'9"	540	4,180	6,500	7,363	161	s.l.	21,000	560	550

Appendix Two

U. S. AIRCRAFT LEND-LEASED TO THE USSR

The first U.S. aircraft sent to Russia were 195 Curtiss Tomahawk (P-40C) fighters brought by ship over the Arctic route to Archangel about October 12, 1941.

These were part of 1080 Tomahawks built for the British, who had sent 324 to the Middle East early in 1941, and had kept the rest as a reserve for training tactical reconnaissance squadrons. They were considered unsuitable for the RAF's Fighter Command, and some had already been given to China and Turkey.

At the same time, thirty Curtiss O-52 observation planes had been shipped, but only nineteen arrived, along with five B-25B medium bombers.

In 1942, the improved Curtiss Kittihawk (P-40E) was shipped. The Arctic route, while the shortest way to Russia, was becoming so dangerous that 248 P-40s were lost on ships sunk by the Germans. Most P-40s were then delivered through Iran, after being shipped around Africa and assembled on the Persian Gulf at Abadan. The first P-40s sent were from British contracts, but army models sent later included 313 P-40Ks, 220 P-40Ms, and 980 P-40Ns.

The aircraft sent in the largest numbers was the Bell P-39 Airacobra. Fighter Command had tried a squadron of these in October 1941, found them unsatisfactory, and released the remainder back to the U.S., or to the Soviet Union. The first batch were ex-British Airacobras shipped via the Arctic early in 1942, but later shipments came by water to Iran, and afterwards were ferried by air through Alaska and Siberia. The U. S. Army models sent were 108 P-39Ds, 40 P-39Ks, 137 P-39Ls, 157 P-39Ms, 1113 P-39Ns, and 3291 P-39Qs. The P-39 was considered superior to the P-40 by its Soviet pilots, of whom the most famous was Pokryshkin.

As the P-39 and P-40 were dropped from production, they were replaced in Soviet shipments by a batch of P-47D Thunderbolts, and most of the Bell P-63 Kingcobras produced. The former came through Iran, but the P-63s came, beginning in June 1944, via the Alaska-Siberia (Alsib) ferry route.

The North American B-25 bombers were delivered by air except for the first five mentioned above, 102 arriving in 1942. More widely used, as a counterpart to the Pe-2, was the Douglas A-20, or Boston, light bomber.

The Douglas C-47 transport, U.S. progenitor of the Li-2, began arriving in the USSR in September 1942, all coming via Alsib. To ease the transition into U.S. aircraft, 30 AT-6C trainers came by water in 1942 and 54 AT-6Fs by Alsib in 1945. A single B-24A was added to the total when stuck in Siberia while ferrying U.S. personnel, along with a lone Curtiss C-46.

The only navy aircraft sent were 138 PBN flying boats, beginning in September 1943, and 48 PBY-6A amphibians in 1945.

A State Department "Report on War Aid Furnished by the United States to the USSR" (Washington, 1945) lists 14,798 army aircraft allocated to the Soviet Union, of which 14,018 were actually delivered. Soviet history usually compares this quantity unfavorably with about 292,000 aircraft built in the U.S. and 142,800 built in the USSR during the 1941–45 wartime period, pointing out that lend-lease aircraft were less than 10 percent of the Soviet production. Aluminum and aviation fuel sent by the U.S. for Soviet aircraft should also be included in the balance.

According to the report mentioned above, the army aircraft sent to the USSR were these, along with the number sent, and the number delivered:

Fighters:	P-39	=	4924/4719
	P-40	=	2430/2097
	P-47	=	203/195
	P-63	=	2421/2400
	Total	=	9978/9438
Bombers:	A-20	=	3125/2908
	B-25	=	870/862
	B-24A	=	1/1
	Total	=	3996/3771
Others:	C-46	=	1/1
	C-47	=	709/707
	O-52	=	30/19
	AT-6	=	84/82
	Total	=	824/809
	Totals	=	14,798/14,018

Shipments:	10/1 /41 to 6/30/42	=	1311
	7/1 /42 to 6/30/43	=	3816
	7/1 /43 to 6/30/44	=	5735
	7/1 /44 to 5/12/45	=	2983
	5/13/45 to 9/ 2/45	=	744
			14,589*

The British contribution to Soviet air strength began with 39 Hurricane II fighters which arrived in Murmansk by September 1941, and were flown by RAF pilots in combat several weeks before being turned over to the 72nd

(* This total is 209 less than on type list; the difference may be the aircraft shipped before October 1, 1941. ED.)

Fighter Air Regiment of the Northern Fleet. Altogether, Britain sent 2952 Hurricanes, 143 Spitfire VB and 1188 Spitfire IX fighters, and about 30 other aircraft, but not all arrived.

This information is offered by the editor so that the reader may make his own estimate of the role of lend-lease.

Appendix Three

PRODUCTION OF SOVIET AND GERMAN AIRCRAFT

Year	Soviet	German
1938	5,469	5,235
1939	10,382	8,295
1940	10,565	10,826
1941	15,735	12,401
1942	25,436	15,409
1943	34,900	24,807
1944	40,300	40,593
1945*	20,900	7,540

SOURCES: 1938–40 data from S. M. Shtemenko, *The Soviet General Staff at War* (Moscow: Progress Publishers, 1970) p. 28, later data from A. Yakovlev, the *Aim of a Lifetime* (Moscow: Progress Publishers, 1972) p. 307, and Cajus Bekker, *Luftwaffe War Diaries* (London: Macdonald, 1967) p. 377.

* January to June only

LIST OF REFERENCES

Most footnotes in the Russian edition are to USSR Defense Ministry archives, and these have been omitted as inaccessible to American readers. For the English edition, this set of references retains the more important Russian published works, especially the six-volume history of the war, and authorities in English used to provide data for the American editor's additions.

Part One (CHAPTERS I TO IV)

1. Information on Soviet aircraft added by the editor is drawn from A. S. Yakovliev, *Fifty Years of Soviet Aircraft Construction* (Moscow: Science Publishers, 1968), also available in translation from NASA, Vaclav Nemecek, *Sovetska Letadla* (Prague: Nase Vojsko, 1969), and John W. R. Taylor (ed.) *Combat Aircraft of the World* (New York: G. P. Putnam's Sons, 1969).
2. Frank Tinker, *Some Still Live* (New York, 1938) has a detailed account of the Americans flying Soviet fighters in Spain.
3. *Istoriya Velikoy Otechestvennoy Voyny Sovetskogo Soyuza 1941–1945.* Moskva, Voenizdat, *History of the Great Patriotic War of the Soviet Union, 1941–1945,* (Moscow: Military Publishing House, 1960), I, 65. Hereafter cited as *Istoriya.*
4. *Ibid,* I, 93. German authorities believed there were about 1500 first-line aircraft in 1933.
5. Nemecek, pp. 43–44; William Green in *Flying Review* (London), January 1970, p. 62.
6. *Istoriya,* I, 414.
7. Cajus Bekker, *Luftwaffe War Diaries* (London: Macdonald, 1967), p. 223.
8. Nemecek, pp. 235–41: Taylor, pp. 571–75.
9. Malcolm Passingham and Waclaw Klepocki, *Profile* ⌗216, *Petyakov Pe-2* (Windsor: Profile Publications, 1971).
10. Nemecek, pp. 175–77: *Flying Review* (London), March 1968, pp. 157–59.
11. *Istoriya,* I, 99.
12. *Ibid.,* I, 450. Strength in summer 1939 was given as 5500 aircraft. P. Zhilin, *They Sealed Their Own Doom* (Moscow: Progress Publishers, 1970).

13. Zhilin, pp. 83, 183.
14. A. N. Lapchinsky, *The Air Army* (Moscow: Military Publishing House, 1939), p. 48.
15. Yu. P. Petrov, *The Construction of a Party-Political Apparatus in the Soviet Army 1921–1940* (Moscow: Military Publishing House, 1954), p. 236.
16. *The Industry of Germany in the Period 1939–1945* (Moscow: Foreign Literature Publishing House, 1956), pp. 106, 108. Bekker, p. 377, gives production as 10,247, including 378 gliders, in 1940; and 12,401, including 1461 gliders, in 1941.
17. USSR Defense Ministry archives data. Data available in the U.S. gives smaller German aircraft stocks. On December 31, 1940, Luftwaffe inventory of combat types showed 7836 on hand, with 4696 of these in active units. In addition, there were 1600 transports (439 with groups) and over 300 liaison aircraft, plus many training aircraft. See *National Archives Microfilm,* captured German OKW (High Command) documents, T-77, roll 80, pages 803556 ff. Partial data for June 28, 1941, after the first week of fighting in Russia, shows 3451 bomber and fighter aircraft (not including over 1000 recon and other types) in units: more fighters, but fewer bombers, than in December. See Charles K. Webster, *Strategic Air Offensive Against Germany 1939–1945* (London: HMSO, 1961), IV, 501–04.
18. Barbarossa Directive text from *Nurenberg Trial; a Collection of Documents* (Moscow: State Law Publishing House, 1952), I, 367.
19. German writers on Luftwaffe deployment are Generalleutnant Hermann Plocher, *German Air Force Versus Russia, 1941,* pp. 30–35; and Richard Suchenwirth, *Historical Turning Points in the German Air Force War Effort,* pp. 75–76 (both published in New York by Arno Press, 1968); and Bekker, p. 373. A Soviet source is Zhilin, pp. 150–52, 167–68. William Green, *Warplanes of the Third Reich* (Garden City, N.Y.: Doubleday, 1970), gives some unit strengths.
    Unit identifications here assembled by the editor from Bekker, Green, Plocher, and other postwar sources.
20. On April 15, one of these planes was forced to land near Rovno, and its equipment was taken by the Russians. *Istoriya,* I, 479; and Zhilin, p. 199.
21. Generalleutnant D. Walter Schwabedissen, *The Russian Air Force in the Eyes of German Commanders* (New York: Arno Press, 1968), p. 11.
22. *Ibid.,* pp. 16–17.
23. *Ibid.,* pp. 18–20.
24. Christoper Shores, *Finnish Air Force* (Canterbury: Osprey, 1970).
25. Bekker, p. 280.
26. Alexander Werth, *Russia at War* (New York: Dutton, 1964), p. 15.
27. See Chapter XX below (p. 440 in Russian text) for losses per sortie. Sorties total 42,000 for all fronts to July 10, and losses were heavier than in later periods.
28. A. I. Yeremenko, *On the Western Front* (Moscow: Military Publishing House, 1959), p. 90.
29. Bekker, p. 283.

30. *Istoriya*, II, 108; and Werth, pp. 203–06.
31. *Istoriya*, Vol. II; cited by Werth, p. 222.
32. Werth, pp. 231–35.
33. Alexander Yakovlev, *The Aim of a Lifetime* (Moscow: Progress Publishers, 1972), p. 166.
34. G. S. Desnitsky, *On Duty in the Sky of the Motherland* (Moscow: Military Publishing House, 1961), p. 53.
35. *Istoriya*, VI, 210.
36. *Flying Review* (London), June 1969, pp. 79–81.
37. *Istoriya*, II, 428.
38. *Ibid.*, II, 449.
39. Bekker, pp. 223, 377.

Part Two (CHAPTERS V TO VIII)

1. Bekker, p. 294.
2. *Istoriya*, III, 114.
3. Hermann Plocher, *German Air Force Versus Russia, 1943* (New York: Arno Press, 1968), p. 367.
4. *Ibid.*, pp. 36–37.
5. Larisa Litvinova, *The Road of Battle and Glory* (Moscow: Foreign Languages Publishing House, n.d.), pp. 231–52; Lt. Col. V. Mitroshenkov, "They Were First," *Soviet Military Review* (Moscow: *Krasnya Zvezda* Publishing House), March 1969, pp. 20–22; Edgar Meos, "Soviet Women Fighter Pilots," *Aircraft Illustrated Extra*, No. 3 (London, n.d.), pp. 38–42.
6. *Istoriya*, III, 243.
7. Plocher, pp. 75–79.
8. B. Nicolas, *Air Journal* (Voiron, France, 1969), Vol. II, No. 3, pp. 4–16, *Icare* (Paris, 1972), No. 62, pp. 36–37, 104.
9. Plocher, pp. 115 ff. and pp. 137 ff. gives the German view of these operations, including a paratroop drop on September 25; there are many differences between the German and Soviet accounts.
10. *Istoriya*, II, 593. These include other Axis losses, as well as German.
11. *Istoriya*, III, 20.

Part III (CHAPTERS IX TO XX)

1. *Istoriya*, IV, 20; and Zhilin, p. 220.
2. Bekker, p. 377, gives German aircraft production as 15,409 in 1942 and 24,807 in 1943, does not include satellite output; while Webster, p. 394, gives 15,556 in 1942 and 25,527 in 1943.
3. See Webster, pp. 501–04, for German strength in combat types.
4. Albert Seaton, *The Russo-German War 1941–45* (London: Arthur Barker Ltd., 1971), pp. 427–31.
5. Paul Carel, *Scorched Earth* (New York: Little, Brown, 1971), p. 553.
6. Shores, appendix.
7. Seaton, p. 458.

8. Zhilin, p. 220.
9. K. Tippelskirch, *History of the Second World War* (Moscow: Foreign Literature Publishing House, 1957), p. 446. In Russian.
10. *The World War of 1939–1945*, p. 475. (This is the only data in Russian footnote.)
11. *Ibid.*, p. 516.
12. Carel, p. 596, lists these generals by name.
13. Edgar Meos, "Escape or Death," *Flying Review* (London), March 1961, pp. 35–36.
14. *Battles of 1939–1945* (Moscow: Foreign Language Publishing House, 1957), p. 237. In Russian.
15. Zdenek Titz, "Lavochins Over Slovakia," *Air Pictorial* (London), March 1966, pp. 92–94.
16. Seaton, p. 547, quoting German data.
17. Zhilin, p. 220; *Istoriya,* V, 27; Seaton, p. 527.
18. *Istoriya,* V, 57.
19. Witold Liss, *Lavochkin La-5 & 7*, Profile ⧉149 (Leatherhead, England, 1967).
20. *Journal of Military History*, No. 5 (1959, p. 87. In Russian).
21. *Istoriya,* V, 290.
22. *Aero Album* (Whittier, California), Winter 1971, p. 8.
23. Werth, pp. 1029–32.
24. *Ibid.*, p. 1040.
25. This quotation is as given in *Istoriya,* V, 594. The original *Times* quotation.
26. Bekker, p. 377.
27. Data from Soviet Defense Ministry archives.
28. Bekker, p. 377 (gliders not included).

INDEX